Navigating Art Therapy

From *Art-making as a Defence* to *Works of Art*, **this anthology will help you navigate your way through the ever growing world of art therapy.**

Art therapy is used in an increasing range of settings and is influenced by a range of disciplines, including psychotherapy, social psychiatry, social work and education. *Navigating Art Therapy* is an essential companion for both seasoned art therapists and those new to the field as it offers a comprehensive guide to key terms and concepts. With contributions from art therapists around the world, entries cover:

- forms of interpretation
- processes of adaptation
- history of art therapy
- the inspiration provided by artworks and popular culture.

This book is an ideal source of reference as the concise, cross-referenced entries enable easy navigation through ideas and terms integral to the discipline. As such, it is invaluable for anyone working in the art therapy field.

Chris Wood is the team leader for the Art Therapy Northern Programme in Sheffield and combines art therapy training in higher education with therapeutic practice in the public sector.

Contributors: Julie Aldridge, Maggie Ambridge, Michael Atkins, Peter Baker, Teresa Boronska, Ani M. Brown, Philippa Brown, Peter Byrne, Caroline Case, Martin Cody, Rupert Cracknell, Simon Critchley, Tessa Dalley, Barrie Damarell, Frank Denning, Jane Dudley, David Edwards, Michael Edwards, Deborah Egan, Deborah Gibson, Andrea Gilroy, Liisa Girard, Alison Goldsmith, Helen Greenwood, Simon Hackett, Penelope Hall, David Hardy, Julie Harper, Margaret Hills de Zárate, Susan Hogan, Marilyn Hoggard, Karen Huckvale, Clare Hughes, Daphne Jackson, Julie

Jackson, Kevin Jones, Debra Kalmanowitz, Riita Laine, Malcolm Learmonth, Sarah A. V. Lewis (née Paget), Marian Liebmann, Bobby Lloyd, Jacky Mahony, Maggie McManamon, Gerry McNeilly, Debbie Michaels, Katrina Millhagen, Janette Moon, Deena Northover, Kate Ogley, Clare Phelan, Alison Poad, Margaret Pracka, Carina Rafael, Laura Richardson, Simon Richardson, Mary-Jayne Rust, Kate Rothwell, Joy Schaverien, Caryl Sibbett, Sally Skaife, Sandra Storey, Colin Teasdale, Kim Thomas, Robin Tipple, Mike Waite, Diane Waller, Sally Weston, Simon Willoughby-Booth, Elaine Wisdom, Chris Wood, Michèle Wood, Pam Wood.

Navigating Art Therapy

A Therapist's Companion

Compiled by Chris Wood

Routledge
Taylor & Francis Group

LONDON AND NEW YORK

First published 2011 by Routledge
27 Church Road, Hove, East Sussex BN3 2FA

Simultaneously published in the USA and Canada
by Routledge
270 Madison Avenue, New York, NY 10016

Routledge is an imprint of the Taylor & Francis Group, an Informa business

Typeset in Times by Garfield Morgan, Swansea, West Glamorgan
Printed and bound in Great Britain by TJ International Ltd, Padstow,
Cornwall
Paperback cover design by Andrew Ward

This publication has been produced with paper manufactured to strict
environmental standards and with pulp derived from sustainable forests.

British Library Cataloguing in Publication Data
A catalogue record for this book is available from the British Library

Library of Congress Cataloging-in-Publication Data
Navigating art therapy : a therapist's companion / compiled by Chris Wood.
    p. ; cm.
  Includes bibliographical references.
  ISBN 978-0-415-22318-8 (hardback) – ISBN 978-0-415-22319-5 (pbk.)
1. Art therapy–Encyclopedias. I. Wood, Chris, 1954-
  [DNLM: 1. Art Therapy. WM 450.5.A8 N318 2010]
  RC489.A7N324 2010
  616.89'1656003–dc22

                                                         2010021283

ISBN: 978-0-415-22318-8 (hbk)
ISBN: 978-0-415-22319-5 (pbk)

Contents

Personal Acknowledgements

All of the contributors have been generous with their time, their thinking, and their encouragement. Colleagues at work (art therapists and others), supervisors, and friends have been tolerant. I really appreciate this. In addition, I value the images loaned to me by clients and colleagues for the cover; it would have been good if it could have been possible to include many more images, but the ones on the cover seem to me to provide a glimpse of the richness of what is seen in art therapy. I also want to acknowledge the tireless work of proofreading by Em Turton.

The biggest acknowledgements though are to my mum, Pam Wood, and my partner Dick Pitt, because they have been both patient and kind and this was crucial. I should also mention that my dad, Harry Wood (who died recently), used to smile at me about this book. When he was a young man he worked on board ships as a navigator, which I now know is relevant to what I have been doing here.

Introduction

This is a reference book. The book is unusual because of the nature of art therapy – a way of working that has new and unusual ways of looking at things and approaching problems. The discipline is special because of the ancient elements of art and imagination. As Bachelard (1958: xxxiii) said: 'Art . . . is an increase of life, a sort of competition of surprises that stimulates our consciousness and keeps it from becoming somnolent.'

Art therapists think carefully about the art made by their clients. Art can reflect things that are unbalancing a life, and do so better than words can, and it can, crucially, provide a means of repairing or getting balance back. Liisa Girard, a Finnish art psychotherapist, introduced me to the concept of isomorphism:

> In logic isomorphism considers similarity of structure. The concept provides a useful way of thinking about looking at art works in therapy. An art therapist can use their capacity for sensing spatial qualities in order to give attention to the isomorphism (or parallels) between the features in the patient's life and relationships, to the events and forms seen on paper or in clay.
>
> (Girard, 2008b: 7)

Another art therapist, John Henzell (1997: 77) wrote: 'The image is isomorphic with our experience because it refers so directly to it while defying any easy paraphrase in words – it must be painstakingly translated.' He also suggests that the image holds the imprint of the meeting between therapist and client: 'A painting, drawing, or sculpture made in therapy [is] part of the very tissue of the session; through them the event itself survives as a material object' (Henzell 1997: 71).

This sensing of spatial qualities and relationships is different from what some might imagine art therapists do. It seems appropriate therefore that there are several entries in this book on forms of interpretation: rarely an easy and certainly not a one-sided process in art therapy. A number of entries in the book are like this – overlapping and interconnected.

Art therapy itself is situated in-between disciplines such as psychiatry, social work, special education, and psychotherapy; though a discipline in its own right, art therapy exists in a hinterland. These are places at the edge of countries, where several borders meet. People who inhabit hinterlands speak several languages because they live their lives crossing backwards and forwards over different borders. Art therapy also contains knowledge of different languages from a wide range of interrelated disciplines. It tends not to have orthodoxy and where it is doing well it tends to be playful. Many entries reflect the multilingual nature of the discipline and include words from the different terminologies of the disciplines on its borders.

The entries

The book is unusual compared with other art therapy literature, because it contains short entries that might become a regular source of reference. Personally, I find dictionaries and anthologies helpful as they make me think again about subjects I know about and introduce me to some I do not. Cross-references help with navigation through the ideas, although this is not always in a straight line: when I look something up, I tend to get interested in other entries on the same page and then follow their list of cross-references as I explore associated ideas.

The process of collecting entries involved asking a wide selection of art therapists at different stages of their careers in Britain, and a few from other parts of Europe and Scandinavia, for concepts they find helpful and inspiring. Many people responded; some sent me concepts that overlapped, but many sent concepts from widely differing areas of practice. It is clear that the range of practice and therapeutic approaches being used in art therapy is expanding, and increasingly adaptations are made in response to the different circumstances of clients' lives and service setting. A number of entries concern the process of adaptation.

For example, frames of reference used for work with children and their families lay the foundations for understanding much work with adults. *Art Therapy with Children: From Infancy to Adolescence* (edited by Case and Dalley, 2008) contains a number of chapters that explain the use of attachment frameworks in art therapy in ways that are relevant to work with adults. Similarly, some entries on work with children indicate fundamental aspects of work with adults.

Children often seem at ease with art-making and playing and are able to quickly grasp the purpose of meetings with an art therapist. I work with adults and some of them initially feel that using art materials is strange. They may not feel they have an artist inside them, but very few would feel that there has never been a time when their imagination was moved. There may have been a story from childhood, a picture hanging in their school, a comic with weekly instalments, a film, an old TV programme, or even a hard-to-distinguish sculpture in front of the town hall; for some it will be the memory of watching a game of football and the ribald humour and songs on the way home. There will be something that has caught their imagination and made them think about their lives, and a number of entries reflect the ways in which art therapists try to acknowledge this.

Art therapists gain sustenance and understanding from the work of artists. There are many entries that refer to the work of artists and some that refer to the artwork made by art therapists themselves, but few mention specific artists. There could never be enough space for such entries. The entries that are included from art, literature, visual culture, and popular culture are only a small number of examples. I hope that these few will stimulate the reader into thinking about inspiration they have found for their work in art that has touched them. Therapists also have to think about sustaining their own health and liveliness and some entries are concerned with how this might be achieved in part by keeping their art-making awake.

The accumulated history of art therapy in Britain has developed during three identifiable historical periods (Waller, 1991; Wood, 1997, 2001a) and the contemporary period. A number of entries (e.g. 'First period') describe these and offer signposts to relevant references. It is intended that the history shows how and when concepts developed and gives an indication of future developments.

During the first period, the focus of art therapy was on the power to be found in expression. During the second period art therapists tried to counter some of the alienating effects of psychiatric institutions by providing in their studios an 'asylum within an asylum'. In the third period, the work of art therapists became more influenced by psychotherapeutic practice and by the problematic transition from asylum to an unknown community; during this time questions of theory, practice, and technique became important. As the work of mental health services moved into the community (1980s–1990s), art therapists were working with more single-handed responsibility for their clients and as a result they sought and found more rigorous explanations for the therapeutic relationship within psychodynamic approaches for work with children and adults (Wood, 2001a). Many art therapists published work during this period.

Each of the three periods had drive and development. They have all contributed in powerful ways to a belief in the possibility of art therapy. The strands of the history were gradually knotted together during three overlapping 20-year periods of the last century (Wood, 1999b, 2001a, 2005, 2010a). The contemporary period is the fabric that has been made from the preceding three, and in it there is an increasing concern to produce systematic evidence for the practice (Gilroy, 2006; Wood, 1999b). Linked entries indicate efforts made to produce specific art therapy evidence and point to the possibilities of finding evidence in generic research. The gold standard of systematic research – the randomised controlled trial (RCT) – is not a straightforward instrument for research in mental health (Barkham, 2007; Gilroy, 2006; Seligman, 1995). The creation of large enough sample sizes for RCTs in art therapy is often problematic because the costs can be prohibitive, but there are increasing numbers of trials undertaken in all areas of art therapy practice. These include work with older people, people with a diagnosis of schizophrenia, people who are depressed, as part of a mindfulness approach in cancer care and general physical health, and outcome studies with children and young people. Some of these are indicated in relevant entries and more results from RCTs in art therapy are published regularly.

The first two periods left art therapists with a legacy of using the same careful approach to therapeutic work, an approach that did not alter in relation to any particular client group. This began to change in the third period, with particular approaches being offered to particular clients. A range of special interest groups for art therapists working with different client needs have developed during the contemporary period. In Britain, these are based within the professional association, and it is likely that the development of such interest groups will continue in different places in the world and that they will help with the creation of evidence.

Another feature of the contemporary period seems to be a concern with the visceral nature of making art and the significance of its materiality for clients. Art therapists throughout the world are extending the range of their practice and making helpful connections with other artists (*Arts in Health* in Britain, for example). They are also considering how social psychiatry agendas are pertinent to the contemporary concern with social inclusion.

Golberg and Thornicroft (1998) demonstrated how real the differences are in the level of mental health service provision between countries that spend 6% and countries that spend 8% of their GDP on mental health. At the beginning of the twenty-first century, Britain saw a period of investment as the government tried to raise levels of health service spending in the UK to those in much of Europe. However, only a small proportion of this investment went to mental health and the current world economic recession almost certainly means that people working in all public sectors will see services affected. The contemporary period in art therapy (from 2000 onwards) seems to be invoking much of what has gone before, but there is a more frank move towards adaptation of therapeutic approaches to the differing circumstances of clients' lives and to the cool waters of recession. This is a response to public service and other service realities and it is likely that the economic situation will mean that these tendencies continue. A number of entries show one response to this, with therapists using time-related approaches and mixed-length case loads.

Currently some art therapists are exploring research concerning the connections between mind and brain and developments in neuroscience and psychotherapy, whereas the professional association BAAT (British Association of Art Therapists) is responding to social economic concerns and pointing to the significance of the *Social Inclusion* and *Arts in Health* agendas in ways that indicate some of the work art therapists might contribute. *New Horizons* (DOH, 2009), reports that one in six people suffer from mental illness.

The range of difficult settings in which many art therapists work mean that they have to understand the limits of what they can do and it is in the interests of their clients that they do so. Nevertheless, although they often adapt the scope of their practice to circumstances, a psychodynamic understanding of the therapeutic relationship is used because it theorises the unconscious in ways that other models (from humanistic and cognitive traditions) do not. For centuries, artists and writers have acknowledged less conscious aspects of human experience. Theories that use only the rational aspects of human behaviour tend to overlook the art-making side of life.

Despite the shifts in focus, which have been made in the profession in response to different periods of history, the fundamental elements of the practice remain: the art-making and the therapeutic relationship, and acknowledgement of the way both of these are influenced by the socio-economic circumstances of the client's life and the therapeutic setting. The active combination of these elements is unique to the profession and one of its strengths.

Throughout their history and unusually amongst those professionals offering forms of psychotherapy, art therapists have consistently attempted to create the circumstances for their practice within public services (hospitals, schools, prisons, homes, and marginalised communities), often with people who would not otherwise have had access to forms of psychological help. This is a part of art therapy practice that is worthy of respect and a part of the practice I am always proud to see. Clients often have complex needs, limited resources, and many are isolated: this means that art therapy is necessarily part of a repertoire of approaches provided by multi-disciplinary teams and that therapists need to be aware of the multicultural health needs of large cities and the concerns of user movements.

Art therapists often seek out settings in which it is possible to work and then do what they can to respond appropriately. Increasing numbers, for example, work in the developing world, but many also work in Western cities with people who feel alienated. One art therapist, Dylis Pugh, when working in the council estates of Sheffield spoke about her art therapy work helping young people find the confidence to begin to access other services.

As a discipline, art therapy is continually developing and the number of people who might connect with it is growing. My hope is that a range of people will find they can make use of the book as a signpost to art therapy ideas, many of which are relevant to mental health in general. I do not and could not claim that the book is a complete reflection of the discipline. It is not intended as a substitute for the original literature but as providing a way of pointing people towards some of the key elements in art therapy and ensuring that they know how to follow up (or navigate to) the connections they find here. Nevertheless, more than 70 art therapists and some colleagues from other disciplines contributed entries. They work with and have experience of a wide range of clients, including many children, families, and adults. The range of their thinking about individual and group work is fascinating and I hope that readers will find, as I have done, that it begins to broaden their understanding of what art therapy is.

Contributors

The abbreviation against the name of the contributor is also used against the entries to indicate which ones they have contributed to. Many contributors have more than one professional qualification, but unless otherwise indicated all are art therapists. The double asterisk in front of their name indicates that the reference list contains some of their publications.

Julie Aldridge: JA
Teacher on the MA Art Therapy course at Crawford College, Cork, Eire.

**Maggie Ambridge: MAm
Worked for many years within an NHS CAMHS team, predominantly in reparative work with children and families. She endeavours to progress her own artwork and is an associate of the Art Therapy Northern Programme.

**Michael Atkins: MAt
Works with an NHS CAMHS team and as a placement supervisor to trainees with the Art Therapy Northern Programme.

Peter Baker: PBa
Works for the NHS in an eating disorders unit and also for Twelves Company, a charity providing art therapy to children and adolescents who have been affected by abuse.

**Teresa Boronska: TBo
BA (Hons) Fine Art, PGCADE, Dip AT, Dip Group Psych, MA Art Therapy: Her journey into the profession came as a consequence of working in schools as an environmental teacher and artist in inner-city London.

**Ani M. Brown: AMB
MA Art Psychotherapy, Cert Psychoanalytic Psychotherapy: Her Goldsmiths MA and advanced studies concerned severely disturbed adolescents and the use of art therapy in family therapy.

Philippa Brown: PBr
BA Hons Art and Design, PG Dip AT, MA History of Art: Since 1994, Programme Leader on MA Art Therapy at University of Hertfordshire; previously worked in mental health for many years.

**Peter Byrne: PB
PhD: Between 1992 and 2002, Course Leader for the MSc in Art Therapy; continues to work at Queen Margaret University, Edinburgh as a senior lecturer.

**Caroline Case: CC
Child psychotherapist (SIHR) working with an NHS CAMHS in Bristol; also an analytical art therapist in private practice. She has published widely on images in therapy, most recently in 2005, 2006, 2007, 2008, and is an associate of the Art Therapy Northern Programme.

Martin Cody: MC
Trained as a sculptor in the late 1970s and as an art therapist in 1985, and has since worked in NHS Adult Psychiatry and Therapeutic Community settings in Middlesex and Birmingham.

Rupert Cracknell: RC
Started work at Withymead and spent most of his working life in the NHS; moved to Ireland and makes a contribution to the Cork Course.

Simon Critchley: SC
Art therapist currently working in the North East of England with young people.

**Tessa Dalley: TD
Experienced art therapist and child and adolescent psychotherapist currently working in an inpatient adolescent unit. She has published a number of books and articles, works as a clinical supervisor, and has a small private practice.

**Barrie Damarell: BD
Professional Lead for the Arts Therapies for Plymouth Primary Care Trust, with 25 years of experience in the context of learning disability. He has published on clinical and supervision practice.

Frank Denning: FD
Has many years experience in the field of mental health as a social worker; he uses his training in group analytic therapy with many clients who would not normally have access to such an approach.

**Jane Dudley: JD
RMN, MA (Gender Studies), Group Analytic Psychotherapist, Psycho-analytic Psychotherapist, Art Psychotherapist: Has worked for the NHS

within adult psychiatry since 1980s. Published widely; politically active with BAAT and Amicus (Unite) and Arts Psychotherapies professional bodies.

**David Edwards: DE
MA, PG Dip AT, BA Hons (Fine Art), HPC Arts Therapist (Art), UKCP Psychodynamic Psychotherapist: Works in a range of NHS and educational settings, mainly with adults; practices privately as a clinical supervisor and lectures on art therapy; published the book *Art Therapy* (2004) and is an associate of the Art Therapy Northern Programme.

**Michael Edwards: MEd (Professor)
Sadly, Michael Edwards died on 13 March 2010. He contributed greatly to the development of art therapy and he was undoubtedly one of a generation of pioneers. He was an analytical psychologist and Professor Emeritus of Art Therapy at Concordia University, Montreal. He trained and worked as an art therapist with the late Irene Champernowne at Withymead and established the first art therapy training in Britain. Later he undertook further training at the C. G. Jung Institute in Zurich, where he was offered the position of curator of the Jung Picture Archives. He was an associate of the Art Therapy Northern Programme.

Deborah Egan: DEg
Photographic designer.

**Deborah Gibson: DG
MA Art Therapy Research; Dip AT; Dip Couns (Person Centred); Cert Supervision: Clinical experience in a variety of mental health settings and lecturer with the Art Therapy Northern Programme. She is interested in teaching and learning and in the interface between the psychodynamic and person-centred approaches.

**Andrea Gilroy: AJG
BA, ATD, DPhil, HPC Arts Therapist (art): Reader in Art Psychotherapy at Goldsmiths; an experienced educator, researcher, editor, and author with wide publication. She maintains a collaborative relationship with the University of Western Sydney through activities as a Research Fellow.

**Liisa Girard: LG
Dip Textiles (UIAH), Dip AT (UIAH), Registered Psychotherapist, Finland: Amongst the first ten art therapists trained in Helsinki in 1974. She used her experience of group work and the work of Dockar-Drysdale with deprived children to contribute to 'Adam's hut' group therapy in a men's acute ward.

Alison Goldsmith: AGol
Experienced art therapist and supervisor.

**Helen Greenwood: HG

BA (Hons), PGCE, Dip AT: Thirty years of work in NHS adult mental health services and in teaching and supervision; now working freelance. Wide publication and for 16 years was an editor for *Inscape* and then the *International Journal of Art Therapy: Inscape*; associate of the Art Therapy Northern Programme.

Simon Hackett: SHack

Addiction Therapist in Leeds before taking his first Art Therapy post in Rotherham Learning Disability Services. Since 2004 he has been Head of Arts Therapies in the Northumberland, Tyne and Wear NHS.

**Penelope Hall: PH

Works with adults and children in various settings; for many years she was a contributor to the Champernowne Trust Course.

**David Hardy: DH

Works with clients in palliative care, men and women with learning disabilities, and adults in the mental health services.

Julie Harper: JHar

Developed an inpatient and peripatetic art therapy service for children suffering from life-threatening illness with CAMHS in Cornwall. In 2004, she received an award from the NHS for services to life-threatened children and their families.

**Margaret Hills de Zárate: MHZ

Course leader for the MSc in Art Therapy at Queen Margaret University, Edinburgh. Her research interests reside in the area of displacement and political violence.

**Susan Hogan: SH (Professor)

Has written extensively on the relationship between the arts and insanity, and the role of the arts in rehabilitation. She is also very interested in the treatment of women within psychiatry.

**Marilyn Hoggard: MH

Experienced art therapist and one of the first deaf therapists to train in the UK.

Karen Huckvale: KH

Works with CAMHS and is contributing to the development of Devon's Service for Looked-After Children. Co-Director of Insider Art, an independent arts and health training and service provider.

Clare Hughes: CH

Has had a varied professional career since leaving Ireland, with many years as a midwife, a degree in fine art, time as a health researcher in New York, and as an artist and art therapist in the NHS; associate of the Art Therapy Northern Programme.

Daphne Jackson: DJ
Trained at Sheffield before taking up her first Art Therapy post in CAMHS; she then worked at Rampton Hospital and now works with adults for Bradford NHS.

**Julie Jackson: JJ
MA AP Research: An art therapist with many years of experience, currently working with the Glasgow homeless team; associate of the Art Therapy Northern Programme.

**Kevin Jones: KJ
Art therapist and psychotherapist who has worked with adult mental health services. He was involved in one of the first Art Therapy RCTs. He is a lecturer on the MA Art Psychotherapy course at Goldsmiths College.

**Debra Kalmanowitz: DK
MA, HPC Arts Therapist (art): Works extensively in the context of trauma, political violence, and social change locally (UK), internationally, and in countries of conflict and change. Currently in Hong Kong, she continues to co-direct ATI (Art Therapy Initiative: www.atinitiative.org).

**Riita Laine: RL
Trained at Hertfordshire, completed her training according to the Finnish psychotherapy requirements in 1995, worked as an art therapist in a psychiatric hospital, and as a private practitioner and supervisor in Helsinki. She has been a chairperson for the Finnish Association for Art Therapists.

**Malcolm Learmonth: ML
Lead Art Psychotherapist and Arts and Environments Development Lead in the Devon NHS, Arts and Health Lead and a Council Member for BAAT, and co-director of Insider Art (an independent arts and health training and service provider).

**Sarah A. V. Lewis (née Paget): SAVL
Worked in Bristol with Michael Donnelly, whose valuing of those on the brink of social and psychological survival became the basis of her chapter in *Art Therapy in Practice* (Lewis, 1990). Lead art therapist at Southmead, Avon and Wiltshire NHS and first research and development specialist nationally for Arts Psychotherapies.

**Marian Liebmann: MLieb
PhD, BA (Hons), MA, CQSW, HPC Arts Therapist (art): Works in art therapy with offenders, women's groups, and community groups, and is currently in an Inner City Team where she has developed work on anger,

conflict, and cultural issues. She teaches and lectures widely on art therapy, being the author of ten books.

**Bobby Lloyd: BL
Works as an artist and child and adolescent art therapist; has worked cross-culturally in the UK, internationally, and in countries of conflict. Increasingly her work focuses on trauma, loss, and social change, and developing practice in response to need. Co-directs the Art Therapy Initiative (ATI: www.atinitiative.org) and is an associate of the Art Therapy Northern Programme.

**Jacky Mahony: JMa
Dip Studio Pottery, PG Dip AT, Adv Dip AT, MA Art Psych, AsT (A): Currently finishing a PhD concerned with the relationship of the therapist's personal art practice to an NHS outpatient art psychotherapy group.

Maggie McManamon: MMc
Worked for 25 years in social services, early years childcare and education, and the civil service. She is currently an Independent Reviewing Officer for looked-after children in Sheffield.

**Gerry McNeilly: GMc
Senior adult psychotherapist, group analyst, and art psychotherapist; currently works for the NHS in south Warwickshire.

**Debbie A. Michaels: DAM
BA, PG Dip, MA, RATh, MBACP (accredited): After a first career in interior design, she trained as an art therapist and psychotherapist. Her experience with adults at the interface of physical and mental health has been applied in the public, voluntary, and private sectors; lecturer with the Art Therapy Northern Programme.

Katrina Millhagen: KM
BA Sociology, PG Dip AT, MA Art Therapy: Worked as a peripatetic art therapist in Sheffield and afterwards in adult and special needs education and community mental health. Since 1999 has been a lecturer with MA Art Therapy at Queen Margaret University, Edinburgh.

Janette Moon: JM
Established an Arts Therapies department within a Neuro-Rehab Unit in Sheffield. Over many years she worked with art therapy courses in Sheffield and maintained her art practice, concentrating on sculpture; associate of the Art Therapy Northern Programme.

Deena Northover: DN
Art and psychoanalytic psychotherapist working for the NHS and in private practice with both adults and young people. She is visiting lecturer and clinical supervisor for art psychotherapists, junior psychiatrists, and

other mental health practitioners; associate of the Art Therapy Northern Programme.

Kate Ogley: KO
Artist working in video and installation, living in Falmouth. She has participated in, organised, and coordinated artist-led initiatives across Cornwall. Her work is concerned with aspects of displacement.

Clare Phelan: CP
Developed services in the Bradford NHS for clients with enduring mental health problems. Her interests are in working with people with a history of psychosis and in what art therapy can provide.

Alison Poad: AP
Originally an occupational therapist who trained as an art therapist (1992, Sheffield). She works for the Devon NHS in adult mental health and has particular interests in mindfulness, art therapy, and measuring outcomes.

Margaret Pracka: MPr
Masters in Philosophy/Sociology in Poland: In Britain she studied and worked initially in social work and then in art therapy. Subsequently she trained at the Tavistock as a Child Psychotherapist and is an associate of the Art Therapy Northern Programme.

**Carina Rafael: CR
Qualified in Edinburgh: Working since 2008 at the Psychiatric Department of Hospital São João, Oporto, Portugal: with adults, especially ex-soldiers with post-traumatic stress disorder and victims of sexual abuse and trauma.

Laura Richardson: LR
BA Eng/Am Lit, BA Fine Art, MA Art Psychotherapy Research: Combines the roles of Professional Lead for Arts Therapies (Adult Services) and Arts Lead in Sheffield NHS (SHSC). She has particular interests in linking her experiences in fine art and art psychotherapy, equality and diversity, and partnership working; an associate of the Art Therapy Northern Programme.

**Simon Richardson: SR
Trained as a fashion designer in 1981 and qualified as an art therapist in 1994. He works to acknowledge the impact of social, cultural, political, and economic influences on the lives of Art Therapy service users; member of editorial team for BAAT's *Newsbriefing* since 1999.

**Kate Rothwell: KR
BA, Dip AT, MA: Works with people who experience severe mental disturbance and challenging behaviour. Art therapist at Kneesworth House Hospital medium secure unit, and previously a lecturer with the Art Therapy course at University of Hertfordshire.

**Mary-Jayne Rust: MJR

Jungian analyst and art therapist. Her work with women with eating problems led her to explore the roots of consumerism, as well as the links between psyche, body, culture, and the land (www.mjrust.net).

**Joy Schaverien: JS (Professor)

PhD: Jungian analyst and analytical art psychotherapist in private practice in the East Midlands, UK. Visiting Professor in Art Psychotherapy with the Art Therapy Northern Programme; professional member of the Society of Analytical Psychology in London (Jungian section) and training therapist and supervisor for the British Association of Psychotherapists. She has published widely.

**Caryl Sibbett: CS

Programme director of MSc Art Psychotherapy (HPC approved), run by the Centre for Psychotherapy, Belfast Health and Social Care Trust, and a lecturer in the School of Education, Queen's University, Belfast. She practises art psychotherapy at the Centre for Psychotherapy and her approach is integrative.

**Sally Skaife: SSk

Programme leader for MA in Art Psychotherapy at Goldsmiths; former member of the *Inscape* editorial group and BAAT chairperson. Research interests include the politics of art therapy, continental philosophy and art therapy and experiential learning in large art therapy groups.

Sandra Storey: SSt

Art therapist with many years of experience, currently working in Yorkshire with men and women with learning disabilities.

**Colin Teasdale: CT

DFA (London), Dip AT, MA (RCA): His Masters at the RCA (1983–1986) concerned work with homeless people in London; Senior Lecturer at University of Hertfordshire (1985–1993); pioneered art therapy at HMP Grendon, a prison providing psychological treatment for personality disordered male offenders (1993–1998). He developed art therapy as part of NHS community teams, in multicultural settings in West London (1999–2003) and recently in West Somerset.

Kim Thomas: KT

Works for NHS in Birmingham and has many years experience in offering individual and group art therapy to people with severe and enduring mental health difficulties. She is a BAAT supervisor and provides educational/ introductory workshops.

**Robin Tipple: RT
Has worked with adults who have learning disabilities, children in a therapeutic community who have experienced abuse, and children with developmental disorders, including Autistic Spectrum Disorders. He has been researching art therapy assessment.

Mike Waite: MWa
Art therapist working in a range of services in Sheffield and Rotherham.

**Diane Waller: DW (Professor)
Professor of Art Psychotherapy at Goldsmiths College and Imperial College London; also a group analytic psychotherapist. Her research interests are the sociology of health professions, the cultural context of and evidence-based practice in psychological therapies, and the history and development of art therapy in Europe. She is a member of the Health Professions Council, UK. In 2007, she was awarded an OBE for Services to Healthcare.

**Sally Weston: SaW
MA AP Research: Worked for 6 years in the Mental Health Services in Bradford. She now works as an art therapist in Neurological Rehabilitation in Sheffield. She has taught on art therapy qualifying courses and with the Art Therapy Northern Programme since 1997.

Simon Willoughby-Booth: SWB
MA (Hons): Lead Art Therapist for Learning Disabilities Service, NHS Lothian, and Professional Lead for Arts Therapies. An NHS clinician for over 30 years with a special interest in forensic issues in learning disabilities. His current research work is on developing self-report outcome measures for use with people who have learning disabilities; he now works freelance. He is a partner at the Health Professions Council.

Elaine Wisdom: EW
Works at Holy Rood House, Centre for Healing and Pastoral Care in North Yorkshire, which has a wide client base. Her practice is holistic and has its roots in the years when she lived in a religious community.

**Chris Wood: CW
PhD: Works with staff and students of the Art Therapy Northern Programme in Sheffield, which provides a base for training and research within the partnership between the Sheffield NHS (SHSC) and local Universities http://www.sct.nhs.uk/training-and-courses/art-therapy-northern-programme. She also works as an art therapist with adult clients of the NHS.

**Michèle Wood: MW
Works at Marie Curie Hospice, Hampstead. She lectured for 7 years at University of Hertfordshire and also worked with both adults and children in mental health, educational, and medical settings. Currently holds a research scholarship and works with the MA Art Therapy Programme, Roehampton University.

Pam Wood: PW
Experienced yoga teacher.

Entries

Entries

Absorption in art-making: CW

Making art can remind a person what it is to be absorbed. When someone is troubled it can be hard to escape an uncomfortable or even miserable self-consciousness. Whether a therapist adopts a gently supportive approach or a more challenging one, an important task of therapy is to enable clients to become creatively absorbed in what they are doing and in their lives. We seem to have a basic need for periods of absorption. They can provide the opposite of alienation. When children play, they are not often self-conscious, but they are absorbed.

After a period of distress, it can be difficult to feel absorbed when alone. Art-making can lead to reverie and a benign sense of absorption. Artists' studios throughout the centuries have contributed to the environmental circumstances and often the company that make absorption possible.

Alienation; Bachelard; Psychosis and; Reverie; Studios; Time disappears

Abuse: The creation of discontinuities of experience: CC

> In the sessions she longs to make something 'nice' but each time there is a downward spiral of barely containable mess, clay goes to slimy, smeared water, paints to murky brown/black mixtures. She is not able to bear the pain of looking at the damage and distress inside, felt depressed, despairing and suicidal under her insistence on 'nice pictures', denying what was actually being made. In the session she flits from one rushed activity to the other, is on the tables, at the windows, out of the door, leaving the room in chaos at the end so that my 'insides' feel tipped upside down or inside out. This evokes the sense I have from her that her world was turned inside out and upside down by the abuse. She no longer knows what is 'good' or 'bad', 'right' or 'wrong', who is to be trusted, what is 'real' and what is 'not real'

. . . A space has developed in the session where she can be 'still'.
There is the possibility that I can think about her, rather than often
feeling left behind in the tail of a tornado as she leaves the session. She
enjoys the sensation of being in my thoughts though it is hard to trust
that I will not lose interest if she is 'not entertaining me' in some way.
She communicates a lot through song and in this session is able to let
me know her fears that she will always be a soiled, abused child, the
'ugly duckling', and wish to be a 'pure swan', a girl to whom abuse has
not happened.

(Case, 2000: 40–47)

*Boundaries; Reparation using Herman; Therapeutic frame; Violation of
body boundaries*

Access to art: CW

Art therapists often work with people who have little access to the kinds of
art found in theatres, galleries, opera houses, and literature. They use wide
definitions of art and include many things that touch the imagination,
including much from the media, popular culture, and even football. Some
might keep a selection of books about the work of artists, photography, etc.
in their studios as a way of trying to broaden access, although others might
consider that this alters the nature of the therapeutic frame in ways that are
unacceptable.

Melvin Bragg (2004) points to a quartet of themes – accidents of
geography; not feeling educated enough; psychological fear and poverty
that keep many people without access to art and the way it describes the
human situation – although he celebrates the ways in which some TV is
improving access.

*Artists; Beuys; Blake; Comic strips; Football; Film Studio; Internet;
Popular culture; Ritual; Social inclusion; Television*

Act of painting: CW

. . . not about paintings, but about the act of painting, and the kinds of
thought that are taken to be embedded in paint itself. Paint records the
most delicate gesture and the most tense. It tells whether the painter
sat or stood or crouched in front of the canvas. Paint is a cast made of
the painter's movements, a portrait of the painter's body and thoughts.
The muddy moods of oil paints are the painter's muddy humours, and
its brilliant transformations are the painter's unexpected discoveries.
Painting is an unspoken and largely uncognized dialogue, where paint

speaks silently in masses and [colours] and the artist responds in moods . . .

(Elkins, 2000: 5)

Paint; Painting

Acting out: DN

'. . . conceived by Freud . . . to describe feelings from the past that are repeated within the transference: the patient "acts it" before us, as it were, instead of reporting it to us' (Freud, 1938: 176, in Laplanche and Pontalis, 1988: 6). Acting out also extends to outside of the transference relationship: 'We must be prepared to find, therefore, that the patient yields to the compulsion to repeat' (Freud, 1915: 151, in Laplanche and Pontalis, 1988: 4).

Acting out is a two-fold notion of *putting outside of oneself* something that should be kept inside and dealt with psychologically. In acting out the tension is drained, so that no trace of the internal conflict remains. The commonly held psychoanalytic view is of the acting out as an attempt to attack or to break off the therapeutic relationship.

Many of the people referred for art psychotherapy act out their feelings in extreme and life-threatening ways. However, once a therapeutic alliance is established it is possible for the patient to express their feelings more creatively, link those feelings to thoughts, and ultimately to understand them and be understood. Their acting out behaviour gradually lessens and sometimes disappears.

Alienation; Images used to convey the 'action' of violence; Therapeutic alliance

Action painting: Impact on art therapy: LR

Action painting was contemporary with Surrealist experiments with 'automatism', and Tachiste adventures in mark-making. In New York during this era, Caroline Pratt (herself influenced by psychoanalysis) and Margaret Naumberg (one of the originators of American art therapy) both founded progressive schools promoting emotional development through spontaneous creativity and self-directed learning. Florence Cane taught at the Walden School from 1920 to 1930. Her approach, influenced by abstract expressionism, used art-making, which combined physical movement, play, work, and discipline, to enable pupils to find their 'essence'.

Whilst some people relish the freedom and physicality of action painting, others associate it with loss of control and catharsis. This can elicit fantasies of using the whole room as the canvas, obliterating the space and all in it with paint. Whilst some fear it might involve complete disinihibition, others express grievance about an ostensible absence of craft, viewing the genre as fraudulent.

For Pollock (Cane's contemporary), who made a dance of throwing paint onto the canvas with sticks and hardened house-paint brushes, process was key: 'I feel nearer, more a part of the painting, since this way I can walk round it, work from the four sides and literally be in the painting' (Hughes, 1980: 313). The American critic Rosenberg described the birth of this form of abstract expressionism:

> At a certain moment the canvas began to appear to one American painter after another as an arena in which to act – rather than as a space in which to reproduce, redesign, analyse, or 'express' an object, actual or imagined.
>
> (Rosenberg, 1952: 45–46)

Rosenberg distinguished these enactments from autistic soothing, and from catharsis, by characterising them as 'dramatic dialogues' between painter and canvas.

Mise-en-scene; Process; Process model

Active imagination: EW

> Active imagination is the opposite of conscious invention . . . *it* uses a different energy described as *dreaming with open-eyes* . . . A new situation is created in which unconscious contents are exposed in the waking state . . . previously unrelated contents become more or less clear and articulate . . .
>
> The process of active imagination itself may have a positive and vitalising effect but the content (as of a dream) may also be painted as well.
>
> (Samuels et al., 1986: 9)

Colours and active imagination

Acute states: CT

I have found the term 'acute states' broad enough to describe and encompass contact with service users suffering from borderline developmental, affective conditions, and behavioural disorders. Art therapists have often been seen to work beneficially in public services settings with people on the margins of receiving treatment, the more difficult clients or patients whose mental states are often acute, heightened, severe, or delicate. Yet, as art therapists, we consistently need to promote and monitor the implications of working with such emotionally toxic material *within* rather than beyond the call of duty. For this reason, art therapists in the UK produced guidelines for working in prisons (Teasdale, 2002).

Clinical guidelines; Clinical guidelines in art therapy; Distributive transference and teamwork; Unhelpful counter-transference in forensic work

Adamson, Edward (1912–1996): CW

When working at Netherne Psychiatric Hospital (Surrey) in the late 1970s I was interested to meet some of the long-term 'patients' who remembered 'Mr Adamson'. He was one of the art therapy pioneers in Britain. He established studios at Netherne from just after the Second World War in 1946 and then worked as a 'hospital artist' for 35 years (Adamson, 1984: 4). The studios and the gallery he had established were still in existence when I was there. The equipment he offered each person who came to a studio was always the same: an easel, a chair, and a frame with two shelves for the same range of art materials. In this way, everyone was offered a small self-contained area in which to work without feeling overlooked.

People who remembered working with Adamson all mentioned the quietness of the studio and his respectful presence. Ironically, it may be that, because of instructions from medical colleagues to avoid interpretation (Waller, 1991: 54), Adamson provided powerful therapeutic containment. His way of inviting people to begin was simple and broadly similar with everyone; he would sit down next to them and ask them if they would like to do some painting.

> The hospital residents who came to the studio were accorded the dignity of helping to cure themselves. The very fact that they came to the studio each day placed a responsibility on their shoulders, rather than allowing them to become the passive recipients of authoritarian care. We were all working very much in the dark in those early days. I must confess that within a few weeks of starting my new job, I was in two minds whether I would have sufficient courage to continue. On looking back I realise that I stayed mainly in response to the overwhelming need of those who queued up everyday outside the studio, eager to begin.
>
> (Adamson, 1984: 2)

> Rich veins of surrealism are discovered in the studio. When, sometimes they [feelings] are fearful and persecuting, painting ventilates them within the safety of the studio.
>
> (Adamson, 1984: 6)

Agency; First period of British art therapy; Lyddiatt

Adaptations of practice: CW

Art therapy is based on clear psychotherapeutic principles; however, applying those principles sometimes requires adaptations of practice, made in response to context, current evidence, and the needs of particular clients. The *Guidelines for Art Therapists Working with Older People with Dementia* (Waller and Sheppard, 2006) provide a clear example:

> . . . In our experience it is possible to use a psychodynamic approach to the benefit of clients, but it needs to be modified.
>   . . . Despite the impairment of clients with dementia, we have observed that normal group processes take place. For example, clients' anxiety before breaks and towards the end of the sessions; testing the group's and therapist's boundaries; beginning to trust each other within and outside the group; being more confident in expressing emotion. The curative factors inherent in group therapy as discussed by Yalom (1983) and others are evident. However, there are some differences . . .
>
>   (Waller and Sheppard, 2006: 5–12)

It is important to ensure that adaptations do not damage the essential elements of the work: the art-making, the therapeutic relationship, and its boundaries. However, if adaptations are thoughtfully made they can aid the development of a therapeutic alliance where none previously existed. Adaptations have meant that art therapists throughout the world have provided a service for clients who might not otherwise have received it. Part of the process of adaptation involves a consideration of how socio-economic circumstances influence the lives of clients.

Adaptations might include: the provision of 'therapeutic care' as opposed to full therapy (Kalmanowitz, and Lloyd, 2005; Papadopoulos, 2002); supportive psychotherapy (Greenwood, 1997; Hartland, 1991); and brief therapy and adaptations based upon evidence from other models (DOH, 2000; Feltham and Dryden, 2006; Roth and Fonagy, 1996). They might also include acknowledgement of class and racial prejudice (Campbell et al., 1999; Wood, 1999a) and a critical consideration of 'psychological mindedness' (Coltart, 1987, 1988).

Addiction and art therapy; Art therapy approaches for particular clients; Brief psychotherapy (three entries)*; Clinical guidelines; Dementia clinical guidelines; Supportive psychotherapy; Therapeutic alliance; Therapeutic care*

Adaptations of practice with adolescents: AMB

A survey (Brown, 2005) showed that 81 out of 86 art therapists adapted their practice with adolescents to focus particularly on issues of engagement, boundaries, and termination of therapy. Both 'flexibility' and 'consistency' were identified as fundamental characteristics for the therapist to display. Therapists might then move between being seen as a safe 'parental' figure or as an ally in response to dependency needs that fluctuate 'moment to moment' within the therapeutic relationship.

Adolescence and neurological research

Addiction: CW

Most addiction literature concerns substance misuse (e.g. drugs and alcohol) but other forms of addiction seem to be developing (e.g. gambling). Addiction is the cause of human misery and death throughout the world; it is interwoven into economic systems, wars, and the ideologies of consumer lifestyles, with massive cost to national economies. The impact of addiction is wide ranging; examples include the inexorable dismantling of former mining communities and the hooking of children for use in the international sex trade. Increasingly health workers throughout the world call for legalisation as a way of defeating the drug barons economically. It is clear that moralising is rarely effective, but it is also clear that offering treatments that work is not straightforward. Governments find it difficult to tackle the health and social problems associated with addiction.

The UK's largest study of drug treatment, the 'National Treatment Outcome Research Study' (Glossop et al., 2001), was published in stages. The study hoped to show 'what works, what doesn't and what may usefully be adapted in order to help ensure that we secure the best treatment results possible'. It is estimated that for every £1 spent on treatment £3 is saved (in terms of crime and other costs), which amounts to at least £5 million a year in the districts included in the study. Art therapists meet many of the UK Government training requirements for drug workers.

Addiction and art therapy

Addiction and art therapy: CW

Waller and Mahony (Mahony and Waller, 1992; Waller and Mahony, 1999) advocate that art therapists should not abandon the roots of their work, but find ways to work alongside drug treatment teams. They discuss the difficulties of addiction; how addicts are stigmatised by labels such as 'addictive' personality traits and how problems that result directly from addiction are overlooked (Waller and Mahony, 1999: 8). Using both British and American art therapy literature, they identify elements of the art-making as being helpful for facilitating expression, protecting defences, and providing containment.

Gilroy (2006) discusses the implicit evidence contained in British and American papers (Dickman et al., 1996; Francis et al., 2003; Juilliard, 1995; Karkou and Sanderson, 1997; Mahony and Waller, 1992; Springham, 1994; Waller and Mahony, 1999):

> These few papers convey the potential for art therapy as a distinctive treatment for clients with addictions. Short-term art therapy groups challenge the assumptions of clients in a manageable way; this links with Karkou and Sanderson's (1997) suggestion that a more task-orientated approach might be appropriate early on in treatment, and distinguishes between longer-term individual and studio-based art therapy where clients can withdraw into narcissistic self-appraisal through art.
>
> (Gilroy, 2006: 124)

Dickson's (2007) thoughtful review of the literature cites a special issue of *The Arts in Psychotherapy* devoted to addiction (1990), an important theme being how art therapy might be *adapted* for inclusion in different treatment modalities. She points to ways in which different approaches worked well together in the programme where she worked: art therapy provided a time to 'assimilate some of the feelings evoked by the intense cognitive input of the programme' (2007: 25).

Adaptations of practice; Addiction

Adhesive identification with animals: CC

This concerns children who locate themselves in animals, usually a family pet. This is a form of adhesive animal identification, used to protect the self and hold it together. The core self of the child is frozen and held protected inside the outer skin of animal identification, which allows animation and interaction with the environment. This defence can protect the self from harm when the strain of 'being human' becomes too great. This taking on of an animal skin has elements of adhesive equation and of 'second skin' phenomena described by Bick (1968). Borrowing an animal skin is both a defence but also a creative leap of imagination as it allows a pathway out of autistic defences towards expression and communication to others, albeit a shape-shifting, camouflaged one (Case, 2005c).

Animals; Animation; Imagery and clay work of confusional or entangled children

Adolescence and neurological research: AMB

Neurological research (Balbernie, 2001; Wilkinson, 2006) has shown that the adolescent brain is more elastic than that of an adult. This suggests that young people have the capacity to (more easily) overcome trauma suffered earlier in life, with appropriate support from a facilitating environment of care, education, and, when necessary, therapeutic treatment.

Adaptations of practice with adolescents; Brain injury; Damage to mental health; Neurological art therapy; Psycho-neuro-immunology

Advertising: CW

Advertising is used to sell commodities and services. Sometimes adverts play on a sense of anxiety, sometimes they simply play. The images get into people's heads and they come into art therapy sessions, as collage material, inspiration, or illustration of contemporary life.

Advertising is on billboards, glossy magazines, and screens. Its design is often beguiling. With music, images, fantasies, and clever puns we are regularly sold ideas about how we might aspire to live. In the 1950s when the industry began in USA, people with psychoanalytic knowledge were hired because an understanding of the unconscious was thought to be useful in constructing the advertising message. Adverts have become increasingly sophisticated (we often have to work out what we are being sold) but the power of advertising remains 'to identify, and beam messages to, people of high anxiety, body consciousness, hostility, passiveness, and so on' (Packard, 1957). Packard's book *The Hidden Persuaders* (1957) was criticised by the industry as being unnecessarily conspiratorial and by academics as being too general, nevertheless a multinational industry understands the power of the image and it spends huge budgets on keeping in step with the *zeitgeist* of the times.

Collage; Popular culture; Visual culture

Advice: CW

Advice is generally one person's opinion about what another should do. Although therapists of most persuasions avoid giving advice, it is sometimes used in 'directive' therapeutic styles such as brief, cognitive, and crisis intervention. The advice here is different from that seen in everyday usage. It tends to be about the means of achieving therapeutic goals and not as instruction about what the goals should be. For example, some therapies advise that clients undertake homework in-between sessions. There is evidence that this can strengthen the outcome (e.g. Bergin and Garfield, 1994; Shelton and Ackermann, 1974). Similarly, art therapists sometimes 'advise' the use of scrapbooks or journals outside sessions. In these, clients collect and mull over the raw material of art-making and their thoughts about the therapy.

Most art therapists work in the public sector with clients who have a complex range of difficulties. Aspects of the work are difficult to contemplate because of the levels of poverty, deprivation, addiction, and uncertainty. In these circumstances, there is a need for vigilance about the dangers of offering advice that is more in the interests of the therapist than of the client. Nevertheless, some work with clients in very trying life circumstances needs to pass into the arena of what Papadopoulos described as 'therapeutic care' (2002), in which some advice might be offered.

Anticipatory guidance in art therapy; Supportive psychotherapy; Therapeutic care

Aesthetic counter-transference: JS

This is a form of counter-transference that is particular to art psychotherapy or other forms of psychotherapy where pictures are made or presented within a therapeutic relationship. The aesthetic effects of such pictures have an impact on the therapist and client as viewers and therefore influence and affect the transference and counter-transference dynamic. The term was introduced in *the Revealing Image* (Schaverien, 1991: 117–122) and developed in *Desire and the Female Therapist: Engendered Gazes in Psychotherapy and Art Therapy* (Schaverien, 1995a: 141). Consideration of this led to the development of the distinction between *diagrammatic* and *embodied* images. These are two different types of image that reflect the depth of psychological engagement of the client within the therapeutic relationship.

Counter-transference; Counter-transference captivity; Diagrammatic image; Embodied image

Aesthetic philosophy in art therapy: CW

Aesthetic philosophy concerns the nature of art. There are few direct references to it within art therapy literature. Nevertheless, it is possible to identify some concepts in art therapy that originate in aesthetic theory (e.g. Aldridge, 1998; Maclagan, 2001; Schaverien, 1991 [citing Cassirer]; Simon, 1992, 1997; Thomson, 1989; Waller, 1974, 2004, 2009b; Wood, 1999b). Case (2000) and Hills (2006) examine the place of beauty in therapeutic work and Jones exmines the sublime (*see* 'Sublime').

Michael Edwards (1989) discussed how formalised, controlled ideals of the neoclassical tradition promoted a sense of a common morality. He suggests that ideas of the time about rationality and reason led to an intolerance of 'the disorderly side of human nature' and that this was reflected in attitudes towards art and in '. . . viewing the expression of inner turmoil as an unforgivable breaking of the rules' (Edwards, 1989: 80). Nevertheless, Neoclassicism contained the seeds of a psychology of art. During the industrial revolution, art, in reaction against industrialisation, became romantic, with the depiction of imagination, fantasy, and dream imagery.

Maclagan (2001) discusses the impact of Surrealism in the early twentieth century and he makes the case for a more aesthetic approach to psychological issues. Peter Byrne (2002) describes the democratisation of art since the beginning of the twentieth century as contributing to the development of art therapy. Literary and art criticism are related to aesthetic philosophy and Wood (1999b) commented that it was surprising that these disciplines are not much used in art therapy. There is evidence that this is changing (e.g. Aldridge, 1998; Byrne, 2002; Gilroy 2008 [citing Rose, 2001]; Hills, 2006; Kalmanowitz and Lloyd, 2005 [citing Adorno]; Maclagan, 2001; Schaverien, 1991 [citing Cassirer]; Wood, 1999b [citing Eagleton]).

Art and materials in contemporary aesthetic philosophy; Visual research

Aetiology or etiology: CW

This refers to the study of causes. Medical and sociological research investigates the causes and origins of disease and human difficulty and the range of factors that might contribute to it. Art therapy, a profession situated in-between psychiatry, social work, and psychotherapy, is aided by accounts of causality, which combine psychiatric, psychological, and sociological understanding (e.g. Papadopoulos, 2002; Warner, 1985).

Agency; Psychiatry, psychoanalysis, poverty, and class

Agency: CW

> The idea of agency is a culturally prescribed framework for thinking about causation . . . Whenever an event is believed to happen because of an 'intention' lodged in the person or thing which initiates the causal sequence, that is an instance of agency.
>
> (Gell, 1998: 17)

Mental health workers in all disciplines are generally trying to enlist the agency of their clients. At times of stress, it can be difficult for a client to believe that they can influence the circumstances of their life, and the circumstances of some lives mean that choices are limited.

In art therapy, it is unquestionably the case that the clients make their own artwork. The therapist may offer the client some ideas about their life;

they may be a part of a significant relationship with the client; they may even suggest themes for the artwork; but they cannot make the client's art for them. The knowledge that the art made is their own can help the client begin to *see or recognise* their own agency.

Gell (1998) offered an additional perspective in using anthropology to provide a theory of the workings of *all* art. 'For many scholars and indeed in much common-sense thinking about art, it is axiomatic that art is a matter of meaning and communication. Gell (1998) suggests that it is instead about *doing* . . .' (Thomas, 1998: viii–ix).

Power; Transferable skills

Aggression: As a component of depression: DN

Psychoanalytic ideas about depression concern *ambivalence about aggression*, self-esteem, and loss. This stems from Freud's *Mourning and Melancholia* (1917), in which he suggested:

> . . . that loss was a central precipitant and precursor (vulnerability factor) in depression. The triggering current loss reawakens earlier childhood losses – either actual or symbolic – and through 'identi-fication with the lost object', the sufferer *attacks himself with reproaches that rightly belong to the loved one who has left him or let him down.*
> (Bateman and Holmes, 2002: 238)

Klein (1940) suggested that individuals might, when faced with external loss in later life, believe themselves as:

> . . . omni-potently to be responsible for loss, due to . . . inherent destructiveness, which has not been integrated with loving feelings. The sado-masochistic element in depression arises from projection and reintrojection of these feelings of envy and hatred. For Winnicott, if the depressive position – or stage of concern – has been achieved, the reaction to loss is grief; if not the reaction is depression.
> (Bateman and Holmes, 2002: 238)

Self-harm

Alchemy: SaW

Alchemy is one of many Arabic precursors to modern science. Artists commonly practised forms of it when experimenting with making colour until the invention of tubes for oil paints (Elkins, 2000). The search for gold

– not the base metal but spiritual enlightenment (perhaps we would also call it self-knowledge) – is the true goal of the alchemist's practice.

Archetype; Crucible

Alienation: CW

Being alienated involves feeling like a disinterested observer of one's own life. It evokes a sense of being *beside oneself* and not present in the tasks in which we are engaged. Processes of alienation mean that it is not straight-forward to distinguish between what comes from the individual and what comes from society. Themes that clients discuss range from the sense of being disconnected from society, not being taken seriously, feelings of isolation, loneliness, and stigma, and the difficulties of paying bills.

Theories of alienation were explored in the work of Marx and followers:

> All these consequences are contained in the definition that the worker is related to the product of his labour as to an alien object. For on this premise it is clear that the more the worker spends himself, the more powerful the alien objective world becomes which he creates over against himself, the poorer he himself – his inner world – becomes, the less belongs to him as his own.
>
> (Marx, 1844: 70)

The voices of many clients are heard in this lament about internal and external influences in their lives that alienate them from themselves and their experiences.

Absorption in art-making; Loneliness; Poverty; Rehabilitation

Amodality: RL

A picture's essence can be recognised in the effect it has on the viewer's mind as well as on her body. An art therapist takes in the pictures through multiple senses, amodally. This translates to a holistic percep-tion, bringing together various sensory modalities (cf. Stern 1985; Kristeva 1989). In addition to using the sense of vision, one 'listens' to the work via one's bodily sensations and attempts to feel their qualities: how the paint has been applied, how the process of creation is visible in the completed work, how the artist has treated his subject, etc. The process of taking in the qualities mediated by the material in the picture happens, as it were, as a physical roaming within the picture, with one's gaze acting as the guide. What one looks at also evokes an olfactory sensation. The loudness and quietness of the picture, its heaviness and lightness, movement and stillness, its temperature and taste may be experienced as auditory: taste, scent and tactile impressions and combinations of them. The viewer lives the picture rather than observing it from a distance . . . The question is: how is this picture, what is it like? Not so much: what is that?

(Laine, 2007: 129)

Amplification; Spatial awareness and empathy

Amplification: RL

Instead of free association, Jung describes a somewhat different approach to the exploration and interpretation of his clients' dreams or visual symbols. This approach he calls amplification. Compared to free association, amplification is a more narrowly defined, more controlled and more focused type of association where one attempts to search for analogies that would expand upon the symbol in question. Amplification is drawing parallels, finding correlation in myths, legends and other fields of science: ethnology, anthropology, history of religion, biology.

Amplification does not aim to explain a symbol. Rather, the objective is to circle around the symbol, to enrich it with new parallels and perspectives, using these to stay close to the meaning without being fixed on any particular interpretation too soon (Jacobi, 1942; Jung, 1961).

(Laine, 2007: 129–130)

Amodality; Circle; Free association through art; Legend; Metaphor
(three entries); *Myth; Popular culture; Symbol*

Analytical art psychotherapy: JS

This term was introduced by Joy Schaverien in *The Revealing Image: Analytical Art Psychotherapy in Theory and Practice* (1991: 6–7). It was first published in her PhD thesis entitled 'Transference and Countertransference in Art Therapy: Mediation, Interpretation and the Aesthetic Object', completed in 1990. This was a new term derived from two sources: Cassirer (1957: 93), who writes of an 'Analytical differentiation' in relation to the creative process; and Jung's (1921) method of psychotherapy, called analytical psychology.

Pictures that play a central role in art psychotherapy or analytical psychotherapy offer a different experience from verbal interpretation. They offer an opportunity for mediation and analytical differentiation. Such pictures are their own interpretation and therefore, in order to establish the centrality of the artwork in this process, a new term was required.

Styles of practice

Anger and art therapy: MLieb

The title of *Art Therapy and Anger* was specifically chosen, rather than 'Art Therapy and Anger Management', 'because there are a variety of views about anger and whether it is a destructive emotion to be "managed" or a constructive emotion to be welcomed and expressed' (Liebmann, 2008: 9).

Art therapy has things to offer in work on anger management: aiding communication; the process of making artwork slows clients down and helps them to reflect more on what is going on; making artwork can also be a less threatening way to approach issues. Doing this work in groups can also offer further benefits: sharing the artwork helps people to realise that they have things in common with each other, thereby overcoming isolation. Doing artwork enables a group to include both those who 'act out' their anger on others and those who 'act in' their anger on themselves; in a verbal group it is often difficult to include both of these in the same group (see more examples in Liebmann, 2008).

Acting out; Conflict resolution; Life of a symbol

Anima and animus: CW

'The inner figure of woman held by a man and the figure of man at work in a woman's psyche . . .' (Samuels et al., 1986: 23). The concepts are taken from Jung, with *anima* being internal to a man and *animus* internal to a woman. A playful image indicating this relationship (showing a woman and her gorilla) was shown on the cover of *Inscape* in 1980.

Animals: CC

Children sometimes bring live animals into the therapy session. Their presence suggests the older part of the child coming into relationship with a younger part, given concrete presence in animal form.

Animal cuddlies and transitional objects appear in children's images when there is a mute entreaty representing feelings that cannot be verbalised or are pre-verbal. Animal images may emerge in child therapy to represent and symbolise a traumatised younger self that is frozen in fear (Case, 2005c).

Animation

Animation: CC

This refers to the energy of experiences with animals and nature seen outside the therapy room. It may be safer for severely deprived children to see animation outside through the therapy room window, rather than work with the energy between therapist and child. This may be a necessary stage before a child can be brought into a state of imaginative play with materials inside the therapy room. The term animation is used in the sense of new imaginative play for each particular child, stimulated by an encounter with nature, an apprehension of beauty, or the sublime (Case, 2005c).

Animals; Comic strips; Film Studio; Sublime

Anthropology of mark-making: EW

This refers to the study of that mark-making tendency that is deeply embedded in all cultures. Indigenous mark-making has been associated, since prehistoric times, with understanding the connections between the interior and exterior. Spiritual and religious rituals have also used mark-making in aspects concerning health, healing, and the sustaining of life.

> Among the oldest traces left by man in the caves one sees marks made by a finger, a sort of streak on the clay surface . . . scribbles, interlacings are also found, with sometimes superimposed drawings of animals . . . The imprint of hands coated with colour used for body painting and placed on rocky walls appear to be the first pictorial attempts . . .
>
> (Houghton Broderick, 1948: 10)

Evolutionary psychology and art-making; Evolutionary psychology and cave art; Marks

Anticipatory guidance in art therapy: KH

Anticipatory guidance involves alerting people to what might happen during therapy. It links with Kelly's (1955) fundamental postulates as a way of helping clients sustain themselves whilst in therapy.

Early attempts at art-making are often characterised by feelings like 'this is completely spoilt, and ruined' as a consequence of some small mark made. The processes of art-making enable the safe practice of surviving those 'it's all gone wrong' moments by re-working, salvaging, or capitalising on a 'mistake' or 'accident'. We learn that we can avoid 'making things worse' and that we can be creative about the potential 'catastrophe', not only surviving it but also incorporating it, often improving the outcome. For example, the paint blot can become the wings, which are just what is needed.

Anticipatory guidance, worse/better paradigm; Consent; Learning circle; Personification

Anticipatory guidance, worse/better paradigm: KH

The desire to be wholly well can inhibit recovery because being really well means learning to manage lots of different feelings and situations rather than simply getting rid of the difficult feelings. Effective management requires a complex understanding of the pattern of one's own emotional system. George Kelly's (1955) personal construct psychology explores how each person characteristically evolves a system for anticipating events.

Three simple diagrams help to explore how feeling better is actually about *managing feeling more* rather than *not feeling bad*. It also allows for discussion about *expecting* to feel worse and how, at times, *feeling* worse can be seen as *being* better. This paradoxical state is similar to stage two of the 'Learning Circle', where feeling stupid is actually proof you have learnt something.

Bumping along the bottom (Figure 1) feeling dreadful is horrible but most people are quick to agree that the gap between feeling bad and feeling dire is not that big. In showing this the therapist clearly demonstrates their understanding that 'it's all awful', which is also good for the therapeutic alliance.

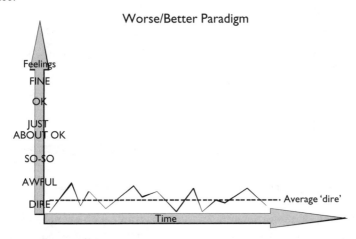

Figure 1 Bumping along the bottom.

What sabotages or really slows progress is being unprepared for the almost vertiginous plunges into feeling dire from positions of feeling so-so or just about OK (Figure 2). Being able to anticipate and develop plans for coping with these times of being plunged into feeling dreadful (Figure 3) can help to reduce their impact and duration.

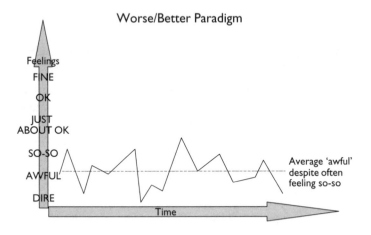

Figure 2 A small improvement.

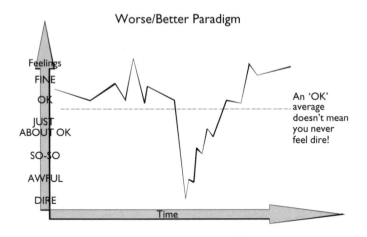

Figure 3 Feeling bad really does feel worse than ever as we get better.

I draw out (scribble) versions of these diagrams with clients and students on a regular basis. I usually ask for and write down their words for feelings to make it as individually relevant as possible. For one client anticipating and regularly plotting the ups and downs of her feelings became a monster's face with an increasingly smiley but very saw-toothed grin. Developing new predictable and familiar patterns to work with when faced with the uncertainty of new or long buried emotions and change is reassuring and empowering.

Anticipatory guidance in art therapy; Learning circle; Personification; Therapeutic alliance; Working through

Anti-psychiatry: CW

Anti-psychiatry became an international movement at the end of the 1960s and it continued intermittently for many years. In the first half of the twentieth century, many psychiatric hospitals had become dumping grounds for people who had lost their way, inpatient stays were too long, and a diagnosis of schizophrenia could mean a person being confined to a back ward for years and possibly for the rest of their lives.

Despite its title, the majority of the people advocating anti-psychiatry were psychiatrists and others working in psychiatry. The movement strengthened social psychiatry ideas. Art therapy and art therapy training in the late 1970s were shaped by both anti-psychiatry and the support gained from social psychiatry teams.

At the height of anti-psychiatry, it was common to blame the families of people diagnosed as schizophrenic and to scapegoat staff working in the hospitals. There was little compassion for families and no sympathy for people doing difficult work.

Laing, Goffman, and Berke (Wood, 1991) were central to the movement in Britain throughout the 1970s and the early 1980s. The work of the Italian psychiatrist Basaglia was important: he helped introduce the reform of the Italian Mental Health Act law 180 in 1978 (Wood, 1985).

Many psychiatrists tried to implement Laing's ideals of democracy into psychiatric working practices and in many places this meant that clients were better treated. The resulting changes contributed (with other factors) to the birth of user movements throughout the world.

Laing and Goffman; Social inclusion; Social psychiatry; User Movements

Archetype: MAm

The OED defines an archetype as a very typical example, an original model (or mould), or a recurrent motif in literature or art. This term is used by Jung from 1919 and is a fundamental concept of analytical psychology. An archetype is thought to structure the psyche, psychosomatically linking body and psyche, instinct and image. As a hypothetical entity, it is evident only through its manifestations.

Archetypes are recognisable in outer behaviours, especially those that cluster around the basic and universal experiences of life, such as birth, marriage, motherhood, death and separation . . . revealing themselves by way of such inner figures as anima, shadow, persona . . . Theoretically, there could be any number of archetypes.

(Samuels et al., 1986: 26)

Archetypal behaviours are most evident at times of crisis when the ego is most vulnerable. They arouse deep feelings and are often related to dreams. Archetypal qualities are found in symbols and this partially accounts for their fascination, utility, and recurrence.

Anima and animus; Procrastination; Symbol

Art and materials in contemporary aesthetic philosophy: KO

The work of Beuys is an example of how art and materials have been used in contemporary philosophy. Beuys came to prominence in the mid-1960s initially with his 'actions', performances, and installations. In these events, he incorporated materials such as felt, fat, dead, and sometimes living animals, earth, honey, and blood. Beuys believed that animals possessed spiritual qualities lost to Western society and could teach us how to live in tune with the natural world. In one of his key performances '*I like America and America likes me*', Beuys spent a week sharing a large cage with a coyote within the Rene Block Gallery in New York. He was driven from the airport in an ambulance, wrapped in felt. Inside the cage with the animal were several Wall Street journals, a length of felt, and a six-foot walking stick. For Beuys the coyote embodied the powers that the white man in America had largely extinguished. During the 1970s Beuys' concerns became increasingly political and didactic; he held debates and gave lectures on what he referred to as his 'expanded concept of art' (Harlan, 2004: 3). He famously stated, 'Everyone is an artist' (Borer, 1996: 17), and tried to bring art into the arena of everyday life. Beuys wished to convey how the creativity inherent in us all has the potential to transform and shape the substance of our lives and the society we live in.

Art materials; Artists; Beuys; Power of myth-making, Beuys and the Tartars; Romanticism; Sculptural materials

Art and sublimation: KJ

The links between sublimation, the role of the ego and super-ego in the internalisation of cultural values, and the renunciation of drive gratification

(Freud, 1917) were central to the Freudian view of cultural and social development (Freud, 1923, 1930). Artists worked on the raw material of their own unconscious conflicts through the art materials, which allowed the audience to identify with these unconscious conflicts as embodied in the artwork and rendered in culturally acceptable symbolic form (Freud, 1907).

Although Freud linked artist, audience, and society, his theory remained ambivalently located in an ahistorical realm, somewhere between sublimation and symptom (Adams, 2003). Despite his valuing of art and his appreciation of the human collective effort of culture, the aesthetic is sometimes reduced to an expression of repressed instinctual conflict, tending toward an illusory wish-fulfilling fantasy aimed at avoiding reality.

Kris responded to this impasse and developed the idea of artistic sublimation as a mature form of defence, which neutralised potentially dangerous drive energies and made them available to the ego. The artist, through a 'regression in the service of the ego', enabled the aesthetic illusion from which neutralised unconscious energies could create socially valued objects. Kris rethought art as an important aspect of the ego's adaptation to the environment (Kris, 1952).

Artists and reparation; Ego mechanisms of defence

Art as a discourse: JMa

This refers to the use of art and art-making as the source of discourse between therapist and clients, as opposed to the more usual focus on the therapeutic relationship. This model of art-making in art therapy modifies unequal power relationships (Greenwood and Layton, 1987; Karkou and Sanderson, 2006; Mahony, 1992) and offers privacy to the group members in their art-making (Haesler, 1989). However, it demands much of the therapist's knowledge about art as well as their counter-transference. Also, not all clients may like the therapist making art (Brooker et al., 2007) and this should be discussed in the assessment and then constantly monitored.

Materials and objects can be taken in and out of the setting to maximise engagement with the art-making, but when using this model it is advisable that works in progress stay in the room. Such an expressive and exploratory practice may be generative, or contrastingly one of documentation, and can involve many forms and media – art-based; codes; formulae; workmanship; mapping; systematic investigation including words, symbols and visual images, physical components; sensation; rhythm and sounds – and all contribute to the total interactional field. The content of the work is not explored and only the process of its making and formal concerns are discussed, with any psychological or emotional links volunteered by clients, not the therapist. The structure of the group dynamically privileges art-

making over verbal interaction. The artwork produced is seen as interpretation in itself, in the group analytic tradition (Foulkes and Anthony,
1965: 258) similar to free association in individual verbal psychotherapy.
The art can be understood as giving visual form to the group matrix and is
multidimensional, forming the operational base of the group. Moreover,
the art-making is characterised by intense engagement and can be thought
of as transforming and materialising autobiography over time in an
integrative process (see Mahony, 2010b).

Absorption in art making; Group analytic approach; Group analytic
psychotherapy; Mythologies and the participant observer; Participative
art practice; Power; Retention of artwork by the client; Rhyme

Art as metaphor: MEd

'Art is a language of metaphor which cannot be stripped down to a basic
explanation and survive' (Edwards, 1978: 13).

Metaphor (three entries)

Art brut: CW

This French term roughly translates as 'raw art' and it is the term used to
describe the movement headed by Dubuffet for recognition of artists
working outside the mainstream art establishment.

> The French term 'brut' is not easily translated into a single English
> word, but it carries with it connotations both of simplicity and natural-
> ness as well as ill-breeding and clownishness. However, this range of
> possibilities is probably one of the reasons that Dubuffet was drawn to
> the word in the first place. The notion of being in the 'natural' or 'raw'
> state lies at the heart of the word and in this sense it is set in opposition
> to 'culture.' However, Dubuffet's early career – not as an artist, but
> working in the family wine business – provides the clue to the most
> celebratory and poetical meaning, namely that like the best champagnes,
> brut here signifies the unadulterated, purest state of things.
>
> (Rhodes, 2000: 23–42)

Subsequently the British writer Roger Cardinal (1972) made the translation
'outsider art'.

Art of the insane; Corbaz; Outsider art

Art made by art therapists: AJG

The art practice of art therapists is a key factor in clinical practice and continuing professional development. Practitioners engage with art in different ways, be it within the context of contemporary art, therapeutic work, or in a quasi-domestic setting (Gilroy, 2005). Some art therapists exhibit their work; some use art as an arena for the reflexive processing of clinical material in supervision and education (Brown et al., 2003, 2007; Lanham, 1998; Rogers, 2002); some use art therapy to think about the nature of the art-making process (Ramm, 2005); some make work alongside their patients (Maclagan, 2005). Others have described their art-making during times of ill health (Halliday, 1988; Sibbett, 2005a) and its use as a visual, practice-based research method (Mahony, 2010b; Sibbett, 2005b).

Art therapists' art practice can have a direct influence on their clinical work: research has shown that an absence of a personal art practice can lead to art therapists' clinical practice becoming more verbally oriented (Gilroy, 1992, 2005). Conversely, clinical practice can have a direct impact on art therapists' art: it may inhibit or enhance the capacity for engagement. For example, the working environments of art therapists can have a deleterious effect and practitioners may become 'visually saturated' with patients' artworks, but equally art therapy rooms can offer opportunities for therapists' art-making and patients' work can be a stimulus for therapists' art.

Therapist's engagement with their own art

Art materials: CW

> In fact anything and everything can be pressed into service, but the directness of the work must not be lost in a welter of variety for its own sake. Too much lavishness can be distracting . . .
>
> (Lyddiatt, 1972: 15)

Art and materials in contemporary aesthetic philosophy; Collage; Rhyme

Art of the insane: CW

During the middle years of the twentieth century the linked ideologies of *art brut* (or *outsider art*) and *the art of the insane* (Cardinal, 1972; Dubuffet, 1995; MacGregor 1989) provided a strange background to the concerns of art therapists. Comment about art made outside the margins (whether of the art establishment or on the edge of sanity) offers much insight into the nature of the work, but some comment is sceptical about art therapy, suspecting it of domesticating the source of creativity and diminishing quality.

MacGregor writes of a 'golden age of psychotic art' and offers his own recommendation of distinctions he thinks should be made, as though they were a description of actual historical processes:

> The meaning of the phrase 'art of the insane' evolved over a long period. In its early usage it implied all drawings, paintings and sculptures made by madmen. Towards the end of the twentieth century, the phrase began to be used in referring to only those rare works perceived as being of unusually high artistic quality or meaning.
>
> (MacGregor, 1989: 6)

Nevertheless, MacGregor usefully discusses how the art made by people on the margins is changing. He points to times when there is an overuse of medication and to the large amount of time that the people whose work he catalogued had for art-making in the old asylums.

Art brut; Corbaz; Géricault and physiognomy; MacGregor; Pell

Art supplies: CW

> Art Supplies connotes . . . all the stuff we struggle mightily to tame and force to behave the way we wish [and which] are often considered passive, inanimate things devoid of an inner vitality . . . *media*, from, the Latin *medius*, meaning 'middle' are those things that stand between imagination and expression, between the mind and the act, the hand and the canvas. Media shuttle between the realm of thought and feeling and the concrete world of events.
>
> (London, 1989: 169)

Knowledge of materials

Art therapy: CW

It is important to consider the audience before offering a definition (the needs of clients, lay-audiences, and therapists differ).

There is a range of possible definitions. The one quoted below (Case and Dalley, 2006) encompasses much. However, art therapists largely work with clients who live difficult lives in difficult circumstances and this means that definitions of art therapy need to include consideration of the context in which the client lives and the therapist works. It is helpful to have a sense of the way human distress is shaped by a world that includes social inequality and discrimination.

Art therapy, or art psychotherapy as it is sometimes called, involves the use of different art media through which a client can express and work through the issues, problems and concerns that have brought her into therapy. In the therapeutic relationship, the art therapist and client are engaged in working together to understand the meaning of the art work produced. For many clients, it is easier to use a non-verbal form of communication and, by relating to the art therapist, make sense of their own experience through the art object, which provides a focus for discussion, analysis, and reflection. As the art work is usually concrete, there is a memory of the therapeutic process in the making of the object and in the interaction between therapist and client. Transference develops within the therapeutic relationship and also between therapist, client and the art work, giving a valuable 'third dimension' or three-way communication (Schaverien 2000).

(Case and Dalley, 2006: 1)

Adaptations of practice

Art therapy and art activities: MLieb

Art therapy and art activities are both valid processes in their own right, but with different emphases. The aim of an art activity is usually the production of a picture, collage, or sculpture. The aim is the completion of the work (and often its exhibition), but along the way participants often gain great benefit. The aim of art therapy is the exploration of a personal problem or situation using art materials, but along the way artworks of great merit may be produced.

Training module in the sensitive use of art for non-art therapists

Art therapy approaches for particular clients: CW

Increasingly, different forms of art therapy practice for clients with specific difficulties are being reported with individuals and groups. Art therapists within BAAT have created a range of special interest groups. The distinguishing of different forms of practice may help the profession in the establishment of an evidence base.

The attempt to determine *what* form of therapy *works for whom* (Roth and Fonagy, 1996) involves a range of adaptations based on the evidence so far of what approach seems to help particular difficulties (e.g. children with ADHD, clients with depression or a history of psychosis, etc.). There are a small but increasing number of randomised control trials showing the benefits of art therapy for people with particular needs (e.g. for people with dementia, schizophrenia, or physical health needs).

Adaptations of practice; Clinical guidelines; Evidence-based practice;
Randomised controlled trials; Styles of practice; What works for whom?

Art therapy object: MC

In longer term, individual, object-relations-orientated art therapy, an art therapy object refers to a hypothetical idea of a particular 'good object' formed and internalised by the patient from his or her experiences of image-making and the therapeutic relationship with the art therapist.

In object relations theory, a securely internalised 'good object' is thought of as loving and caring for the self, and being loved by and cared for by the self.

Cracked pots; Object; Object relations theories

Art therapy RCTs: CW

A randomised controlled trial (RCT) is not a straightforward instrument for research in mental health (Barkham, 2007; Gilroy, 2006; Seligman, 1995; Wood, 1999b), but it is the one recognised internationally as a 'gold standard' for systematic research. The creation of large enough sample sizes for RCTs in art therapy is often problematic because the costs can be prohibitive, but there are increasing numbers of trials undertaken in all areas of art therapy practice. These include:

- with older people (Waller et al., 2006);
- with people with a diagnosis of schizophrenia (Richardson et al., 2007; and the large HTA-funded Matisse project that is ongoing);
- with people who are depressed (Bell and Robbins, 2007; Thyme, 2007);
- as part of a mindfulness approach in cancer care and general physical health (Cohen, 2006; Monti, 2006; Oster, 2006);
- and an increasing number of outcome studies with children and young people (e.g. Rosal, 1993; Sanders et al., 2000).

The art therapy RCTs are the result of art therapists working collaboratively with teams of researchers. Results from RCTs in art therapy are published regularly in electronic sources.

Case studies; Collaborative research teams; Evidence-based practice;
Quantitative research; Randomised controlled trials; What works for
whom?

Artists: CW

As indicated in the introduction, the work of many artists in the visual arts, music, literature, and film are a source of understanding and inspiration in art therapy.

Artists and reparation; Bachelard; Beuys; Blake; Bourgeois; Complexity and pain contained in an artwork; Géricault and physiognomy; Rodin and drawing; Wilde's Dorian Gray

Artists and reparation: MAm

For many artists and writers, the products of their art may be seen as a reparative re-working of childhood experiences. They include Paula Rego, Louise Bourgeois, Alice Miller, Maya Angelou, and Tracey Emin. Griselda Pollock, quoting Lubaina Himid in *After Mourning comes Revenge*, writes of the revenge following a sense of loss:

> To mourn the loss . . . is to examine the meaning of what is felt as lost . . . and to free the creative subject for action . . . Artistic practice is . . . more than a therapeutic process. It requires mourning to be accomplished – for there to be departure from the trauma – for the artist to release her creativity.
>
> (Pollock, 1999: 189)

The stories and poetry of Maya Angelou are testimony to the creativity released from a history of communal pain and mourning. Paula Rego (King and Bradley, 2001) describes her childhood as 'intense' in the sense that 'everything seemed significant and important'. As a solitary, only child her early experience of being read to, as well as making up her own stories, became combined visually in her images: images that tell a story, often depicting a darkly comic side. Her stark and enduring representations of female suffering (exemplified in the abortion pictures) reveal a sensitive acknowledgement of the bleak suffering of girls and women. In the most desperate and humiliating situations, she reveals the ultimate strength of women. John McEwan (1992) writes of her 'black moods' and her child-hood struggle between good manners and inward revolt. Rego herself describes her 'flight into story telling' – 'You paint to fight injustice'.

Art and sublimation; Bourgeois

Art-making as a defence: CW

> . . . some art therapists . . . assert that 'art is inherently therapeutic.'
> While as an art psychotherapist I would like to think this were true the
> evidence convinces me otherwise. Painting [art-making] in therapy is
> no more or less therapeutic than any other aspect of the therapy
> process and is subject to the same resistances and difficulties that limit
> therapeutic change. A more realistic view might be to say that art is
> potentially highly therapeutic. This acknowledgement that art is not a
> universal panacea of sublimation liberates the therapist from idealised
> notions of omnipotence and allows for the varying degrees to which
> clients can utilise the creative process.
>
> (Mann, 1990a: 7)

Defend or abwehr; Sublimation theories

Art-making leftovers: KM

By definition 'leftovers' are often neglected from consideration, but placing
value on and taking into account 'discarded' art objects, or even 'leftovers'
from the art process, can lead to useful discoveries for clients.

Scissors

Artwork and outcome measures: HG

Greenwood et al. (2007) brought the qualitative process data of categorised
artwork together with clinical outcome data in a single case study of a
patient seen for 6 years of long-term art therapy. Using a standard evaluation instrument CORE-OM (Clinical Outcome in Routine Evaluation
Outcome Measure) before each session, the process of change in therapy
was monitored. After therapy ended, data from researchers and the art
therapist were examined together. The study demonstrated a relationship
between the type of art and the level of psychological distress indicated by
the standard outcome measure. Seven distinct phases of art were identified,
including 'no art', and generally one theme tended to lead to the next.
Awareness and naming of the different categories arose within the therapy
process. In contrast, the CORE scores showed great variability from one
session to the next. The researchers suggested that the type of artwork
might be a better indication of overall progress than single-session
CORE scores.

Outcome measures

Artworks and discourses of men and women with learning disabilities: BD and RT

Difference, social isolation, loss, vulnerability to abuse, and exploitation all have a presence in the artworks and discourses of men and women with learning disabilities. The loss experienced is not only in relation to the death of significant others but is the loss of opportunities that in other contexts would be perceived as rights. Rees (1998) makes this explicit in *Drawing on Difference*, the first British book dedicated to art therapy in the context of learning disability. 'Secondary handicap' material and expressions of loss permeate the whole therapeutic space, affecting the client's relationships to the materials, the art therapist, and indeed the very fabric of the art room. Any or all of these aspects can at times become targets for split-off unbearable and projected aspects of disability (e.g. the pens that refuse to work properly, the damaged brush, and the 'stupid therapist'). The artworks may also visually indicate or represent damage, perhaps through the absence of some vital aspect or some form of distortion.

Difference can be shown, for example, through the repeated absence of an element in an image or a sense of isolation in the spatial treatment of an artwork. The experience of being observed so much and being seen as unlike others is conveyed by the human figure represented as a passive object for the gaze of an unseen observer, and the representation of the 'handicapped smile' (Sinason, 1992).

Emotional life for men and women with learning disabilities; In the box; Learning disabilities; Secondary handicap

Assessment and formulation: CW

Roth and Fonagy (1996) describe assessment and formulation as the 'complicated tasks of assessment and treatment planning'. Assessment involves making an educated prediction about the prospects for therapy with a particular client. This is different from assessing a person. Increasing autonomy and regulation in psychotherapeutic work of all kinds have meant that there has been an increasing focus on the processes involved in assessment (Mace, 1995: 1).

Considerations that are important in art therapy assessments can be summarised as the client's capacity to use art materials (an inability would not necessarily exclude someone) and the client's capacity to engage in the process of therapy (at whatever level). Many of the considerations involved in making generic assessments for mental health work and psychotherapy are also relevant in work with children and with adults. In addition, it is helpful to consider that: 'The assessment is a significant process in its own right – not just assessment for something else – and should be viewed as a brief intervention with therapeutic potential' (M. Pracka, 2009, lecture notes).

Formulation is the process of developing information gained during the assessment process into a plan for the therapy. The formulation needs to be theoretically coherent and based on available evidence (D. Gibson, 2009, lecture notes).

Brief dynamic art psychotherapy; Evidence-based practice; Health Professions Council; Materials and image in assessment

Attachment framework: TBo

The *International Attachment Network* at University College London had its first seminars in 1998. These presentations related to the foundations of the work already set out by John Bowlby. Daniel Steel introduced these seminars, the first of which discussed the findings of Mary Ainsworth and her work with parent and child called the 'Strange Situation'. Her findings related to the several categories of attachment that parent and child could engage in. Understanding these different attachment styles offers further tools through which to attune to clients. Other influences from an attachment framework included Mario Marrone. His book, *Attachment and Interaction* (Marrone, 1998), presents a comprehensive introduction to the development of attachment theory. His findings on parenting styles and his ideas on iatrogenia and the persecutory therapist are of particular use in supervision. Travarthen (biologist) offers further understanding of attunement. His videos on the musicality of babies and the timing of parental interaction show how crucial this is in allowing the baby time to digest and respond to stimuli. Other influences in this framework are Stern, Sore, Shroufe, de Zulueta, and Fonagy, among others. The seminars offered great help to those working with children in child protection. Boronska's work on art therapy from an attachment perspective includes a paper discussing two sibling groups (Boronska, 2000) and another concerning the sibling bond (in Case and Dalley, 2008).

The Bowlby Centre is a useful link for art therapists: (http://thebowlby centre.org.uk/aboutCAPPhome.htm).

Assessment and formulation; Child development

Attraction to and copying pictures: CC

An attraction to a particular artist's pictures may represent an unconscious investment, related to the matching of an inner experience, as well as the unconscious beginnings of one's own image-making. The image that a child chooses usually depicts an inner-world landscape or experience and the recreation or 'copying' of the image helps to begin a process of developing emotional literacy. In this way, images that children 'find' or bring to the session help to find forms for inner feeling (Case, 2008).

Artists

Audit: AJG

Audit is essentially a series of practical, quality assurance procedures, which aim to ensure that clinical work, based on the best available evidence, is implemented, monitored, and continually improved in a cyclic, multistepped process. Audit measures the quality of services and care offered to the public, changing and improving that which is demonstrably lacking and following up any necessary changes to ensure their implementation. It can have a problem-solving remit but it can also be a means through which practitioners can formalise their continuing process of critical self-reflection about services and practices. It is at the heart of developing an evidence base to practice, being a means of checking that 'the right thing has been done' and 'that it has been done right' (Parry, 1998).

Audit data can be collected in a variety of ways: retrospectively through documents (e.g. on demographics) or through brief questionnaires that can be analysed simply and speedily. Audit can support the improvement of care and ensure that practice is kept up-to-date through the continuing professional development of staff. Nevertheless, it is also a self-referential system and a direct consequence of fiscal imperatives and new managerialism operating upon public sector work since the 1980s (Power, 1998; Shore & Wright, 2000). Art therapists need to maintain their political awareness when engaging with every aspect of the audit process (Gilroy, 2006).

Clinical guidelines; Evidence-based practice; Outcome measures

Autistic spectrum disorders and art therapy: SWB

Autism is not a single condition; however, individuals on the autistic spectrum usually have significant difficulties in three areas: communication, imagination, and socialisation. Art therapists' thinking about autism has often been subsumed under the general field of work with people who have learning disabilities, but Evans and Dubowski (2001), Stack (1996), and Fox (1998) have explored issues specifically related to autism, and the contribution of art therapy to the development of object relations and symbol formation.

Artworks and discourses of men and women with learning disabilities;
Communication with men and women with learning disabilities

Bachelard, Gaston (1884–1962): CW

This extraordinary French Professor of Physics and Chemistry was gifted in independently using scientific and poetical forms of explanation. In *The Poetics of Space* (Bachelard, 1958) and *On Poetic Imagination and Reverie* in (Bachelard, 1967) he discusses the possibilities for thinking in images, and he explores the relationship between interior and external space. Art therapists often refer to Bachelard's poetical writing.

> Of course, thanks to the house, a great many of our memories are housed, and if the house is a bit elaborate, if it has a cellar and a garret, nooks and corridors, our memories have refuges that are all the more clearly delineated. All our lives we come back to them in our daydreams.
>
> Bachelard, 1967: 8)

Agency; Blank sheet; Reverie

Balint groups and image consultation groups: RL

Balint groups were developed by Michael and Enid Balint as a way of providing a feasible form of group-based psychotherapeutic training for general practitioners (Balint and Balint, 1961). The groups provided a method for helping GPs think about the impact of psychological issues on the health of their patients.

Image consultation groups take a similar approach:

> In their own way, everyone was an expert on what they themselves saw, experienced and were able to take in. The client emerged as the most important person, as the protagonist.
>
> There is a resemblance between Balint groups and image consultation. In both groups, there is an emphasis on trying to listen to and recognise one's feelings and associations in relation to the presented case; however, in image consultation the case consists primarily of the client's pictures. While a Balint group attempts to get away from an illness-centred towards a patient-centred approach (Trenkel, 1994), one might say that image consultation is image-centred when compared to typical supervision . . .
>
> (Laine, 2007: 123)

Supervision

Baring the phenomenon: JS

This term refers to the otherwise inarticulable quality of artworks, which sometimes reveal that which cannot be adequately translated into words. Sometimes in a picture, the phenomenon is bared – the image is uncloaked. The term is adapted and changed from Cassirer's original meaning (1957) by Schaverien (Schaverien, 1991: 107) to make it applicable for analytical art psychotherapy.

Analytical art psychotherapy; Therapeutic precision; Without recourse to words

Beuys, Joseph (1921–1984): KO

Joseph Beuys was one of the most important German artists of the twentieth century. His career spanned 30 years of intensive activity. His work and ideas continue to influence developments in many aspects of contemporary art. The body of work includes installations, drawings, performances, actions, lectures, and public debates. He also worked colla-boratively with others to found organisations such as the Democratic Student Party in 1969, which he claimed was his finest sculpture. Beuys had a charismatic personality and presented himself as a shaman-like figure with a considerable following. The 'wound' is a recurring theme in his work. He says, 'I realized the part the artist can play in indicating the traumas of a time and initiating a healing process' (Rosenthal, 1984: 33). He believed in the redeeming and transforming qualities of creativity. He drew his ideas from disparate influences that included Shamanism, Norse mythology, folklore, the natural sciences, philosophy, and ecology.

The following are useful websites relating to Beuys:

- http://img127.imageshack.us/my.php?image=morepg8.png
- http://img127.imageshack.us/img127/7150/morepg8.th.png
- www.ImageShack.us

Art and materials in contemporary aesthetic philosophy; Artists; Power of myth-making, Beuys and the Tartars

Blake, William (1757–1827): CW

Although William Blake is now much celebrated, the visions of the artist and poet meant he was an outsider during his lifetime. Ackroyd (1995: 196) suggests he had 'something of madness' about him and that his marriage to a servant put him outside the art academy of his day.

Blake's personal symbolism often inverts accepted norms and often refers to angels. He had a life-long struggle against poverty and for recognition, and as a result themes in his work resonate with those expressed by many art therapy clients. Ackroyd (1995) compares Blake's gothic gestures with the excitement provoked today by science fiction, with its dark stars and dark forces.

He was unusually aware of the horrors of slavery. More radical than many abolitionists of his day, he thought that the 'physical enslavement of Africans was a consequence of the British elite's own mental enslavement' (Bindman, 2007: 20). Throughout his life, he warned of ways in which we mentally enslave ourselves and he advocated that only poetry and art could protect us.

Artists; Géricault and physiognomy; Mind-forged manacles; Muse and duence; *Popular culture; Romanticism*

Blank periods or threshold difficulty: MEd

> For almost all of one year, Fridays were days of agony and yet they were set aside for what I most wanted to do – paint from the imagination, or the unconscious, as we never called it then. The reality was that hour-by-hour, week-by-week I would keep company with a blank or nearly blank canvas and scratch out a few desultory drawings which were my desperate and increasingly despairing attempts to come up with an idea 'good enough' to paint. Image after image was rejected. Nothing was ever good enough, so I could never get started . . .
>
> For me, just one vital link was missing. I needed somebody to tell me on those Fridays simply to begin painting, without paying too much attention to what I was doing, to teach me to suspend my critical faculties, be prepared for anything and just paint. I needed to develop a body of work, an opus that could be worked upon as raw material, or *prima materia*, as the alchemists would have said. Without this opus, directly from my psyche I tried to rely upon what my consciousness knew about art, and was depressed by its aridity. What I needed but didn't know it, was . . . an *art therapist* . . . somebody to unlock my self-consciousness and help me to establish an unpremeditated and judgment-free flow of images. *Not*, you will note, an art therapist to *interpret* my scanty collection of pictures, let alone my behaviour. Somebody nevertheless, on my side, who would help me to trust *whatever* my imagination came up with, not judge it.
>
> (Edwards, 1998a)

Alchemy; Blank sheet; Block; Procrastination

Blank sheet of paper: MEd

A blank sheet of paper can be as difficult to deal with as trying to fit into a complex and unfamiliar dance or musical pattern because, in its blankness, it throws all the responsibility onto the would-be writer or artist. Every mark is attributable. There is nowhere to hide.

Archetype; Blank periods; Block; Drawing a line; Procrastination

Bleulers: Psychiatrists father and son: CW

Barham's account (1995) of the work of the Swiss psychiatrists Eugen Bleuler (1857–1939) and Manfred Bleuler (1903–1994) is empathic. Eugen Bleuler laid the foundations for combining psychotherapeutic and psycho-social approaches in work with the most disturbed patients and he never gave up the struggle to reconcile the organic and the psychological psychiatric traditions. However, Barham reports that this struggle 'over-whelmed' Eugen towards the end.

It is on the life of Manfred Bleuler that Barham mainly focuses, since Manfred Bleuler's major work (1972) gives the most incisive account to date of the history of schizophrenia. It shows that the characteristic dialogue of psychiatry is between a professional class and a pauper class. Implicit and powerful in its contemporary relevance is the 'gripping account of the ideological force field in which the whole problem of schizophrenia is entrapped' (Barham, 1995: 27). Bleuler's writing is full of moving accounts of his thoughtful encounters with his schizophrenic patients.

That the work of the Bleulers was conducted over more than a 20-year period means that it is almost certainly the longest research undertaken with this client group. In describing their work, Barham is proposing that clinical hope in the field of schizophrenia is well grounded, but he is indicating that political support for such work is less secure. The central issues described by the Bleulers in their work remain relevant and the same 'ideological force field' is the context for much work in psychiatry, psy-chology, and art therapy. The case they made is from a position of practice.

*Class; Evidence-based practice; Kraepelin and perceptions of
schizophrenia; Psychiatry, psychoanalysis, poverty, and class*

Block: LR

To describe the aspect of depression that makes creative work impossible as 'block' suggests that creativity is still alive, but the channels between the internal source, the conscious mind, and the hand have been interrupted.

Robert (pseudonym) described how he used to gaze into the eyes of his portraits and feel deeply connected with them. He explained that to draw was now for him 'just going through the motions' – a meaningless exercise (in his view). Not painting now left him feeling powerless: '. . . for the artist, the disruption of creative abilities is characteristically a loss even more bitter than that of a beloved person . . . because it tends to rob him of the central goals that characterise his being' (Gedo, 1989: 58).

Wood (1986) writes about the fear that can be engendered by the expectation to make artwork, citing Herbert Read's phrase 'milk white panic'. Sometimes an indirect approach to creative paralysis can be helpful, as performance anxiety can make an internal critic fierce. Periods of simply observing and not trying to draw or make anything at all, and periods of 'mulling' and researching, seem as important as 'hands on' production. At other times, 'dry periods' can be interrupted by shifting the medium, for example from painting to collage, photography, or words. There are of course no formulas or simple answers to this perennial difficulty.

Blank periods; Procrastination

Borderline personality disorder (BPD): DN

BPD is summarised in diagnostic systems as a 'pervasive pattern of instability of interpersonal relationships, self-image, and affects, and marked impulsivity beginning by early adulthood and present in a variety of contexts' (American Psychiatric Association, 1994: 301.83). It is characterised by intense but unstable personal relationships; self-destructiveness; frantic alternating between extremes of idealisation and devaluation; efforts to avoid real or imagined abandonment; chronic feelings of emptiness; recurrent suicidal behaviour; mood instability; inappropriate anger; transient paranoid ideation and identity disturbance. Diagnosis does not necessarily lead us to an understanding of the underlying causes or the experiences:

> . . . there is an increasing interest in the nature of borderline disorders and their treatment by modified psychoanalytic methods. Indeed it appears that this may well be one of the major contributions of psychoanalysis to contemporary psychiatry.
>
> (Bateman and Holmes, 2002: 222)

Kernberg (1984) offers the concept of a Borderline Personality Organisation (BPO). Fonagy (1991) suggests that people with borderline conditions *may* lack what he calls 'mentalizing capacity'. Gunderson and Sabo (1993) indicate that one-third of BPD patients fulfil the criteria for post-traumatic stress disorder, having been subjected to physical and sexual abuse in childhood or being the survivors of traumatic loss.

Mentalisation; Post-traumatic stress disorder and art psychotherapy

Boundaries: MAm

Boundaries can describe the physical limits of the therapy space; they can also describe the personal, social, or professional limits between the therapist and the client. These can encompass stated or unstated 'rules', which are necessary for the physical and psychical protection of both parties.

Judith Lewis Herman provides a useful description of boundaries in a therapeutic relationship:

> Secure boundaries create a safe arena where the work of recovery can proceed. The therapist agrees to be available to the patient within limits that are clear, reasonable, and tolerable for both. The boundaries of therapy exist for the benefit and protection of both parties and are based upon a recognition of both the therapist's and the patient's legitimate needs. These boundaries include an explicit understanding that the therapy contract precludes any other form of social relationship, a clear definition of the frequency and duration of therapy sessions, and clear ground rules regarding emergency contact outside of regularly scheduled sessions.
>
> (Herman, 1994: 194)

Boundaries can also refer to elements of the image in therapy, which appear as barriers, edges, or encapsulations.

Abuse; Lateness; Picture within the frame; Professional conduct and misconduct; Therapeutic frame; Violation of body boundaries

Bourgeois, Louise: JM

The work of Louise Bourgeois often represents the making of sculpture as a symbolic enactment and catharsis giving form to memory. With a life spanning Freud, Bachelard, and Postmodernism, she described her practice and work as talismans and containers for early traumatic memories and experiences:

> Once a sculpture is done, it has served its purpose and has eliminated the anxieties that I had. The anxieties are gone forever. They will never

come back. I know it. It works. In 'She Fox', the material didn't give anything. To hunt, to seduce, to deal with a stone is really to deal with terrific resistance.

(Bourgeois, 1998: 143).

Artists; Bachelard; Invocations; Sculptural materials; Three-dimensional form

Brain injury and art therapy: SaW

One reason for including art therapy as a part of a repertoire of approaches for people with brain injuries is to respond to those who cannot take advantage of solely verbal psychological work. Difficulties can include problems with memory, speech, and understanding, lack of insight, and ability to plan or initiate activities independently.

Prigatano (1991) records how his clients repeatedly ask questions about whether they can live a worthwhile life after the changes that brain injury brings. Many years of practice have convinced him that expression through the arts within therapy can help clients to recover a sense of meaning (Prigatano, 1991, 1999). Art therapists working in neuro-rehabilitation also offer testimonies supported by client words and images (McGraw, 1989; Von Sass Hyde, 2002; Wisdom, 1997).

Some American art therapists concentrate on positive cognitive changes caused by engagement in art-making. Del Giacco (www.brainyart.com) developed a structured programme of activities. Garner (1966) points to the unique combination of art-making and a therapeutic relationship to address complex interactions of neurological, cognitive, and psychological issues experienced after brain injury.

It has been estimated that between 25–50% of people suffer a major depressive illness after brain injury (Butler and Satz, 1999), sometimes some years after the event. Since the 1970s, statistical evidence indicates that patients receiving psychological help have 'improved function beyond what could be expected from spontaneous healing or traditional rehabilitation' (Davis, 1983, cited in McGraw, 1989).

Adolescence and neurological research; Damage to mental health; Neurological art therapy; Psycho-neuro-immunology; Stroke and trauma

Brief and short-term art psychotherapy: LR

Art psychotherapists use a range of time frames, from Michel Wood's (1990) 'Art therapy in one session' to interventions bounded by inpatient stays, and where possible and appropriate more open-ended work. Approaches include the psychodynamic (McClelland, 1992; Springham, 1992; M. Wood, 1990), cognitive-behavioural (Loth-Rozum and Malchiodi, 2003), and integrative (Atlas et al., 1992; Luzzatto, 1997; Riley, 1999). Adapting to the context, Luzzatto (1997) integrates Hill's (1948) open studio model with a Foulksian (Foulkes, 1964) emphasis on accommodating diversity, and Springham (1992) describes his Yalom-influenced time-limited closed group in a detoxification programme setting. McClelland (1992) stresses the particular importance of team ownership when using a process-oriented approach. By contrast, Loth-Rozum and Malchiodi (2003) are influenced by cognitive-behavioural therapy (Beck, 1976; Ellis, 1993) using a primarily educational focus, whilst Riley (1999) and Riley and Malchiodi (2003) recommend solution-focused brief models (Shazer, 1988), where strengths rather than problems are the focus. The aim is to reduce young people's shame about needing help, with the time limit itself offering hope of recovery.

The Richardson and Jones (Ruddy and Milnes, 2003) randomised control group trial into art therapy for schizophrenia studied the effects of short-term group art therapy, with some evidence of sustained engagement by the participants. The reviewers recommend further studies and larger sample sizes, but the National Institute for Health and Clinical Excellence (NICE) schizophrenia guidelines (2009) cited the study as part of its recommendations for the use of art therapies.

All the writers stress the care needed in calibrating an appropriate depth for vulnerable individuals, suggesting a thorough assessment process.

Brief and short-term psychotherapy; Brief dynamic art psychotherapy; Supportive psychotherapy; Themes; Therapeutic care; Time-related processing; Unconscious and art-making in brief work; Witness and witnessing

Brief and short-term psychotherapy: LR

Whilst brief and short-term psychotherapy have existed since Freud's time, very diverse views exist on minimum effective therapy length. Malan (1976) defined this as less than 50 sessions, Mann (1973) suggested 12, but Feltham and Dryden (2006) identified 1–25 sessions. The Department of Health states that 'Therapies of fewer than eight sessions are unlikely to be optimally effective for most moderate to severe mental health problems. Often sixteen sessions are required for symptomatic relief and more for lasting change' (DOH, 2001a: 2). An in-depth treatment of the large and diverse body of literature on assessment for briefer approaches is beyond the scope of this entry; however, further reading is essential for practitioners.

In the 1990s 'Care in the community' and the U.S. 'managed care' provided difficult-to-resist incentives to tailor inpatient therapy to shorter admissions. Yalom's (1983) influence is widespread in his advocacy of working in the present, regarding each session as complete in itself – making psychotherapy practicable under these circumstances.

Brief and short-term art psychotherapy; Brief dynamic art psychotherapy; Supportive psychotherapy; Themes; Therapeutic care; Time-related processing; Unconscious and art-making in brief work; Witness and witnessing

Brief dynamic art psychotherapy: DN

This is a model influenced by Mark Aveline's approach (2001) when faced with mounting waiting lists.

Aveline reminds us of the enduring contributions of psychoanalysis:

> . . . that tend to be forgotten when under attack for being 'endless in time and endless in goal' . . . careful attention to meaning, the importance of complex motivation and psychological conflict in determining behaviour, the distortion through use of mental mechanisms of reality perception (self and others) and the crucial importance of childhood experience in development.
>
> (Aveline, 2001: 380)

Assessment and formulation are fundamental. With time constraints, the therapist and patient are often more actively involved in agreeing the core issues and the issues to exclude. The frame (focus, structure, time limits, and materials) is then set out and agreed. Focus,

> together with the urgency confirmed by the constraint of a time-limit, form the two principal ingredients in the demonstrated success of this approach . . . successful outcome correlates with early positive therapeutic alliance . . . therapist activity, the prompt addressing of negative transference and focused work with intrapsychic and interpersonal conflicts of central importance to the patient.
>
> (Aveline, 2001: 375)

Working with these principles and the use of art materials enables the patient to re-address past trauma from a focus on present-day issues and problems. The focus and structure of the session is negotiated and agreed at the beginning of each session, but the art-making is usually non-directive. The disposal of the image also forms an essential component of the therapy.

Early on patients are invited to think about how the abusive, traumatic events they have endured affect their behaviour in their present internal and external worlds and relationships, and how these may be unwittingly repeated and enacted. As Aveline puts it: 'The stern demand of explorative psychotherapy is to see and accept one's own contribution to problems in living and to make changes' (2001: 378).

Assessment and formulation; Brief and short-term art psychotherapy; Brief and short-term psychotherapy; Disposal; Disposal and endings in brief work; Retention of artwork by client

British Association of Art Therapists (BAAT): CW

BAAT is the professional association representing art therapists in Britain. It works to promote the development of the profession. The British Association has been established for 50 years and has been successful in gaining recognition from the NHS, Social Services, Home Office, Department of Education, and registration of practitioners with the Health Professions Council. BAAT members are concerned with promoting both the interests of their clients and those of the profession. BAAT produces a range of publications, including ethical guidelines, a journal, website, and a web-based research forum (known as ATPRN). It also hosts conferences, special interest groups, and many organisational meetings.

Many art therapists at different points in their careers have worked, often unpaid, for BAAT because they believe in the work and wish to support, promote, and develop understanding about art therapy and its potential benefits. The history of BAAT's development is described by Diane Waller (1991).

Websites are a good source of information about the work of other professional associations throughout the world and the BAAT website can be found at http://www.baat.org/

Health Professions Council; Organisations regulating and representing art therapists; Professional conduct and misconduct; Professional titles; Trade unions

Case studies: AJG

Research-based case studies can be qualitative, quantitative, or a mixture of the two. They come in a number of different forms, ranging from discursive narratives to outcome-oriented experiments, from inquiry about individual casework to investigation of a group, and from exploration of a number of similar cases to examination of a number of matched individuals. They are amongst the most practicable and accessible means of art therapy research.

Single case studies or case reports describe 'unusual or exemplary cases' (Higgins, 1996: 68). They are often retrospective but can be concurrent and rely on a detailed narrative by the therapist, and sometimes by the client too (Dalley et al., 1993) as well as by others involved with the individual and their care. The researcher may or may not be the clinician and it is possible to collaborate, to varying degrees, with the client, their families/ carers, and colleagues in the research.

Research-based case studies can draw on different kinds of data: the artworks, the therapist's notes, colleagues' notes, and other documents relevant to the case. These can be subjected to different kinds of analysis. For example, discourse or grounded theory can be used to analyse the various texts; artworks can be analysed ichnographically (see Panofsky, 1972) or be viewed through different theoretical 'lenses'. Visual displays of artworks can be curated and viewed by client and therapist together or by different personnel whose views are documented as part of the research. Rose (2001) usefully outlines a structure that examines artworks according to their site of production, the modalities used in their production, and the methods used for understanding an image (i.e. how it is 'audienced').

Different degrees of collaboration can also be part of case study research; for example, client and therapist can agree at the outset to document their experiences using journals, both visually and in text, and a co-authored text or display may result. When there is consent, sessions can be filmed and/or recorded and reviewed by client and therapist together.

Note-keeping; Qualitative research; Review with images; Single-case experimental designs

Catharsis: CW

The emotional release that can accompany art-making in therapy is some-times described as a catharsis. Although in his *Poetics* Aristotle described catharsis as the release and purification of difficult emotions and therein one of the main purposes of tragedy – the audience experiences this emo-tional release when watching tragic drama – such release need not only be about difficult feelings:

> What exactly is the nature of catharsis? Scholars have offered many different interpretations . . . Some argue that it is an intellectual 'clari-fication': the audience learns something about humanity, and learning produces pleasure. According to this view, catharsis is a fundamentally cognitive experience: we gain a clearer and better sense of the world, and thus end up feeling better and wiser when the tragedy draws to a close. Other scholars argue that catharsis is a 'purgation' of the emo-tions, a release of strong feelings that leaves us feeling drained but also relieved.
>
> (Nightingale, 2006: 45)

Bourgeois

Challenging behaviour: People with learning disabilities: SWB

This is behaviour that challenges us and the situation or circumstances of the person with learning disabilities and can include verbal or physical aggression, destruction of property, or self-injurious behaviour. It is a communication by the individual that may mean 'I don't like this' or 'I don't understand this'. It is always a means of expression to which we must listen and it is neither random nor just naughtiness. Art therapists such as Cole (1984), Fox (1998), Loake (1984), and Stack (1996) have confronted and explored the issues posed by working with challenging behaviours in art therapy and the positive effect that therapy may make in offering alternative ways to communicate and be heard.

Communication with men and women with learning disabilities; Therapeutic alliance; Working alliance with men and women with learning disabilities

Champernowne, Irene (1901–1976): CW

Irene Champernowne was analysed by both C. G. Jung and Toni Wolff in Zurich. This led:

> . . . her to expressing her own dreams through painting. One of her 'spontaneous' paintings is reproduced in Jung's (1958) monograph on *Flying Saucers*. She was also influenced by the colleague H. G. Baynes who was already (1940) encouraging patients to paint their dreams and fantasies, discussed in Jung's Tavistock Lectures, delivered in London in 1935.
>
> (M. Edwards, 2005)

Her vision and energy resulted in the Withymead therapeutic community being established in the 1940s (Stevens, 1986). Champernowne's thinking on psychosis was described in a lecture:

> It is true that in therapeutic practice many of the creative forms arise from the depths of the psyche – a place where the universal experience . . . originates. This is true particularly of the psychotic patient whose ego has already been flooded with images and experiences; overwhelmed quite often by archetypal patterns, and thus deprived of the simple human ways of living and loving . . . But my experience of many series of paintings of this archetypal nature . . . is that they have had little effect upon the individual painter's total way of living . . . The ego is already too drowned in the unconscious experiences . . .
>
> (Champernowne, 1971: 8)

Archetype; Psychosis and art therapy; Withymead centre

Child development: MPr

This is the process by which a child grows and changes during childhood. It is a continuous process and each stage is dependent upon and influenced by the previous one. It does not take place in isolation, but in the context of relationships that may be constantly changing. A developmental model aids in understanding how mental life develops in the move from infancy to adulthood, through stages of inter-uterine life, birth, babyhood, toddlerhood, latency, puberty, adolescence, and young adulthood. During the time as a young adult, the sense of self as a separate individual is strengthened, and dependency upon parents and peer group diminishes. This separateness of self enables mature adulthood relationships to grow and develop.

The book edited by Case and Dalley (2008), *Art Therapy with Children: From Infancy to Adolescence*, focuses on normal developmental processes and describes the work of art therapists with children and their families in different developmental stages. Hindele and Vaciago Smith (1999) and Waddell (1998) carefully consider the work of emotional development at each stage from a psychoanalytic perspective.

Attachment framework; Maturation in adolescence and the uses of art therapy

Circle: DJ

The circle is a global and ancient image that can evoke complex arrays of meaning. It has long been understood as a figure of totality, be this God, man, or molecule. As it is infinitely symmetrical, it can readily symbolise perfection. Associations that are more mundane tend also to be positive. To see something 'in the round' is to take a balanced and comprehensive perspective, for instance King Arthur's Round Table famously denied precedence to any one position. All that is within may be brought into relationship; it is all-inclusive and embracing. Yet it also excludes: the division of inside from outside is intrinsic to its form.

The circle is common in religious architecture. Stone circles, rose windows, stupas, and Islamic domes all reflect its cosmic symbolism, as do the circles of dance and of ritual where the practice of moving in a circle defines a sacred space. The process of circumambulation may figure the movements of heavenly bodies through the sky or represent the journey of an individual soul, but it suggests also the sense of containment and protection yielded by the circle form. Just as the seasons rotate through the year, conversely, the vicious circle illustrates both movement and containment deployed to the worst effect.

Gestalt therapy, Rita Simon, and Jung all use the circle to map aspects of the psyche.

Gestalt in art and psychotherapy; Life of a symbol; Simon, Rita

Class: CW

Despite widespread pronouncements that we have seen the end of class divisions or that they are no longer significant, most people still have an idea of the class from which they originated that deeply shapes their sense of identity. The absence of social class from discussion in the world of psychotherapy might be explained by the tendency to invoke the inner world as the only rightful concern of therapy.

Many government surveys throughout the world have recorded great differences in wealth and their impact on physical and mental health. Poverty may be a part of what a public sector client needs to voice to a therapist. Many art therapists working with children or adults have seen its stunting effects in their clients' lives.

Psychotherapeutic work is often the preserve of the few. Although members of a range of disciplines in the public sector have counselling and psychotherapeutic skills, the circumstances in public services often make it difficult for them to provide properly contained work. As a consequence of the difficulties of access, the range of people considered suitable for such therapy is not much tested and often is artificially constrained (by prejudice) along class lines (Wood, 1999a).

Access to art; Bleulers; Deserving and undeserving; Poverty; Psychiatry, psychoanalysis, poverty, and class; Race and culture

Clay: SAVL

Clay is an immediate, plastic medium for expression.

Peat; Terracotta

Clinical guidelines: AJG

The development of clinical guidelines is one of the key ways that a discipline can demonstrate that its practice is evidence based. The aim of a clinical guideline is to assist practitioners, members of the multidisciplinary team, and users in the identification of the best clinical process that will lead to the optimum outcomes. They are 'systematically developed statements' (Mann, 1996b: 4), 'decision-making tools' (Cape and Parry, 2000: 172) that act as an *aide-memoire* for practice in relation to specific illnesses or problems in particular circumstances. They state the 'right thing to do': seeking not to restrict or prescribe a clinical approach, but rather to guide practitioners through a multiplicity of theories, approaches, and research findings, whilst respecting the final judgement of the clinician. Clinical guidelines are therefore usually prospective, addressing certain disorders with specific client populations, particular problems encountered in clinical work, assessment/triage decisions, and treatment decisions. Their development requires a rigorous process of literature searching, a critical appraisal of the literature, a systematic review of the literature using appropriate 'levels of evidence', and a distillation of the evidence into recommendations that comprise the guideline. Guidelines may be local or national, an example of a national clinical guideline being Parry's (2001) guideline on assessment and choice of appropriate treatment in psychological therapies and counselling. In Britain the National Institute for Health and Clinical Excellence (NICE) issues clinical guidelines based on available evidence (http://www.nice.org.uk).

Clinical guidelines in art therapy

Clinical guidelines in art therapy: CW

Clinical art therapy guidelines in Britain include those for working with people in prisons (Teasdale, 2002), with elderly people with dementia (Waller and Sheppard, 2006), and those for the use of artwork with people who have a history of psychosis (Brooker et al., 2007).

Clinical guidelines

Collaborative research teams: CW

Funded research studies nearly always involve a team of people working together with a range of expertise in research. There is collaboration over things like calculations, methods, questionnaires, and therapy and user experience. Most art therapists find it reassuring to realise that very little larger scale research is undertaken by an individual.

Art therapy RCTs; Randomised controlled trials; Research critical appraisal

Collage: CH

The term collage derives from the pasted paper compositions, *papier-collés*, associated with a wide variety of Cubist compositions. They represent the most inventive phase of the Georges Braque and Pablo Picasso partnership and their experiments with creating a new art practice that played with and subverted pictorial realism. This game, whose rules both artists constantly changed, was labelled 'Cubism'. They made use of wallpaper, oilcloth, newspaper, tobacco, and matchbox covers, as well as labels of goods in common usage. This made the viewer turn away from nostalgia to face the reality of the modern world and the political tensions that led to the First World War. Collage gained a political significance.

Collage is deeply connected with the process and chemistry of paper-making, industrial technology, and mass production that have evolved in many cultures. From its early roots in folk art, collage has been a medium widely practised without special training; it has reflected people's lives and derived strength from the immediacy of ordinary material in everyday use. It has enabled free association, experimentation, and a shortcut to problem-solving. It frees the artist's imagination and moves it away from reliance on traditional art materials, thereby providing a new and more playful way of expression.

The ready-made words and images available in magazines may offer a choice for image-making when other art materials fail adequately to engage the client, or if the client feels unable to use paint and conventional drawing materials. The familiarity and immediacy of such ordinary materials as newspapers and magazines, cards, and assorted coloured paper scraps can be less threatening than a blank sheet of white paper and its association with past failures with drawing and painting.

Art and materials in contemporary aesthetic philosophy; Art materials;
Words written on a picture

Colouring: CW

> Colouring is an interesting activity when considered therapeutically, as it can be a potentially cathartic experience as defences are eroded and inner feelings emerge to the surface. Conversely, colouring in can be understood to be blotting out, filling in, covering up. Once again, the image expressed this ambiguity and the possibility of holding opposites.
>
> (Dalley et al., 1993: 83)

Absorption in art-making; Catharsis; Colours and active imagination

Colours and active imagination: DE

> We have only to look at the drawings of patients who supplement their analysis by active imagination to see that colours are feeling values. Mostly, to begin with, only a pencil or pen is used to make rapid

sketches of dreams, sudden ideas, and fantasies. But from a certain moment . . . the patients begin to make use of colour . . . [and] merely intellectual interest gives way to emotional participation.

(Jung, 1955–1956: 248)

Active imagination; Colouring

Comic strips: MLieb

One technique I have found valuable in helping offenders when looking specifically at offending behaviour is the use of narrative 'comic strips' (Liebmann 1990, 1994). Often offenders say that their crime 'just happened', as if they had no control over it. The 'comic strip' technique can help offenders describe their crime, as seen from their point of view. This can then help them to become more aware of the events leading up to the crime, and then to see where they might have acted differently – and could do so another time if in similar circumstances. This process can also help to pinpoint patterns in offences, which may not be obvious from talking about them, and suggest areas for future work (e.g. work on anger, self-esteem, empathy, etc.).

Anger and art therapy; Animation; Offenders using art therapy; Popular culture

Communication with men and women with learning disabilities: SHack

'Many people with learning disabilities have difficulties with communication, and if they are unable to express themselves verbally, they may be treated as though they experience no feelings' (Hollins and Esterhuyzen, 1997: 497). Sometimes communication difficulties can place constraints on people with learning disabilities accessing a range of psychological therapies. It could be argued that it is the particular skill of the art therapist to facilitate many levels of communication in this work. Despite having a number of ways of communicating, some people attending therapy may not be able to name or speak about their emotions or feelings. Aiding communication through making artwork and using pictures or symbols can be the key to allowing exploratory therapy to function. Communicating and being understood can become a predominant and painful theme for people with learning disabilities in therapy.

Ironically, in one group a man who had no verbal communication became a key spokesperson. He would reflect on the mood and artwork by pointing to emotion picture symbols or using his electronic communication device. I recall becoming aware of a powerful group dynamic at play that seemed to be giving a voice to the voiceless. I was impressed by the group members' patience in listening to others and their efforts to tell their own stories.

Artworks and discourses of men and women with learning disabilities

Complex homelessness: An art therapy model: JJ

The optimum model for art therapy with people who have complex homelessness issues should be culturally sensitive, (O'Connor, 2005; Bentley, 1997; Ravenhill, 2004), informed by the principles of 'therapeutic care' (McNaughton, 2005; Papadopoulos, 2002), whilst following a trauma theory structure (Dass-Brailsford, 2007; Herman, 2001). This enables the main issues underpinning complex homelessness to be addressed e.g. the lack of early childhood containment and trauma affecting psychological functioning.

(Jackson, 2007: 42)

Adaptations of practice; Trauma and homelessness

Complexity and pain contained in an artwork: TD

Remembrance of the First Holy Communion, is the work [of] Marislow Balka . . .

A small figure stands beside an occasional table covered with a tablecloth with some exquisite detail of lace. He is tidily dressed, with a shirt buttoned neatly at the neck, and the suit of a boy, with short rather than long trousers; on his lower legs he wears long white socks, pulled up but nevertheless a little wrinkled. One of his knees is bloody, and on closer examination there is a mark of lipstick/blood – carnal and innocent. The boy is seemingly in command of himself, standing poised, but with a slightly shambolic air, one hand resting on the table. His head is turned in expectation. His shoelaces are undone. Two things disturb the image. On the table, embedded, hidden, but on the surface, as if in a gravestone, is a photograph of a child: First Communion, which after all witnesses the birth of the adult, equally signifies the death of the child. Above the boy's left breast, like a pocket handkerchief, is an opening with soft red fabric – a pincushion, an open wound, a heart. The boy is standing on a bed of sharp nails, holding the table. On further inspection there is a mutilated finger on his shoulder, which gives the impression of a shell within a soft body. At the back there is an open space leading down to his bottom – an open chasm of emptiness or nothing inside. The simultaneous expression of complex and difficult feelings into an object: a contained space, the image provides the container, thinking can be done and meaning can be found . . . ways of seeing that we see every day in our therapeutic work – painful, inexpressible thoughts expressed in forms and objects . . . The dilemmas of life can be contained in one object, these awful, difficult, painful things put in a form that can then be understood.

(Dalley, 2000: 97)

Abuse; Artists; Rites of passage

Computers in the art room: MWa

The standard of digital hardware and creative software now available to facilitators or clients with a grasp on computing can be a useful and creative tool in the art room. Creating or manipulating images with computers can engage, excite, and inspire the artist. Computers have the potential to show images and image-making in a very different light. They offer the opportunity to develop, expand, and edit existing images and ideas to the user's desire whilst documenting each step of the journey. They also have the benefit of retaining an original image in its unaltered state.

Digital photography; Typewriter and blackboard

Concentration: PW

To concentrate is to stop speaking and simply look for a time: '. . . focus on an image . . . or place an object in front of you. Devote all of your attention to this image or object. And don't forget to breathe. Breathing . . . another way to concentrate' (O'Hara, 1995: 83–84).

Reflection

Conflict resolution: MLieb

Conflict resolution work is based on humanistic ideas and values that emphasise such concepts as:

- listening to others, for feelings as well as facts;
- cooperation with others, valuing their contributions;
- looking for common ground rather than for differences;
- affirmation of self and others as a necessary basis for resolving conflict;
- speaking for oneself rather than accusing others;
- separating the problem from the people.

These ideas are extremely useful in working with other staff, with clients, and in helping clients to resolve conflicts in their own lives. They also inform the values of mediation (see Liebmann, 1996, 2000).

Art (and the arts in general) have long been used to portray and describe conflict, and art therapy has been acknowledged as a medium that can be used for looking at internal and external conflicts. Often this leads to insights that can in turn help to resolve conflicts, or at least view them in a different way. There is also the possibility of using well-known art therapy techniques in a slightly different way, to look directly at some of the components of conflict (e.g. comic strips, dangerous journey, sharing paper, and the squiggle game).

Anger and art therapy; Comic strips; Journeying; Sharing paper;
Squiggle game

Confusional or entangled children: CC

Tustin (1992) gave names to two types of state. She used the term 'encapsulated' to describe the state of autistic withdrawal, and the term 'entangled' to describe psychotic confusion.

Autistic spectrum disorders; Psychosis and art therapy; Psychotic
processes; Symbolic equation

Consent: CW

Consent is given when a client agrees to 'treatment'. 'The focus on consent has increased in recent years because of the European Human Rights Act (particularly Article 3) which enshrines the rights of the individual to determine what happens to them' (BAAT, http://www.baat.org).

It is important for a therapist to do their utmost to ensure that a client understands what they are agreeing to when they consent to therapy. BAAT recommends that in addition to the therapist offering a verbal explanation they provide the client with an explanatory leaflet. It is then necessary to record the client's consent (BAAT: Art Therapy, Note-Writing and the Law pack).

Leaflets

Container/contained: TD

... Bion's ideas of the container/contained informs us ... (Bion 1963) ... Based on the idea of projective identification ... Bion thinks that when the infant feels assaulted by feelings he cannot manage he has fantasies of evacuating them into his primary object, his mother. If she is capable of understanding and accepting these feelings without her own balance being too disturbed, she can 'contain' the feelings and behave in a way towards her infant that makes the difficult feelings more accept-able . . . Mother/therapist can process and digest unacceptable, intolerable feelings and these can then be introjected in a manageable, acceptable form.

. . . making an image and understanding its meaning within the safety of a therapeutic relationship can have the same containing function. Unacceptable feelings/anxieties/fantasies can be expressed into an image and these can be held in this image over time or until the client is ready to take them back in an acceptable form. A client spontaneously creates an image or object, and at the time, it is not possible to understand or make sense of it. The meaning is held by and therefore contained in the image in the sense that those unacceptable, intolerable feelings can be taken in at a later stage when the client is ready.

(Dalley, 2000: 92)

Containment

Containment: DE

Once the child or client has a sense of someone [or something] with this containing function within, the capacity for thought and for tolerating bad feelings is increased . . . The ability to hold and contain sense without simply evacuating it into someone else has then been taken in. A sense of space and time is created; experience does not have to be rejected or incorporated immediately but can be held for a while. Thoughts and thinking become possible . . .

(J. Segal, 1992: 122)

Container/contained

Containment and counter-transference: HG

Containment is a psychoanalytic concept used by Wilfred Bion in 1962 and introduced to art therapy literature in the 1980s. It was applied to experi-ences in a group for patients with psychotic illnesses (Greenwood and Layton, 1987). Bion developed Melanie Klein's ideas of projective identi-fication. The infant projects bad feelings/anxieties into a good breast. Through a process of reverie and digestion, the mother thinks about them and modifies them so that they can be given back in a form that is tolerable to the child. Bion links this to the development of a capacity to think.

As therapists, we can try to understand what we are containing for patients by considering our counter-transference. If this can be articulated then the patient may be able to start to think about the intolerable feelings that they pushed (and so got rid of) into the therapist. Even without a clear verbal interpretation, containment can be communicated by body language and simply by the continued presence of the therapist struggling to understand. On the other hand, if the therapist goes off sick the patient gets a message that his unwanted feelings were not contained and were dangerous.

Art therapists have found the concept of containment a useful model of working with psychosis and other levels of disturbance. The concept links with Winnicott's idea of 'holding'.

Container/contained; Containment

Contemporary period of art therapy: CW

In this period art therapists are weaving together the three main strands of the profession's earlier history: a belief in the power of expression; a social psychiatry (and social inclusion) understanding of context; and clarity about psychotherapeutic principles. This is all in conjunction with efforts to produce research and evidence of effectiveness. There is a surprisingly long list of different therapeutic approaches and adaptations being used by art therapists and not all of these include the idea of an unconscious. The extensiveness of the models being used means that art therapists can reasonably claim to share evidence of effectiveness produced for other psychological approaches.

The fundamental elements of art therapy practice remain the art-making and the therapeutic relationship, and the way both of these are anchored by the socio-economic circumstances of the client's life and the therapeutic setting. The combination of these elements is unique to the profession and part of its strength.

Noticeably, discussions in this period include the material qualities inherent in art-making and the participative practices by the therapist (e.g. Aldridge, 1998; Allen; 1992; Case, 2005a; Gilroy, 2008; Greenwood et al., 2007; Hyland Moon, 2007; Maclagan, 2001; Mahony, 1999, 2001, 2010a, 2010b; Richardson, 1997; Waller, 2009a; Wood, 1999b, 2005).

A strong continuing tendency is the way in which art therapists are adapting their practice in efforts to meet the wide-ranging mental health needs of city populations.

Adaptations of practice; Adaptations of practice with adolescents; First, second and third periods of British art therapy (three entries); *Future cities; Participative art practice*

Context and practice: MLieb

Art therapy work arises from the interaction between therapist, the client, and the whole context that is the art therapy room – the place of the mental health team (or other service) within the community (the client's community and the wider community). This means working with different clients in quite different ways, using themes with some and not with others, and employing different materials and starting points. The aim is for the client to find their own way to their own goal, and from this quest a pattern usually emerges. This can mean that theory develops out of practice rather than being applied to it in a pre-determined way, and insights from many traditions can be relevant and useful.

Adaptations of practice; Adaptations of practice with adolescents; Art therapy approaches for particular clients; Contemporary period of art therapy

Continuous projection and difficulties in symbolising: TD

> . . . A deep . . . disturbance will prevent symbolic thinking, and therefore pretend blood made by the child in the battle becomes blood, play fighting becomes fighting. There is no distinction between fantasy and reality and this becomes dangerous both for client and therapist. It is the task of the therapist to hold the thinking and contain the feelings . . .
>
> Many times symbolic acting out can be expressed through the art materials and this must be contained, not controlled, through understanding and interpretation. When the use of art materials becomes out of control . . . it is essential to set limits in order to contain the anxiety so that thinking can take place, and not a continual splurging out which is in essence an attack of thinking . . .
>
> (Dalley, 2000: 93)

Container/contained; Projective identification; Symbolic equation

Coping strategies that use dreams and art-making: DK and BL

Play and dreams are referred to as 'natural healing processes' (Punamaki, 2000). These form essential mediating factors contributing to the resiliency of an individual. The psychoanalyst Christopher Bollas (1999) draws parallels between aspects of dreaming and the creative process in which the painter, composer, or poet transfers psychic reality into another realm, an altered external actuality and something indeed that has not existed before. The artist at times feels an internal transformation taking place. This might explain something of the motivation of the painters, actors, musicians, and audiences we met in Sarajevo during the Bosnian conflict in 1994, who regularly risked their lives or persisted in making or participating in art despite the associated dangers. It also explains something of what we try to facilitate in art therapy environments in such contexts: the ability of an individual to symbolise, solve creative problems, imagine, and be in touch with a repertoire of emotions, all of which draw on a wide range of different coping strategies. Access to art-making and other forms of creativity encourages the development of an individual's imagination, spontaneity, and sense of their own identity. The art-making and the art itself can serve as a bridge between the past and the present, between traumatic memories and good memories, between that which can be given words and that which yet cannot (entry adapted from Kalmanowitz and Lloyd, 2005: 23).

Resilience and the psychosocial model; Therapists' engagement with their own art; Visceral

Corbaz, Aloïse: CW

Aloïse Corbaz is a female Outsider Artist. She:

> . . . was well educated and had worked as a teacher and governess before her increasing mental disorder led to her being committed to a Swiss psychiatric hospital in 1918. Her symptoms were bound up with her struggles with religion and sexuality, including an unrequited love for the German Emperor Wilhelm II, to whom she wrote passionate love letters. Her imagery is unremittingly sexual in nature. The central figures are always women attended by their male lovers. Invariably these are highly stylized representations; famous lovers from history and opera whom Corbaz reveals in their transcendent forms. They are the creatures of another world created, inhabited and controlled by the artist.
>
> Corbaz's method of representation grew out of, and reinforced her alienation from, the world outside her fantasies. Her figures are iconic and, even though they are usually in close physical contact, remain fundamentally self-contained. The characteristic lack of illusionistic depth in her pictures contributes to their other-worldliness. Michel Thevoz has argued that the flat surface of the paper is, for Corbaz, 'a solace and a refuge' in which a reality with only one viewpoint – the artist's – is admissible.
>
> (Rhodes, 2000: 76–77)

Art brut; Art of the insane; MacGregor; Outsider art

Cosmologies or underlying beliefs: CW

The identification of a client's underlying beliefs is often a part of the art therapist's work:

> Our understanding of why things happen, how they can be controlled, derives from our beliefs about how the universe works – our cosmology. Cosmologies involve ideas about cause and effect. For examples, if our understanding of how the world works incorporates a belief in spirits, then very probably we will attribute part of what happens to their actions. If our cosmology incorporates a belief in germs, then again, we will probably attribute something of what happens to their actions. These examples are not mutually exclusive: many people consider that both spirits and germs affect their lives.
>
> The things we make, just as much as the things we do, express our beliefs. Sometimes – as is the case of a carved figure of a divinity – this may be easily apparent. A stethoscope also embodies cosmology: it is based on ideas about how human bodies work, and about the importance of hearing what goes on in them. Thinking about objects in these terms enables us to reflect on the nature of our own and other's beliefs and practices.
>
> (British Museum Exhibition Catalogue, 2003: 6)

Cradle to grave

Counter-transference: FD

> One technical term, which is often used, and probably abused, is 'counter-transference'. It is a term, which should apply to the unconsciously motivated feeling, which the analyst is having about the analysand in the analytic situation. The term should be correctly used . . . This is not a pedantic matter; it is dictated by the fact that our chosen tools as it were are words. If we use them wrongly we soon find ourselves in the position of a sculptor using a blunt instrument.
>
> Someone mentioned to me a boy patient who 'doodled' on the table as if he were writing or drawing. The analyst might find it worthwhile doing something of this kind on paper dating it, say, April 15th, and putting it aside. Then at a later date say, May 1st, instead of looking at notes made in a more conventional manner, one could write down one's interpretations of the squiggles or marks made on April 15th. In that way one can make use of one's conscious activities of May 1st to interpret the unconscious productions of April 15th. Drawing upon his own conscious and unconscious, the analyst would not be confusing

two different analytic procedures; they are both recognised frames of mind and there is, therefore a technical disciplinary framework.

(Bion, 1973–1974)

Aesthetic counter-transference; Counter-transference captivity; Reflective counter-transference; Transference and counter-transference in group analytic art therapy

Counter-transference captivity: HG

This refers to moments of fear and suspense in the therapeutic relationship where the therapist may feel pinned to the spot and alert to some unknown danger. It is as if there is only a narrowly defined line along which the therapist can proceed. For example, the therapist may be expected to hear of the patients' experiences as they tell them, but show no interest in what they might mean for the patient and no concern to look at things from another angle. Or, for example, the patient may expect the therapist to keep quiet, tread carefully, and not let anything happen. The patient seeks only an empathic response and finds the therapist's objective view intolerable. Thus, the therapist is not free to think.

The psychoanalyst Ronald Britton provides useful understanding and discusses the therapist's need for a place in his mind that he could step sideways into and from which he could look at things. 'It is the attempted integration of subjective and objective ways of thinking in the patient or the bringing together of empathic understanding and intellectual comprehension by the analyst that is believed to cause a catastrophe' (Britton, 1998: 43).

Britton's ideas are rooted in the primal family triangle and the development of the oedipal situation, exemplifying knowledge.

Aesthetic counter-transference; Counter-transference; Reflective counter-transference; Scapegoat transference; Scapegoat transference and projective identification

Cracked pots: HG

This was a phrase used to discuss art therapy and psychosis in a case study of a woman diagnosed with schizophrenia who had had a pre-frontal leucotomy. She made clay pots that cracked as they dried. She would glue, paint, and varnish the pots, developing a design from the cracks. She referred to the cracks as being like her broken heart.

The word crack-pot was a colloquialism from about 1860, which denoted a pretentiously useless, worthless person. Crack-brain was indicative of craziness: a soft-headed person. A crack is defined as a flaw, deficiency, unsoundness. However, there is also another meaning: we talk of 'cracking up' as a breakdown, but 'crack' is also used to praise highly, in the phrase 'crack shot', for example. In the case study (Greenwood, 1994) the patient experienced fragmentation and potential annihilation through the process of making clay pots. But she developed them so they remained intact, albeit cracked. She saw them as both ridiculous and also as works of art. They were all painted the same colour and they developed meaning as a family to which, in time, she made a loving relationship.

Art therapy object; Psychosis and art therapy

Cradle to grave: The NHS: CW

'From cradle to grave' was the phrase used by William Beveridge at the inception of the British NHS to indicate the life-long nature of health needs. The exhibition *Living and Dying* (2003) considered a range of world-views or cosmologies about health care from different cultural vantage points:

> When a group of people share the same set of ideas, then very often everyone in the group takes those ideas for granted and rarely questions how effective they are. Modern secular British society draws its cosmology from science: it sees most of what happens as a comprehensible in terms of the physical world, rather than as a consequence of the actions of non-material being such as spirits. As a result of this emphasis on the physical, notions of individual well-being have become more and more focused on a scientific or medical understanding of the human body.
>
> 'Cradle to Grave', an art work made by Susie Freeman, Liz Lee and David Critchley (Pharmacopoeia), looks at a contemporary British approach to well-being. Two lengths of knitted fabric, one for a man and one for a woman, lie side by side. Knitted into each piece of fabric are examples of all the prescribed pills that this man and woman might take in their lifetime. Lying alongside are family photographs, documents and other medical interventions such as hearing aid, which mark the progress of their lives. Based on actual medical records, the installation is a stark demonstration of a specific approach to well-being as distinctive as any in the exhibition. The average British citizen takes more than 20,000 pills over the period of their lifetime. Certain medicines such as paracetamol are taken the world over, but the volume of pill-taking documented here suggests a particular focus on the physical body.
>
> (British Museum Exhibition Catalogue, 2003: 12)

This has implications for perceptions of physical health, but it also influences views about mental health. It can lead clients to be passive if they simply accede to taking pills. Effective physical and mental health care depends upon the active engagement of the client.

Agency; Cosmologies; Mental health; Sickness/health

Creation of art in therapy: MEd

In relation to the effect of the therapist's approach on the client's creativity:

> . . . 'innocence' achieves much more than it gives up in foregoing the attempt to reproduce a pre-envisaged imitation of art. This is not deliberate neo-primitivism nor blind regression either, one of which is likely to be too conscious and the other not conscious enough. If the psyche is attended to and honoured, the result may, unintentionally and paradoxically, touch the soul of art. By abandoning preconceptions and concentrating on inner promptings, we let in true creativity, on a modest scale.
>
> . . . for such 'artless' creation to take place freely there has to be privacy and security in the setting and trust in the process. The former requires the sense of a 'framed' space; the latter usually means a suspending criticism, concentration upon doing one's best for the image, showing willingness to incorporate 'mistakes' . . .
>
> (M. Edwards, 1999)

Absorption in art-making; Anticipatory guidance in art therapy; Jung on creation; Therapeutic frame

Creative life: CH

> . . . from where, Tobey wrote, can release from all this rigidity of pattern come? To me, it must come from the creative life. That life which draws upon the vital forces within us, gives us power to begin to think and feel for ourselves, in our own individual way. The beginning of the creative life is the beginning of faith in oneself, the will to experience and order the phenomena about us.
>
> (Leach, 1978: 166)

A person who seeks the help of an art therapist might begin to express themselves through the use of art materials. The creative spark and the faith in self that are needed to undertake life-enhancing changes might be found in both the art-making and the therapeutic alliance.

Agency; Therapeutic alliance

Creativity in the person-centred approach: DG

Carl Rogers (1902–1987), seen as the founder of client-centred therapy, writes:

> All therapeutic approaches are of course centrally interested in the client, and in this sense might be thought of as client-centred. But the term 'client-centred' has, for our group, a technical meaning not often explicated. Many therapeutic systems consider the achievement of an empathic grasp of the client's private world only a preliminary to the real work of the therapist. For these therapists, coming to understand the client's phenomenal universe is rather like taking a history; it is a first step. Instead, the client-centred therapist aims to remain within this phenomenal universe throughout the entire course of therapy and holds that stepping outside it only retards therapeutic gain.
>
> (Rogers, 1966: 185)

Within the person-centred approach, Carl Rogers makes the following propositions for human psychological development:

- creativity – innate creativity;
- actualising tendency – innate ability to be self-actualising;
- perceived reality/organismic valuing;
- symbolising (or ignoring, denying, distorting) experience in relation to self-concept.

Otto Rank (1932) looked at creativity as a tool to understand life experiences and to integrate them.

Rollo May (1953) had a humanistic understanding of creativity. He states that an authentic creative process is one that brings something new into being, which in turn enlarges human consciousness.

Cosmologies; Person-centred approach to art therapy

Cross-cultural influences: Taoism and nature: ML

Cross-cultural influences may inform and enrich art therapy practice. For example, the movement of energy in Tai chi can be compared to the movement of energy in making art and there are manifold ways in which the linking of stories and cultural traditions can help us practise:

> Even among lifelong city dwellers, nature as a source of art therapy imagery is extremely common, with the spontaneous production of trees, mountains, animals, birds, rivers, flowers and the sea.

We can look at such imagery as 'projective': describing what is inside as if it were outside. Taoism offers a less rigid border between 'in' and 'out'. We are as much 'inside' nature as it is 'outside' us. In and out have a reciprocal flow, and is a continuum. Our inner nature seems to articulate itself spontaneously in images of the world.

. . . The roots of Taoism go back to animism, which seems to be a fundamental human belief structure. The world is animated ('ensouled' we might say), and populated by intelligences, spirits benevolent and malign. Traditional cultures, from a western point of view, have been patronised for this 'child-like' level of 'projection'. The fact is that there may well turn out to be a very high survival value in this view. No animist or Taoist would contemplate radioactive waste.

(Learmonth, 1999: 192–194)

Linking personal and political; Therapy ceremony and tea ceremony; Vitality

Crucible: SaW

The importance of the crucible as a vessel suitable for containing material being worked at high temperatures is common to both steel-making and alchemy. The word is useful when explaining why a *protected space* is important in art therapy. In his workshops, Michael Edwards has pointed to the idea of the crucible as a metaphor to indicate that showing artwork while art therapy groups were in progress might mean that something vital to the group process could be lost (*or exploded*).

The steady holding of the processes in the group and in the therapist invoke the qualities of the crucible, until transformation of the elements can take place. Once this happens, the crucible is opened and the new element is poured out. This opening is a process that needs to be executed skilfully, in relation to both staff and clients, ensuring that fellow staff have sufficient knowledge about the therapy and that clients understand that the protected space in therapy is within the context of a team.

Alchemy; Container/contained; Metaphor (linguistic and visual)

Curating and visual research: AJG

Art therapy research can draw on curatorial processes as a discreet means of investigating the artworks made in art therapy. Art therapists can collaborate with their clients and curate private, retrospective, visual displays of artworks to examine key images and events, perhaps with an accompanying audiotape of the process [with appropriate consent]. Such displays might also be viewed by other audiences such as supervisors, other art therapists, and multidisciplinary teams, with their responses and reflections being recorded.

The curatorial process can move beyond the chronological development in which images are usually presented to displays that are curated according to a particular theme or topic. Working with artworks from art therapy in this way can afford new learning about the relationships between images and a more nuanced view of art therapy that reflects the shifts, plateaus, and links that are not apparent in a chronological display. Paying attention to the curatorial process and to what is enabled, or inhibited, by differing locations can inform how artworks are audienced in different places at different times. For example, Duncan (1995) explores how space constructs the viewer and involves him or her in different kinds of viewing practices or 'civilizing rituals'.

Looking and visual research; Visual research methods

Cutting out and cutting up: CC

When cutting out, children discover the cut-out shape and the shape left by the cut-out object: they may realise with surprise that they have two shapes. This can signal the beginning of a sense of separation in children who are merged with mother or another parental figure. A cut-out shape can look like different objects when moved around. This is important for playing with imaginative ideas and learning about different perspectives: things are not just black and white (Case, 2002).

In children with separation difficulties it is sometimes possible to see that the background paper is experienced as the mother environment or foetal sea and the cutting out as the coming onto land or being born psychologically. For example: 'The next month Alison wanted a mermaid cut out and as she took her from me she said. "She's still wet," shaking her, as if she had come out of the water in being cut out of the paper' (Case, 2005b).

Cutting up may have to do with the severing of mental and physical links and the wish to limit connections that can be made when the material is very painful. Sometimes images are cut out and stuck onto another piece of paper. This could represent an island of experience or memory that cannot be assimilated, which when it is given shape can be explored with the therapist and integrated.

Children also build up layers of paper, often hiding an image inside the layers. These hidden images could represent aspects of the self or others that they feel must be kept secret, or protected, and yet they also want to bring them to the session to be communicated. There is sometimes a tension between cutting up and cutting out when there is a struggle between destructive versus creative urges (Case, 2002, 2005a).

Acting out; Scissors; Self-harm; Vantage points

Damage to mental health: CW

In 2008, the World Health Organization (WHO, http://www.who.int.mental _health/en/) launched a campaign to improve mental health services internationally, asserting that with proper care, psychosocial assistance, and medication tens of millions could be treated for depression, schizophrenia, and epilepsy, prevented from suicide, and begin to lead normal lives – even where resources are scarce. The statistics cited by WHO may fluctuate, but the structural concerns they indicate will not change quickly:

- Mental, neurological, and behavioural disorders are common to all countries and cause immense suffering. People with these disorders are often subjected to social isolation, poor quality of life, and increased mortality. These disorders are the cause of great economic and social costs.
- Hundreds of millions of people worldwide are affected by mental, behavioural, neurological, and substance-use disorders. For example, estimates made by WHO in 2002 showed that 154 million people globally suffer from depression and 25 million people from schizophrenia; 91 million people are affected by alcohol use disorders and 15 million by drug use disorders. A recently published WHO report shows that 50 million people suffer from epilepsy and 24 million from Alzheimer and other dementias.
- In addition to the above figures, many other disorders affect the nervous system or produce neurological sequelae. Projections based on a WHO study show that worldwide in 2005: 326 million people suffer from migraine; 61 million from cerebrovascular diseases; 18 million from neuro-infections or neurological sequelae of infections. The number of people with neurological sequelae of nutritional disorders and neuropathies (352 million) and neurological sequelae secondary to injuries (170 million) also add substantially to the above burden.
- About 877,000 people die by suicide every year.
- One in four patients visiting a health service has at least one mental, neurological, or behavioural disorder but most of these disorders are neither diagnosed nor treated.
- Mental illnesses affect and are affected by chronic conditions such as cancer, heart and cardiovascular diseases, diabetes, and HIV/AIDS. Untreated, they bring about unhealthy behaviour, non-compliance with prescribed medical regimens, diminished immune functioning, and poor prognosis.
- Cost-effective treatments exist for most disorders and, if correctly applied, could enable most of those affected to become functioning members of society.
- Barriers to effective treatment of mental illness include lack of recognition of the seriousness of mental illness and lack of understanding about

the benefits of services. Policy-makers, insurance companies, health and labour policies, and the public at large all discriminate between physical and mental problems.

- Most middle- and low-income countries devote less than 1% of their health expenditure to mental health. Consequently mental health policies, legislation, community care facilities, and treatments for people with mental illness are not given the priority they deserve.

Brain injury; Health; Mental health; Mental health treatments;
Neurological art therapy; Psycho-neuro-immunology; Stroke and trauma

Deaf clients and scene-setting: MH

Whilst a hearing person describes a story and the actions simultaneously, a deaf person is often more systematic and sequential in their description. They first describe the background using sign language and give a detailed description of everything in the story before embarking on the actions. This is described as 'setting the scene'. Although it may be seen as a time-consuming/lengthy way of using therapeutic space, it is extremely important, often providing a backdrop for what is happening in the client's life and also a context for what is being communicated, which can help both client and therapist to understand one another.

Setting the scene is evident in some of the images done by deaf children and adults within art therapy sessions.

Adaptations of practice; Context and practice; Deaf clients and the
invisible screen

Deaf clients and the invisible screen: MH

When the client is deaf, the notion of an 'invisible screen' between them and the therapist may be helpful. If sign language is being used then 'scene-setting' takes place and the image of a scene is initially created and described through sign language and held in a space between the client and the therapist. This space can be described as an invisible screen and once it is 'held' by the therapist and the client they can point to different aspects of the scene that has been set and to the form of communication that it provides. When the deaf client is comfortable within this way of communicating, the therapist might encourage him or her to use art materials to transfer the image from the invisible screen and make things from the screen materialise into art form.

Deaf clients and scene-setting

Death images: JHar

When a child is approaching their own death there will be signs in the imagery of their artwork. Sometimes this may happen before the child is thought to need palliative care. The unconscious appears to prepare the body for dying.

Six-year-old Katy was very ill. She was unable to sit up. She kneaded a piece of plasticine in her hand as she lay on her hospital bed. She handed it to me saying, 'Look, it has turned into a candle that has almost burnt down'. This 'candle' could have been so easily extinguished. Terminally ill children appear to have an intuitive and pre-conscious awareness that they only have a short time left to live.

Gentle dragon; Monsters, dragons, and demons

Deconstruction: SSk

This term is from the French philosopher Derrida (1976), who thought that Western metaphysics (all that addresses questions outside the realm of science, e.g. truth, aesthetics, morality) is logocentric and seeking a central truth through which all can be understood. In addition to the idea of a central truth is the idea of there being various fundamentals that stem from that central truth, such as the notion of freedom and the importance of authority and order. These then create binaries with what they seek to exclude. Deconstruction is the process of showing that the side of the binary that is excluded continues to determine the assertions that are being made.

Although there are aspects in common, deconstruction differs from psychoanalysis in that traditional psychoanalysis relies on an idea of the unconscious that underlies all manifest behaviour. It also differs from the modes in art therapy theory of construing binaries as potentially creative: the theory of dialectics (Skaife 1995, 2000), the attraction and repulsion of opposites (McNeilly, 2006), creative tensions (Case and Dalley, 2006), contrary perspectives (McNiff, 1998). In Western philosophy these all derive essentially from Hegel (1770–1831). Sarup (1993) usefully distinguishes between Hegel's dialectics and deconstruction:

> Hegel's idealist method consists in resolving by sublation the contradictions between the binary oppositions. Derrida stresses the point that it is not enough simply to neutralize the binary oppositions of metaphysics. Deconstruction involves reversal and displacement . . .
>
> (Sarup, 1993: 51)

Deconstruction is a useful tool to use for working with the binaries that have become ingrained in our theorising of art therapy, (e.g. inner and outer, unconscious and conscious, embodied image and diagrammatic image). It is also a useful way of thinking about the relationship that talking can have with art-making, and vice versa, each one deconstructing the other.

Dialectical theory

Defend or *abwehr*: KM

Abwehr is a term used by Freud, which is often translated as 'to defend'. The word 'defend', however, can point to protection as an outer process: that there is an outer 'enemy' against which individuals must defend themselves (as though fighting on the battlements). *Abwehr* refers much more to inner processes of defence. The word can also be translated as 'to parry' or 'to ward off', both suggesting an active role for the client. The therapist can unwittingly support and contribute to processes of 'warding off'. The imagery may be borne out of a conscious or unconscious attempt to ward off feelings, or efforts to assuage the therapist.

Abuse; Art-making as a defence

Delight and disgust in the abject: LR

Julia Kristeva (1982: 2) uses her childhood experience of baulking at the skin on a cup of hot milk, given to her by her parents, to point to the essential role that the defining of the boundaries of delight and disgust plays in the process of individuation.

The interplay of attraction and revulsion, caught in an irresolvable dynamic, lies at the heart of the concept of 'the abject'. Barbara Creed links the term to the processes of distinction of human from non-human, permissible from taboo, and the sacred from the profane. She explains the process by which human beings expel substances such as faeces, urine, or unfit food, which would be harmful if retained (Creed, 1993: 8).

However, our human dilemma lies in the fact that it is not possible to deny completely that which is expelled, as rejected substances have to be acknowledged and dealt with in some way if further risks are to be avoided.

Aggression: As a component of depression; Mourning and melancholia; Mourning the lost object; Mutative metaphor(s); Sublimation theories in psychoanalysis; Visceral

Dementia art therapy clinical guidelines: DW

These guidelines (Waller and Sheppard, 2006) aim both to inform good art therapy practice with older people with dementia and to broaden and encourage the use of art therapy with this client care-group.

The problems facing older people in day and residential care are of great concern to the persons themselves, their carers, and to health and social care staff. It is a major challenge to improve their quality of living by providing services, which take into account emotional as well as physical needs. Constructing an approach to dementia that goes beyond basic care to addressing the painful and at times unmanageable feelings of loss, frustration and rage, which arise from this condition, requires more evidence-based practice than has previously been available. However, there is some evidence that Art Therapy offers older people with moderate to severe dementia a nonverbal route for emotional expression whilst encouraging maintenance of identity and self-empowerment . . .

(Waller and Sheppard, 2006: 5)

The guidelines include discussion of many facets of the work: memory and language impairment, the impact of routine on groups, institutional issues, realistic assessment, and establishing the working space and the art materials.

For an example of an art therapy RCT in this area of work, see Waller et al. (2006).

Art therapy approaches for particular clients; Dementia impact on client and therapist

Dementia impact on client and therapist: DW

Working with people with dementia requires working with confusion and this can result in the therapist also becoming confused and experiencing memory difficulties and at times an overwhelming sense of being trapped or feeling helpless. Expectations have to be realistic. It is possible for a therapist to take pleasure in small changes, but to realise that the client may not have the same understanding of that pleasure.

Some clients with dementia are aware of their cognitive difficulties and find this intensely painful. Indeed, our research has convinced us that dementia clients' emotional memory is more resistant to deterioration than their memory for names and places, but the difficulty remains in finding a means of communicating or expressing feelings. Sometimes frustration and sense of loss are very powerful, so much so that it can lead to a 'shut down' of feelings. The art therapist needs to be aware of this and remain sensitive in helping the client to manage their extreme distress.

(Waller and Sheppard, 2006: 12)

Dementia art therapy clinical guidelines; Transference in palliative care

Deserving and undeserving: The Poor Law, the workhouse, and the asylum: CW

In Britain the *Ordinance of Labourers* of 1349 distinguished between 'sturdy beggars' who were considered as fit for work and the 'deserving poor' who were not considered fit because they were ill, too young, or old. Anyone found helping a sturdy beggar to 'avoid' work by providing food or charity risked imprisonment. This distinction survived and was then repeated in the Poor Law of 1834 in which the deterrent of the workhouse was introduced. It is possible to uncover the problematic distinction between notions of the 'deserving' and the 'undeserving' in all subsequent attitudes, policies, and legislation concerning 'provision' for the poor, the unemployed, and the insane (Wood, 2001a).

Evidence of differences in treatment offered to people from different economic backgrounds appears from 1787, when 'hysteria' amongst female textile workers halted production in their factory. It is recorded that a 'cure' was found and production resumed because of the ministrations of a Dr W. St. Clare who was called to the factory with an electric shock machine (*The Gentleman's Magazine*, 1787).

The influence of the Industrial Revolution during the late 1700s produced profound social changes. Large parts of the population moved from small rural workshops towards urban industry. The workhouses were gradually to become an undesirable economic threat to the new factory owners and a number were converted to asylums.

Cradle to grave; Psychiatry, psychoanalysis, poverty, and class

Destructive narcissism: HG

This is a psychoanalytical concept developed by Herbert Rosenfeld in 1971. Destructive aspects of the self are idealised and submitted to, and they capture the positive, dependent aspects of the self. Severe negative reactions occur when progress is made in therapy and when dependency on the therapist begins to develop. It is as if defences against the growth of the therapeutic relationship are developed: the work of the therapist is devalued and feelings of need and vulnerability become intolerable. There may be an overwhelming wish to destroy the therapist, who becomes, via transference, the object and the source of life and goodness. Death or non-existence may be idealised as a solution to problems (Greenwood, 2000).

Defend

Diagnostic systems in psychiatry: CW

The American Psychiatric Association (APA) and the World Health Organization (WHO) systems of classification come from different histories of psychiatry. Different historical periods have seen major revisions to their systems of classification, hence we have four editions of the APA's *Diagnostic and Statistical Manual* (DSM) and ten editions of WHO's *International Classification of Diseases* (ICD). These manuals are widely used as guides to mental illness.

Many professionals and service users strongly want to avoid the use of psychiatric classification in ways that label people and make them feel discriminated against and less-than-human. Overly rigid adherence to psychiatric classification contributes at times to bad practice and overprescription of medication, yet large numbers of psychiatrists and other team members do not claim that diagnosis indicates much about the direction that treatment might take. They tend to see diagnosis as an obligation and a first step, with actual treatment requiring a more sophisticated holistic approach.

What diagnosis might provide is an indication of stressors influencing mental health. Without some system of classification, it would be difficult to make international comparisons, which enable better understanding of how poverty, employment or unemployment, physical ill health, women's health, and education influence mental health. This seems to be the position of the WHO.

However, repeated challenges to classification and derogatory forms of labelling means that classification is subject to healthy processes of modification. For example, currently the *Voices* User Movement is campaigning against the use of the term 'schizophrenia' because it has long-standing negative connotations.

DSM systems of diagnosis; ICD systems of psychiatric diagnosis; Ideology and psychiatric diagnosis; Kraepelin and perceptions of schizophrenia; Psychiatric diagnosis as labelling; User Movements

Diagrammatic image: JS

The *diagrammatic* image is like a 'sign' in that it refers to something outside of itself. It is often a simple line drawing, a semi-conscious form of communication made with the therapist in mind, in order to recount some feeling state, dream, or memory. The picture may be of rather poor aesthetic quality and it may use only line or pin figures. Like a map, it is an aid for telling the therapist about a dream or memory; it records the basic relationships but in itself it effects little change. The diagrammatic image alone is insufficient and it may need words, spoken or written, to express its meaning in full. Feeling may be evoked in relation to such a picture, but it does not transform the psychological state of the artist (Schaverien, 1991).

Aesthetic counter-transference; Embodied image

Dialectical theory: SSk

This contains the idea that an argument always has a counter-argument, which is resolved by a synthesis that sets up a further counter-argument. This theory was developed by Hegel (1770–1831). As well as being widely used as a method of understanding political history, it has been used for thinking about processes in psychotherapy (Blackwell, 1994a; Nitsun, 1996; Ogden, 1988, 1992a 1992b); and art therapy (Skaife, 2000).

Ogden's proposition is of a self that is never static but always moving through conflict and its resolution, in a process of becoming. This has been related to the interplay between conscious and unconscious factors in making a piece of artwork and the paradoxical experience in art therapy of being alone with the artwork but also in the presence of other people. In art therapy, the artwork is simultaneously about communication with others, but also about a place in which one communicates with a divided self: the maker and the observer (Skaife, 2000).

Deconstruction

Digital photography: MAt

Michael Atkins (2007) considers the uses of digital photography in relation to recording client's artwork in the context of data protection legislation and ethical practice. He describes benefits to both therapists and clients in using this technology alongside existing art therapy practice.

He considers some of the benefits, which include photographs forming a valuable record of client's progress and as an aide-memoire for the therapist, and CDs may be 'written' and given to clients at the end of therapy.

Computers in the art room

Directive and non-directive styles of work: CW

During the early 1980s art therapists who actively offered clients a theme for exploration in their artwork were described as using a 'directive' approach. Those who waited and apparently responded more passively to whatever clients made were described as using a 'non-directive' approach.

McNeilly's (1984a, 1984b, 1987) and Robert's (1983) papers on non-directive approaches in groups were published. The papers provoked an indignant response from art therapists wishing to defend the use of themes (Liebmann et al., 1985: 23–25).

In 1984, Gerry McNeilly was the main advocate for a non-directive approach, but he subsequently advocated (1987) that a crude opposition between directive and non-directive styles was not helpful. The tension between the two approaches may relate to tensions between public-sector psychiatric practice and private-sector analytic practice. Those who challenged McNeilly as being too uncompromising did so from a public-sector perspective, whereas in 1984 McNeilly was writing shortly after his group analytic training. By the time McNeilly modified his position in 1987, he may have integrated his group analytic training into his considerable public-sector experience. Greenwood and Layton's papers in 1987 and 1988 began to adapt group process knowledge to the circumstances of the public sector using both directive and non-directive methods with long-term clients who had a history of psychosis. Also Teasdale (1995a) proposed an 'emergent theme-centred approach' that suggests a 'middle ground' position. This shows one of the histories of adaptation common in art therapy.

Group analytic approach to art therapy; Themes

Disposal and endings in brief work: DN

Disposal can be a potent component of brief focused work. For instance, an identified core issue might be to want to have better control of intrusive thoughts, memories, or flashbacks of an abusive nature. It can then be cathartic or empowering to create and then destroy, throw away, or to find another way to dispose of an image that is a concrete representative of the unwanted feelings. In this way, an alternative means of managing hitherto unmanageable feelings can be made concrete. It can then become easier to internalise this process over time as a model for containing, mastering, and managing other unwanted and difficult feelings that can continue outside therapy (Segal, 1975, 1978a).

Agency; Brief psychotherapy (three entries)*; Disposal of artwork; Power; Unconscious and art-making in brief work*

Disposal of artwork: DE

The question of what happens to an artwork after art therapy has ended is a complex one. Clients dispose of their images and artworks during or after sessions by all manner of means and for all manner of reasons. The fate of an image after the session has ended, or after therapy has ended, may therefore involve it being displayed, offered as a gift, or possibly being destroyed. In each case, the fate of the image or object has meaning and significance.

A picture may be kept by the client, left with the therapist, or a conscious decision may be made to destroy the pictures. The point is that, when these decisions are consciously arrived at, in negotiation with the therapist, they may be important markers for acknowledging the importance of the ending of therapy.

(Schaverien, 1991: 115)

More often than not clients dispose of their artwork by leaving it with the art therapist. Sometimes these artworks are left with the explicit intention of being collected or returned to later. At other times they may be forgotten or abandoned, the process of making images in art therapy having served its purpose.

Disposal and endings in brief work; Endings; Retention of artwork by client

Dissociation: MAm

The Latin *dissociare* means 'separate'; in Latin the prefix *'dis'* indicates separation, whereas *'sociare'* means 'unite' or 'join together'. Dissociation is about detachment from an unbearable situation. It involves an attempt to deny that an unbearable situation is happening or that the person is present in that situation.

Dissociation is the process whereby normally integrated streams of thought or consciousness are kept apart and communication between them restricted. This last ditch defence takes place in the face of repeated and overwhelming trauma (Mollon, 1996).

Dissociation and counter-transference:

> . . . the therapists . . . experienced similar feelings in sessions – a physical sensation of extreme weariness and inability to be effective was significant at one stage . . . this can often be a sign of dissociative states . . . no real feelings are expressed in the verbal account of what ought to be very distressing experiences. In this situation, non verbal work may give more clues . . . (the child's) images reflected her experience . . . helpless disembodied heads, all unable to act.
>
> (Ambridge, 2001a: 80)

Abuse; Counter-transference; Defend; Psychosis and art therapy

Distributive transference and the importance of teamwork: CT

Forensic psychiatrist and analyst Christopher Cordess (1996) highlights the importance of processing therapy with adults in acute states *as part of teamwork* rather than lone endeavour in order to contain overt, covert, and benign or malignant transference and counter-transference material. He explained how this 'allows a sharing of the transferential burden, and allows the team, when it works well, to be of greater support and help to some patients than any one individual therapist' (1996: 97). Teasdale (1997, 2002) advocates the importance of integrating art therapy into the service in which it is situated, in order to contribute to the effectiveness of therapy and to the protection of all when working with personality-disordered offenders.

Borderline personality disorder

Dolls: CW

European dolls have mainly been used as toys. In other parts of the world dolls are part of continuing traditions of religious and magical significance. The history of dolls and their making is an example of how meaning is attributed to different materials, forms of play, and symbols.

In Japan, early dolls were made of wood and used to ward off evil spirits. Now they are dressed as warriors and legendary figures to be used in boys' festivals and theatre. The simplest Indian dolls are very similar to the earliest Egyptian dolls, being made of flat rectangles of wood, but they also incorporate other local materials such as pith, clay, papier-mâché, cow dung, bronze, rag, and vegetable fibres. It was traditional in India to give elaborately dressed dolls to child brides. In China, dolls were originally made as idols or fetishes and so were considered unsuitable for children.

Healing dolls made of paper or straw have been used since ancient times: for example, placed in the bed of a sick child and then thrown into the sea, as a way of transferring the sickness.

Invocations; Materials and image in assessment; Play; Play technique

Drawing: DEg

These thoughts on drawing are taken from those gathered by *The Campaign for Drawing* and John Ruskin's charity *The Guild of St George* (founded in 1878):

- 'I would rather teach drawing that my pupils may learn to love nature, than teach them looking at nature that they may learn to draw' (John Ruskin).
- 'If you can draw, even a little bit, you can express all kinds of ideas that might otherwise be lost – delights, frustrations, whatever torments you or pleases you' (David Hockney).
- '. . . drawing is the act of thought' (Richard MacCormac, architect).
- 'To young children drawing is as natural an activity as running and playing, but as we grow and develop, in general we drop the drawing,

why? It's sad that so many people lose this ability (Gerald Scarfe, cartoonist).

- 'In pictures you can express things you can't say in words.' (Robbie Cattery, kitchen fitter).
- 'When you get drawing, you're young again' (Stan Foot, pensioner aged 80).
- 'Drawing is thinking through the pencil' (Deborah Eagan, photographic designer).

Drawing a line; Rodin and drawing

Drawing a line: MEd

Drawing an *actual* line can be a powerfully committing experience. We have all experienced how the first line on a blank sheet of paper focuses commitment in that moment. There are many familiar situations, especially in games in which the 'line' is observed as a significant representation of a rule. Paul Klee coined the idea of 'taking a line for a walk'. One thinks too of: the *Caucasian Chalk Circle* in Brecht, where the line focuses the need for decision (and the outcome is surprising and compensatory); circles drawn to make magic or to keep a situation safe from evil; the deadly but inaccurate line of the cartoonist; and the loss of subtlety, but strengthening effect, when line is added to wash in painting (Edwards, 2001).

Blank sheet of paper; Circle; Drawing

Drawings made by clients: CW

The discipline of drawing endows that fantasy with an element of reality, thus lending it greater weight and greater driving power. And actually these crude pictures do produce effects which, I must admit, are rather difficult to describe. When a patient has seen once or twice how he is freed from a wretched state of mind by working at a symbolical picture, he will thenceforward turn to this means of release whenever things go badly with him. In this way something invaluable is won, namely a growth of independence, a step towards psychological maturity.

(Jung, 1933: 80)

Agency; Transcendent function

Dreams: MAm

Freud described dreams as providing a royal road into the unconscious (1900). Both Freud and Jung made a distinction between different types of dream. Freud distinguishes simple from complex dreams. Simple dreams are those in which the residues of the day are processed, whilst complex dreams can be wish-fulfilling, hallucinatory, or regressive. Jung, when discussing cultures in which dreams were an accepted means of making decisions, points out that there are two distinct kinds of dream that merit different kinds of attention: the great vision, which is meaningful and of collective importance, and might feel life-changing; and the smaller and more ordinary dream.

Even when the action of the dream cannot be recalled upon waking, a residual trace often remains and the dream may be remembered later when its significance enters consciousness.

- 'Many artists, too, cultivate the memory of dreams and recreate them in their pictures' (Schaverien, 1999: 57).
- 'The dream and the dreamer are inextricably linked and the unconscious functions satisfactorily only when the attitude of the conscious EGO is one of exploration and readiness for collaboration . . . To understand the dream's meaning I must stick as close as possible to the dream image' (Jung, 1918: 320).
- 'In *passive fantasy* the image occurs as an involuntary intrusion. It is unexpected. It comes to a person. It is presented. Often it is unwelcome when it represents dissociated psychic elements which are not consistent with a conscious attitude. Nightmares are one instant, but the intrusion can occur when awake' (Hobson, 1985: 100).
- 'A sequence of dreams might at first seem opaque. However, like pictures, viewed in retrospect they may reveal the paradoxically chaotic logic of the psyche' (Schaverien, 2002: 4).

Dissociation; Psychoanalytic accounts of the unconscious; Spontaneous art; Unconscious

DSM systems of diagnosis: CW

DSM IV (*Diagnostic and Statistical Manual*) contains information about all classified mental health disorders for children and adults. It also lists known causes of these disorders, statistics in terms of gender, age at onset, and prognosis, as well as some research concerning the optimal treatment approaches.

In some ways the DSM is more sophisticated than the ICD system because it uses five axes with which to arrive at a working diagnosis. When used well this can provide a five-dimensional approach to diagnosing a client. The axes are intended to help in providing the fullest picture of the client and their difficulties, and were introduced in part to try to minimise the tendency in American psychiatry to give worse diagnoses to those with a lower socio-economic status.

Christian Perring discusses preparations for the DSM V:

> DSM, it is a book that is hard to ignore . . . They [psychiatrists] were trained with it, they have to use it in their professional work and it is occasionally helpful to refer to when talking with patients, but they often don't think it provides any deep insights into mental illness, and there are many parts of it they do not believe in at all . . . However, it is the document that has been adopted by most bureaucratic and legislative organizations . . . to determine when people should be entitled to treatment or their psychological state may be relevant to assessing their responsibilities for their actions . . . what sorts of changes to DSM will best serve psychiatry and society . . . ?
>
> (Perring, 2003)

Diagnostic systems in psychiatry; ICD systems of psychiatric diagnosis

Eating disorders: CW

Eating disorder work was politicised by the feminist approach of the North London Women's Therapy Centre (NLWTC) (Lawrence, 1984; Orbach, 1986). This linked psychotherapeutic and political ideas to explain the prevalence of eating disorders. Arts therapists were influenced and have described a range of approaches (e.g. Dokter, 1994; Levens, 1995; Rust, 1992; Schaverien, 1995a; Waller, 1993). Michèle Wood's review of art therapy eating disorder work was prophetic in anticipating contemporary concerns:

> The question of the effectiveness of art therapy in the treatment of eating disorders raised by Waller back in 1983 is one that has not been directly addressed in the subsequent literature. Writers have tended to concentrate on describing why art therapy may be effective, rather than on evaluating whether it really is. Only Luzzatto [1994] presents a case in which the art therapy sessions were the main agent for therapeutic change and that this change was maintained, as reported by the client's general practitioner three years after therapy had ended.
>
> In 1984 Murphy pointed out that art therapy cannot work in isolation and that it had to be part of a multidisciplinary approach to the treatment of a condition as complex as anorexia. A valid appraisal of the efficacy of art therapy would need to take into account the contributions of other therapists and treatment methods that the client may have experienced alongside the art therapy.
>
> (Wood, 1996: 18)

Art therapy approaches for particular clients; Collaborative research teams; Distributive transference and teamwork; Eating disorders: themes-based art therapy groups in specialised teams; Evidence-based practice; Transactional object in eating disorders

Eating disorders: Themes-based art therapy groups in specialised teams: PBa

Themes are suggestions of a focus for the group and the art-making. They are aimed at maximising engagement and containment of the potential for acted-out aggression. At first the themes encourage playful exploration, and then they are used to increase the level of disclosure by exploring life events and family make-up. The benefits seem linked to curative factors that Yalom (1985) identifies as: instillation of hope, universality, development of socialising techniques, imparting of information, interpersonal learning, group cohesiveness, and catharsis.

Theme-based work contributes to the directive approach used by teams in overcoming the defensive stance people with anorexia can exhibit, especially at the beginning of their treatment. Willner identifies that the anorexic person not only starves themselves of food but also of feelings: 'Anorexia nervosa is itself a massively defensive psychopathology, characterised by "keeping out", both literally through ruthless self-starvation and psychically through emotional imperviousness' (Willner, 2002: 125).

This can also be likened to addiction in that patients seem to have little or no desire to stop what they are doing. Being anorexic can be experienced as being more beneficial than not. This is why motivational enhancement therapy (MET) is sometimes offered as a way for the patients to overcome the lack of motivation to engage in treatment. This resistance is a reason why some work in such teams has an element of compulsion. Supervision can play a vital role here in helping the therapist to deal with the resulting counter-transference.

Addiction; Distributive transference and teamwork; Eating disorders; Themes; Transactional object in eating disorders

Ego and id: CW

'Ego' and 'id' are part of a theoretical lingo, but the main purpose of psychoanalysis is to help us deal with the least theoretical aspects of our mind – with that in us which is most primitive, most irrational, and can be expressed, if at all, only in the most ordinary, least complicated language. The distinction between the 'I' and the 'it' is immediately clear to us, and hardly needs psychoanalytic explanation, since we are aware of it from our way of talking about ourselves. For example,

when we say, 'I went there,' we know exactly what we were doing and
why we did it. But when we say 'It pulled me in that direction,' we
express the feeling that something in us – we don't know what – forced
us to behave in a certain way . . . When a person suffering from
depression says 'It got me again' or 'It makes life unbearable!' he gives
clear expression to his feeling that neither his intellect nor his conscious
mind nor his will accounts for what is happening to him – that he has
been overcome by forces within him which are beyond his ken and his
control.

(Bettelheim, 1982: 52–57)

Bettelheim's book *Freud and Man's Soul* (1982) does much to dispel the
complications that were due to the original translations of Freud's work.
He points to the ways in which Freud used everyday language to explain
how he understood the workings of the mind. For example, as children all
Germans have the experience of being referred to by the pronoun *es*. This
means that the expression *das es* can remind German readers how they were
referred to (diminutively and maybe affectionately) as children before they
learned to repress sexual, aggressive, and illogical impulses. Consequently,
they may have a more ready understanding of the way Freud used the term
as one for the unconscious. The attempts by English translators to couch
Freud's work in scientific Latinised language mean that too often these
connotations are lost on English-speaking audiences.

Super-ego

Ego mechanisms of defence: HG

Defence mechanisms were initially described by Freud as one of the major
functions of the ego. His ideas were developed by his daughter, Anna Freud
(1966). Subsequently, there has been confusion over definition. In 1987 a
list of defence mechanisms were included in DSM III-R and these were
divided into groups of psychotic, immature, neurotic, and mature. At one
end of the spectrum psychotic defences, such as denial, alter the perception
of external reality. At the other end of the scale, mature defences often
appear more adaptive than pathological – sublimation and humour are
examples. People employ several defences from different levels at any one
time. It is interesting that someone with a diagnosis of psychosis will
employ psychotic defences, but they also have a capacity to develop mature
defences, and in particular sublimation and humour often emerge in the
context of art therapy.

Defend or abwehr; Ego and id; Sublimation theories in art therapy;
Sublimation theories in psychoanalysis

Ehrenzweig, Anton: SSk

Anton Ehrenzweig's *Hidden Order of Art* (1967) has influenced the thinking of many art therapists, for example, Simon (1992), Dalley et al. (1987) and Maclagan (2001). Ehrenzweig wanted to show that the 'unconscious scanning', which he saw as located in Freud's primary process, was superior as a means of 'finding out' than the secondary process, that is, analytic thought. He saw unconscious scanning as involving a syncretistic grasp of whole objects, common to small children but replaced by analytic vision when latency set in. Thus, like Freud, he equated syncretistic vision with libido and analytic vision with thought processes. In the creative adult these two processes, the differentiated and undifferentiated modes, alternate fruitfully. In Ehrenzweig's work these functions seem to have separate body locations – analytic in the mind; syncretistic in the body – and they all belong to the subject of the artist, with the matter of what is to be perceived as passive. Ehrenzweig believed that there was a 'hidden order' in this individual unconscious. Maclagan (2001) discusses how Ehrenzweig's ideas tend towards understanding art as a symbolic representation of the unconscious, which puts its aesthetic aspect as secondary. The mind/body split in Ehrenzweig's work reflects the dominant climate in which art is considered secondary to verbalisation as a means of thinking and reflecting and intrapersonal dynamics are seen as being prior to social dynamics. This has implications for any art therapy theory that is derived from the work of Ehrenzweig.

Amodality; Free association through art; Spatial awareness and empathy; Spontaneous art; Visceral

Embodied/embodiment: MAm

David Maclagan, building on Schaverien's work, explores the embodied aspects of aesthetic responses, that:

> involve the body at a number of interacting levels' including 'reciprocity . . . but they also involve complex exchanges between our response to the material aesthetic qualities of a painting and responses that are both physical (such as gut reactions) and psychological (in the form of phantasies about the physical).
>
> (Maclagan, 2001: 48)

Joy Schaverien (1991) considers the artist's relationship to the artwork and describes an important distinction between the diagrammatic and the embodied image.

Diagrammatic image; Embodied image; Spatial awareness and empathy; Visceral

Embodied image: JS

The embodied image is a picture (or work of art) that articulates a feeling state that can be conveyed in no other way. It is profoundly symbolic and no other mode of expression can be substituted for it. The embodiment takes account of the whole picture as a profound and irreducible entity, which has been called the 'art symbol' (Langer, 1957). This is different from the symbols that appear in pictures, which may be treated more like signs. In creating such an image the client becomes totally engaged in its making and it is as if the picture seems to lead, becoming rather different than originally intended. Often such a picture reveals some previously unconscious element in the psyche. The embodied image may begin with the intention of conveying a mental image or a dream, for example, but as it progresses the picture leads on from the original image or dream. Similarly it may be based in a memory but, again, as it is made the memory develops, revealing aspects that were previously unconscious. The point about the embodied image is that, in the process of its creation, feeling becomes 'live' in the present. This may be understood to be a result of an unconscious transference of 'attributes and states'. The aesthetic quality of such a picture may be commensurate with the engagement of the artist/patient within the transference (Schaverien, 1991).

Absorption in art-making; Diagrammatic image; Embodied/embodiment

Emotional life for men and women with learning disabilities: BD and RT

Like everyone, the learning-disabled experience adversity during periods of transition and, for them, developmental demands are particularly perplexing. In infancy, there is the difficulty of relating to the mother, and later the father, in an atmosphere of anxiety, grief, and loss. There is the difficulty of asserting autonomy and establishing trust when needs can only be met through dependency, and the further difficulty of developing social and communicative skills with the disadvantages of impairments. Beginning school and engaging with peers, and entering the culture, are difficult because they demand learning. Adolescence is confusing because of the ambivalence of others towards the sexuality of people with learning disabilities, and achieving a measure of independence through the engagement in new relationships is hazardous. Life transitions can be hindered by the absence of adequate rites of passage. Leaving home, experiencing the diversities of youth, work, marriage, children, or perhaps the choice of rejecting these in favour of alternatives, are largely out of reach for people with learning disabilities. Often for the learning-disabled person change, instead of being a gradual exposure to a new way of being in the world, happens catastrophically, perhaps through the death of a parent, which can also lead to the loss of home and community. Therefore, many learning-disabled children, youngsters, and adults, both men and women, need to have therapeutic support to manage such stresses.

Child development; In the box; Learning disabilities; Secondary handicap; Stupidity; Therapeutic care

Empathy: CW

This is the ability to identify with and thereby understand another person's feelings or difficulties:

> Psychotherapists have paid less attention to formal training in estab-lishing and maintaining rapport than counsellors. Methods of training in attending skills have been described by Ivey and Simek-Downing (1980) and of training in empathy by Kagan (1980).
>
> (Tantam, 1995: 9)

Empathy as a core condition of therapeutic work is strongly associated with the person-centred approach of Rogers.

Despite the complications of agreeing frames of reference for researching the concept, it is regularly cited as contributing, if modestly, to a good outcome (e.g. Tantam, 1995: 10). 'An aesthetic approach is a form of empathy' (Girard, 2008b: 8).

Comic strips; Kindness; Person-centred approach; Projective identification and empathy; Shame; Spatial awareness and empathy

Endings: DE

A central aim of art therapy is to make a satisfactory ending in order to help the client make a new beginning – in effect, to move on. It follows from this that from the very beginning of therapy both the client and the art therapist are inevitably moving towards ending and parting. Ending art therapy usually represents a compromise between hoped-for changes and the limitations within which the client and art therapist have been working. The ambivalent feelings clients often have about ending may find expres-sion in the way images made in art therapy are disposed of: whether, for example, they are destroyed, abandoned, or taken away at the end of therapy as valued objects.

Ending therapy can raise many difficult issues for both therapist and client (Edwards, 1997), with perhaps the most powerful feelings touched upon being those associated with loss. The link between ending and loss is a potent one, especially if the feelings aroused by previous losses were experienced as traumatic or overwhelming. An ending experienced as a loss may leave the client feeling bereft, vulnerable, or needy. As art therapy draws to a close, feelings of anger, rejection, or abandonment experienced by the client in response to previous losses may be triggered. Similar feelings may also be experienced by the client at the end of each session or before a break in therapy. For some clients, therefore, ending may prove particularly difficult and requires patience and humility on the part of the therapist (C. Wood, 1990).

Disposal and endings in brief work; Disposal of artwork

Erotic transference and counter-transference: CW

Schaverien writes: '. . . the emergence of eros, which is generated in the transference in psychotherapy or in relation to pictures, is purposeful. It is a sign of life and a move towards individuation for therapist as well as client' (1995a: xii). The subject concerns vitality in general (Mann, 1997; Mclay, 2008).

Entries on Transference

European art therapy: DW

> . . . there is a growing interest in art therapy as a mode of treatment for emotional and psychiatric problems throughout Europe and that, although in some countries, for example in Switzerland, Germany and France, there exists an extensive body of literature and several training programmes, it is only in the UK where art therapy has passed through the stage of being an occupational group to becoming recognized as a profession by state registration.
>
> (Waller, 1998: 129)

At a European Conference discussion about state regulation in 1997:

> . . . Many people feared that this would destroy the creativity inherent in the discipline. Others, however, pressed for codes of practice and ethics in the interests of public protection. Some felt an alliance with psychotherapy would be logical, others wanted to stay firmly with art and artists. The outcome of this debate, which lasted for two hours and involved many speakers from the audience, was a request for more of the same kinds of debate at future congresses . . .
>
> (Waller, 1998: 144)

The International Society for Psychopathologie of Expression and Art Therapy (SIPE) founded in 1959 by Robert Volmat, works in Europe for the promotion of understanding between the various specialists interested in the field (http://online-art-therapy.com). Similarly the *European Consortium for Arts Therapies Education* (ECArTE) exists to promote the development of art therapies education: (http://ecarte.info/).

Organisations regulating and representing art therapists; Ritual

Evidence-based practice: AJG

Evidence-based practice (EBP) is a paradigm that amounts to a social movement (Sturdee, 2001) concerning policy, purchasing, and practice in health, social, educational, and criminal justice systems. Its origins are in evidence-based medicine (EBM). It is, essentially, a socio-political response to two issues that dominate health care: first, the management of provision for an increasing population with diminishing resources; second, the proliferation and variation in clinical practices and treatment outcomes that combines with a lack of supporting empirical evidence demonstrating the clinical and cost-effectiveness of these same practices. EBP therefore aims to demonstrate that 'the procedures adopted by a profession are safe, effective and cost-effective' (Roth and Fonagy, 1996: 1) through the integration of individual expertise with the best available evidence from systematic research. The fundamental principle is that practitioners in all areas of health, social, educational, and criminal justice provision can only be assured that they are practising to the best of their abilities through constantly reviewing, updating, and adjusting their practices according to the latest research findings. Decisions about provision at the level of both policy-making and local purchasing should follow the same principle, ensuring that the public receives what are demonstrably the most effective treatments, care, education, and rehabilitation, delivered in the most efficient way.

Audit; Clinical guidelines; Quantitative research; Randomised controlled trials; Research critical appraisal; Systematic review; What works for whom?

Evolutionary psychology and art-making: ML

Evolutionary psychology attempts to explain how evolutionary pressures, and adaptive responses to them, have shaped us as a species. Theories are hotly debated because it is difficult to be precise about the relative influence of genetic and cultural factors.

Many of the precursors of art-making are not human specific. Animal play and, in all probability, dreams feature safe rehearsals of potentially life and death skills: chasing and being chased, for instance. But, even in animals, imaginative play can reach sophisticated levels. There is at least one well-documented instance of a young wild chimpanzee apparently adopting a log 'doll'. Here, play seems to be rehearsing social skills that, no less than chasing and being chased, are survival skills.

If this behaviour is observable in apes, it can be fairly confidently predicted that it would have been present in proto-humans. Archaeological records suggest that creative problem-solving took place alongside sophisticated tool-making and use. It is fiercely debated whether anything identifiable as 'art' was made by any hominid species before Homo sapiens. There are some suggestive objects and examples of what could have been deliberate burial rituals, possibly indicating creative symbolic thinking by Neanderthals. Thus, it seems highly likely that processes core to art therapy practice – imagination, play, visual problem-solving, and quite possibly symbolic thinking – were in place as resources very early in human development.

Evolutionary psychology and cave art

Evolutionary psychology and cave art: ML

It was in the Upper Palaeolithic period, about 30,000 years ago, when the masterpieces of cave art and sculpture were made. It is clear from the vigour, skill, and intensity of this art that image-making seems to be practically an identifier for our species. While animals have been known to make use of art materials, art-making itself would appear to be species-specific behaviour. That the early works were created in hard living circumstances implies that they were not regarded as a luxury; also that art-making as a human behaviour is seen across cultures and time implies its universal significance.

Thinking about the adaptive value of the origins of art-making is not new. The subject interested some writers who were influential on early art therapy thinking, for instance Herbert Reed (1937), who suggested that the intense observation of animals in cave art would make the artists and the observers better equipped to catch them. While this makes sense, it still does not seem enough of an explanation. Mithen (1996) makes a case to suggest that cognitive fluidity enabled people to cross their 'social intelligence' with their 'natural history intelligence' and lead to the domestication of animals. The survival value of being able to think across modes in order to devise new solutions is obvious, and art-making was at the heart of it. Ellen Dissanayake, writing from an anthropological and art history background, has specifically made the links between art-making, transitions, distress, and adaptation in her books *'What is Art For?'* (1985) and *'Homo Aestheticus'*

(1995). 'In extreme situations,' she argues, 'humans have always looked to the arts to shape and control perplexity and suffering' (1995: 157).

Anthropology of mark-making; Evolutionary psychology and art-making

Expression: TD

'The process of art therapy is based on the recognition that man's fundamental thoughts and feelings, derived from the unconscious, reach expression in images rather than words' (Naumburg, 1958: 511). When used therapeutically in this way, art is a means of non-verbal communication, a way of stating mixed, poorly understood feelings in an attempt to bring them into clarity and order.

(Dalley et al., 1987: 2)

Ehrenzweig; Free association through art; Kramer; Lyddiatt; Naumburg; Spontaneous art; Techniques of art therapy

Facture: CW

This word is ancient. It refers to the manner or style of how something is physically made. It is used in the French language, particularly in relation to academic schools of painting. The French phrase *'belle facture'* describes the beautiful handling of painterly or surface materials. In *Psychological Aesthetics* (2001), David Maclagan uses this word in making a stylishly argued case for art therapists to direct more of their attention towards the physical, material formation of clients' work.

Embodied/embodiment; Intersubjectivity; Irigaray; Rhyme; Visceral

Family work: MLieb

Ideas about families have undergone a major shift during the last 20 years. The concept of a nuclear family (of two married adults, one male and one female, with two children) as the norm has given way to a broader view of family that, includes single-parent families, 'reconstituted' families, gay and lesbian couples with children, grandparent-led families, and the wider networks of many cultures now living in the UK. Thus, 'family' can include all of these and any group living together in close proximity or with close ties.

There are many ways of working with families in art therapy – either with members of the family individually (e.g. play therapy for very young children, art therapy for older children and young people, and verbal counselling or therapy for adults) or with families as a whole. It can be used with or as part of family therapy work. Sometimes group art therapy can help families to examine how they relate to each other in the present, and suggest ways forward.

Social inclusion; Social psychiatry

Fear (of the image): EW

There may be fear of the image as a powerfully revealing tool of the imagination and unconscious. This can invoke a perception of danger and the possible disintegration of a carefully worked at, hard-won method of coping. There may also be fear of the potential pain involved in the perceived and/or actual loss of self. All of this can be mingled with a sense of the powerful nature of the image, a sense of awe and of being awe-full.

Defend or abwehr: Wilde's Dorian Gray

Female body: LR

Jenny Saville, in her painting 'Plan 1993' (Rosenthal et al., 1998: 161), presents an imposing female nude with contour lines, from what seems to be a small child's perspective. Her curves, shadows, dimples, pubic hair, and veins are all shown in detail and through this positioning and the suggestion of body as landscape there is an impression of a vastness that can barely be contained by the canvas. The overwhelming proximity evokes the primal ambivalence of the very young, who both desire to be enveloped and at the same time have an existential fear of being smothered. Saville here draws attention to mixed feelings about maternal power and the mature female body.

She also describes women's ambivalence towards their own bodies in a culture where female beauty is defined as the barely pubescent. In the 1998 Channel 4 series *'Vile Bodies'*, she gave her manifesto:

> We have to work at making ideas of beauty more complex . . . Our bodies have become like a commodity. We're always trying to take our bodies in and make the frame as narrow as possible, whereas I was trying to push the limits of my body.
>
> (Townsend, 1998)

Alienation; Eating disorders; Fear (of the image); Female gaze; Feminist art therapy; Gaze; Gaze and glance; Male gaze

Female gaze: LR

The prevalence of 'the male gaze' throughout Western art history leaves women with what Griselda Pollock terms 'a structuring absence' (1995:

14–17) of visual language for their experience, and a vacuum of cultural reference for female power and active potential. The unmet need for a 'female gaze' has provided a spur for many female artists.

American photographer Cindy Sherman cast herself in a variety of roles when constructing photographs, which at first glance resemble film stills, glamour photographs, pornographic centrefolds, and history portraits. Using facial expressions, prostheses, and masquerade, she exposes and challenges cultural expectations. The effect in her *Untitled* portraits of 2000 (Dickinson, 2004: 19) is to highlight a cultural mindset that only recognises the sexuality of older women if they wear youthful disguise, but in a double-bind finds older women grotesque in their attempts to do so. She sets up the conditions for both repudiation and empathy between herself as subject and the female viewer.

Behind the co-option of images of women lies the baby's dependency on the mother's gaze to develop a healthy sense of self. In *Playing and Reality*, Winnicott builds on Lacan's (1949) work, *Le Stade du Mirroir*, in his reference to the mother's mirroring role in 'giving back to the baby the baby's own self' (Winnicott, 1971b: 138).

Alienation; Eating disorders; Female body; Feminist art therapy; Gaze; Gaze and glance; Lacan; Male gaze

Feminist art therapy: SH

In terms of feminist art therapy, this is primarily an enhanced awareness of women's issues and misogynist discourses (particularly negative psychiatric discourses about women's 'instability'). Sometimes, when using directive art therapy, it is possible to introduce exercises that can help participants to reflect on their sexuality and gender. For example, I offer a workshop in which I ask participants to bring in two images from any sources (newspapers, art books, magazines, etc.) that relate to their sense of sexuality and gender (be that male, female, gay, lesbian, or transgender). I ask them to bring in two images, one they like and another that makes them feel uncomfortable. These images form the basis of the session, and it is an opportunity to look at how sexuality and gender are represented and to explore how participants feel about these images that surround us in our daily lives.

Some art therapists work with women-only groups to more readily allow women to explore unique aspects of their experience, such as pregnancy and childbirth (Hogan, 2010), or collective trauma such as breast cancer or rape (Malchiodi, 1997). However, to maintain feminist awareness is, arguably, an important aspect of good practice and should form an integral part of training.

There are two main approaches to feminist altheory, though they are not mutually exclusive:

- Feminist standpoint theory: Feminism is the principle of advocating social, political, and other rights of women as equal to those of men (Alvesson and Skoldberg, 2000).
- Postmodernist feminism: There is no one postmodern feminist method, so I would describe postmodern feminist methodology as postmodern methodology with a focus on the experiences of women (postmodernists could use standpoint techniques as part of a wider research strategy so that the two are not mutually exclusive).

Alienation; Directive and non-directive styles of work; Eating disorders; Female body; Female gaze; Irigaray

Fetish: JS

The origins of the term fetish are in sorcery. A fetish is a doll or an object made with the intention of conveying some desired effect. It may be experienced as 'alive' with influence for good or ill. In psychoanalysis, the term fetish has come to be commonly associated with sexual perversion. In psychoanalysis a fetish is an object of attachment that is linked to the person's sexuality in some fundamental way (Freud, 1928). In sexual perversion fetishisation is a 'dehumanising of objects out of fear' (Stoller, 1975: 124). The transformation of the object into a fetish is a way of dealing with desire and it might be understood to be a substitute for relating. The fetish is an object that indicates a self-referential state and so the relationship to it has an obsessional quality. It may, as in sorcery, influence others but it is not relational – it does not expect a response.

The original, magical, sense of the fetish may mean that some pictures made by patients are attributed magical powers of influence (particularly when made by those suffering a psychotic state). The image may be a substitute for thought – an enactment out of the unconscious state – and so it stands for 'the thing' in a magical sense. In art theory, the term fetishistic is sometimes used to describe repetitive marks in a painting. Therefore, when the art object is experienced as a fetish, it is not necessarily nor solely linked to sexuality (although this is not excluded). The fetish, associated with a part of a person, is a sign; it stands for something outside of itself. The picture, invested as a fetish, offers an opportunity for enactment of part-object relating. The temporary attribution of 'life' in a picture may offer a means through which the non-human element may become embodied and then conscious. This is described in detail in *Art, Psychotherapy, and Psychosis* (Schaverien, 1997).

Dolls; Invocations; Symbolic equation

Film Studio Ghibli and Miyazaki (Hayao): MAt

There is a great deal to be said for Hayao Miyazaki and Studio Ghibli (www.onlineghibli.com), but better than reading about the work of this master of Japanese animation (Anime) is to watch it.

These films can be discovered on DVD (www.studioghiblidvd.co.uk) since the success of the Oscar-winning *Spirited Away* in 2002. Offering an antidote to the strident, CGI (computer-generated image) world of many big-budget children's movies, where effects take precedence over story or character, Ghibli work consists of beautifully realised and largely hand-drawn animated films.

There are powerful stories with richly drawn and complex characters carrying a deep emotional resonance, touching on loss, friendship, the destructiveness of human nature, and the plight of the natural world. They are also great fun and full of action, humour, and adventure. Whilst they frequently contain talking animals, these are from folk tales and myth, not Disney.

Pom Poko is a humorous and magical film about raccoons confronting urban development, which also contains realism as change takes its toll on their community. This film is a thought-provoking exploration of the responses to an external threat, offering no easy answers or solutions. Other films include *Princess Mononoke, My Neighbour Totoro* and *Grave of the Fireflies*.

For art therapists these films offer an antidote to cynicism. They do this without shying away from painful realities and with a lightness of touch that does not patronise. Above all, children are treated with respect, childhood is valued, and imagination and magic are cherished.

Internet; Myth; Popular culture; Visual Culture

First period of British art therapy history: CW

In late nineteenth and early twentieth century art, it is possible to see a growing concern with the outreaches of human experience. Two World Wars had compounded a general sense that a simplistic or innocent under-standing of the surface of human experience does not explain enough. It was into this reeling world that what became known as art therapy emerged in Europe.

In the four periods of British Art Therapy history (Wood, 1997, 2001a), the first period was situated at the end of the impact of these wars, between the late 1930s and the end of the 1950s. Adrian Hill, a British art therapy pioneer, wrote *Art versus Illness* in 1945 (Hill, 1948). His work developed from an art education approach to one that gradually became more psychologically minded. The same might also be said of his contemporary, Arthur Segal, in his wish to forge links between medics and artists.

Although published later, Edward Adamson (1984) and E. M. Lyddiatt (1972) both wrote accounts of their work during this first period. There is repeated evidence in the early writings of art therapists of their insistence on being with clients (no matter how disturbed) in as ordinary a manner as possible. Respectfulness is implicit in much of this work and, given the damage that people with mental illness feel due to discrimination, this provided real balm and a good place to begin. There are many people working in the psychiatric services who continue to understand this. Such understanding seems to have less to do with different professional training than the personal attitudes of the people concerned. However, the lineage of the moral treatment philosophy (Wood 1997, 2001a) is strong and this has had an influence in the histories and practices of a range of psychiatric disciplines, including art therapy.

Lyddiatt's particular approach involved attending to the 'ever-present phenomenon' of the unconscious in everyone. Some of the underlying Jungian inspiration for Lyddiatt's work resonates with what was developed at Withymead.

Adamson; Champernowne; Lyddiatt; Moral treatment; Second period of British art therapy; Withymead centre

Fool images: MJR

The image, or archetype, of the Fool embodies the energy of leaping into the creative unknown. Most people will have come across the Fool in the plays of Shakespeare or in the Tarot cards, and the image lives on as the joker in playing cards. Like the hero, the Fool embodies action, but does not ride out in battle. The Fool can be male or female.

In Shakespeare's play *King Lear*, he is the only person who can get through to Lear in his most tragic time. Lear is the epitome of the broken down Old King whose ego rules. The only way to make Lear see his folly is for the Fool to speak in riddles, the language of the unconscious. The Fool symbolises the forces of chaos and license, while the king represents those of law and order.

Fools set off with gay abandon, with the innocence of a child coming into the world, full of trust, alive, playful, and completely open to whatever comes their way in the present moment. This openness invites synchronicity. The Fool is the energy in all of us that is seeking to become full individuals and carries vital, fresh inspiration without judgement.

The image is double edged, the fool is carefree: in stepping off the cliff, will they fly or do they not see the danger coming? Political activists are regularly characterised as foolish because of this tension. Yet Jung, in

Memories Dreams and Reflections (1961), describes how he consciously submitted to an experience like that of 'stepping of the cliff' just after his famous break with Freud. He struggled with feeling foolish, but what followed was a deep change in his life.

Erotic transference and counter-transference; Life of a symbol; Linking personal and political; Stone

Football: DE

The game of Association Football (or soccer) is played and watched by millions across the globe and has come to assume a place of vital import-ance in the lives of individuals both young and old, male and female, all of whom may live in very different economic, social, political, and cultural circumstances (Oakley, 2007). Wherever it is played, football embodies many of the ethical principles that infuse and regulate social conduct. Football provides, as Blackwell comments:

> The basis of many values and beliefs of British culture and the language in which they are represented: 'Fair play' . . . 'Being on the ball', 'Foul play' . . . Sport is culture, and no understanding of contemporary culture can be complete without an understanding of sport. This fact is often overlooked in cultural studies.
>
> (Blackwell, 1994b: 227)

Blackwell's sentiments are echoed by McIntosh (1987: 16), who argues: 'Sport, no less than art and literature, is bound up with the moral code and values of a community.' That so large a proportion of the world's popu-lation has adopted these values and beliefs says much about the intrinsic appeal of Association Football, an appeal that cannot entirely be accounted for by media manipulation, cultural imperialism, or the workings of international capitalism. Pickford (1940: 129) comments: 'No group which took it up was forced to play football as a religious, moral, or political duty to any other group.'

Internet; Play; Popular culture

Formative function of the art medium: JS

> Cassirer demonstrates how it is, in part, through the making of tools and eventually artefacts that the 'I comes to grips with the world' (Cassirer, 1955: 200) . . . It is this *formative* function of the art medium that offers a way of bringing unconscious material to consciousness

and it is through this process that a symbolic attitude may begin to develop from an undifferentiated state.

(Schaverien, 1995a: 123)

Agency; Intersubjectivity; Scapegoat transference; Three-dimensional form; Unconscious

Free association through art: TD

The implication of using art as a form of free association may be more far-reaching and can be more fully developed than dream analysis, for it is the privilege of the artist to combine the ambiguity of dreaming with the tensions of being fully awake. Ehrenzweig describes this in the following way:

'Something like a true conversation takes place between the artist and the work. The medium, by frustrating the artist's purely conscious intentions allows him to contact more submerged parts of his own personality and draw them up for contemplation. While the artist struggles with his medium, unknown to himself, he wrestles with his unconscious personality revealed by the work of art. Taking back from the work on a conscious level what has been projected onto it on an unconscious level is perhaps the most fruitful and painful result of creativity' (Ehrenzweig, 1967: 57).

(Dalley et al., 1987: 3)

Ehrenzweig

Freudian symbols: DE

Arising out of his study of dreams, Freud came to the view that it is through symbols that repressed or forbidden ideas, feelings, and wishes are able to avoid censorship and reach consciousness. As Bateman and Holmes (2002: 129) comment: 'Freud seemed to believe that due to "primal repression" some aspects of life could only be represented indirectly via symbols, thus putting repression and the potentiality for neurosis at the heart of dreaming, creativity and cultural life generally.'

However, as Rycroft (1981: 73–74) notes:

All this would be plain sailing if Freudian theory had not introduced a confusing complication by asserting that the symbols occurring in dreams differ radically from other symbols . . . True symbols, in the strict psychoanalytical sense, being those which represent ideas, feelings and wishes that have been repressed. 'Only what is repressed is symbolised; only what is repressed needs to be symbolised.'

According to Freudian theory, the number of things needing to be symbolised is relatively small and largely restricted to family relationships, the body, and sexual activity. Moreover, so-called Freudian symbols function by analogy, that is, symbol and object resemble each other. Thus the penis might be represented in a dream by objects that 'resemble it in shape – things, accordingly, that are long and up-standing, such as sticks, umbrellas, posts, trees and so on' (Freud, 1915–1917: 188).

Enormously influential though they have undoubtedly been, Freud's views on the nature and function of symbolisation have been substantially revised by later psychoanalysts. Carl Jung, Melanie Klein, Marion Milner, Charles Rycroft, Hanna Segal, and Donald Winnicott, amongst others, regarded Freud's view of symbolism as too narrow and have sought to differentiate between the healthy and pathological use of symbols. Nevertheless, the view that a picture, like a dream, is the symbolic expression of the neurotic and conflicted inner world of the artist has proved extraordinarily persistent.

Sublimation theories; Symbol; Symbolic equation; Symbolisation

Future cities: CW

One demographic fact that makes it hard to organise and deliver services is that the world population is in the midst of a demographic crossing. From 2007 onwards more people are living in cities than in rural areas (predicted by the UN in 2003). A London conference in 1998 brought together mental health workers from some of the largest cities in the world. The aim was to address what the sheer size of cities would mean to the future of mental health. The largest cities hold almost unfathomable numbers of people (between 18 and 28 million). The metropolis is becoming the megalopolis:

> Megalopolises are not only cities grown big: they are likely to be different creatures – in the same vein as adults are not big children although they continue to belong to the same biological species . . . It is an amazing fact that governments of the world, faced with rampant urbanization, have not developed a strategy for the provision of health care in cities. In some 30 years four-fifths of the world population – in developed and developing countries will be living in urban areas. This represents a steady growth for industrialised countries and a revolutionary change for most of the others. It is easy to predict that this change will bring new health problems or magnify those currently facing health care in an unprecedented manner: it is also possible that a well formulated plan of action to counter these problems might make it easier to deal with them.
> (Sartorius, 1998: 3)

Contemporary period of art therapy; Mental health treatments; Poverty

Gaze: MAm

Verb: to look steadily and intently; noun: a steady intent look (OED).

Joy Schaverien has written eloquently on the subject of the gaze, in particular the 'engendered gaze', referring both to 'the gaze engendered through looking at pictures and that which is influenced by the gender of the artist', in the context of transference and counter-transference in a psychotherapeutic relationship. She writes: 'The gender of the "Other" is influential in all therapeutic relationships but particularly so when the gaze becomes engaged through pictorial imagery' (Schaverien, 1995a: 12–13).

Robert F. Hobson, in *Forms of Feeling*, writes about 'the taboo on looking':

> Try looking deeply and intensely into the eyes of someone you do not know well. You will become aware of the deep-seated taboo on the look of intimacy . . . intimate looking can lead to an escalation of emotion . . . There is a need for both distance and contact. We move towards and away from others within our personal space . . . The taboo on the stare is perhaps biologically based, built in by evolution . . . it is not always easy for some psychotherapists to avoid using wittingly or unwittingly, sexual attractiveness (heterosexual and/or homosexual) as a gratifying, collusive means of avoiding unpleasant significant conflicts. The sexual look and the taboo are very open to manipulative exploitation.
>
> (Hobson, 1985: 123–125)

Concentration; Female gaze; Gaze and glance; Male gaze; Shame

Gaze and glance: LR

Berger's groundbreaking *Ways of Seeing* (1972) questioned the stance of Western art that the arrangement of the viewer and the subject are value-free givens. He explored how the viewer had always been assumed to be male, and how a woman in a painting or photograph was arranged to be the object of the male gaze. He discusses how women internalise this: 'A woman must continually watch herself' (Berger, 1972: 46).

This leaves female experience largely outside the cultural record, with the male standpoint as 'normal' and the female as 'other'. Pollock voices a passionate desire:

> To write across the texts of history, the desire of women to be seen, in art, the uncomfortable complexity of the pain and injuries of class, race and gender – as subjects of history and subjects in history.
>
> (Pollock, 1995: 14–17)

Bryson (1983), in seeking out concealed cultural references and in appreciating social and political context alongside image content, suggests two attitudes of looking at art. One of these is 'the gaze' (1983: 164), described as a distanced, god-like omniscience, which he finds makes galleries little more than 'archives of pleasure' waiting to be 'cruised'. An alternative way of seeing is 'the glance', 'a sideways look whose attention is always elsewhere' (1983: 94) that offers opportunities to question the authority of illusionistic art and to subvert white, male-centred, Eurocentric visual codes.

This strategy of looking in a questioning way seems particularly suited to art psychotherapists as it opens up opportunities for seeing below the surface and beyond the official line.

Female gaze; Feminist art therapy; Gaze; Irigaray; Male gaze; Power

Gentle dragon: JHar

A young man suffering from muscular dystrophy returned to a piece of artwork he had created two years before. It was a large, fearsome, papier-mâché dragon standing one metre high. His hands were considerably weaker than when he first made the dragon, so it was with great difficulty that he softened the fearsome features and added a pair of wings, completing it two days before his death.

Death images; Monsters, dragons, and demons

Géricault and physiognomy: CW

In the course of a period of depression, Géricault became friendly with a Dr Georget who treated him. This led to the painter becoming a hospital artist for a time; thus a project was devised to portray certain typical psychiatric illnesses, as they were understood.

(M. Edwards, 1989: 81)

Five of his portraits of the 'insane' remain and they are wonderfully executed. MacGregor (1989) includes them as amongst the most significant masterpieces of the nineteenth century. They situate Géricault's unique contribution to the development of a psychologically penetrating French Realism, although doing nothing for diagnosis based on physiognomy (psychiatric diagnosis based upon a person's appearance). Instead, ironically perhaps, Géricault contributes to a dawning consciousness about the nature of psychosis and a realistic view of its ubiquitous aspects. The shared humanity of those patients who sat for Géricault's portraits is seen across time.

History of psychiatry's use of art; Psychosis and art therapy;
Romanticism

Gestalt in art and psychotherapy: DG

Gestalt concerns perception and process and, when used in psychology, is both experiential and cognitive, aiming for improved awareness and contact with the environment. Latner (1992: 14) shows that it arises from a humanistic perspective and the philosophies of existentialism and phenomenology.

In Arnheim's (1969) discussion of art, its appreciation, and perception he used Gestalt psychology. He suggests that seeing is an active and dynamic activity and, through seeing, the mind orders the surface and the three-dimensional illusion of an image. It understands the contextual space in which the image is viewed and something of the cultural context in which it is not only viewed but also made (Arnheim, 1954).

The application of Gestalt to art psychotherapy becomes apparent in Clarkson's (1999: 2) description of the approach as: 'particularly characterised by the use of metaphor, fantasy and imagery, working with body posture and movement, enactment and visualisation, time distortion and the full expression of feelings involving the whole body'.

The classic view of Gestalt therapy is of the exploration and healing of splits within the client's psyche by dynamic use of two chairs (with the client being asked to move backwards and forwards between them) in order to gain new literal and metaphorical perspectives (Perls et al., 1951). Within the frame of art psychotherapy this can be achieved by the therapist *actively* directing the client to enter, in fantasy, elements of an image and to live that experience in the here-and-now moment.

Circle; Metaphor (linguistic and *visual); Personification*

Graffiti and art therapy: SC

Graffiti is a potent form of expression. It is part of popular culture and a language of communication accessible to people who do not have an art background. Like images made in art therapy, graffiti is not always aesthetically pleasing and it can be an external projection of uncomfortable feelings.

There is little academic literature in which the use of graffiti by art therapists is described. Exceptions include Sue Morter's (1997) work with psychiatric patients and troubled adolescents, Hagood's (1992) and Mackie's (1992) work with offenders, the research of Klingman et al. (2000) into graffiti as spontaneous expression of grief, and Kirsten Bolton's MA Thesis (2005).

Graffiti can be a way of dealing with difficult feeling (Othen-Price, 2006). It can be used in claiming ownership of or destroying and rebuilding an environment, symbolising the deconstruction and reconstruction of ego and identity during adolescence (Critchley, 2007). It may also be a defensive response to external threats. 'Tagging' is repetitive and emotionally inexpressive, and 'wildstyle' graffiti can be hard to read. 'Writers' who have moved on to more artistic 'pieces' may also revert back to the more basic and soothing activity of 'tagging' when stressed (MacDonald, 2001: 76), and may never reveal their true identity.

One way to engage with 'hard to reach' groups such as troubled adolescents could be to work within environments where they produce graffiti. Although this may lead to difficulties setting boundaries, well-structured sessions in community settings could lead to greater numbers of adolescents making use of art therapy who would otherwise not attend (Critchley, 2007).

Adaptations of practice with adolescents; Popular culture; Social, economic, and cultural context for adolescence

Griffins, gargoyles, and gremlins: CW

Throughout history there have been images of griffins and gargoyles, which suggests that people have been thinking about how to deal with what they represent for a long time.

'Monsters' come in all manner of wonderful shapes, colours, and sizes. They can inspire art-making. The smaller creature of a personal gremlin (seen in recent literacy adverts) that nags and undermines is also suited to art and play. A conscious self-help approach is one that some art therapy clients find useful; however, 'monsters' are not always created consciously and so are not necessarily accessed through self-help approaches.

Ego and id; Gestalt in art and psychotherapy; Monsters, Dragons, and demons; Personification; Popular culture; Super-ego

Group analytic approach to art therapy (after Foulkes): GMc

Within a group analytic approach to art therapy, there is the adventure of finding direction from initial chaos and this will lead the group down a conscious road to the unconscious. When I start to conduct a new group, I now simply say: 'I would like you to use the art materials in the room to express whatever you wish.' In subsequent groups, members come into the room and start work with the available materials without any further instruction from me. In the initial decision-making phases, I neither encourage nor discourage any decision the group is moving towards, except on those rare occasions when there is in operation a group resistance of a destructive nature. I interpret this resistance.

The responses to my initial request for a new group to make use of the materials available are numerous, including panic, petrification, anxiety, uncertainty, and anger towards me for not making it easy. By avoiding the trap of not colluding with dependency needs, I am now at risk of demanding too much independence from a beginning group. After the images have been produced there is a pregnant silence, whose implication is that I should assume responsibility for what they have done. I remain silent and the frustration of the group increases. Freedom is at stake. Eventually they start to work and tentatively take the first steps towards working as an analytic group.

As each group becomes accustomed to this way of working, self-disclosure becomes less threatening, with people relating more to their feelings and the images they have conjured up. Resonance manifests itself more and on a deeper level. Personal initiative becomes increasingly evident (McNeilly, 1984a, 1984b, 2006).

Group analytic psychotherapy; Resonance; Symbols and collective imagery in group analytic art therapy; Themes; Transference and counter-transference in group analytic art therapy

Group analytic psychotherapy citing Foulkes: FD

What is group-analytic psychotherapy? . . . it is *not* psychoanalysis of individuals in a group. Nor is it the psychological treatment of a group by a psychoanalyst. It is a form of psychotherapy *by* the group, *of* the group, including its conductor. Hence the name: group-analytic psychotherapy.

(Foulkes, 1975: 3)

Group analytic approach to art therapy; Group matrix in visual form

Group coherence: PBr

A common understanding or feeling generated in a therapeutic group.

Group conductor role: DW

Through their own experience in therapy, the group leader should have learned how to tolerate distressing experiences and to enable the group to do the same. To sum up, the major functions of the group conductor are to:

- establish and sustain the group's boundaries (selection and preparation of members, organising of the group room, receiving apologies, etc.);

- model and maintain a therapeutic group culture; i.e. one in which tolerance and a permissive, accepting attitude prevails;
- provide an understanding of the events of the session and encourage group members to do the same;
- note and remind members of their progress and change since being in the group;
- encourage members to take responsibility for their actions;
- predict (and possibly prevent) undesirable developments, such as scapegoating, victimisation, acting out, premature termination of member, misleading feedback being given;
- involve silent members – preferably by pointing out how the group process has enabled a member to remain 'the silent one';
- increase cohesiveness (by drawing attention to similarities between members in the group);
- provide hope for members (it helps members to realise that the group is an orderly process and that the leader has some coherent sense of the group's long-term development).

(Waller, 1993: 44)

Group analytic approach to art therapy; Group interactive art therapy; Group work models in art therapy; Interpersonal learning in groups; Therapy for the therapist

Group interactive art therapy: DW

In summary . . . curative factors are contained within a group interactive model, in which the making of images facilitates interaction among members and the therapist and stimulates the creativity of participants. The model also involves awareness of the group as a 'system' and willingness to use the social and cultural context of the group and its images as material for the group. As in verbal group therapy, the conductor avoids focussing on the individual, or on the overt 'content' of the session, but encourages the members to interact, being aware of the symbolic, metaphoric messages arising both from the images and the relationships among the members themselves.

(Waller, 1993: 40)

Group conductor role

Group matrix in visual form: JMa

Art-making in a group can provide a multidimensional, non-verbal discourse with layers that relate to both the group and individual. This can give visual form to the group matrix. Over time, self-initiated, sustained art-making facilitates the process (compared, for instance, to an image made in each session for discussion). With sustained, durational art-making where the content is not actively explored for meaning, the artwork produced can be understood as an interpretation in itself in the group analytic tradition (Foulkes and Anthony, 1965: 258), similar to free association in individual verbal psychotherapy (Mahony, 2010a).

As a construct, the group matrix is conceived as providing a concert of interactions at all levels of the mind between two or more people, which, like an orchestra, provides the experience of the *group as a whole* (Foulkes and Anthony, 1965: 26). As the network of all individual mental processes in a group, the matrix displays the total interactional field transmitting and communicating a complex social situation, which, it has to be remembered, is a contrived one and deeply influenced by the therapist.

Group analytic psychotherapy

Group process knowledge in art therapy: CW

Group process work involves the therapist giving their main attention to processes in the group (e.g. Bion, 1961; Foulkes, 1964; Yalom, 1985). The development of group process knowledge in art therapy has been gradual and varied. Art therapists used open-studio groups throughout the period from the 1940s to the end of the 1970s and accounts made in this period show an understanding of some group process, but often work focused on the position of the individual client and not the group. During the late 1980s and the 1990s more art therapists adopted a group analytic perspective after Foulkes. This allows for a movement backwards and forwards between an individual and a group focus, which is well suited to many aspects of art therapy group practice.

The move of psychiatry into the community during the late 1980s and 1990s came during a time of economic restraint in Britain and this posed many challenges. There was a need for art therapists to develop their skills in ways that enabled them to work more on their own, away from a team setting. Deco (1998) writes that as art therapists left the institutional containment of the old hospital studios, the focus of the work necessarily had to shift. More reliance was placed upon psychotherapeutic and group process knowledge. A range of adapted art therapy group practice is now used. This is described in a number of books and many articles (see next entry). Organisational group process issues are also becoming a feature of art therapy literature and training: see entries on 'Menzies-Lyth' and 'Groups and organisations'.

Adaptations of practice; Group work models in art therapy; Groups and organisations; Menzies-Lyth

Group work models in art therapy: MLieb

Art therapy groups can provide a combination of individual and group experiences that draw on the traditions of both group work and art therapy. These include:

- Open studio approach (Adamson, 1984).
- Theme-based groups (Barber, 2002; Campbell, 1993; Liebmann, 2003; Ross, 1997).
- Group analytic art therapy (McNeilly, 1984a, 1984b, 1987, 1989, 2000, 2006).
- Group interactive art therapy (Waller, 1993).
- Art psychotherapy groups (Deco, 1998; Skaife and Huet, 1998).

This 'typology' is not a watertight classification, so there may be art therapy groups that include features from several of the above types. Many art therapists also work in different ways with different groups. It is up to each art therapist to assess which approach suits their group and situation best.

Adaptations of practice; Assessment; Group analytic approach to art therapy; Group interactive art therapy

Groups and organisations: DAM

Although primarily concerned with understanding human behaviour in terms of the individual psyche at the intrapersonal level, psychoanalysis has always been concerned with human relations in groups and organisations. Freud (1921) believed that individual and group psychology could not be absolutely differentiated, because the psychology of the individual is itself a function of the relationship between one person and another. Klein's approach suggested that adult experience reproduces defences against early anxieties, which shape the way we forge relations with our outside world. Projective processes create perceptions of the social world, which in turn, through introjective processes, precipitate social forms in the individual. Jaques (1955), Bion (1961), Menzies-Lyth (1959, 1988), and Hinshelwood (1987), among others, have argued that these primitive, psychotic processes play a large role in our lives, claiming that much, if not most, of our group behaviour and institutional arrangements is specifically and exquisitely designed to avoid consciously experiencing anxiety (Young, 1994). Using Klein's (1946) concept of projective identification, the link can be made between an individual's behaviour and organisational dynamics. This enables us to understand the structure, process, culture, and environment of a group or organisation in terms of the unconscious defence mechanisms developed by its members to cope with individual and collective anxiety

(Donati, 1989; Hinshelwood and Skogstad, 2000; Obholzer and Roberts, 1994; Skogstad, 1997).

Menzies-Lyth

Health: CW

'Health is a state of complete physical, mental, and social well-being and not merely the absence of disease or infirmity' (World Health Organization: 1946, http://www.who.int.mental_health/en/). This definition has not been amended since it was agreed in 1946.

Future cities; Mental Health; Mental health treatments; Poverty

Health Professions Council (HPC): CW

The HPC in Britain is a regulator of a number of health professions. It aims to protect the people ('the public') who use the services of the health professions it regulates. It does this by making good practice and good conduct a condition of registration and by investigating and adjudicating instances of malpractice.

Professions regulated by the HPC have at least one title that is protected in law and this makes it illegal for a person to use a professional title unless they are qualified. Art therapy became a registered profession in Britain during 1997. The protected professional titles are art therapist and art psychotherapist.

Although HPC documentation (www.hpc-uk.org/) makes it clear that the Council's primary aim is to protect the public, there are clearly some benefits for the professions. A level of public credibility is gained by professionals who submit themselves to regular scrutiny of their training, professional skill, behaviour, and health. In addition, because HPC staff have no professional allegiances, professional clannishness is less likely to cloud the judgement of those charged with regulating registration and protecting clients by judging fitness to practice.

Registration must be renewed every year; this involves paying a registration fee, making the commitment to maintain standards of practice and conduct, keeping a log, and providing evidence of continuing professional development (CPD).

The HPC does not register medics and nurses, but they do have their own legally binding registration systems. Clinical psychologists have recently become registered with the HPC. Psychotherapists other than art therapists/ art psychotherapists are not currently regulated beyond their professional associations, although negotiations with the HPC are taking place.

Organisations regulating and representing art therapists

Heterosexism and the heterosexual lens: JD

Heterosexism is a term coined by Morin in 1977, which Long (1996) uses when she asks that we address heterosexism within clinical supervision and to bring attention to issues of diversity. Gay and lesbian families have been the 'poor relations' in that there is little consideration of the differences and similarities of their life cycle patterns compared to those of heterosexual families (Long, 1996: 382). Dudley (2001) used Long's (1996) term 'heterosexual lens' to discuss the impact on therapy of a therapist being blinded by it.

She suggested that systems (including those in art psychotherapy) seek to impose heterosexual values to the exclusion and denial of other sexualities. This imposition includes influencing the art that might be created, causing art to be modified or hidden.

Those excluded have:

> . . . created rival cultural and symbolic systems . . . different sensibilities and consciousness . . . expressed in a variety of cultural forms, lyrics and music, oral tradition, humour as well as fiction and art.
>
> . . . although mainstream culture has a vested interest in keeping alternative cultures out of record and invisible, stigmatised groups also have their own motives for keeping their cultural products and conventions hidden; for self protection, to prevent co-optation and to create a safe cultural space, a world over which they have some control.
>
> (Vance, 1991: 13)

Female gaze; Feminist art therapy; Gaze and glance; Internet; Male gaze

Heuristic research: LR

The Greek word *heuriskein*, to discover, provides the root for *eureka!*, 'I have found it!' This was shouted by Archimedes, who whilst bathing discovered the principle of finding the weight of an irregular object through water displacement. This story recognises that breakthroughs often occur when the enquirer is in a state of informal, or even unconscious, engagement with their material and illustrates what might be described as the 'incubation' stage in creative process (Adams, 1979).

Moustakas (1990) recommends 'indwelling', an intensive introspection combining conscious and unconscious processes with the following stages: initial engagement, immersion, incubation, illumination, explication, and ultimately creative synthesis combining conscious and unconscious processes. This is personal identification in the manner of Salk, the American biologist who imagined himself as an immune system working with a cancer cell. Moustakas recommends journal-style 'self-conversations' (1990: 17) to capture these inner encounters with the material.

Heuristic enquiries lend themselves to the visual, the metaphorical, and the narrative. McNiff (1998: 54), Mahony (2001), and Rogers (2002) demonstrate how heuristic methodology stimulates insight. Rogers courageously used her own art and clinical work to explore how her art-making enabled her to experience her feelings in clinical work without 'cutting them off' (2002: 70). This enabled her to empathise with people facing the harsh realities of dementia.

Dementia impact on client and therapist; Metaphor (linguistic and *visual); Sense of self; Visual heuristic research*

Hierarchies of evidence: AJG

Evidence-based medicine has clear hierarchies of evidence described in its literature, but what constitutes the 'best' evidence, what is considered as valid 'evidence', and what evidence is available varies from one profession to another, therefore evidence hierarchies vary too. A simple hierarchy of evidence has been described by the NHS Executive (Mann, 1996a: 16) but this, like many others, privileges the research orthodoxies of medicine, specifically the evidence-derived randomised controlled trials (RCTs), and does not acknowledge evidence from qualitative research. Examples of reviews that use this kind of evidence hierarchy are issued by the Cochrane Collaboration, this being an international organisation that maintains and disseminates up-to-date research-based information about different healthcare interventions. Running in parallel to this is the Campbell Collaboration, which reviews research in education, social, and criminal justice systems. Quantitative research is similarly privileged by the Campbell Collaboration but their hierarchy of evidence includes qualitative research if it is part of a quantitative study. It is therefore important that appropriate hierarchies are devised that have meaning within a discipline's research profile. A hierarchy of evidence for art therapy has been proposed (Gilroy, 2006) that enables quantitative and qualitative research to be included in a systematic review alongside other, academically rigorous, art therapy literature and the views of experts, practitioners, and service users.

Audit; Clinical guidelines; Evidence-based practice; Randomised controlled trials; Research critical appraisal; What works for whom?

Hill (Adrian) on painting: DW

In 1945, Hill's book *Art Versus Illness* was published . . . it is interesting to note how he considered painting to be helpful to patients:
   'To redress the injuries of a morbid introspection, the bitterness and resentment may have to be released by encouraging the sufferers to

express their exacerbation in pictorial form, while anxiety and distress in another case may well be deflected and a more hopeful mental attitude established by inciting the very opposite type of picture making and that in the form of a sequence of paintings . . . never invite a recital of their physical disabilities and forebodings, but concentrate their attention on ways and means for their immediate mental emancipation' (Hill, 1945: 33).

Here we see a basic agreement with Naumburg and Kramer that feelings can be externalised through painting, but the emphasis is on distracting the patient from those feelings, or 'morbid introspection' as Hill puts it.

(Waller, 1991: 7)

Art therapy approaches for particular clients; Kramer; Naumburg

History of psychiatry's use of art: CW

During the nineteenth century, a number of medics felt that artwork could make 'the patient's insanity, visible and concrete' (MacGregor, 1989: 33). John Haslam, 'Apothecary of Bethlam Hospital', published his *Illustrations of Madness* in 1810. His title explained his purpose, which was to use the art and writing produced by patients to demonstrate their insanity. A similar aspiration of the time was to use a patient's physiognomy (facial appearance) to confirm insanity, yet Dr Georget, who commissioned portraits of the insane for this purpose, was not convinced that they looked any different from people in good health.

Géricault and physiognomy; MacGregor; Simon, Paul-Max

Homework

See: *Advice; Journals/sketchbooks*

ICD systems of psychiatric diagnosis: CW

The *International Statistical Classification of Diseases and Related Health Problems* (ICD) provides codes to classify diseases and a wide variety of signs, symptoms, social circumstances, and external causes of injury or disease. Every health condition (physical and mental) can be assigned to a category and given a code.

The World Health Organization (WHO) publishes the ICD codes and they are used worldwide as a way of recording morbidity and mortality statistics. The system of classification is intended to promote international comparability in healthcare statistics. The advancement of health care and wider, fairer access to health and health care in the world can be said to depend in part on the systematic provision of this kind of information.

ICD 10 has not superseded ICD 9 in all respects, and aspects of both are still used. The system is not as multidimensional as the American system of classification, *Diagnostic and Statistical Manuals* (DSM) published by the American Psychiatric Association (APA). Consequently, WHO is working with the Americans to bring the DSM and the mental health sections of ICD into alignment, but differences remain. For research purposes, it can be helpful to compare definitions given by both systems. There is also a Chinese system of classification, although this is increasingly based on Western systems.

A fully revised ICD 11 is planned for 2011, but minor updates are recorded every year. There is considerable ongoing debate about the uses of diagnostic systems amongst people working in psychiatry and in user movements.

Diagnostic systems in psychiatry; DSM systems of diagnosis; Ideology and psychiatric diagnosis

Id: CW

See: *Ego and id*

Ideology and psychiatric diagnosis: CW

R. M. Young (1999) described revisions of DSM II into DSM III during the Nixon Reagan era as being the result of a 'palace-coup' that was pushing for an objectivist biological account of psychiatry:

> . . . if you are a student coming to these matters for the first time, you can easily be led to believe that the terms of reference of DSM-III or the newer DSM-IV are simply common sense reality and the only natural and appropriate way of thinking about psychiatry.

He points out that:

> . . . the ideological determination of ways of thinking in the human sciences does not always militate toward conservatism . . . Homosexuality, which featured as a mental disease in *DSM-II*, simply did not feature in *DSM-III* (Shorter, 1997: 303–5) . . . it was de-pathologized as a result of the rise of the gay and lesbian movement for the rights of the homosexual. This is a striking example of how social and political forces change our concepts of who is ill and who is just different.
>
> (Young, 1999)

Bleulers; Diagnostic systems in psychiatry; DSM system of psychiatric diagnosis; Heterosexism and heterosexual lens; Psychiatric diagnosis as labelling; Psychiatry, psychoanalysis, poverty, and class; User Movements

Image in law citing **BAAT: CW**

BAAT proposes that images have 'non-literal, non-fixed' meanings. Thus, as potential legal evidence, the art therapy image may be contrasted to other types of images, such as an 'X-ray' image, as shown in Table 1. Art

Table 1 Comparison of art therapy image with X-ray image

Art therapy/image product	X-ray
• Meaning is context specific	• Meaning is not context specific
• Images cannot stand alone	• Image can stand alone
• Meaning cannot be agreed by all art therapists, in any context	• Meaning is agreed by any trained professional, anywhere
• Meaning is elusive and changeable	• Meaning is fixed and agreed consensually
• Words cannot be ascribed to specific imagery	• Words can be ascribed and to specific imagery

therapists should caution those wishing to see the images (or art objects) produced in art therapy as freestanding evidence (BAAT, Art Therapy, Note-Writing and the Law).

Imagery and clay work of confusional or entangled children: **CC**

The importance of working with clay is that it is on the ground and firm, solid. Clay can enable both a metaphoric but also a concrete experience. The term 'concretising' often seems to be used in a negative way, as something that we should grow out of or something that ill people do. It is seen as limiting, since the play of symbol and metaphor is not available to those who can only think concretely.

A confusional child's drawing and painting can have a lyrical quality, with names woven into the image: one may see images that look as if they are representational but, in fact, they show the 'equative feelings' of children in states of mind where there is to be 'no differentiation'. This adhesive relationship can be represented by a literally gluey picture. It eventually becomes possible to begin putting these feelings into words. The first images to be made after a chaotic period allow what was being protected by the aggressive behaviour to emerge and be articulated (Case, 2005b).

Adhesive identification with animals; Confusional or entangled children; Metaphor (three entries); Psychosis and art therapy; Psychotic processes; Symbolic equation

Images used to convey the 'action' of violence: KR

Patients who feel profoundly distrustful of others and who do not readily articulate their experiences verbally sometimes make images that seem to be used to convey the 'action' of violence. The art-making process is an inter-mediate arena mediating between therapist and patient. This arena can be safely 'attacked' by the patient making a visual depiction of aggressive desires. Perhaps this is particularly, although not exclusively, helpful to people diagnosed as 'personality disordered'.

Art-making within a therapeutic relationship means that destructive and traumatic impulses can be experienced, whilst being held in the process, rather than being acted on. This can enable an increase in the capacity to tolerate disturbing feelings, and possibly this can facilitate a reduction of risk for people who act out their internal disturbance by putting their own and others' lives and well-being at risk through violent behaviour.

Acting out; Anger and art therapy; Borderline personality disorder; Container/contained; Continuous projection and difficulties in symbolising; Kramer; Mediating function of the art object; Mentalisation

Immanent articulation: JS

As an artwork is viewed by its maker it begins to become familiar. The artist begins to understand the 'immanent articulation' of the picture. This is a half-formed understanding of the psychological implications of the visual impact of the picture. Its meaning is nearly conscious. This is the beginning of differentiation.

This term is borrowed from Cassirer's *The Philosophy of Symbolic Forms* (1957: 61) and quoted and adapted by Schaverien in *The Revealing Image* (1991: 108).

Baring the phenomena; Life of the picture; Naumburg; Retention of artwork by client

In the box: loss and bereavement for people with a learning disability: SHack

At this time in his therapy, James (pseudonym) showed some acceptance of the loss of his father and was able to depict him in a coffin. He said very little about this image but took care to point out the individual elements of his father's body that he had chosen to include in his drawing. Looking at the image, he said 'dad in box', and pointing in turn to each part of the drawing James continued to describe the image by saying, 'box in ground'. Then later, placing his fingers on the page near his dad's head, he said 'blue lips' and in the chest area he said 'heart'. James's father had died following a sudden heart attack on a family holiday.

Within art therapy, people are able to generate their own ways of naming and speaking about death. They frequently address the subject without skirting around the edges. Given the choice and the opportunity, many adults with learning disabilities can place their loved ones 'in the box'. Essential to this is the careful attention and effort given to understanding their experience of real, and occasionally debilitating, grief. The more common alternative is having meaning placed upon their experiences by others and not having the space to feel for themselves.

Communication with men and women with learning disabilities; Emotional life for men and women with learning disabilities; Learning disabilities

Inner art: CW

Michael Edwards writes about the private quality of much of the work on view in *The Inner Eye* exhibition (Elliot, 1978). He suggests that it was made as part of a process of private contemplation, with possibly only one person other than the artist originally being able to see the work. He names such art 'inner' art and describes three sets of circumstances in which it might emerge.

Firstly, he suggests that such work may be a spontaneous occurrence; secondly, that it may arise because of being invited to paint dreams and fantasies by a psychotherapist; and thirdly, he suggests that inner work may develop out of 'a planned therapeutic environment where art materials are freely available and an art therapist is providing encouragement, support or sympathetic non-interference' (Edwards, 1978: 14). It is possible to compare this idea of 'inner art' from the second period with Lyddiatt's earlier idea of 'spontaneous' art put forward during the first period of British art therapy history.

Lyddiatt; Second period of British art therapy; Spontaneous art

Inner autonomy: KM

A fundamental aspect of art therapy is the client's *inner struggle for autonomy*. The nature of this struggle influences all aspects of the art therapy process: the meeting between therapist and client, their relationship, the art-making process, and the art object. Inner autonomy implies getting in contact with oneself and noticing one's feelings and difficulties, which do not depend on outer affirmation or the gaining of power and the approval of others. When art therapists encourage clients to focus on inner feelings and needs that have become neglected, it can sometimes relieve a client's sense of self-betrayal as they begin to pay more attention to themselves.

In order to facilitate the client's discovery of a greater sense of inner autonomy, the therapist will try, when appropriate, to avoid contributing to the client's self-deception (in which they 'ward off' uncomfortable feelings) but 'paradoxically' the therapist will also want to avoid an overly *directive approach* so that the client can come to their own conclusions. The quest to rediscover a sense of inner autonomy and vitality is often a struggle that is described (if not always at first seen) in their artwork.

Agency; Defend or abwehr; Directive and non-directive styles of work; Vitality

Internet use and mental health: CW

The uses of the internet and its impact on mental health are complex. For example, suicide sites are potentially tragic. Some eating disorder sites perpetuate ideas about starving being desirable. Cyber-bullying is developing particularly amongst young people. More generally, there are aspects of internet technology that contribute to confusion about public and private spheres of life, and this potentially can make people vulnerable in ways that have not previously been encountered.

There are, however, also many life-enhancing aspects of internet use that, for example, counter isolation, challenge oppression, and help in gaining knowledge. The internet has provided the forum for powerful new developments in culture: for example, in discussion groups and in different forms of art-making made in response to popular culture and other events. Internet use can be interactive and not as passive as watching TV. Nevertheless, the internet is a tool that is not yet fully understood in terms of its impact on mental health and culture.

Computers in the art room; Mental health; Popular culture; Visual culture

Interpersonal learning in groups: DW

Irving Yalom . . . developed concepts of interpersonal learning which are thoroughly and clearly outlined in his book, *The Theory and Practice of Group Psychotherapy*, first published in 1975. According to Yalom, the group provides a forum in which the patient can explore and develop his relationships with others, resulting in greater trust and improved social skills. Yalom based his theory of interpersonal learning on Stack Sullivan's interpersonal theory of psychiatry. He maintained that psychiatric symptoms and problems originate in and express themselves as disturbed interpersonal relationships. Yalom emphasises two concepts: (a) the group as a social microcosm and (b) the corrective emotional experience.

'Social microcosm' refers to a group process, which resembles customary everyday functioning, in which patients tend to behave in their usual maladaptive way. It is by observing and drawing attention to these behaviour patterns in the group that the therapist and other group members can have a 'corrective emotional experience', thus helping each other to change. This process has been summarised by Bloch and Crouch as follows:

'the patient takes the risk, emboldened by the group's supportive structure, of expressing some strong emotion to one or more group members, including, perhaps, the therapist. Within the context of the here-and-now, the protagonist is able to reflect on the emotional experience he has undergone and to become aware, with the aid of fellow-members, how appropriate his reactions were. This awareness paves the way for an improvement in interpersonal relating' (1985: 77).

(Waller, 1993: 26)

Group interactive art therapy

Interpretation as a participant in the process: TD

Whether working with individuals or groups, art therapists are participants as well as observers in this therapeutic process. By working together and discussing the art work produced in the sessions, the therapist must help the client make sense of his or her own painting. This does not imply direct analysis or interpretation, but mutual suggestion and exploration, by both client and therapist, of the meaning of the images. The solidity and concrete nature of the art form provides a clear visual arena for therapeutic work and some obvious starting points for interpretation. Interpretation should be approached with caution, however, for, despite the apparent advantages in having such a tangible focus, art forms are statements on many different levels, and this tends to exacerbate the risk of error or misunderstanding.

. . . Even the most experienced art therapist cannot be totally confident about correct interpretation without active participation and co-operation from the client within the therapeutic encounter. As the painting is unique to the 'artist', it is only he or she who can ultimately come to understand its full significance.

(Dalley, 1984: xx–xxi)

Interpretation perspectives; Interpretations, Jung's approach

Interpretation perspectives: DE

Part of the attraction of psychoanalytic interpretation is that it has its own devious form of logic, yet is at the same time beyond normal standards of proof. By conjuring up the mirage of an alternative 'unconscious' intentionality which is in competition with consciousness, psychoanalysis (at least in its classical, Freudian forms) sets up modes of explaining a painting's hidden meaning that in effect act out a rivalry with the creative work they are purporting to analyse . . . the psychoanalytic privileging of depth over surface also has the effect of splitting the 'superficial' aesthetic level of a painting from its deep unconscious meaning.

(Maclagan, 2001: 13)

A good interpretation, one could say, is something the patient can entertain in his mind. It is not a password.

(Phillips, 1988: 143)

My own method is to be as passive as possible. I never attempt to interpret a person's work, particularly when he or she is painting. I feel that this would alter the relationship between us . . . There is a great temptation to ascribe all sorts of psychological meanings to paintings, quite independently of their originators. This often leads to the interpreter unwittingly projecting his or her own feelings onto the paper. This can also have the result of eliciting paintings which obligingly mirror the particular psychological orientation of the therapist.

(Adamson, 1984: 7)

It appalls me to think how much deep change I have prevented or delayed in patients . . . by my personal need to interpret. If only we can wait, the patient arrives at understanding creatively and with immense joy, and I now enjoy this joy more than I used to enjoy the sense of having been clever. I think I interpret mainly to let the patient know the limits of my understanding. The principle is that it is the patient and only the patient who has the answers.

(Winnicott, 1971b: 101–102)

Interpretation as a participant in the process; Interpretations, Jung's approach

Interpretations, Jung's approach: MEd

In interpreting a dream, picture, poem, or other form of active imagination Jung's methodology was to 'amplify' the image rather than try to restrict it to a basic meaning. In this sense he did not 'draw the line' as settling for one or other reductive interpretation but, by gathering information and associations, he would build up a frame of reference that was inclusive, with a view to arriving at a comprehensive and subtle understanding of whatever dream or image was being considered. This was a hermeneutic method. It is a method of successive approximations using analogies and metaphors, trying to use the known to help to understand the unknown.

Amplification; Interpretation as a participant in the process;
Interpretation perspectives; Metaphor (framed and unframed);
Transferable skills

Intersubjectivity: SSk

The concept of intersubjectivity has its roots in the work of the philosopher Martin Heidegger (1962), who challenged the subject/object split that the French Philosopher Rene Descartes had introduced with his notion of doubt. Descartes famously posited that all he could be sure of was his ability to think (Descartes and Maclean, 2006). This notion creates a split between the thinking subject and what is thought about; it is, however, the basis of all scientific thought. An intersubjective understanding of our relations with others has it that from the beginning we are only ourselves in relation to another. We do not have a subjectivity that is separate from the way we are perceived as objects by others, and the relationship between ourselves as subjects and as objects is a reflexive one. Thus our individuality is entirely dependent on our relations with others and is never fixed. We exist in an intersubjective field. Merleau-Ponty (1962) related intersubjectivity to the way in which we perceive the physical world, believing that as embodied beings our primary experience of the world and one another is through our senses. Our relationship with the world around us, like our original relationship with a caregiver, is an interactive one. Like the physical world, we are material beings and it is through our engagement with the correspondences between ourselves and the world that we develop. Making art, then, is a manipulation of media that corresponds both to ourselves and to the world around us, bringing about an interactive, intersubjective process through which we can 'become'.

Facture; Formative function of the art medium; Sense of self

Intuition: RL

 . . . Wilfred Bion (1984a, 1984b) draws a parallel between intuition and our other senses: hearing, vision, taste, smell, touch. He speaks of intuition as the potential for sensing and identifying emotional states . . .

Bion (1962) discusses obstacles to intuition, calling them 'opacities' (1962, 315; Calvino, 1998: 14). He considers this to be a state permeated by memory, desire and understanding. He calls the opposite of this state 'transparency', where the therapist's ability to record to memory and retrieve from memory is functioning but her mind is not overcrowded with memories. The therapist's mind has room to take in the atmosphere of the client's pictures. The tendency to hold onto theoretical views, interpretive formulas or the client's life history can easily obstruct intuition if these become the starting points for looking and the therapist begins to use the pictures as evidence for what is already known.

(Laine, 2007: 127)

Empathy; Interpretation perspectives; Kindness; Supervision; Therapeutic alliance; Transference; Vitality

Invocations, ex-votas, or *retrablos:* CW

Some work made by art therapy clients can be viewed as a form of invocation. For example, small paintings or art objects are hung as tokens of thanks, prayer, or offering in Catholic churches. Similar offerings are used in many cultures and religions throughout the world (e.g. Daoism).

Sometimes things hanging alongside ex-votas range from lockets of hair and other mementos to abandoned crutches. Ex-votas are often made by people without any art training and so are not parts of an established art tradition, but come from practices handed on through generations. Sometimes it seems they have been painted with such passion that they are intended as magical invocations, although they seem to function on a number of levels.

They have influenced a range of artists. Freda Kahlo's paintings of her father Wilhelm include some that seem like ex-votas, in the ways they combine portrait and text as an offering.

Art brut; Dolls; Drawing a line; Fetish; Film Studio; Magical thinking; Outsider art; Talisman transference; Transactional object

Irigaray, feminism, and art therapy: SSk

Luce Irigaray (born 1932) is of interest to art therapists as she relates male/female dynamics to the difference between sound and vision, or non-figurative talk and art. Her ideas are helpful in considering the relationship between art and interpersonal talking in art therapy. Irigaray's aim is to work at creating a culture of two subjects. She regards this as two tasks:

to develop a female culture and to develop a culture that embraces two different subjects. This venture coincides with the two tasks that I consider important for art therapy: to develop what art therapy has to offer that tends to be hidden in dominant therapeutic discourses, that is, the significance of perception and materiality; and to explore the relations between two languages whose difference could be thought of as based in gendered terms. Irigaray (2004) argues for seeing women as different from men, rather than just for equality for women (as she sees De Beauvoir as having done). If women are not seen as different, and therefore having different symbolisations, they are only seen in relation to men and men's symbolic systems (e.g. Freud's Oedipus complex being too directly related to girls).

Irigaray firmly centres her arguments in intersubjectivity, which, like Merleau-Ponty, she understands as embedded in the 'material' that she sees as also neglected because of the dominance of the masculine in Western philosophy. Irigaray maintains that acknowledgment of the difference between the two genders, carnal as well as cultural, might yield fecundity.

Intersubjectivity; Feminist art therapy

Journals/sketchbooks: CW

There is a journal/sketchbook tradition in fine art, where many lines of enquiry are pursued alongside making: for example, the reflective journal of Mexican surrealist Frieda Kahlo (2006) and the practice of German conceptual artist Joseph Beuys, who made use of process maps chalked onto blackboards. Also, ordinarily, many art students keep a journal. Art therapists sometimes refer to this tradition when they ask clients to consider keeping a journal/sketchbook or 'scrapbook' of their thoughts and feelings (whether inspirational or difficult), because these books can be stores for the raw material of art-making.

Journals and scrapbooks can also be enlivening as a form of reflexive practice for practitioners (Pell MA Research Thesis, 2008).

Advice; Art as a discourse; Homework

Journeying: CW

A sense of journeying is present in much of Goldsworthy's (2007) work, e.g. 'Night Path'. A sense of journeying seems to be an archetypal element in much client work.

Archetype; Conflict resolution

Jung on creation: MEd

> Analysis of artists consistently shows not only the strength of the creative impulse arising from the unconscious, but also its wild and wilful character. The biographies of great artists make it abundantly clear that the creative urge is often so imperious that it battens on their humanity and yokes everything to the service of the work, even at the cost of health and happiness.
>
> (Jung, 1950: *CW15*)

Here Jung explicitly says that 'the creative urge' might be a threat to *humanity*. This apparently contradicts the idea that the act of creation, as in the art therapies, might be life-enhancing. At various times in his writings Jung seems to be struggling with this question.

Muse and duende

Jung's personal uses of art: MEd

Of all the major psychologists, Jung gave unparalleled importance to pictorial image-making, both in his personal life and in the kind of therapy he advocated. He tells us that as a schoolboy he showed some artistic ability and a preoccupation with symbolic images (1961); later, about the time he qualified as a psychiatrist, he made landscape paintings around Paris, which show signs of some natural talent. Following his traumatic break with Freud, he found respite in building stone structures on the Zurich lakeshore, and after the death of his wife, and at other times of crisis, he turned to carving, drawing, and painting. For Jung, such activity was not a simple matter of taking one's mind off problems by escaping into image-making. He believed that working with dream and fantasy material pictorially could, significantly and dynamically, change the inner situation from which pain and conflict had arisen. He tells us that he first began to advocate this activity to his patients in 1916. He would tell them to disregard conventional ideas about art and instead to give full attention and respect to the inner image, whatever it might be. By coincidence in that same year, 1916, and also in Zurich, the Dada movement was founded on the premise of an insurrection against all that was pompous, conventional, or even boring in the arts and, in a very particular sense, an attempt to get back to nature. It was also anti-war. Subsequently, as we know, these ideas led Ernst, Breton, and others to become intensely interested in the unconscious and voluntarily to enter into the apparent conflict between 'dream and reality'. Thus, 'surrealism' entered our vocabulary. Jung was initially wary of Dada, perhaps because he had reservations about 'invoking the unconscious', although he later showed some interest.

Art made by art therapists; Stone; Therapists' engagement with their own art practice; Transcendent function

Keening: CW

Keening is a term used to describe the weeping and wailing of people who are grieving. It originates in mythology and was used to describe Banshee women in Celtic cultures who anticipate the imminent death of people with wailing sounds that continue after the death. The sounds made are different in different cultures. In some they take the form of ear-splitting screaming, in some loud wailing, and in others a rhythmic lament.

The possibility of a range of forms of 'keening' can help in understanding what is happening when distress becomes a persistent cry of pain.

Mind-forged manacles

Kindness: CW

'A sign of health in the mind', Donald Winnicott wrote in 1970, 'is the ability of one individual to enter imaginatively and accurately into the thoughts and feelings and hope and fears of another person; also to allow the other person to do the same to us.' To live well, we must be able to imaginatively identify with other people, and allow them to identify with us. Unkindness involves a failure of the imagination so acute that it threatens not just our happiness but our sanity. Caring about others, as Jean-Jaques Rousseau argued, is what makes us fully human. We depend on each other not just for our survival but for our very being. The self without sympathetic attachments is either a fiction or a lunatic.

(Phillips and Taylor, 2009: 97)

Empathy; Intuition

Klein and creativity: DE

Melanie Klein (1882–1960) was an original and controversial psychoanalyst who developed a very different way of thinking about the internal world to that proposed by Freud (Grosskurth, 1987; Hinshelwood, 1989; Klein, 1975; Segal, 1978b). Klein's model of the unconscious mind grew out of her work with children using what she termed 'The Psycho-Analytic Play Technique' (Klein, 1955, in Mitchell, 1986). It was through this technique that Klein was able to gain access to a child's unconscious and alleviate their fears. In the consulting room the children Klein worked with had access to play materials such as water, pencils, paper, and paints, and his or her own set of toys, including small wooden human figures in two sizes, a train, a car, and so on. Through observing the ways in which a child played with these toys, Klein recognised that:

> [T]he brick, the little figure, the car not only represent things which interest the child in themselves, but in his play with them they always have a variety of symbolical meanings as well which are bound up with his phantasies, wishes, and experiences . . . Play analysis had shown that symbolism enabled the child to transfer not only interests, but also phantasies, anxieties and guilt to objects other than people. Thus a great deal of relief is experienced in play and this is one of the things which make it so essential for the child.
>
> (Mitchell, 1986: 51–52)

Through her work with children, Klein came to the view that play was a defence against anxiety, its primary function being to provide relief through the externalisation of unconscious phantasy. Klein's contribution to understanding the means by which a child or adult is able to use objects and materials to represent, express, or control internal feeling states symbolically has been enormously influential in advancing psychoanalytic thinking about aesthetics and creativity (Glover, 2000). Whereas Freud focused almost exclusively on the symbolic content of art, and in so doing ignored its aesthetic qualities, Klein explored the function of symbols and the psychological processes involved in their creation. As a result of Klein's work, much greater attention is now paid to the importance of pre-verbal experience and forms of communication when working with very disturbed or regressed clients. Klein was also largely responsible for developing ways of thinking about the nature of the physical encounter with art and our emotional response to this, ideas that were later elaborated by the psychoanalyst Hanna Segal (1957, 1991) and the art critic Adrian Stokes (1965, 1972).

Projective identification: A Kleinian perspective; Reparation: A Kleinian perspective; Unconscious phantasy

Knowledge of materials: CW

> In order to create a department of this kind, one should have a fundamental knowledge of technique and materials, and then forget it all . . . one must then be ready to be led by the unconscious . . . Generally speaking, people who want to work spontaneously should not study technique . . . It can happen that artistic skill blots out what the unconscious is trying to say.
>
> (Lyddiatt, 1972: 20)

How can participants express themselves visually, though when they have no idea of the potential of materials and when their idea of art is painting by Rembrandt or Leonardo da Vinci or other *old masters?*.

(Waller, 1991: 52)

Art and materials in contemporary aesthetic philosophy; Collage;
Materials and image in assessment; Milner on using art materials;
Simplicity of materials; Size of materials

Kraepelin and perceptions of schizophrenia: CW

Emil Kraepelin (1856–1926) was a pioneer psychiatrist who contributed to the scientific ethos of the discipline. He believed in the organic causes of mental illness. After analysing thousands of case studies, he introduced diagnostic categories for schizophrenia. He held that degeneration was inherent in the condition.

Therapeutic nihilism, extended hospital stays and coercive management within the asylum walls, and poverty and unemployment beyond them, during these years of the late nineteenth-century Great Depression combined to limit the chances of recovery from dementia praecox. Few psychiatrists since Kraepelin . . . found the course of schizophrenia to be so malignant as originally portrayed. As Kraepelin's classification was adopted around the world, nevertheless, so was the impression that the illness was inevitably progressive and incurable. To varying degrees the same view holds sway today – that without treatment the outlook is hopeless – despite considerable evidence to the contrary.

(Warner, 1985: 13–14)

Bleulers; Diagnostic systems in psychiatry

Kramer, Edith: DW

Edith Kramer was a contemporary of Naumburg's and an art teacher by background. She is considered by some to be the founder of art therapy, or at least as essential to its development as Naumburg. Kramer still teaches on courses in New York and elsewhere.

Kramer considered that it was the art activity itself that had inherent 'healing' properties, and this gave the opportunity to externalise, re-experience, and resolve conflicting feelings . . .

Unlike Naumburg, Kramer did not work with the transference, but preferred to focus on the art object as a 'container of emotions' and she related to the patient through their art.

She herself was influenced by Freudian psychoanalysis, believing that art could be a means of sublimating feelings, but she felt this to be positive, in that, for example, out of destructive and aggressive feelings could emerge an object (drawing, painting, model, etc.) which would symbolise these feelings and thus prevent them being acted out.

Both Naumburg and Kramer were practising in the USA during the 1940s at the same time as Adrian Hill and others were introducing the concept of art therapy to British hospitals and sanatoriums . . . the same divergence was emerging in Britain between those who placed emphasis on the image-making as therapeutic in itself (Hill et al.) and those who saw the art object as both integrative and healing, and also as an aspect of the transference relationship between the therapist and patient (Champernowne et al.).

(Waller, 1991: 6–7)

First period of British art therapy; Hill on painting; Images used to convey the 'action' of violence; Naumburg; Sublimation theories in art therapy

Kusama and the artist's experience of psychosis: CW

The work of the artist Yayoi Kusama offers a visual representation of some aspects of the experience of psychosis. Discussions of her exhibitions contain echoes of accounts by outsider artists and the thoughts of people who have a history of psychosis.

Yayoi Kusama's visual art, with very few exceptions, shares a common vocabulary of dense, repetitive patterns made from cell-like clusters she calls 'Infinity Nets'. Whether these patterns are made of polka dots, phallic-shaped tubers, postal stickers or even dry macaroni, they reflect the artist's self-described obsession with nets, dots, food and sex, with pattern used as a means of self-obliteration. Kusama's unceasing restatement of the 'Infinity Net' is, however, also a reaffirmation of her persona, a defiant 'I exist' (Tatehata, 1993). The youngest of four children, Yayoi Kusama was born . . . 1929 in . . . Japan, into a prosperous and conservative family. This meant that the crucial years of her early adolescence coincided with Japan's involvement in the Second World War. From an early age Kusama suffered from bouts of mental illness and hallucinations. She has traced the origins of the 'Infinity Net' and polka-dot motif back to these episodes, during which she remembers seeing a red flower pattern 'dissolving and accumulating, proliferating and separating', filling 'the room, my body, the entire universe' until 'my self was eliminated, and I had returned and been reduced to the infinity of eternal time and the absolute of space'.

By the artist's own emphatic [statements], the experience of mental illness is central to every aspect of her work, from her imagery to her prolific production of paintings, sculptures, drawings and objects to prints, ceramics, novellas and books of poetry. At times a crippling burden, the illness is also a generative force. Kusama herself describes it as 'a weapon' not so much the subject of her work as it is the engine that drives it.

(Hoptman, 2000: 3–4)

Champernowne; Marks; Psychosis and art therapy; Transactional object in psychosis

Lacan, Jacques (1901–1981): KJ

In his famous 'Return to Freud' (Lacan, 1977), Lacan replaced parts of Freud's theoretical framework with ideas from surrealism, European philosophy, structural anthropology, and linguistics. For Lacan, the unconscious was less an internal than an intersubjective realm with language expressing desire.

Lacan provokes relevant ideas for art therapy relating language to the non-verbal, and the role of signification through the body, images, and speech. He argued against the reductive interpretations of classical psychoanalysis in relation to art, asserting that it was not the place of psychoanalysis to interpret the artist's psychology through the artwork or to provide the master key to its hidden content. Instead, art can have something of the analyst's function, producing the same unsettling effect as an interpretation. He is less interested in what psychoanalysis can tell us about art than in what art tells us about psychoanalysis (Wright, 1998).

Criticised as 'phallocentric', Lacan's ideas have influenced feminism, film theory, cultural studies, and literary criticism. His work is notorious for the labyrinthine density of writing, his variable length sessions (which saw him lose his membership of the international association for psychoanalysis), and his attempts to systematise psychoanalytic concepts through diverse theoretical models, including anthropology, linguistics, and mathematical topology (Turkle, 1992).

Schaverien (1995a) used Lacan to consider the engendered gaze in *Desire and the Female Therapist*. Maclagan has written about art as one way of attempting to bridge or fill the disturbing emptiness of the inevitable gap that appears between the symbolic order and what it seeks to symbolise (Maclagan, 2001).

Female gaze; Gaze and glance; Male gaze; Sublimation theories in art therapy; Sublimation theories in psychoanalysis; Sublime

Laing, Joyce: DW

Joyce Laing, with Ralf Pickford, was one of the founder members of *'Société Internationale de Psychopathologie de l'Expression'* in Scotland. She founded the first art therapy department in a psychiatric hospital in Scotland, at the Ross Clinic in Aberdeen, and became well-known for her work at the Barlinnie Special Unit, a progressive prison that was organised on therapeutic community lines. She was in charge of the arts and art therapy at Barlinnie (Carrel and Laing, 1982: 56–61). She worked with the notorious criminal Jimmy Boyle, helping him to transform into a talented sculptor.

> Joyce Laing was the first woman to work in the Unit and it was a combination of her warmth, energy, and non-conformity after years without feminine presence which initially engaged the men, though at first they had precious little interest in 'arty' things. Then, in exasperation, Joyce Laing took in a few pounds of sculptor's clay. Jimmy Boyle was hooked (Tisdall, 1983: 64).
>
> (Waller, 2009a: 4)

Negative space; Offenders using art therapy; Sculptural materials;
Sculpture; Three-dimensional form

Laing, R. D. and Goffman, E.: CW

The psychiatrist R. D. Laing had a marked influence on psychiatric practice in the last years of the twentieth century. He:

> ... took the problem of human suffering seriously, though he approached it with humour. His work at the Tavistock meant that his criticisms of some of the more reified aspects of psychoanalytical relationships were well informed. He suggested that there could be more democracy in therapeutic relationships and this may have appealed to art therapists who were working at the time.
>
> (Wood, 1991: 17)

He wrote about the plight of people diagnosed as 'schizophrenic'. International sales of his books were very high over a long period – particularly *The Divided Self* (1959) and *The Self and Others* (1961). Although he made no claim to offer 'a comprehensive theory of schizophrenia' (Laing, 1959: 9), or to recommend forms of therapy for people with psychoses, he nevertheless advanced insightful ideas about psychotic experiences. His descriptions of the forms that can be assumed by psychotic despair – 'engulfment', 'implosion', and 'petrification' – are helpful.

Some in the psychiatric establishment saw Laing as proposing the non-existence of madness. This is a persistent misconception that may explain the force of the reaction against him. Yet Laing himself made only the modest claim that it is 'far more possible than is generally supposed to understand people diagnosed as psychotic' (Laing, 1959: 11).

Criticisms include Sedgwick (1982) from a sociological perspective and Mitchell (1975) from a psychoanalytic perspective in *Psychoanalysis and Feminism*.

In keeping with the ethos of the 1960s, Goffman drew attention to the concerns of patients or, as he put it, the 'inmates'. In *Asylums* Goffman (1961) considers the assault on the person's sense of self upon admission to a mental hospital and discusses what he saw as the institution's mortification processes.

Laing was concerned with how a person's family and social relationship networks influence their sense of security in the world, but he tended *not* to look beyond the family, whereas Goffman's project was more widely sociological.

Anti-psychiatry; Kraepelin; Moral treatment; Psychosis and art therapy; Second period of British art therapy; Social action art therapy; Social inclusion; Social psychiatry

Lateness: CW

Commitment to begin the therapeutic process has a physical basis in terms of actual attendance and an emotional one in terms of the decision to make use of the sessions. The lateness can be understood as one way of testing this out for the client and is common in the early stages of therapy. It raises questions in the client about how much he wants to come, how acceptable he will be to the therapist and is an expression of ambivalence about the undertaking of treatment.

(Dalley et al., 1993: 40)

Boundaries; Therapeutic frame

Leaflets: PBa

Art therapy leaflets are written for referrers, clients, work colleagues, or others interested in learning more about art therapy. They summarise the provision of art therapy in its various settings and help to prepare a person for art therapy, clearing up any misunderstandings they may have. A brief description of art therapy and information about the potential experience of becoming an art therapy client will vary according to the client groups for whom the therapy is provided. Some leaflets display a picture of a client's artwork or the type of pictures that could be made, which helps to communicate what attending art therapy might be like. Leaflets can also help clients to understand issues of consent.

Consent

Learning circle: KH

Kelly's personal construct theory explores how people evolve predictive systems for anticipating events, enabling them to respond quickly to situations: 'man seeks to predict, and thus control, the course of events. It follows, then, that the constructs, which he formulates, are intended to aid him in his predictive efforts' (Kelly, 1955: 12).

Managing change can be stressful. Change and learning can be more easily managed by understanding the basic stages of learning a new skill. A therapist anticipating what is likely to happen next in the process can help to contain some of the anxiety of not knowing.

One form of guidance is the 'learning circle', whose cited origins are as old as Confucius and Socrates. Figure 4 illustrates my version. Having found pre-prepared handouts ineffective, I draw this 'live' with clients and students using individual examples encouraging them to identify the stages.

A 13-year-old I worked with demonstrated the model's capacity for re-framing anxiety. Soon after making a learning circle poster for her bed-room, she told me: 'Now I love the bit where I hate it because it means I'll be able to do it soon!'

Art-making and art therapy model ways of learning about learning. This can help in rehearsing not knowing and in not being able to do something, and surviving that.

Anticipatory guidance in art therapy; Anticipatory Guidance, worse/better paradigm; Circle

Learning disabilities: Art therapy as psychotherapy: BD and RT

The first *Inscape* article on art therapy with people who have a learning difficulty was written by Cortazzie and Gunsburg (1969), who were con-cerned with trying to help patients from the 'back wards' of a large institution. In the late 1970s and early 1980s, Stott and Males (1984) argued that art materials offered people with learning disabilities the opportunity to express themselves and develop communication that was not reliant on verbal skills. Along with other British pioneers, their writing led to the

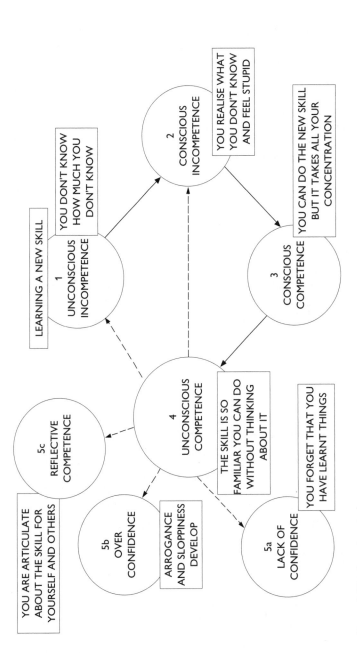

Figure 4 The learning circle.

search for psychotherapeutic approaches to art therapy for people with learning disabilities. In November 1984 a conference entitled 'Art Therapy as Psychotherapy in Relation to the Mentally Handicapped?' at Hertfordshire College of Art and Design explored this. The very title expresses ambivalence about this work, but most presentations placed psychodynamic emphasis on the therapeutic relationship. Many criticised the diet of 'training' offered to people with learning disabilities (Whitehurst, 1984), non-directive approaches were recommended (Loake, 1984), and an object relations approach using Winnicott and Klein was proposed (Hallam, 1984; Hughes, 1988). Hughes (1988) developed her use of Winnicott, and Gray (1985) in her *Inscape* case study discusses 'conscious and unconscious' processes through the artwork of a man with moderate learning disabilities. Goldsmith (1986) recognised differing uses for art materials and their importance in promoting thinking, arguing the possibilities of multiple meaning and interpretation. Strand (1990) used group analysis techniques to counter isolation and demonstrate peer-learning for people with learning disabilities. Dubowski (1985) and Rees (1995) researched art-making by the more severely disabled, and Tipple (1992, 1993) examined both expression in the pre-representational work of the severely disabled and transference phenomena with the moderately disabled.

Artworks and discourses of men and women with learning disabilities; Emotional life for men and women with learning disabilities; In the box; Looking-down ritual; Secondary handicap; Stupidity; Working alliance with men and women with learning disabilities

Learning disability definitions: SWB

UK definitions of learning disability feature in two government policy documents: *Valuing People* (DOH, 2001b) and *The Same as You?* (Scottish Executive, 2000). They state: 'People with learning disabilities have a significant, lifelong condition that started before adulthood, that affected their development and which means they need help to: understand information; learn skills; and cope independently' (Scottish Executive, 2000: 1–3). In the United States, the term (from DSM IV) is mental retardation with a similar definition: a disability characterised by significant limitations both in intellectual functioning and in adaptive behaviour as expressed in conceptual, social, and practical adaptive skills. The terminology used to describe and define this group of people has been explored by therapists, academics, polemicists; disability rights groups, and art therapists (Rees, 1998). Societal views are influenced historically and in part constructed through the terminology: subnormal, retarded, trainable, low grade, mental defective, idiot, feeble minded; all are terms with legal, medical, and academic respectability. Art therapists have actively contested this stereotypical and pejorative view for over 20 years (Hallam, 1983, 1984; Loake, 1984; Manners, 1989; Rees, 1998) and volubly propose that people with learning disabilities are people first, equally entitled to access the full range of opportunities as other members of society, including suitable therapy services.

Diagnostic systems in psychiatry; Looking down in disability;
Measurement of men and women with learning disabilities

Legend: JA

A story handed down through generations that although lacking accurate historical evidence, has gained popular acceptance as truth.

One such legend concerns Saint Gobnait (literally 'Little Mouth'), who remains a focus of devotion in Ireland. She is known to have established a nunnery in the sixth century in County Cork. This much is recorded, but many stories have passed into the oral tradition, including one concerning her angelic guidance on the placing of her community.

Gobnait was urged to wander by land until she saw nine white deer grazing together, indicating her 'place of resurrection'. In Celtic lore, nine is seen as an incorruptible number, white represents purity or holiness, and deer are divine messengers. This achieved, she was clearly a force to be reckoned with in her determination to maintain her convent's physical and spiritual boundaries. Tales recount cattle rustlers successfully deterred by her sending swarms of attacking bees. Others tell of an invader intent on building a castle, but on seeing the walls rising Gobnait hurled a ball of polished agate, destroying it each time it neared completion. This ball can still be seen and touched in the wall of her church. Extraordinary feats of protection and the creation of safe space may resonate for present-day therapists.

Myth

Life of a symbol: AGoI

The symbol is alive only so long as it is pregnant with meaning. But once its meaning has been born out of it, once that expression is found which formulates the thing sought, expected, or divined even better than the hitherto accepted symbol, then the symbol is dead, i.e., it possesses only an historical significance.

(Jung, 1921, *CW 6*: para. 816)

Metaphor (framed and unframed); Symbol; Symbolisation

Life of the picture: JS

The stages outlined by Schaverien (1991) help in a consideration of the life of the picture for the client (Identification; Familiarisation; Acknowledgement; Assimilation; and Disposal):

> . . . all involve active participation of the therapist. However, this activity may appear passive; her or his role is mainly one of 'holding' (Winnicott 1971). The role is a response to the stage of the relationship of the client to her or his picture. Thus, in the stages of identification and familiarisation, the therapist will accompany the client in viewing the pictures. She or he will observe the effect the picture has on the client, and may even use this observation to make a comment. This is different from entering into the picture in an intrusive manner. It may be, for example, that something about the picture is obvious to the therapist immediately, but the client has not realised that there is this, alternative, way of viewing the image. It is important for the therapist to wait for the client to perceive this for her or himself, and only to intervene and point it out once there has been time for the realisation to dawn at the client's own pace.
>
> (Schaverien, 1991: 106)

Baring the phenomenon; Disposal (two entries)*; Immanent articulation; Inner art; Push-and-pull effect; Vitality*

Liminality: CS

Consistent with the findings of Little et al. (1998), liminality is a valuable lens through which to view experiences of cancer, and indeed other illness experiences and life transitions, and also aids exploration in art therapy (Sibbett, 2005a, 2005b, 2006).

Sibbett discusses liminality of thresholds in life and in death:

> Rites of passage are fundamentally characterized by the liminal phase (Mahdi *et al.* 1996), which is the most important as it is the core of where transition occurs (Lertzman 2002). Turner outlined key characteristics of liminality experienced by 'threshold people' (1995: 95) including:
>
> 1. *Limbo* – 'ambiguity', 'social limbo', being 'out of time' (Turner, 1982: 24), 'neither here nor there . . . betwixt and between' (Turner 1995: 95).
> 2. *Power/powerless* – 'submissiveness and silence' (Turner 1995: 103), structural inferiority and outsiderhood (Turner 1975: 231), reduced status, 'passive' (Turner 1995: 95).

3. *Playing* – 'playful experience' (Turner 1988: 124–5), 'ludic (or playful) events' and use of 'multi-vocal symbols' (Turner 1982: 27); experience of 'flow' (Turner 1982: 55–8), potentially transforming, possibility (Turner 1986: 42, 1990: 11–12).

4. *Communitas* – 'intense comradeship', 'communion' (Turner 1995: 95–6).

5. *Embodied experience* – experiencing physiological 'ordeals' (Turner 1995: 103), 'pain and suffering' (Turner 1995: 107), stigma, 'effacement' (Turner 1982: 26), 'polluting' (Turner 1967: 97), 'sexlessness' (Turner 1995: 102), androgyny (Turner 1967: 98), involving 'performance' and 'expression' such as in 'acts' and 'works of art' (Turner 1982: 12–15).

(Sibbett, 2005b: 13–14)

Mentalisation; Mindfulness; Power; Rites of Passage; Sustaining the therapist in cancer care

Linking personal and political: MJR

Listening to a client's dream (about finding herself left alone amidst a consumed forest), I was aware of my own association to the clear-cutting of rainforests of the world. But my client made no mention of this and I was in two minds whether to raise it. Eventually I told her my association, at which point she said that I am 'bringing my green agenda into the room'. I felt angry with her comment, and my irritation blocked me from finding a satisfactory response. Thinking she was not ready to talk about these issues, I left it.

This was some years ago, before climate change had hit the headlines. With hindsight, I can see other ways through. What if I had made a comment that linked inner and outer realities, something like: 'I wonder if your dream is saying something about our collective desire to consume as if there was no tomorrow?' In this way, I am acknowledging that we are all caught in something together; eating problems are not simply an individual or familial experience (Rust, 1992).

Fool images; Stone

Literature review

See: *Research critical appraisal*

Living and dying: CW

People all over the world respond to the challenges of life in marvellously exuberant and creative ways. In the process, they make and use many beautiful and extraordinary objects, and also, sometimes, invest quite ordinary things with an importance and significance that goes beyond appearance.

(British Museum Exhibition Catalogue, 2003: 5)

Cosmologies; Cradle to grave

Loneliness: CW

Many art therapy clients live in extreme isolation. For some, if they did not get out of their beds for a week few people would know. The dislocation and isolation of mental health service users can be understood as coming from the historical development of modern societies. 'By the time we reach the twentieth century . . . the socio-historically conditioned circumstances of the individual's atomised, privatised life are characterised, a-historically, as the "human condition"' (Mészáros, 1970: 255).

Some treatment policies reflect this, although current psychosocial approaches for long-term clients have led to more support and there is less pejorative discussion of dependency needs. Nevertheless, some clients continue to berate themselves because they cannot manage to feel content with meagre rations of human contact and comfort. They tend to think that this is evidence of their own internal inadequacy:

> . . . alienation and reification, by producing the deceiving appearance of the individual's independence, self-sufficiency and autonomy, confers a value *per se* on the world of the individual, in abstraction from its relationships with society, with the 'outside world'. Now the fictitious 'individual autonomy' represents the positive pole of morality and social relations count only as 'interference', as mere negativity.
>
> (Mészáros, 1970: 258)

Shortly before her political demise Margaret Thatcher's (1987) pronouncement, 'There is no such thing as society, there are only individuals', seemed to corroborate this impression of loneliness being part of the zeitgeist. It can be helpful to situate the craziness of this in the society and not in the individual.

Absorption in art-making; Alienation; Poverty; Social inclusion

Looked-after children (also called children in care): MMc

Children become 'looked-after' when their birth parents cannot provide ongoing care on a temporary or permanent basis. This can happen as a result of voluntary agreement or as the result of a court order. Depending on individual circumstances, children may be placed with kinship carers (family), network carers (extended family/friends), foster carers, or in residential provision.

Most young people in care come from families in difficulty and are separated from them because they cannot provide adequate care. Many are affected by distressing and damaging experiences, including physical and sexual abuse and neglect; some may have experienced the illness or death of a parent; whilst others have disabilities and complex needs. Vulnerable unaccompanied minors seeking asylum in the UK also become 'looked-after'. A tiny minority of children and young people are in care because of offences they have committed (less than 2% in 2000). There are about 60,000 children and young people who are looked after by local authorities in England (Department for Children, Schools, and Families) and 80,000 in Britain (http://www.issuk.org.uk/what_we_do/state_care.php).

A coordinated approach is needed across all children's services. Through '*Every Child Matters*' (http://www.everychildmatters.gov.uk) local areas are reforming their multi-agency support for vulnerable children and young people to offer better prevention and earlier intervention. Central government, local authorities and their partners in children's trusts, individual professionals, and carers all share responsibility for ensuring the best for children and young people in care – as they would for their own children. Children in care should be cared about, not just cared for (HMSO, 2006).

Outcome measures for 'looked-after children'; Poverty; Social inclusion

Looking: DW

So, how do we look at the art which is produced in art therapy? This is a question that greatly preoccupies art therapists. David Maclagan addresses this . . . in *Psychological Aesthetics*. 'Although art therapy work was produced under the aegis of "art" it was effectively insulated from the outside world of art, or at least connected with it only peripherally and incidentally . . .' (Maclagan, 2001: 87).

The culture of the art school, the art studio and the art therapy room are nowadays rarely even similar . . . It is important, as art therapists, to think about these issues, and about our preferences, why we like to work in some media and why we like or respond to some art objects and images rather than others and why this is so. It may be that practical necessities dictate how we can use materials with clients. We cannot approach any object, be it in the street, in a gallery or in an art therapy session without the influence of our socio-cultural context . . .

Those of us who encourage our patients to use images in their therapy will witness the production of a huge variety: from the smallest tentative marks to bold paintings and sculptures and group art works which may fill a room. We will be immersed in the context in which they are produced, and this will impact on us . . .

(Waller, 2009a)

Non-art; Seeing and looking

Looking and visual research: AJG

Looking at and analysing the role and function of images is at the heart of much art therapy research, particularly when it is casework based. Schaverien demonstrated this approach in her detailed analysis of a client's pictures in *The Revealing Image* (Schaverien, 1991). In a later text Schaverien (1993) outlines the procedure she used to analyse her client's artworks systematically in a chronological, retrospective review. This considered the marks, form, and colour of each image, the documentation of change and development, and the 'evidence' of therapeutic process, all of which enabled her to compare the client's and her (the art therapist's) experiences. Description, detailed looking, and a clustering of the images according to their subject matter, the art materials used, and the kinds of marks made characterise this kind of visual research, all of which should, as Schaverien states and shows, be analysed within a specific theoretical framework.

This visual method draws on a mixture of anthropological and art historical research traditions (e.g. Panofsky, 1972; Rose, 2001).

Case studies; Curating and visual research; Mythologies and the participant observer; Review with images; Visual research methods

Looking down in disability: BD

The physically disabled person, using a wheelchair, is familiar with the power expressed through the intimidating downward gaze of others. This overt gaze is rendered latent, but no less powerful, in the context of learning disability. There are few other groups of people more closely and continuously observed than the learning disabled and it seems routine for the most meticulous and intimate observations to take place into every area of life imaginable.

In this context, the downward-looking scopic has become a controlling observational gaze, the effect of which is well described by Foucault:

There is no need for arms, physical violence, material constraints. Just a gaze, an inspecting gaze, a gaze which every individual under its weight will end by interiorising to the point that he is his own overseer, each individual thus exercising surveillance over and against himself.

(Foucault, cited in Butler and Parr, 1999: 208)

In supervision, similar dynamics might dwell in the horizontality of the artworks. The familiar triangle of the supervisor, supervisee, and artwork places stress on the latter to represent the absent client. The problem of looking down in supervision is that it closely mirrors both the power relationship described earlier and the learning disabled person's experience of life as a marginalised and isolated figure inhabiting a kind of underclass.

The vertical elevation of artworks in art therapy practice, a simple act requiring little energy, not only enables an empowering eye-to-eye relationship with the client, but also holds the possibility of challenging unconscious constructions of the learning disabled person whilst simultaneously interrupting a re-enactment of the client's oppressive experience mediated through surveillance.

Gaze and glance; Looking-down ritual; Power

Looking-down ritual: BD

There is a ritual embedded in art therapy practice whereby art objects (mostly two-dimensional) are laid horizontally upon the floor or table. This daily practice by art therapists appears to run contrary to the conventional way of looking at pictures in our homes and in the gallery where they are most often displayed vertically and at eye level upon a wall. But what does it say about the client-artist when we privilege the horizontal over the vertical? Holding images vertically has the power to validate artworks and enable them to be seen (Damarell, 2006).

Gaze and glance; Looking down in disability

Lyddiatt, E. M.: CW

Lyddiatt was a friend and colleague of Champernowne, and had undergone Jungian Analysis. In 1971 she published *Spontaneous Painting and Modelling*, the first British book to be devoted entirely to the practice of art therapy, although it is not titled as such.

. . . Her book was reviewed in *The Times* (3rd March 1971) . . . The reviewer concluded that 'Spontaneous painting is not a universal remedy but it is clear that it should be practised much more widely than it is' . . .

(Waller, 1991: 10–11)

Martina Thomson (1989) offers a moving account of her apprenticeship as an art therapist with Lyddiatt, one of the pioneers of British art therapy from the 1950s. She describes the chaotic, rich muddle found in Lyddiatt's art rooms, in sharp contrast to the cool order of Adamson's rooms. Thomson remembers her saying with a smile, 'my house is a mess but my dreams are in order', suggesting this as expressive of her approach to making art.

> Even if it is an over-simplification it may sometimes be a useful plan to describe spontaneous painting in three stages: firstly, imaginative material is given form; secondly, it 'works back' on the maker and is experienced; and thirdly, one feels more alive. Often these stages blend.
>
> (Lyddiatt, 1972: 6)

Later she describes her understanding of the content of pictures as 'exceedingly complex'. For her, intellectual understanding is not the key and, quoting Jung, she identifies that 'the important thing is not to interpret and understand fantasies but primarily to experience them' (Jung, cited in Lyddiatt 1972: 10). Her writing gives the impression of honesty and humour about her doubts.

Adamson; First period of British art therapy; Inner art; Withymead

MacGregor, John: CW

MacGregor's passionate and wonderfully illustrated research into the 'the golden age of psychotic art' in *The Discovery of the Art of the Insane* (1989) is justifiably famous.

He defines what he sees as 'essential to a truly psychotic art:

> The drawings and paintings that form the focus of events described in this study were without exception created in response to a spontaneous impulse arising from within the individual personality. The tremendous fascination that they exerted on artists and physicians in the nineteenth and twentieth centuries derived from this purity of impulse and content.
>
> (MacGregor, 1989: 10)

MacGregor was doing his PhD research during the second period of British art therapy history, although publication was not until 1989. He defines the 'art of the insane' as only consisting of those rare works made during lifetimes of incarceration by artists such as Wolfli, Aloise, and Emile Nolde. He does not include all works by people who go 'mad' in the category. His conclusion is to invoke a moral obligation upon physicians to anticipate the rare emergence of a 'schizophrenic master' and create for them 'an environment in which creativity and independent growth exists, whatever form it may take' (MacGregor, 1989: 103).

He expects the production of art by severely mentally ill people soon to cease almost entirely, seeing the conditions for its creation as: prolonged hospitalisation; prolonged psychosis (i.e. before the use of medication); and the absence of therapy. He seems to dismiss the creativity of the majority. In addition, one comment suggests careless ignorance about art therapy: 'much of what is done in the name of art therapy has little to do with either therapy or art' (MacGregor, 1989: 189).

Art of the insane; Second period of British art therapy

Magical thinking: MAm

'Magical thinking is evident in our dreams and fantasies. This type of thinking is inherent in childhood and is typified by the game of peek-a-boo' (Schaverien, 1999: 57).

Witness and witnessing

Making meaning: DK and BL

'Meaninglessness inhibits fullness of life and is therefore equivalent to illness. Meaning makes a great many things endurable – perhaps everything' (Jung, 1953–1966).

This theme runs throughout our work as art therapists, and more specifically our work within the context of political violence. Meaning making is fundamental to being human and can take many forms – for example, it can be the ability to place the experience in an external context, to understand the experience through the eye of faith, or to hear the experience while retelling it.

For many, the act of giving testimony and being witnessed is essential to making meaning. Many of the press reports coming out of South Africa while the Truth and Reconciliation Commission was in process (1990s) described how comforted the witnesses felt *just to finally be heard*. Sometimes in art therapy when the story is told and heard through the image it confirms for the individual that it did actually take place and was not, as they may have begun to fear, in their imagination.

Victor Frankl (1984), who survived concentration camps (World War II), describes making meaning as basic to our understanding of the will to live. He writes:

. . . to live is to suffer, to survive is to find meaning in the suffering . . . But no man can tell another what this purpose is. Each must find out for himself, and must accept the responsibility that his answer pre- scribes. If he succeeds he will continue to grow in spite of all indignities.

(Frankl 1984: 11–12)

This entry was adapted from Kalmanowitz and Lloyd (2005: 24–26).

Coping strategies that use dreams and art-making; Narrative; Remembering and forgetting; Witness and witnessing in art therapy

Male gaze: LR

In *Ways of Seeing* John Berger (1972) explores the sexual politics of look- ing, exposing the gendered codes of representation that pervade Western art. 'Women are depicted in a different way from men – not because the feminine is different from the masculine – but because the "ideal" spectator is always assumed to be male and the image of the woman is designed to flatter him' (Berger, 1972: 64).

There results a visual economy where women internalise the male observer, treating themselves as sights. This hidden code (presented as 'value-free') may be termed 'the male gaze'. Berger distinguishes this from Indian, Persian, African, and Pre-Columbian art traditions where sexual attraction is depicted more equally.

He uses Peter Lely's 1618 portrait of Nell Gwynne for illustration. The painting is not about Nell; instead its subject is a flattering display of the power and virility of Charles II (Berger, 1972: 52). Virginia Woolf summed up the role that women have traditionally played as tools of the male psyche: 'Women have served all these centuries as looking glasses possess- ing the magic and delicious power of reflecting the figure of man at twice the natural size' (Isaak, 1996: 225).

Contemporary artists such as Cindy Sherman, Jenny Saville, Louise Bourgeois, Mona Hatoum, and Tracy Emin, amongst others, seek to reclaim female subject-hood. Historic and contemporary gay male artists also challenge unstated power assumptions. For example, David Hockney, whose 1960s paintings of young men in the shower attained mainstream acceptability; the American photographer Robert Mapplethorpe and Japanese performance artist and photographer Yasumasa Morimura also work to disrupt the dynamic.

Female gaze; Gaze and glance; Looking down in disability; Looking-down ritual; Male socialisation; Men using art therapy

Male socialisation: MLieb

Male therapists have described how men are taught to switch off their emotions and then find it hard to relate to others (Hodson, 1984). This causes much damage to men's and women's lives. Verbal communication skills are often lacking and not always encouraged (Miedzian, 1992). Often men look to women for emotional support (Lee, 1991). Biddulph (1994) relates this and male reliance on stereotyping to 'under-fathering', often carried on from generation to generation. Other authors (e.g. Miedzian, 1992) chart the ways in which male violence is an outcome of stereotypical attitudes, and is learned through example, the media, toys, and sport. These findings apply across all social classes, even if the manifestations differ in some respects.

In her research on adult male survivors of childhood sexual abuse, Kim Etherington (1995) looks at the factors of male socialisation that make it difficult to admit vulnerability or to ask for therapy. Several of her research subjects saw themselves as failures as men for having allowed themselves (as they saw it) to be abused in the first place. This led them to minimise the harm done and to block off their feelings about the abuse and about themselves. Instead, they often opted for alcohol and drugs to soothe the pain. In addition, while some men cannot face group work – often because of issues of abuse, which they find too shameful to share – many men seem to engage well in group art therapy.

Men using art therapy

Marks: CW

'Marks can be rudimentary dots, lines, and shapes made with wet or dry materials on paper or other surfaces' (Philippa Brown: original entry). Laura Richardson elaborates:

> When 'Doreen' (pseudonym) arrived at the day hospital she was mute. Four days on, she came into a particularly busy open art therapy group. I helped her settle in, but there were many calls on my attention so I spent less time with her than planned. She did not speak and glancing I saw her still empty paper. As I approached, 'Doreen' took her brush and made a mark. 'Ah' she said, 'I do exist then'. This small dot allayed and helped her communicate her doubt.

Drawing a line

Masks: KM

Definitions of 'mask' include a covering for the face involving the eyes, mouth, or whole face. To mask means to conceal or disguise things (e.g. true

motives or feelings). Such 'masks' may be created internally through conscious or unconscious *warding off* processes in response to fears about
unknown feelings. We need to be aware of the possibility of the artwork itself
offering clients a variety of 'masks' to hide behind. Clients may on occasion
even use the artwork to *ward off* difficulties or to abstract their feelings.

Art-making as a defence; Defend or abwehr; Inner autonomy

Masquerade: LR

Masquerade, is an artistic mode of enquiry with roots in allegorical
painting, theatre, and folk traditions that involves the enactment of archetypes and can be seen as a meeting point for visual art, performance,
drama, and therapy.

Since its earliest development, photography inspired experimentation with
identity, illusion, and reality. Claims to realism, combined with its potential
as a performance tool, have allowed photographers to satirise or document
social mores. Julia Margaret Cameron in the 1860s (J. Cox, 1996: 26–27) and
Francis Benjamin Johnson in the 1890s (Marien, 2002: 166) played with
gendered signifiers and androgyny. Joan Rivière's (www.ncf.edu/hassold/
WomenArtists/rivière) influential Freudian essay of 1929, *Womanliness as
Masquerade*, inspired Surrealist Claude Cahun to use many guises to
examine plural identities. Her rallying cry 'exalt the imagination of the
wardrobe mistress!' in her essay of 1930, *Aveux non Avenus* (*Unavowed
Avowals*), led her to both pare down her physical image by shaving her head
and to adopt the guises of doll, guru, boxer, and dandy. 'Conceiving oneself
otherwise in order to become what one is' (Leperlier, in Dexter and Bush,
1994: 20).

Dramatists such as Brecht and Boal pursued masquerade for raising
political consciousness. The Brechtian-influenced British artist Jo Spence
made work from the 1970s to the 1990s challenging cultural stereotypes of
older working class women, developing an approach termed 'phototherapy'
that involved enacting multiple facets of experience and identity.

Gaze and glance; Heterosexism and the heterosexual lens

Materials and image in assessment: KT

The assessment process, perhaps similarly to brief work, can be an intensive
and focused experience. The concentrated nature of the initial meeting often
contains much of what the person's future therapy will address.

One of the main tasks is to provide enough information and experience
for the client to be able to consent to therapy. Enabling someone to give
informed consent in such a short period of time is not straightforward, but

can be facilitated if they have a 'good enough' experience of containment during assessment, and I believe this includes an introduction to the art materials. For some this may simply involve sitting near the materials, looking at them, and wondering if they dare touch.

It is during assessment that many clients first encounter the idea of using art materials as a reflective process, which can be both exciting and scary. Image-making can give the client an opportunity to make tangible space for themselves, where they can see what they are thinking and feeling. This offers a means of giving form to experiences that may previously have existed inside their head. McNiff writes: 'Making and contemplating art are fundamental means of helping people become more conscious of their experience' (McNiff, 1998: 100).

These early encounters allow the client and the therapist to assess whether a safe and containing-enough relationship can begin to be established. It is helpful to think of the image in assessment as a potential meeting place between the client and therapist, and also the client and their 'self'.

Assessment and formulation; Brief and short-term art psychotherapy; Consent; Milner on using art materials; Typewriter and blackboard

Maturation in adolescence and the uses of art therapy: AMB

The psychological tasks of adolescent development include identity formation, integrating previous trauma and conflicts from early attachment, establishing sexual identity, and maintaining the continuity of a sense of self. When unresolved difficulties emerge from early attachments, infantile and oedipal anxieties increase and this leads to an increased need for psychological defences to cope with maintaining equilibrium and continuity of the self or 'ego' (Blos, 1962).

In the 'normal' adolescent, conflicts between satisfying and controlling impulses may be intensely projected into relationships with others, which then become imbued with intensity and difficulty. In the disturbed young person these may be acted out (in forms of self-harm or violence) with risk to themselves or others, resulting in the extremes of behaviours that quickly become disturbing to peers, family members, and other adults.

Copley (1993: 109) explains that the psychologically maturing young person exhibits a decrease in the use of the defence mechanisms of splitting and projection, a developing self-perception of being a whole person, a personal and actual sexual identity, and sustains an intimate relationship with a partner. Winnicott (1965a) indicates that the process of psychological maturation, which begins in adolescence, continues to evolve throughout the life cycle and that this may be powerfully re-evoked at times of transition or significant life events. He also stresses the central significance of the therapeutic environment (Winnicott, 1965a: 80). The wide range of art materials in the art therapy environment creates the potential for intense emotional engagement in the therapy. This is potentially exciting, creative, and/or terrifying since it may re-evoke and bring to life the internal, unconscious world of the young person.

The intensity of interaction with adolescents can be acutely exhausting and co-working with other clinicians or therapists can be a significant means of containing the anxieties of adolescents in groups as well as the counter-transference feelings of the therapists, which may threaten to overwhelm (Waterfield and Brown, 1996).

Adaptations of practice with adolescents; Child development

Measurement of men and women with learning disabilities: BD and RT

The World Health Organization defines mental handicap and learning disability as an 'incomplete or insufficient general development of mental capacities'. The concept of intelligence and IQ scores determine levels and diagnoses: 50–70 = mild, 35–50 = moderate, 20–35 = severe, and below 20 = profound. It is important to note that the people to whom the labels are applied often object to such descriptions, preferring to emphasise the whole person rather than solely their intellect.

What tests measure has long been a subject of debate; early attempts disadvantaged the educationally deprived, and modern tests measuring different kinds of cognitive activity (e.g. sequential and simultaneous reasoning, spatial perception and non-verbal concept formation, verbal reasoning) are also criticised for their conceptual assumptions (see Gardner, 1983). Because some children remain impossible to test, developmental scales and observation may remain the basis on which the label is applied. There are of course recognised syndromes that have physical attributes and the learning disabled often suffer from other handicaps and difficulties, such as sensory impairments and epilepsy.

The terms impairment, disability, and handicap seem to be often confused. In language concerned with the field of 'learning disability', impairment indicates damage to the brain and central nervous system. A disability is a functional incapacity (e.g. difficulties with cognition diminish the capacity for understanding and intellectual activity) presumed to follow from impairment. A handicap represents the disadvantage arising from the impairment and disability (e.g. the inability to read and write).

Learning disability definitions

Mediating function of the art object: JS

> As concrete objects within the therapeutic setting they mediate in the actual space in-between client and therapist. With the psychotic client, the mediating function of the art object is especially significant. Relating directly to another human being may be experienced as far too threatening to a fragile personality, but to relate through a mediating object may be possible.
>
> (Schaverien, 1997: 34)

Images used to convey the 'action' of violence; Transactional object in psychosis

Men using art therapy: MLieb

Art therapy has much to offer men, but they have some difficulties in accessing it because of factors connected with their socialisation and how they are seen in society. The norms of therapy – openness about feelings, communication, self-reflection, intimacy – are areas where some men have difficulties.

Art therapy has a special role in providing a bridge to the skills listed above by giving time for an activity (with very visible boundaries), which may feel safer and more purposeful (in being active) than verbal therapy. The following points may help men in particular:

- Art therapy provides an active phase, which can then lead more easily to reflection.
- It is necessary that the extra difficulties that men may have in accessing therapy, in particular the vulnerability ('un-macho-ness') of being a client, be recognised. Perhaps literature, in which men speak about the benefits of therapy, could help to reassure those who are cautious and wary about art therapy.
- The 'art part' of an art therapy session is likely to be the more important part for many men, especially at the beginning of therapy.
- Some structure may be helpful in containing some men's anxiety about the unfamiliar world of feelings.
- Some men may find group work easier than individual work, because it is less intimate and the solidarity makes up for feelings of being 'deficient men' for needing therapy.

Of course, there is a great overlap between the experiences of men, and these reflections may be relevant to some women too. In the same way that the criminal justice system makes very few provisions for the 'special needs' of women, maybe the mental health system needs to pay more attention to the 'special needs' of men.

Class; Health; Male socialisation; Mental health treatments; Patient choice (two entries)*; Unhelpful counter-transference in forensic work*

Mental health: CW

Mental health is defined as a state of well-being in which every individual realizes his or her own potential, can cope with the normal stresses of life, can work productively and fruitfully, and is able to make a contribution to her or his community.

(WHO: http://www.who.int/mental_health/en/)

WHO is currently appealing internationally to governments to increase their support for mental health services. This is part of a series of six reviews on global mental health published in the journal *The Lancet*. All of the associated papers and commentaries can be accessed freely at the following website: http://www.thelancet.com/online/focus/mental_health/collection.

Damage to mental health; Mental health treatments

Mental health treatments: CW

The World Health Organization (WHO) reports that cost-effective treatments exist for most disorders and, if correctly applied, could enable most of those affected to become functioning members of society.

Barriers to effective treatment of mental illness include lack of recognition of the seriousness of mental illness and lack of understanding about the benefits of services. Policy-makers, insurance companies, health and labour policies, and the public at large all discriminate between physical and mental problems.

Most middle and low-income countries devote less than 1% of their health expenditure to mental health. Consequently mental health policies, legislation, community care facilities, and treatments for people with mental illness are not given the priority they deserve.

The recently launched mental health Global Action Programme (mhGAP) focuses on forging strategic partnerships to enhance countries worldwide in their:

... capacity to combat stigma, reduce the burden of mental disorders and promote mental health ... through combined action in education, social welfare, justice, rural development and women's affairs, it is important to ensure that policies and interventions are evidence-based and reflect commitment to equity, ethics, human rights and gender equality.

(WHO: http://www.who.int/mental_health/en/)

Future cities; Health; Mental health; Poverty

Mentalisation: DN

Mentalisation describes our capacity to focus on mental states within ourselves or in others, particularly when we look for explanations of behaviour. It is, 'a mostly preconscious, imaginative mental activity. It is imaginative because we have to imagine what other people might be thinking or feeling' (Bateman and Fonagy, 2006: 1).

Of the deficits associated with borderline personality disorder (BPD), Bateman and Fonagy suggest that these: 'may be direct consequences of not perceiving the mental states of others with sufficient accuracy or the re-emergence of non-mentalising modes of social cognition' (Bateman and Fonagy, 2006: 18).

Art psychotherapists Franks and Whitaker (2007) devised a 'Joint Therapy Programme' for clients with BPD. They combine group art psychotherapy with individual verbal psychotherapy. Comparison of pre and post-therapy CORE-OM (Clinical Outcome and Routine Evaluation Outcome Measure: http://www.coreims.co.uk) scores demonstrated symptoms remaining considerably lower than at pre-therapy and important increases in functioning scores. They concluded that for their clients '. . . visual dialogue, often unspoken, both with themselves and with others . . . forms a basis of a hypothesis about self which is then tested within the group . . .' (2007: 14). In addition they 'realised how the image becomes central in the mentalisation process, and how it enables clients to observe their sense of self emerging, along with others perceiving them as thinking and feeling . . .' (Franks and Whitaker, 2007: 4).

Borderline personality disorder

Menzies-Lyth: CP

Psychoanalyst Isabel Menzies-Lyth's article entitled 'The Functioning of Social Systems as a Defence against Anxiety' (1959) has been used by art therapists to explore the defence mechanisms that can operate within institutions:

... a social defence mechanism develops over time as a result of collu-
sive interaction and agreement, often unconscious, between members of
the organisation as to what form it shall take. The socially structured
defence mechanisms then tend to become an aspect of external reality
with which old and new members of the institution must come to terms.

(Menzies Lyth, 1988: 51)

She describes how socially constructed defence mechanisms develop in the
culture, structure, and mode of functioning of an organisation. These
defence mechanisms can be buried in the history of an institution, so that
the reasons for them are not clearly remembered. They can influence all
staff, including art therapists.

Menzies-Lyth's original work considered defence mechanisms in the field
of physical health. Her study was about nurses defending themselves in
relation to unacknowledged matters of life and death.

Groups and organisations

Metaphor (framed and unframed): DE

When metaphors emerge in therapy, either in the client's conversation or
through their image-making, our attention is drawn to the ways in which
they reveal and possibly limit the client's thinking.

Henzell (1984) draws a helpful distinction between 'framed' and
'unframed' metaphors in relation to this:

A framed metaphor is open to inspection, indeed it might be said to
invite it; its frame prefaces with 'as if'. An 'unframed' metaphor is
closed ... the particular way an action is expressive, the figurative
allusions involved, remain covert and unconscious, or unassimilated to
conscious examination and criticism.

(Henzell, 1984: 25)

Through becoming aware of the ways in which 'unframed' metaphors limit
thinking and feeling, and through creating new metaphors, the client may
be able to transcend the literal. 'The arrival of a new metaphor may be the
point at which a whole new conceptual scheme can be adopted' (Knights,
1995: 67).

Metaphor (linguistic and visual); Symbolic equation

Metaphor (linguistic): CW

> The word *metaphor* comes from the Greek word *metaphora* derived from *meta* meaning 'over', and *pherein*, 'to carry'. It refers to a particular set of linguistic processes whereby aspects of one object are 'carried over' or transferred to another object, so that the second object is spoken of as if it were the first. There are various types of metaphor, and the number of 'objects' involved can vary, but the general procedure of 'transference' remains the same.
>
> (Hawkes, 1972: 1)

Metaphor (framed and unframed); Metaphor (visual); Transference

Metaphor (visual): DE

Visual metaphors function in much the same way as linguistic metaphors. In art therapy, clients frequently draw or paint metaphorically in order to express or evoke a mood or feeling. A picture of an isolated tree might, for instance, suggest a feeling of loneliness or despair, and an erupting volcano might suggest anger.

Metaphor shapes the way we think and feel, and how we express or communicate our thoughts and feelings to others, including our experience and understanding of psychological distress (Lakoff and Johnson, 1980; Leary, 1992). The language of psychoanalysis is 'saturated' with metaphors: 'object relations', 'splitting', 'projection', 'boundaries', 'containment', and 'transference'. Indeed, as Arlow (1979) points out, psychoanalysis is essentially a metaphorical enterprise:

> Transference, perhaps the most significant instrumentality of psychoanalytic technique, and metaphor both mean exactly the same thing. They both refer to the carrying over of meaning from one set of situations to another. The transference in the psychoanalytic situation represents a metaphorical misapprehension of the relationship to the analyst.
>
> (Arlow, 1979: 382)

Metaphorical thinking is so pervasive that we are often barely conscious of its influence. The idea that the mind is a machine, for example, has proved to be an extraordinarily persistent one and continues to find expression in 'metaphors that have their origin in nineteenth century mechanics; in such terms "blowing your stack", "losing your cool", "boiling over", "letting off steam"' (Winslade, 1996).

Boundaries; Containment; Containment and counter-transference;
Metaphor (framed and unframed); Metaphor (linguistic); Mind-forged

manacles; Mutative metaphor; Object relations (three entries)*; Transference*

Milner (Marion) on outline: DE

While making and thinking about the drawings discussed in *On Not Being Able to Paint*, Marion Milner (1950) became fascinated by the idea of outline, and more particularly with what an artificial thing an outline is. Setting out to test this proposition she produced a drawing of two jugs that was to turn up again and again in her thinking about art and psychoanalysis. It is worth quoting, here, her account of how this drawing came into existence:

> I noticed that the effort needed in order to see the edges of objects as they really look stirred a dim fear, a fear of what might happen if one let go one's mental hold on the outline which kept everything separate and in its place and it was similar to that fear of a wide focus of attention which I had noticed in earlier experiments.
>
> After thinking about this I woke one morning and saw two jugs on the table. Without any mental struggle I saw the edges in relation to each other and how gaily they seemed almost to ripple now they were freed from this grimly practical business of enclosing an object and keeping it in place.
>
> (Milner, 1996: 8)

Drawing a line; Milner on using art materials; On Not Being Able to Paint*; Potential Space or intermediate area*

Milner (Marion) on the therapeutic frame: DE

It was the psychoanalyst Marion Milner who introduced the concept of the therapeutic 'frame' in her 1952 paper 'Aspects of Symbolism and Comprehension of the Not-Self'. In this paper Milner discusses the importance of boundaries by drawing an analogy between the analytic situation and a picture frame. Milner saw that the frame 'marks off the different kind of reality that is within it from that which is outside it' (Milner, 1952: 183). That is, frames or boundaries help to distinguish between the world of the imagination and the world of facts and tangible objects:

> It is the existence of this frame that makes possible the full development of that creative illusion that analysts call the transference. Also the central idea underlying psycho-analytic technique is that it is by means of this illusion that a better adaptation to the world outside is ultimately developed.
>
> (Milner, 1952: 183)

Boundaries; Lateness; Picture within the frame; Therapeutic frame

Milner (Marion) on using art materials: DE

An artist's work is essentially concerned with the giving of life to the bit of 'dead' matter of the external world which is the chosen medium. For, in a sense, what the artist idealises primarily, is his medium. He is in love with it; and this fact may also lead to difficulties through exaggerated ideas about what the medium can do. But if he loves it enough so that he submits himself to its real qualities, at the same time as imposing his will upon it, the finished product may justify the idealisation.

(Milner, 1950: 151)

Materials; Milner on outline; On Not Being Able to Paint*; Picture within the frame*

Mind-forged manacles: CW

The artist William Blake was also a campaigner against slavery. In his poem 'London', included in *Songs of Innocence and Experience* (1794), he introduced the phrase 'mind-forged manacles' to make metaphorical use of the ankle and wrist restraints placed on slaves (Bindman, 2007). This pointed to forms of mental slavery that are self-forged and self-inflicted. In other poems, this idea is elaborated to include the 'chaining of desire'.

Blake; Géricault and physiognomy; Metaphor (visual and *linguistic); Romanticism*

Mindfulness: AP

'Mindfulness means paying attention in a particular way: on purpose, in the present moment, and non-judgmentally' (John Kabat-Zinn, cited in Segal et al., 2002: 121).

It is rooted in Buddhist practice (e.g. Nhat Hanh, 2008) and most frequently taught through meditation practices, which encourage focusing sequentially on awareness of breathing, bodily sensations, sights, sounds, and tastes.

When distressed, we are often caught up in thinking about the past or negatively predicting the future. Mindfulness is not about ignoring distress or defending against emotions. Instead, it offers a way of creating a more balanced perspective by allowing room for feelings and experiences whilst helping us stay in touch with what is happening 'now': the only point in time that we can affect. Learning about mindfulness can help us:

- highlight how much time we spend in the inner world at the expense of noting our surroundings or how we actually live;
- acknowledge, without judgement or denial, the reality of our situation; awareness of how the present aids choice and change;
- address thought and behaviour patterns by recognising choice; choose our focus of attention.

The approach has a number of applications to art therapy. An example of an RCT for a mindfulness-based art therapy (MBAT) is that of Monti (2006).

Absorption in art-making; Adaptations of practice; Concentration

Mise-en-scene in the therapy room: CC

There are some tableaux scenes that show an unconscious conflict coming to the surface, such as the scenes in drawings, or with little toys on a tabletop, or in the sand. There are others that re-create traumatic scenes using the whole therapy room as a stage, in what I have called '*mise-en-scene*' with the child as film or stage director and then as principal actor (Case, 1994). Internal objects take position in relation to each other. There may be a sense that these are becoming unfrozen, after trauma. However, sometimes the trauma is re-created and then enacted by the child, leaving the therapist to experience being a witness to these events and feeling the accompanying emotions.

Houzel (1995) has written about the search for containment of those parts of the self that have never been contained (Case, 2003, 2005b).

Play; Studios

Monotype or monoprint techniques: CH

A monoprint is normally taken from an inked plate by two main methods (Palmer, 1975). In one, the image is drawn onto the plate with ink or paint, with the paper placed carefully on top, pressed down with the hand or a roller, and then removed. Alternatively, the plate is inked evenly with a roller and the image is drawn with a stick, brush, cotton bud, or other implement. Additional material, such as leaves or flat shapes, can be added and these emerge as white areas on the paper.

Muller-White (2002: 149) recommends 'mystery monotype', a method adopted by Paul Klee where he laid paper over the plate, drawing with pencil or ballpoint to transfer the ink. This means of print is unlike other forms (e.g. etching, engraving, lithography, and lino printing) because it produces an individual impression. It is so close to painting because it is not possible to know exactly what will emerge once printed. It has sustained many artists since the seventeenth century. Preble and Preble (1994: 169) call monoprint 'a non-traditional, process-oriented practice'. The variety and fluidity of the process allows focus on creative expression and personal exploration, freeing the client to 'develop some mastery of intense feelings and still feel safe and contained' (Muller-White, 2002: 19).

Many print-making processes do not require any drawing or painting skills and so allow the development of creative play and invention. Mono-printing might be considered when a client or group is stuck, or resistance builds against using conventional materials. The technique offers a relief from the 'milk white panic' that some patients experience when first faced with conventional art materials (Wood, 1986). Patients readily respond, and many go on to amplify the image with paint and other materials. Prints can be collected into a book as a way of providing additional containment.

Print-making without a press

Monsters, dragons, and demons: JHar

Children often describe and depict their illness or other bad things that invade their lives and bodies as a monster.

- Amanda: A 5-year-old who clearly described the invasion of her brain by a tumour in images of a monster who repeatedly attacked her, splitting her head in two.
- Susan: An 8-year-old who, whilst being treated for leukaemia, painted little ducks chasing a huge 'crocodile-like' creature from the duck pond. These images heralded her return to health.
- Daniel: A distressed 4-year-old, was to have his art therapy at home because his parents were coping with nursing his brother who was terminally ill. On my first visit, Daniel opened the door to me, and said: 'Come in but be careful where you put your feet because this house is full of monsters.'

Cradle to grave; Death images; Gentle dragon; Health; Liminality;
Living and dying; Mental health; Psycho-neuro-immunology

Moral treatment: CW

Moral treatment is a part of the history of much work in mental health. With its introduction, respect for the patient was heightened. It came into being during reforms following the French Revolution, being argued for by Pinel with *Traité* (1801) and by Tuke in England with his *Description of the Retreat* (1813). Both recommended it on grounds of humanity and efficacy, at a time when the treatment of mental patients was terrible. It faded away because of socio-economic factors in the wake of the industrial revolution some 50–60 years later.

Samuel Tuke's *Description* (1813) was a modest and yet influential account of the moral treatment approach adopted for the treatment of 'insane persons'. It suggests a gentle, good-humoured approach to the care of people with mental disorders. It encompasses care in all matters – medical, diet (including a little alcohol), and the atmosphere of surroundings.

In Tuke's lifetime, the methods developed at the York Retreat were widely adopted in several countries (especially America) and by many interpretations seen as successful. However, as Warner (1985) indicated, despite their success in Britain and America, the methods of moral treatment gradually fell into disuse during the second part of the industrial revolution. Warner suggests that there is an instructive comparison to be made between this disuse of moral treatment and the gradual decline of social psychiatry during the later years of the twentieth century.

Power of the patient in moral treatment; Social psychiatry

Mourning and melancholia: CW

'In mourning, the world has become poor and empty; in melancholia it is the ego that has become so' (Freud, 1917: 206).

Aggression; Mourning the lost object

Mourning the lost object: DN

'The idea that suppressed mourning leads to psychological difficulties and, conversely, that facing loss and expressing grief are curative, is central to much psychoanalytic work' (Bateman and Holmes, 1995: 72). In his paper 'Mourning and Melancholia' Freud (1917) paralleled normal grief following the loss of a loved one, with depression, 'the work of mourning involves the paradox that in acknowledging what is lost, the bereaved person is at the same time reclaiming it.'

(Bateman and Holmes, 1995: 72)

Melanie Klein was deeply affected by the death of her son and realised that:

what was at stake in loss was the integrity of the whole inner world. She therefore linked loss with internalisation . . . Klein is sensitive to the feeling that with loss 'all' feels lost, and to the continuities between the handling of loss in childhood and adult responses to separation.

Where loss can be mourned (including in healthy protest) then the lost object is 'reinstated' internally. This leads to an enrichment of the inner world which can balance the sadness about what has gone; where it cannot, depletion and depression may follow.

(Bateman and Holmes, 2002: 73)

Mourning and melancholia; Mourning with a therapist

Mourning with a therapist: DN

Mrs Y's mother died when Mrs Y was in her early twenties. Her mother had been an invalid throughout her life and Mrs Y had learnt to suppress her feelings. It is only now, 25 years after her mother's death, that Mrs Y is able to mourn her mother as she begins to be able to 'internalise' her therapist as an object with whom she can rage as well as trust.

X was aged 6 years when his mother died after a brief illness. He and his half-brother were left in the care of the social services. He was brought to therapy because he smeared his faeces on walls, ate from rubbish bins, and became mute. After smearing clay for some weeks alongside an art psychotherapist, he was able to use paints and words to express his anger, grief, and his longing for a new family.

Bateman and Holmes explain that much therapy 'centres around this regaining and reinstatement of lost objects', including the therapy itself and the therapist, 'so that finally, at successful termination, the patient will have internalised a therapeutic function, even though the relationship with the therapist has come to an end' (Bateman and Holmes, 2002: 73).

Mourning and melancholia; Mourning the lost object

Muse and *duende*: MHZ

There is something pagan, and even demonic, about *duende*. It is a spirit of art, the opposite of Muse. Where Muse brings golden inspiration, *duende* brings blood. The Muse speaks of life, yet *duende* sings of death. It is not inspiration, it is a struggle, a dark force, having very little to do with outer beauty; a struggle present in the artist's soul, the struggle of knowing that death is imminent. *Duende* colours the artist's work with gut-wrenching authenticity, painful hues, and the tones that produce strong, vibrant art.

Federico García Lorca first developed the concept of *duende* in a lecture he gave in 1930. It is a concept in Spanish art and especially in flamenco, having to do with emotion, expression, and authenticity. *Tener duende* can be loosely translated as 'having soul'.

Blake; Romanticism

Mutative metaphor(s): CT

Group analyst Murray Cox (1996) used this term to describe the process of therapy being flexible rather than static, in that therapist and client(s) insight and understanding of the meanings of the session material increase over time. The same principle can be applied to discourse in art therapy where associations will evolve as the content of imagery and associated discussion develops. Art therapy's advantage over purely verbal therapy is that the image provides a tangible physical record that can be reviewed alongside other images. This potential for interlinking develops meaning, enhancing the therapy as a reflective, attachment-based learning process. Teasdale (1997) refers to utilising this transitional phenomenon in working with offenders in forensic settings.

Looking and visual research; Metaphor (three entries)*; Review with images*

Myth: JA

A myth is a traditional story, often concerning fabulous or supernatural beings, frequently serving to explain natural phenomena or the origins of a people. It may also denote a fictitious story or an unfounded belief. Our high-tech culture may tend to diminish the social and psychological value of myths that embody the beliefs, aspirations, and perceptions of groups of people. Since living in Ireland, a country renowned for its musical and story-telling traditions, where the ability to turn a phrase or to have a 'party piece' is still admired, I have a renewed sense of the everyday reality of collective myth-making.

Legend; Mythologies and the participant observer

Mythologies and the participant observer: SR

For Richardson (1997) the ideas of the anthropologist James Dow and the philosopher Ludwig Wittgenstein contribute to a potential theoretical framework for a model of the therapist as 'participant observer' in art therapy. In 'Universal Aspects of Symbolic Healing' Dow (1986) argues that any effective process of 'symbolic healing' requires the client and therapist to interact in a shared 'mythic world'. This is a product of the client's 'myth-ologies' – experiential truths contained in things like religious beliefs or cultural practices that generally have greater personal significance than 'objective' or empirical truths. In *Philosophical Investigations* Wittgenstein (1978) argues that language is not simply an abstract system of signs, but is essentially cultural in nature. People become bound together via the shared 'language games' and 'forms of life' through which they interact.

In *Colourful Language* Richardson (1997) uses these ideas to show how the therapist can engage with marginalised people, such as adults with learning disabilities, in ways that are inclusive and meaningful. The art therapist's sensitive use of the art materials with their client, far from detracting from therapeutic aims, can create communication or a 'form of life' that facilitates the client's full participation in the process. As art therapists work with increasingly diverse client groups, it is possible to make the case for a spectrum of practice in which the needs of the client provide the criteria for deciding when or how the art therapist might use the art materials.

Adaptation of practice; Art as a discourse; Participative art practice

Narrative: JA

Art therapy can engender a deep interest in narrative forms. Legend and myth in particular prove to be a rich imaginal source and repository of collective wisdom. Romantic poet Samuel Taylor Coleridge (1815) offers the following definition:

> The common end of all narrative . . . is to convert a series into a whole: to make those events, which in real or imagined history move on in a straight line, assume to our understanding a circular motion – the snake with a tail in its mouth.

> (Coleridge, cited in Ryan, 2002)

Legend; Myth

Naumburg: DW

Margaret Naumburg is considered to have been one of the founders, if not the founder, of art therapy in the USA. In her first published monograph in 1947 (*Studies of the Free Art Expression of Behaviour Disturbed Children as a Means of Diagnosis and Therapy*) she draws on case histories compiled between 1943 and 1945, referring to 'free art expression' rather than art therapy, and seeming to view the art activity and art objects as concrete versions of a dream:

> The techniques of art therapy are based on the knowledge that every individual, whether trained or untrained in art, has a latent capacity to project his inner conflicts into visual form. As patients picture such

inner experiences, it frequently happens that they become more verbally articulate.

(Naumburg 1958: 511)

The emphasis, then, is on the images that arise from the patient's unconscious and that contain conflicts. Once these conflicts are made concrete, they can be understood, which in turn would assist in their resolution. Image-making, because it taps pre-verbal feelings, is more able to produce this resolution than words.

In her later books, Naumburg developed a 'dynamic' model of art therapy, which made use of the transference relationship between patient and therapist, suggesting that art or spontaneous image-making was a means to furthering therapeutic communication.

Both Margaret Naumburg and her sister Florence were influenced by the 'child art' movement in art education, which stressed the importance to the child of allowing spontaneous image-making to take place. Both believed that everyone had the capacity to become an artist, or at least to be visually creative. Eleanor Ulman, writing in the *American Journal of Art Therapy* in 1983, following the death of Naumburg aged 93, commented:

> It was Naumburg who was responsible – almost single-handed – for the emergence of art therapy as a profession. In the 1950s she initiated the first art therapy training courses and she strove mightily in the 1960s for the development of full scale graduate training for art therapists.
>
> (Ulman, 1983: 122–123)

This entry is based on Waller (1991: 5–6).

Action painting; Hill on painting; Kramer; Schools establishing art therapy; Schools using art therapy

Negative space: MAm

Betty Edwards writes: 'Negative Space: the area around positive form, which shares edges with the forms. Negative space is bounded on the outer edges by the format' (2001: 276). Dictionary definitions of 'negative' and of 'space' are interesting in that they suggest a tension between what is seen and unseen, wanted and unwanted, recognised and unrecognised, good and bad. They also hint at potential for expansion or movement – unoccupied ground, freedom and scope, reversal, creation of positive from negative. Negative spaces in artwork may be potent indicators of alternatives that have not yet been explored.

Milner on outline

Negative transference: DN

In the case of 'Dora', Freud (1915) realised how trauma can be re-lived:

> re-experienced, re-enacted, as in real life – in the transference to the analyst. And Freud was able to write up his case . . . as a cautionary tale that demonstrated in a new way the importance of transference: the very detailed way in which the past could be witnessed.
>
> (Hinshelwood, 1989: 464)

In brief dynamic psychotherapy, successful outcome correlates with the 'prompt addressing of negative transference' (Aveline, 2001). Its interpretation is vital when therapy is threatened by the patient's negative feelings towards the therapist or the therapeutic frame (Banon et al., 2001; Roth and Fonagy, 1996).

It can be uncomfortable to receive these powerful feelings, but addressing these within the therapeutic relationship can facilitate positive outcomes. If ignored or unrecognised, 'acting out' can escalate and the therapy itself can break down. It is also worth noting that both positive and negative interpretations can have a greater impact on patients with borderline personality disorder (BPD) than on people diagnosed with BPD (Piper et al., 1991).

In my experience, negative feelings representing past or current significant persons that are transferred to me could seem initially insignificant. However, on further examination they can be regarded as direct unconscious communications. These have ranged from late arrivals to missed appointments, delayed payment (in private practice), and 'gifts' of dead flowers.

One patient always felt abandoned during breaks in therapy and in various ways would attempt to 'run away' from me and the abandoned part of herself. As a child she ran away and on her return she would be beaten. If we had not been able to address the negative feelings from her relationship with her mother in a benign and non-retaliatory way, her therapy might have ended prematurely.

Transference

Neurological art therapy: DAM

The lightning strike of acute stroke or 'brain attack' combines a potentially devastating impact on physical and cognitive capacities with a shattering of self. The sufferer may be catapulted back to a helpless state, facing the shame and humiliation associated with a loss of control, autonomy, and independence. Miller (1993, 1998) suggests that 'it is this shattered self that effective psychotherapy with clients who are neuro-psychologically impaired must fundamentally address' (in Langer et al., 1999: 28).

The body of psychoanalytic ideas relating to early development is particularly relevant. This pre-verbal stage, where environment is experienced through bodily sensations (Weir, 1987), is characterised by helplessness and dependence. Development of the infant's separate sense of self and identity takes place within the physical and psychological 'holding' or 'containment' provided by the maternal environment and attunement to the infant's needs (Bion, 1962b; Klein, 1946; Segal, 1975; Stern, 1985; Winnicott, 1965b). According to Winnicott (1971b), it is this maternal 'holding' that is the 'potential' space in which the true creative self is allowed to emerge. 'This if reflected back, *but only if reflected back* . . . eventually enables himself or herself to postulate the existence of the self' (Winnicott 1971: 64). *Good-enough* holding provides the infant with the sense of being and of an integrated self lodged in his own body (Abram, 1996).

In art psychotherapy the image-making process and how the image is received within the 'holding' of the therapeutic relationship mirror this early relationship (Milner, 1969, in Case and Dalley, 1992). The making of a mark contains the flow of activity and mirrors it back, functioning 'as a very primitive type of external object' (Milner, 1955: 92), forming the basis for communication. The therapist's presence produces a complementary triangulation in the mirroring process. Specific neurological references are Wilkinson (2006) and Hass-Cohen and Carr (2008); see also www.art-therapy-in-neurology.co.

Adolescence and neurological research; Brain injury; Damage to mental health; Marks; Psycho-neuro-immunology; Stroke and trauma

Non-art: DW

The categories of 'art' and 'non-art' can be seen as elements of social organisation, of processes that are value laden, part of the dominant structures within society. How we view art can have a significant impact on the person who makes it, especially where an object, precious and meaningful to its maker, can be perceived as 'rubbish' and thrown away because it does not look like 'real art'.

Kelly (1984) in *Community, Art and the State: Storming the Citadels* suggests that:

> Art is an ideological construction; . . . 'art' functions as one of a series of categories whose purpose is to assist in the construction and maintenance of a hierarchy of values . . . Thus there are activities which may be interesting and rewarding in their own right but which

will never, no matter what standard they reach, be accorded the status of art.

(Kelly, 1984: 54)

Kelly explains that the process by which this happens is 'profoundly political'. The result is a hierarchy of activities, some of which are regarded as 'real art' and others as 'hobbies'. Certain art forms such as 'naïve art', 'prisoners' art', 'psychiatric art', and more recently 'community art' remain on the margins of 'real art' and can then be justifiably exhibited without aspiration to being judged as in the 'mainstream'. So the expectations of the visitors are to some extent shaped in advance of the visit.

'Art' can best be seen as a term used to describe a network of interrelated activities, of cultural practices, and not as a label to be wielded in a limiting or excluding way. I agree with Thomashoff (2004: 73), when he says: 'A work of art is a work of art, whoever created it.'

This entry is adapted from Waller (2009a).

Aesthetic philosophy in art therapy; Hierarchies of evidence; Looking; Works of art

Non-directive approach

See*: Directive and non-directive styles of work; Group analytic approach to art therapy*

Note-keeping citing BAAT: CW

'Clinical notes should describe *what* happened but do not give emphasis to detailing *how* in technical terms . . . Above all you must be sure that your clinical notes fulfil their purpose of clearly evidencing the duty of care at the heart of your intervention' (BAAT: Art Therapy, Note-Writing and the Law).

Useful clinical notes are written in well-reasoned, jargon-free language in which opinions are clearly indicated and distinguished from the factual description of what happened. In addition, they are usually brief. Principles for electronic clinical notes are similarly concerned with evidencing the duty of care and with clarity. Handwritten notes use clear protocols of legibility, black ink, signature, and date.

Clinical notes remain on a client's record for many years and so it is important when writing them to consider prospective audiences (including that of the client) and to write respectfully. BAAT guidance helpfully clarifies distinctions between clinical notes and case studies.

Case studies; Consent

Novel citing Boyd: CW

> The novel is in good health . . . If you want to understand human beings and this strange adventure, this tragic-comic adventure we are all embarked upon in our life-span, the novel does the human condition better than any other art form, so as long as people are curious about their lives, they will always read novels . . .

> (Boyd, 2007)

Access to art

Object: DE

The term 'object' is a technical one and its usage in psychoanalytic literature is in many ways misleading and dissatisfying. As Rycroft (1979: 100) also makes clear:

> In psycho-analytical writings, objects are nearly always persons, parts of persons, or symbols of one or the other. This terminology confuses readers who are more familiar with 'objects' in the sense of 'thing', i.e. that which is not a person.

In the psychoanalytic literature the word 'object' appears both alone and in numerous compound forms, including; object loss, object love, object choice, whole object, part object, good object, bad object, transitional object, object relations(hip), and so on. Charles Rycroft (1979) defines the word object as: 'That towards which action or desire is directed; that which the subject requires in order to achieve instinctual satisfaction; that to which the subject relates himself' (1979: 100).

Object relations theories; Object relationships

Object relations: Destructive narcissism/negative therapeutic reaction: DAM

When there is a failure to differentiate in early development, problems can arise in adulthood, which result in a difficulty discriminating between self and other and between phantasy and reality. Where, due to complex factors, secure attachments to 'good' objects have not been made, there can be tendencies toward fusion states and a pervasive splitting of good and bad (borderline personality), or towards refuge in a grandiose omnipotent self (narcissistic personality). In both, there is an attempt to return to the perfection of an early oneness with the object (Robbins, 2001). Rosenfeld (1987: 106) describes forms of destructive narcissistic organisation that ' . . .

are directed against life and destroy the links between objects and the self, by attacking or killing off part of the self, but they are also destructive to any good objects by trying to devalue and eliminate them as important'. Steiner (1993) illuminates this with his concept of 'psychic retreats' – mental hiding places that protect the individual from catastrophic persecution anxieties stirred up by destructive envious feelings. He suggests that '. . . anxiety about acknowledging new developments is particularly acute in those patients where a narcissistic organisation has created a hiding place which provides a protection from exposure and avoids the need to test achievements against reality' (Steiner, 2001: 1). However, he maintains that '. . . the development of a greater sense of integration leads to a shift in the nature of anxieties and emergence from the retreat then gives rise to contact with depressive feelings such as guilt, remorse, and despair which can be even more unbearable' (Steiner, 2001: 1).

This can lead to an envious and deadly attack on the life in the client and in the therapeutic relationship, which symbolises the potential for making new, creative links and connections (Bion, 1959).

Object relation theories; Object relationships

Object relations: Schizoid anxieties and claustrophobic symptoms: DAM

Ideas about schizoid anxieties are helpful when thinking about claustrophobic symptoms, which manifest in therapy as a fear of being trapped and unable to breathe. Fairbairn (1952) suggested that the schizoid problem is 'love made hungry'. Guntrip (1986: 29) describes this as a fear of 'destroying and losing the love object through being so devouringly hungry'. This anxiety is projected into the object, which is then experienced as suffocating. Guntrip differentiates this from depressive anxiety, which he describes as the '. . . fear of loving lest one's hate should destroy. Schizoid aloofness is the fear of loving lest one's love or need of love should destroy, which is far worse' (Guntrip, 1986: 24).

Object relations theories; Object relationships; Paranoid-schizoid and depressive 'positions'

Object relations theories: DE

Human beings are, by nature, social. We need, and depend upon, relationships with others in order to survive and develop. Clients seen in art therapy frequently complain of feeling disconnected or alienated from themselves or other people. At other times, they may feel overwhelmed or persecuted by them.

Many consider that the origins of these difficulties reside in past relationship problems – in those desires, fears, losses, and deprivations that the client previously experienced in relation to significant people in their lives. Although opinions vary on the mechanisms and processes involved, it is believed that these past experiences, both good and bad, are internalised and incorporated into our 'inner world'. Within contemporary psychoanalysis, and to a significant extent within [British] art therapy too, the main theoretical model used to understand these mechanisms and processes is drawn from object relations theory (Gomez, 1997).

According to Greenberg and Mitchell (1983: 11–12):

> The term 'object relations theory', in its broadest sense, refers to attempts within psychoanalysis to . . . confront the potentially confounding observation that people live simultaneously in an external and an internal world, and that the relationship between the two ranges from the most fluid intermingling to the most rigid separation. The term thus designates theories, or aspects of theories, concerned with exploring the relationship between real, external people and internal images and residues of relations with them . . . Approaches to these problems constitute the major focus of psychoanalytic theorising over the past several decades.

Although often grouped together as though constituting a specific school, so-called object relations theorists such as Klein, Fairbairn, Winnicott, and Guntrip in the UK, and Mahler, Kohut, and Kernberg in the USA, are allied less by an agreed set of ideas than by a similar philosophy regarding the human potential for relationship. Central to this philosophy is the shared belief that from the moment of conception human beings are in relationship with another person or persons and that the impetus for growth and development through relationships is the prime motivation for life.

Kindness; Klein and Creativity; Object; Object relationships

Object relationships: DE

The terms 'object relationships' and 'object relations' are often used interchangeably in the psychoanalytic literature. According to Laplanche and Pontalis (1973: 277), the term object relation(ship) is one:

> Enjoying a very wide currency in present-day psycho-analysis as a designation [name] for the subject's mode of relation to his world; this relation is the entire complex outcome of a particular organisation of the personality, of an apprehension of objects that is to some extent or

other phantasied, and of certain special types of defence. We may speak of the object-relationships of a specific subject, but also of types of object-relationship by reference either to points in development (e.g., an oral object-relationship) or else to psychopathology (e.g., a melancholic object-relationship).

What is usually being referred to when we speak of 'object relationships' is an 'interrelationship'. 'That is, a relationship 'involving not only the way the subject constitutes his objects but also the way these objects shape his actions' (Laplanche and Pontalis, 1973: 278).

As Laplanche and Pontalis also note: 'An approach such as Melanie Klein's lends even more weight to this idea: objects (projected, introjected) actually act upon the subject – they persecute him, reassure him, etc.' (1973: 278).

Object relations theories are therefore primarily concerned with: 'The relation of the subject to his [or her] objects, not simply with the relationship between the subject and the object, which is an interpersonal relationship' (Kohon, 1988: 20). In other words, what object relations theories encompass is not only the impact that 'real' people have on the development of personality, but: 'The specific way in which the subject apprehends his relationships with his objects (both internal and external) . . . [this] implies an unconscious relationship to these objects' (Kohon, 1988: 20).

Despite the terminology, object relations are primarily concerned with the structure and content of our internal and interpersonal relationships. The theories focus upon, and give due consideration to, the means by which we build up our inner world of objects from internal representations of past important relationships and experiences, and the ways in which these influence – and sometimes distort – our relationships with external reality in the present.

Object; Object relations (three entries)*; Object relationships*

Offenders using art therapy: MLieb

Art therapy with offenders is a growing area of work (Liebmann, 1990, 1994; Teasdale, 1999, 2002). Although art therapy in prisons has waxed and waned according to funding availability, it is now more established in Mental Health Secure Units. It is particularly valuable for a group of people who often have poor verbal skills and tend to 'act out' rather than explain their feelings and needs. Using art therapy can be a safe channel for expression of such feelings and leads to greater awareness.

Comic strips; Images used to convey the 'action' of violence;
Mental health

On Not Being Able to Paint by Marion Milner: DE

In the late 1930s, Milner began making the free association or doodle drawings she was later to write about in *On Not Being Able to Paint* (1950). Prompted in part by her educational work, the challenge Milner initially set herself was to study an area of learning she herself had failed to master:

> Always, ever since early childhood, I had been interested in learning how to paint. But in spite of having acquired some technical facility in representing the appearance of objects my efforts had always tended to peter out in a maze of uncertainties about what a painter is really trying to do.
>
> (Milner, 1950: xvii)

What fascinated but also troubled Milner about the images she produced was her discovery that by letting hand and eye do exactly what pleased them without any conscious working to a preconceived intention she was capable of producing drawings entirely different from those she had been taught or, indeed, expected herself to make. One such drawing, started in a mood of 'furious frustration', turned out to be highly organised rather than, as expected, chaotic. Another drawing, on this occasion of a group of stately beech trees, became two stunted thorn bushes in a snowy crag blasted by a raging blizzard. As Milner records:

> This discovery had at first been so disconcerting that I had tried to forget about it; for it seemed to threaten, not only all familiar beliefs about will-power and conscious effort, but also, as I suppose all irruptions from the unconscious mind do, it threatened one's sense of oneself as a more or less known entity.
>
> (Milner, 1950: xvii–xviii)

What reading *On Not Being Able to Paint* helps us to understand is the nature of those fears that inhibit creativity, especially the fear of chaos and the unknown. The lesson Milner seeks to share with her reader through her own struggle to make images is the importance of abandoning self-consciousness, and blurring the boundary between 'me' and 'not me', in order to create something original and meaningful. As Milner puts it: 'it was only when I had discarded this wish to copy that the resulting drawing or painting had any life in it, any of the sense of a living integrated structure existing in its own right' (1950: 154).

Attraction to and copying pictures; Milner on using art materials

Organisations regulating and representing art therapists: CW

Organisations concerned with the work of art therapists in Britain have different primary functions. The Health Professions Council (HPC) protects the public by regulating and registering therapists who cannot work without maintaining their registration.

The professional association BAAT (British Association of Art Therapists) develops, promotes, and represents the work of the profession, whilst trade unions represent and protect individual professionals.

Regulation and representation follow different patterns, although with similar principles in different countries.

British Association of Art Therapists; Health; Health Professions Council; Professional conduct and misconduct; Trade unions

Outcome measures: LR

These are evaluation instruments that enable clinicians and clients to measure the effects of their work in a systematic way. Standard evaluation measures have shortcomings, but they provide recognisable comparisons with other national and international information. The following is not a comprehensive list, but it can offer a useful departure point for finding a recognised instrument that fits a particular situation:

- Clinical Outcomes in Routine Evaluation (CORE), including CORE-YP for young people and CORE-LD for men and women with learning disabilities (http://www.coreims.co.uk).
- Euroqol (EQ-5D) measures quality of life, consisting of five dimensions where users rate their mobility, self-care, usual activities, pain/discomfort, anxiety/depression (Euroqol Group, 2008).
- Health of the Nation family of measures, designed for adults (HoNOS), children and young people (HoNOSCA), older adults (HoNOS 65+), people with learning disabilities (HoNOS-LD), and those with acquired brain injuries (HoNOS-ABI) (http://www.rcpsych.ac.uk/researchand trainingunit/honos.aspx/).
- Strengths and Difficulties Questionnaire (SDQ), designed for children and young people (http://www.sdqinfo.com/).

Artwork and outcome measures; Diagnostic systems in psychiatry; Outcomes for 'looked-after children'

Outcomes for 'looked-after children': MMc

Looked-after children are not a homogenous group and some will successfully move towards fulfilled personal lives and careers. However, despite improvements in outcomes in recent years, there remains a gap between those in care and outcomes for all children:

- In 2006, only 12% of children in care achieved five A*–C grades at GCSE (or equivalent) compared to 59% of all children.
- Their health is poorer than that of other children: 45% of children in care are assessed as having a mental health disorder compared with 10% of the general population.
- Over 50% of children in care responding to a 2007 consultation identified difficulties in accessing positive activities.
- 9.6% of children in care aged 10 years or over were cautioned or convicted for an offence during that year – almost three times the rate for all children of this age.
- 30% of care leavers aged 19 years were not in education, employment, or training (NEET).
- Some groups of children are overrepresented in the care population – for example, disabled children and some ethnic minorities.

However, on a positive note there is 'Evidence from international research that outcomes get better when young people get older and settle into adulthood, especially those who have had stability and skilled help' (Mike Stein, *The Guardian*, 2006, Wednesday December 6).

Looked-after children; Outcome measures; Poverty

Outsider art: CW

Roger Cardinal (1972) used this term to translate *art brut* and the movement associated with Dubuffet:

> First, the makers of *art brut* are outsiders, mentally and/or socially. Second, their work is conceived and produced outside the field of 'fine arts' in its usual sense as referring to the network of schools, galleries, museums, etc., it is also conceived without any regard for the usual recipients of works of art, or indeed without regard for any recipient at all. Third, the subjects, techniques and systems of figuration have little connection with those handed down by tradition or current in the fashionable art of the day; they stem rather from personal invention.
>
> (Thévoz, 1995: 11–12)

By way of his continued collecting activity and a sustained polemic in favour of art created outside the mainstream, Dubuffet assumed the position of arbiter of the scope of Art Brut and the relative quality of its inclusions. In this way a position that had originally been born of a desire to escape the straightjacket of the art market now threatened, ironically, to develop into an 'alternative' orthodoxy . . .

(Rhodes, 2000: 14)

This was consolidated by Dubuffet's establishment of the permanent collection at Lausanne in Switzerland, from which art was not allowed to be exhibited elsewhere for fear of it being shown alongside mainstream work:

Dubuffet's search for an art that lay entirely outside cultural concerns was doomed to failure from the start for no one can create from a position oblivious to the world around. However, he established the idea of this 'non-cultural' production not as something he believed existed, but as an ideal aspiration.

(Rhodes, 2000: 14)

Art brut; Art of the insane; Invocations; Non-art

Paint: CW

'Shit is not the only excretion that paint recalls, and the alchemists were right to stress that ultimately it is blood and since blood carries the spirit, paint becomes a trope for life' (Elkins, 2000: 192).

Act of painting; Painting

Painting: CW

In the end, what is painting? Is it the framed object, with its entourage of historical meanings, the gossip about its painter, and the ledgers and letters and files and reports and reviews and books it inspired? Or is painting a verb, a name for what happens when paint moves across a blank surface?

(Elkins, 2000: 192)

Act of painting; Case studies; Looking and visual research; Paint; Review with images

Palliative care: MW

Palliative care is an approach that improves the quality of life for patients and their families who are facing the problems associated with life-threatening illness. This is done through the prevention and relief of suffering by means of early identification and impeccable assessment and treatment of pain and other problems, physical, psychosocial, and spiritual. World Health

Organization (http://www.who.int/cancer/palliative/en/) thinking on palliative care includes some of the following:

- provides relief from pain and other distressing symptoms;
- affirms life and regards dying as a normal process;
- intends neither to hasten nor postpone death;
- integrates the psychological and spiritual aspects of patient care;
- offers a support system to help patients live as actively as possible until death;
- offers a support system to help the family cope during the patient's illness and in their own bereavement;
- uses a team approach to address the needs of patients and their families, including bereavement counselling, if indicated;
- will enhance quality of life, and may also positively influence the course of illness;
- is applicable early in the course of illness, in conjunction with other therapies that are intended to prolong life, such as chemotherapy or radiation therapy, and includes those investigations needed to better understand and manage distressing clinical complications.

Death images; Liminality; Sustaining the therapist in cancer care; Time disappears; Transference in palliative care

Paranoid-schizoid and depressive 'positions': DN

Melanie Klein described two 'positions' of mental life – the 'paranoid-schizoid' and the 'depressive'.

> In essence the Kleinian 'positions' are constellations of phantasies, anxieties, and defences which are mobilised to protect the individual from internal destructiveness. In the earlier, paranoid-schizoid position the focus of the anxiety is on threats of annihilation and disintegration, and the infant attempts to organise these experiences by the use of splitting and projection. Bad experiences are split off and projected into the object, which is then felt to be persecuting, dangerous, and especially threatening to the good experiences. In order to protect the good experiences, they too may be projected into the object which then becomes idealised.
>
> (Bateman and Holmes, 2002: 39)

Where primary processes dominate polarisations can occur (e.g. idealisation versus denigration, or 'all or nothing' thinking). When feelings and thoughts are evacuated on a large scale, emptiness can prevail.

In the later depressive position, anxiety is not so much about the survival of the self but the survival of the object upon whom one depends. The individual realises that the frustrating and hated object is also one that satisfies and is loved. Recognition that they are one and the same leads to ambivalence and guilt . . . there is a constant oscillation between the two, a third 'borderline' position has also been described.

(Bateman and Holmes, 2002: 38–39)

In this way, the individual achieves a more mature developmental position that can integrate both 'good' and 'bad' experiences and feelings towards the object and self.

Object relations (three entries); *Object relationships*

Participative art practice: JMa

This term is used to describe the therapist's personal art practice, which takes place alongside clients as part of the art-making in a studio-based group. This practice implies more equality in the relationship between therapist and group members and their interchanges than is usual. The term, and the theoretical discussion it provokes, augments ideas about the ways counter-transference can be transmitted in the therapist's artwork (Lachman-Chapin, 1979; Haesler, 1989). However, the therapist thoroughly examining what takes place regarding counter-transference is seen as essential (Haesler, 1989; Mahony, 1992). The mutual and non-verbal visual discourse of the art-making is then elucidated. The discourse is enhanced by thinking of it as an expressive and exploratory art practice by all concerned; when this is sustained over time, it appears to be transformative (Mahony, 2010a).

Art as a discourse; Group (eight entries); *Mythologies and the participant observer; Power*

Patient choice and influence in research: LR

Thornicroft et al. (2002) in their consultation of 40 service users from the South London and Maudsley NHS Trust approached the questions of patient choice from a research priority perspective, noticing a divergence between service users and funders. They identify several underresearched areas: arts therapies; advocacy; treatment choice; complementary therapies; exercise; information; approaches to combat stigma; and the relationship between the environment and patient care. The Care Services Improvement Partnership (CSIP, 2006) also called for better information to assist meaningful choice. They suggested that local services should include creative arts alongside talking therapies, counselling, support groups, massage, and exercise as complements or alternatives to medication.

The Department of Health (DOH, 2004: 7) noted the popularity of a wide range of psychotherapies but identified widespread confusion about the meaning of the word 'psychotherapy', which undermined choice. Their earlier document *Treatment Choice in Psychological Therapies* (DOH, 2001a) set out a range of recommendations on evidence-based practice. This quest for hard evidence generates a ranking system prioritising meta-studies of randomised control trials over interventions with a developing body of evidence and more qualitative data. This has the effect of channelling recommendations towards interventions that are already proven at this level. This explains, in part, the overwhelming emphasis on the further development of cognitive-behavioural therapies in *Improving Access to Psychological Therapies (IAPT)* (DOH, 2007).

While some studies have noted a demand for improved access to art psychotherapy, better resources for more quantitative studies are still required (e.g. MATISSE HTA Project, 2007). In order to assist informed choice there remains a continuing need for all kinds of evidence for the specific benefits of art psychotherapy, amongst the many strands of arts, and psychological therapy practice.

Art therapy; Mental health; Mental health treatments; Patient choice in treatment; User Movements

Patient choice in treatment: LR

The Blair Labour government advocated patient choice with regard to treatment options as a key element in health service modernisation. In 2000 *The NHS Plan* announced movement away from 'a 1940's system operating in a 21st century world' (DOH, 2000: 26), citing long waiting lists, uneven quality and service provision, 'old fashioned' gate-keeping, and unbalanced power relationships between staff and service users as the effects of under-investment. Influenced by the 1990s Conservative policy of 'the internal market', the aim was to ensure a choice between public and private providers of surgery. This quest for improved efficiency and cost-effectiveness through patient and carer empowerment has generated the tariff system *Payment by Results*, which seeks to standardise charges for every health intervention.

Whilst the initial focus was on physical health, independent mental health campaigners seized the opportunity to call for improved options in mental health. Researching the approaches valued by mental health service users, Faulkner and Layzell (2000: 26) published their *Strategies for Living* project. Respondents identified the following areas as helpful in times of distress: relationships with family, friends, and mental health professionals; the support of fellow sufferers; medication; talking therapies; complementary treatments; exercise; interests and activities. Mind (2002) built on this in their *My Choice Campaign*, finding that 54% of 178 respondents felt they had insufficient choice. Of a range of alternatives or complements to medication, the top five chosen were counselling, group therapy, art therapies, psychotherapy, and aromatherapy. Mind recommended a diversity of approaches to meet individual needs.

Mental health; Mental health treatments; Patient choice and influence in research; User Movements

Peat: RC

Peat has similarities to clay since both are accumulations over aeons, reflecting a fundamental relationship between humanity and the earth and the locations and peculiar features of the places where people live. There are many images: the peat bog; the people who use peat; peat digging; peat drying; transportation of the peat; and the smell of peat burning. A thick sticky tar exudes from its burning, which penetrates the walls of the old cottages. Peat brings to us a sense of the depth of materiality, and brings us into relationship with the instability of all material.

The late Michael Lynch introduced art therapists in Eire to its uses as a material. He was quite specific about the creamy density that is needed for work with peat in this way.

Peat's shamanic dimension draws all the above to experience the fecundity of the earth; a local expression is personified in the Hag of Beara; an Earth Deity (in West Cork) who is said to have been changed to stone by a priest, and at the same time evokes something concerning our dance in life with death.

Art and materials in contemporary aesthetic philosophy; Clay; Sand; Terracotta

Pell, Cynthia (1933–1977): CW

The life of this artist, who was a patient for many of her adult years, is described in two small privately published books (Dower and Williams, 2000). Family, friends, and fellow artists composed one of the books and, in it, photographs of Pell's images are interspersed with their memories of her. The art therapist Brita von Awigbergk introduces the other book and, in this, the artist's work is amongst the memories of staff who worked with her at Bexley Psychiatric Hospital. The art in both books is vibrant. The subtle contrast between the two books challenges our perceptions of the difference between a person and a mental patient. Pell's images eloquently portray aspects of experience that haunt most lives: they show fear, misery, loss, and love. She drew and painted friends and fellow patients; many of her images include the physical details of the large mental hospital environment.

Art brut; Art of the insane; First period of British art therapy; Outsider art

Person-centred approach to art therapy: DG

The person-centred approach to art therapy is one in which the relationship between client, therapist, and image is considered in the here-and-now with three particular qualities or attitudes being held in mind by the art therapist, namely: *empathy, congruence,* and *unconditional positive regard* (frequently misunderstood and misquoted as the 'core conditions'). Three additional elements must be present for the work to be helpfully therapeutic: that the client and therapist are in psychological contact; that the patient or client is in a state of incongruence; and that s/he must be able to, at least to a minimal degree, perceive the therapist's empathic understanding and unconditional positive regard (Rogers, 1959: 213).

Within the person-centred framework, creativity in its broadest sense is thought to arise from three inner conditions: extensionality or openness to experience; an internal locus of evaluation; and the person's ability to play with ideas and to enter a place of reverie. Rogers (1959) suggests that a nurturing environment is essential for creativity to thrive and that creativity is one of the hallmarks of a congruent and fully functioning person. Liesle Silverstone (1995) and Pat Allen (1995) have written about a person-centred approach to art therapy.

Creativity in the person-centred approach; Journeying

Personification: KH

The personification of feeling states provides the possibility to 'talk with' the feeling in the form of a person, creature, or thing. Named horrors are sometimes easier to deal with than unnamed ones, especially if they have a face, even if it comes with many teeth. Image-making is another way of naming.

Animals; Anticipatory guidance (two entries)*; Gestalt in art and psychotherapy; Griffins, gargoyles, and gremlins; Learning circle; Monsters, dragons, and demons*

Picture within the frame: DE

'The picture within the frame is the space where transferences may be illustrated, revealed and enacted . . . The picture, safely contained within the boundaries of the edges of the paper, reveals the imaginal world' (Schaverien, 1991: 77).

Metaphor (three entries); *Milner on the therapeutic frame; Potential space; Therapeutic frame; Transference*

Play: CW

> The natural thing is playing, and the highly sophisticated twentieth-century phenomenon is psychoanalysis. It must be of value to the analyst to be constantly reminded not only of what is owed to Freud but also of what we owe to the natural and universal thing called playing.
>
> (Winnicott, 1971a: 48)

It is interesting, given their very different styles of work, that Winnicott (Independent School) and Klein comment on the centrality of play in their therapeutic work:

> As I look back over the papers that mark the development of my own thought and understanding I can see that my present interest in play in the relationship of trust that may develop between the baby and the mother was always a feature of my consultative technique . . .
>
> (Winnicott, 1971a: 48)

> I have been prompted by the consideration that my work with both children and adults, and my contributions to psycho-analytic theory as a whole, derive ultimately from the play technique, evolved with young children.
>
> (Klein, 1955, cited in Mitchell, 1986: 35)

Much of what art therapists do is about helping a client to remember and, where possible, re-store their sense of imagination and play (Wood, 1986). In a wide literature we are told that, play is the hallmark of health in children and in adults. Perhaps therapists of all persuasions (hearing, as they do, about a lot of unhappiness) need reminding occasionally of Winnicott's dictum:

> Psychotherapy takes place in the overlap of two areas of playing, that of the patient and that the therapist. Psychotherapy has to do with

two people playing together. The corollary of this is that where playing is not possible then the work done by the therapist is directed towards bringing the patient from a state of not being able to play into a state of being able to play.

(Winnicott, 1971b: 38)

Here Winnicott cites the absence of play as being the only real symptom worth attending to.

Dolls; Football; Play technique

Play technique: CW

The play technique introduced by Klein from 1955 has had wide-ranging impact. She developed it because of working with clients who had very little language (i.e. with very young children or with children who were autistic). She thought the play technique was comparable to the way Freud used free association to gain access to the unconscious. Klein's main diagnostic method was to find a way of understanding the nature of the client's anxiety:

> . . . my attention from the beginning focused on the child's anxieties and that it was by means of interpreting their contents that I found myself able to diminish anxiety. In order to do this, full use had to be made of the symbolic language of play which I recognized to be an essential part of the child's mode of expression. As we have seen, the bricks, the little figure, the car not only represent things which interest the child in themselves, but in his play with them they always have a variety of symbolical meanings as well which are bound up with his phantasies, wishes, and experiences. This archaic mode of expression is also the language with which we are familiar in dreams, and it was by approaching the play of the child in a way similar to Freud's inter-pretation of dreams that I found I could get access to the child's unconscious. But we have to consider each child's use of symbols . . . mere generalized translations of symbols are meaningless.
>
> (Klein, 1955, cited in Mitchell, 1986: 51)

There are clear parallels here for art therapy.

Free association through art; Dolls

Pleasure: MC

Often the dialogue between therapist and client in individual art therapy is concerned with the pleasure that comes from experiences of interest, curiosity, creativity, mutuality, thinking, and understanding of what art is made. It is a particular case of the triangular relationship in art therapy.

Mental health; Mindfulness; Play; Reverie; Triangular relationship;
Vitality

Popular culture: CW

> For those legions of us born into working and lower middle class cultures the stuff of aesthetic is more likely to be found in things like television, both in its content and in its form as a medium, in other forms of mass entertainment and leisure, in the urban and suburban landscapes we inhabit, in the objects we buy or covet, in advertising and commercial design, and in popular music.
>
> (Richards, 1992: 10)

The work of Barry Richards challenges the high art concerns of psychoanalysis, yet his project also attempts to harness some of the knowledge provided by it in relation to popular culture. Art therapists can make use of such a project because there is reason to explore widely in seeking further understanding of the many artworks made by our clients. As with entries on artists, it is not possible to include all the examples from popular culture that might inspire art-making.

Access to art; Advertising; Dolls; Film Studio; Football; Internet;
Television; Visual culture

Portable Studio: DK and BL

'Portable Studio' is an idea developed by Debra Kalmanowitz and Bobby Lloyd during work in the former Yugoslavia in the 1990s, a region at the time fragmented and in places still hostile (Kalmanowitz and Lloyd, 1997, 1999). They described 'Portable Studio' as based on the premise that the internal structure they carried with them as art therapists could allow for work to physically take place in a wide range of settings that, in the former Yugoslavia, extended from the refugee camp dining room and bedroom to the hills surrounding the camp, and at one point the local town rubbish dump. This internal structure comprises a number of key elements, including an attitude both to the art and the individual making it. Central is a belief in the individual as possessing internal resources rooted in experience, resilience, and culture, rather than being a powerless victim for whom the therapist alone holds the solutions. In addition, the internal structure of the

Portable Studio includes attentiveness to the art-making and its ability to provide a form, which can contain the individual's experience as well as an understanding that images potentially hold multiple meanings and that the therapist, in her active alertness (Learmonth, 1994), holds this potentiality. The internal structure can also provide an environment that allows for creative expression as well as sustained immersion (McNiff, 1992) in the art-making (Kalmanowitz and Lloyd, 1999).

Absorption in art-making; Adaptations of practice; Making meaning; Psychosocial approach; Remembering and forgetting; Resilience and the psychosocial model; Therapeutic frame; Training module in the sensitive use of art for non-art therapists

Postmodernist art therapy: SH

The ramifications of postmodernist theory for art therapy practice are complex, but postmodernist therapists are interested in resisting reductive interpretations of their clients' work and demeanour. Furthermore, they might see the client themselves as constituted by discourses, which are internalised and enacted. There is no 'true self' in this model of thinking. Any idea of 'self-hood' is mobile and shifting – an enactment within an inter-textual arena.

One model of therapy, which is quite compatible with postmodernist thought, is the group-interactionist model (Waller, 1993). The theory underpinning this method is particularly influenced by Harry Stack Sullivan (1953), Foulkes (1964), and Yalom (1985), who regard interactions with 'significant others' as more important to the aetiology of disease than early childhood experiences, and indeed personality is seen in a constant state of flux rather than laid down in early childhood (Waller, 1991: 22). These ideas draw on symbolic interactionist thought: 'People create and continually re-create themselves in contact with others; indeed, the self *is* ultimately a process' (Alvesson and Skoldberg, 2000: 14).

Philosophically, this method and approach is rather different from those that see psychological development as universal, and the aetiology of disease as laid down in early childhood and as resulting in collective psychological states. Postmodernist therapists are not looking to uncover supposedly universal psychological developmental aspects in their clients; these are regarded fundamentally as seductive explanatory fictions. The interactionist approach is arguably more in keeping with poststructuralist developments in psychology and the social sciences.

Interpersonal learning in groups; Reductive interpretation; Sense of self; Social psychiatry

Post-traumatic stress disorder (PTSD) and art psychotherapy: DN

Psychodynamic art psychotherapy can have good outcomes for sufferers of PTSD who have not been responsive to cognitive-behavioural therapy (CBT) and other models. Treatments last for a maximum of a year and are once-weekly. Caroline Garland writes that it is this connection of the past with the present 'that is part of what makes the after-effects of trauma so hard to undo' (1998: 13).

Mr D, a man in his thirties, was diagnosed as suffering PTSD following a violent assault on him by several drunken people in front of his heavily pregnant wife. Consequently he suffered a depressive breakdown with frequent flashbacks to the assault and became withdrawn and suicidal. The CBT he had undertaken did not alleviate the cumulative trauma of his violent childhood, which pervaded his inner world. During the course of the art psychotherapy we were able to link his feelings of anger and helplessness at the more recent trauma to similar but unexpressed childhood feelings. These were repeated when, as a young man, he continued to be assaulted by his father and failed also to protect his mother from similar assaults. Following 9 months of weekly sessions Mr D's flashbacks were almost non-existent, he was much more communicative with me, and his marital relationship was much improved due to him being more communicative with his wife and more involved with childcare. Both he and his imagery became more expansive. His increased understanding of how external events had re-evoked an internalised violence enabled Mr D to begin to establish a more benign and reflective inner world.

Brain injury; Brief dynamic art psychotherapy; Complex homelessness; Dissociation; Mentalisation; Mise-en-scene in the therapy room; Negative transference; Stroke and trauma; Trauma

Potential space or intermediate area: DN

In *Playing and Reality* Winnicott (1971b) wrote:

> [it] is useful then to think of a third area of human living, one *neither inside the individual nor outside in the world of shared reality*. This intermediate living can be thought of as occupying a potential space . . . This potential space varies greatly from individual to individual, and its foundation is the baby's trust in the mother experienced over a long enough period at the critical stage of the separation of the not-me from the me, when the establishment of an autonomous self is at the initial stage.
>
> (1971b: 110)

This 'third area' forms the 'playground' for the infant and caregiver. 'I call this a playground because play starts here. The playground is a potential space between the mother and baby or joining mother and baby' (Winnicott, 1971b: 47).

Milner (1978) also described Winnicott's drawing games (that he called the squiggle game) used to structure sessions:

> Each account of those drawing sessions with the child exemplifies as well his beautiful concept of potential space – an essentially pictorial concept, although he defines it as what happens between two people when there is trust and reliability.
>
> (Milner, 1978: 39)

Absorption in art-making; Intersubjectivity; Object relations theories; Milner on the therapeutic frame; Play; Squiggle game; Winnicott

Poverty: CW

There is strong contemporary evidence (Elo, 2009) showing that lower class people die younger and, because the stressors of lower class life are greater, there is more likelihood of physical and mental illness. Internationally studies show that schizophrenia and other mental disorders are more common in the lower classes (e.g. Warner, 1985: 33–56; Weich and Lewis, 1998). Warner (1985) points to the way the changing social circumstances and fortunes of upper caste members of Developing World cultures tend to mean that they have high rates of mental disorder. Theories of social causation as opposed to social drift are the best explanation for this. It is likely, however, that whereas for the majority the strains of lower socio-economic status contribute to the higher levels of serious mental disorders, downward social drift after the onset of mental illness can account for a proportion of the social class gradient.

To substantiate the idea that socio-economic factors influence the course and appearance of schizophrenia, Warner points to a meta-analysis of 68 follow-up studies conducted in Europe and North America since the beginning of the 1900s. He also indicates how recovery rates were significantly lower during the Great Depression of the 1920s and 1930s in USA, Europe, and Scandinavia, providing a clear example of the influence of poverty and class (Warner, 1985: 73, 77, 79).

Bleulers; Looked-after children

Power: CW

> Power is in fact the medium of our social existence, the dynamic which moves the apparatus of our relationship with each other . . . It is the

power of others which either hurts or supports us, our own power which enables us to establish an at least precarious perch from which to survey and deal with the world.

(Smail, 1995: 348)

The power of professionals and the power of clients are rarely in balance. Art therapists are often in situations where their position means that they work with clients who have lost power. Examples include someone without liberty under a mental health section, parents who fear the removal of their child, and elderly people who feel patronised by aspects of public services that they rely upon. It is important to acknowledge the power imbalance if a client is to believe us. It is not helpful to behave as though power differentials do not exist. A small number of texts address the specific issues of power in therapy relationships (e.g. Smail, 1995; Proctor, 2002) and art therapy (e.g. Campbell et al., 1999; Hogan, 1997; Weston, 1999; Wood, 1999a).

Agency; Alienation; Art as a discourse; Liminality; Mythologies and the participant observer; Participative art practice; Power of the patient in moral treatment; Premature interpretation

Power of myth-making, Beuys, and the Tartars: CR and PB

Rafael and Byrne discuss the power of myth-making in relation to the artist Joseph Beuys. Their paper outlines his history from being a German pilot in the Second World War. The story of his air crash and rescue by the Tartars, who wrapped him in fat and felt (materials he later used in his artwork), is well known. Yet Rafael and Byrne provide evidence that this story is not true and that Beuys actually spent 9 months in a British prisoner of war camp:

> It is possible to argue that Beuys could either have gone through a psychosis that led to a healing psychological journey or he might have created this myth consciously and deliberately. It is not possible to give an objective explanation as there is not enough information . . . it is only possible to speculate.
>
> A decade following the war Beuys had recovered from his post-war depression by drawing compulsively. His psychological and physical wounds seem to be ritualised through performance re-enactment and be directed towards self/social and world healing and go beyond what in rational terms seems an unbearable and irredeemable catastrophe . . .
>
> Beuys may have suffered from trauma, as literature and his artwork seem to suggest this possibility . . . Papadopoulos (2002) suggests that if we understand trauma as dual definition: as a wound and as an

opportunity for a fresh start . . . trauma survivors can be empowered and facilitate their own healing.

Beuys's myth . . . created around the Tartars, permitted reinvention and possibly it was the impulse necessary to overcome the traumatic experiences of war . . .

(Rafael and Byrne, forthcoming)

Beuys; Trauma; War wounds; Witness and witnessing

Power of the patient in moral treatment: CW

Moral treatment was based on practical experience and gradual modification in response to three areas of inquiry:

> I. By what means the power of the patient to control the disorder, is strengthened and assisted.
> II. What modes of coercion are employed, when restraint is absolutely necessary.
> III. By what means the general comfort of the insane is promoted.
>
> (Tuke, 1813: 138)

These three questions incisively foretell areas of inquiry that have been important in the treatment of people with mental health difficulties. Considering the power of the patient to control their disorder introduced the potential agency of the person being treated. This is important because so much in the history of mental illness has tended to discredit a patient's contribution to his or her 'own' recovery.

Tuke's book refers to Pinel's *Traité Medico-philosophique sur L'Aliénation Mentale* (1801). The phrase '*traitement moral'* is taken from this work but it is not well translated by the phrase 'moral treatment'. Pinel's phrase translates more closely as 'treatment through emotions' (K. Jones, in Tuke, 1813[1996]: xi).

Belief in the possibilities of the patient's own power was epitomised in the methods used by the York Retreat. William Tuke's daughter-in-law gave one of the descriptions of the Retreat that does most to convey the quality of its work. She suggested the name 'Retreat' as opposed to a 'Hospital' or 'Asylum'. She wanted to describe 'a quiet haven in which the shattered bark might find the means of reparation' (cited by Kathleen Jones, 1972).

Throughout its history art therapy has placed at the centre of its practice a sense of the client's own agency in the therapeutic relationship and their active engagement with making art. In this, the profession might claim lineage with a moral treatment approach.

Agency; Moral treatment; Power; Social inclusion; Social psychiatry

Premature interpretation citing Dalley, Rifkind, and Terry: CW

> . . . premature interpretation can be destructive and damaging and is more often than not due to the therapist's own need for understanding and answers more than the client's. As art therapists we have to be sensitive to the clumsiness and inappropriateness of casual interpretation or chance remark – *naming an image* in words can cause great distress and anxiety when the client may be struggling to depict something entirely different . . . Any important material will re-emerge in subsequent sessions and remaining in a state of 'not knowing' is crucial in the interaction between therapist and client to allow the understanding and symbolism of images and material to emerge in their own time.
>
> One is reminded of the importance of Bion's work in helping us as therapists to 'live in the question' and not close down possibilities of meaning.
>
> (Dalley et al., 1993: 114)

Interpretation as a participant in the process; Interpretation perspectives; Interpretations, Jung's approach; Power; Reductive interpretation

Print-making without a press in art therapy: CH

There are a variety of print-making processes. These can be employed in art therapy and be very effective in many situations. Common inexpensive materials can be used safely without the need for chemicals or sharp instruments. Print-making can offer a supplement or alternative to the many methods of art-making for the client.

Monotype techniques

Process: EW

This is a series of changes that lead to development. Examples include the process of growth – a method of doing something in which there are a number of steps. *Procession* in the theological sense is the act of proceeding from a source – emanating. 'So process can mean that which once started moves on, almost, it might be said, to take on a life of its own, as in, *the living process of the unconscious*' (Dr Roger Grainger, personal communication).

The second meaning of 'process' – to walk in formal procession – may be thought of both as the emerging process and that which is unfolding through and within it. This might be thought of in terms of *how* the making is carried out and also in the unfolding of *what* is made.

[If a person's process is blocked or stuck in some way, if they are not engaged with or in process, there is at least a part of the person that is not alive or is struggling for life. This could be the entry point of therapy.]

Process model for art therapy; Unfolding

Process model for art therapy: DW

> . . . a 'process' model is . . . how I personally see art therapy: that is, as providing the opportunity for a recipient to experience their own conflicts through the combination of image-making and a close rela-tionship with the therapist, and thus to have the possibility of resolving them and gaining the power to change – and moreover, to continue to be able to do so. This is opposed to a view of therapy which suggests a 'once and for all' cure.
>
> (Waller, 1991: xiv).

Brief (three entries); *Process; Time-related processing*

Procrastination: MEd

The American painter Rauschenberg described his way of working (making the stage sets) for a particular ballet. He would collect whatever he could find around the theatre area in the hour or so before the performance began, then he would have only the programme interval to put together a new-every-time three-dimensional collage. It succeeded wonderfully well on the night I was there, but as a way of working it is the opposite to what most people's super-egos or other busybodies advise. If commissioned for a painting he would procrastinate until there was not enough time left and then complete it in frenzy. He presented a rationalisation for leaving things to the last minute – his own particular rite of passage. My understanding is that it was Rauschenberg's only way out for finding a way in, a deliberate way of frustrating a stultifying consciousness. It is a dangerous thought, but I wonder if the function of procrastination is to drive us over the edge, to a wilder but potentially more creative place, when we get too desperate to contain our built-up anxiety.

There is an extraordinary range of occasions in which we are faced with entrance and exit decisions, dilemmas, or opportunities. It is often said that stage fright can heighten performance. We can put this down to the stimu-lation of fear-induced adrenalin. From the perspective of depth psychology I would say that creating an 'impossible' situation – without sending it completely out of control – shifts the balance from the personal towards the archetypal. New energies usually arise not from the familiar, the nos-talgic image, but from the uncomfortably unfamiliar. Sometimes we have to learn to love what is not recognised. Without the disruption of discord there would be no stories, no music, no art, and no therapy. Once again the arts, myths, and fairy stories can show us the way to change and from change to find some resolution.

Archetype; Blank sheet; Block; Journeying; Super-ego

Professional conduct and misconduct: CW

Although the spectre of misconduct and de-registration is nerve wracking, most people understand that upholding principles of good professional conduct is in the interests of clients. The principles of professional conduct for art therapists are outlined in the Health Professions Council (HPC) document known as SCPE (Standards of Conduct, Performance and Ethics, newly revised in July 2008), available online:

> If you make informed, reasonable and professional judgements about your practice, with the best interests of your service users as your prime concern, and you can justify your decisions if you are asked to, it is very unlikely that you will not meet our standards.

The HPC website address is: www.hpc-uk.org.

Health Professions Council

Professional titles: Arts psychotherapies and Arts therapies: JD

Which professional titles are used involve political and pragmatic decisions. The long-standing debate suggesting that the professions should use the title 'Arts Psychotherapies' as opposed to 'Arts Therapies' was re-opened by Jane Dudley (2004a, 2004b). National negotiations with the Department of Health (DOH) and the Unions to achieve the best pay levels for 'Arts Psychotherapists' had re-opened at this time and there was a big struggle to help the DOH understand what it is that 'Arts Therapists' do. The name 'Arts Therapists' includes music therapists, dance-movement therapists, and dramatherapists. When the title 'Arts Psychotherapists' was used there was more immediate understanding of the practice within the DOH and negotiations moved on swiftly (www.baat.org/AFC).

The Health Professions Council (www.hpc-uk.org/) showed that the public had little idea as to what 'Art Therapy' consisted of, consequently Jane Dudley proposed that at the national level the professions have the one title – 'Arts Psychotherapists' – because in her view 'Arts Psycho-therapy' best described the professional practice.

[Pragmatically it seems wise to use the protected title with the most likelihood of being understood in any given context, and this is unlikely to change.]

British Association of Art Therapists; Health Professions Council;
Organisations regulating and representing art therapists; Trade unions

Professionalization: DW

The ideas which led to the development of art therapy had existed for a long time, but at a certain point they were taken up and started to permeate the health system (in the case of the UK during the Second World War). Professions tend to follow the same processes, starting out as loosely organized groups of people with similar ideas and aims, then becoming more formally structured into an association or associations and societies, which begin to design training programmes. The founders and then the followers (graduates of these programmes) gradually identify a body of knowledge and practice, which then becomes a segment, splitting off from the 'parent' profession and either joining up with another, or setting up its own systems. So there is never a point when a profession (or indeed a Society) is a static thing, otherwise it would stagnate and die.

The development of art therapy in the UK has followed this pattern although it is unusual in that it has had only one professional association, formed in 1963 and linked very early on with the trades union movement. This association [*British Association of Art Therapists*] (BAAT) also took on the role of a learned society, with educational aims, and a pressure group for patients' rights. This unity of purpose and grass roots aspect of British art therapy certainly helped in the struggle towards recognition of the discipline and regulation. Nevertheless, as is only to be expected, the emergence of the profession has been characterized by dilemmas and paradoxes, or by 'uneasy alliances', perhaps the most significant of all being between art and therapy.

(Waller, 2009a: 8)

British Association of Art Therapists; European art therapy; Health
Professions Council; Trade unions

Projective identification: DN

. . . In association with this unconscious projective fantasy there is an interpersonal interaction by means of which the recipient is pressured to think, feel, and behave in a manner congruent with the ejected feelings and the self- and object-representations embodied in the projective fantasy. In other words, the recipient is pressured to engage in an identification with a specific, disowned aspect of the projector.

(Ogden, 1982: 1–2)

In a therapy session the therapist may notice feeling compelled to behave or speak in a particular way, which may feel at odds with their usual feeling state. For example, when working with an eating disordered young woman I found myself handing her bite-sized portions of clay rather than my usual handfuls and felt as if I was having to coax her into accepting these morsels. She had disowned and *projected* the needy part of herself and projected it into me and made me the *recipient* of the part of her that could feel tempted into wanting my therapy 'food'. I became *identified* with the part of her that did not want to feel any need.

Projective identification: A Kleinian perspective; Projective identification and empathy; Scapegoat transference and projective identification

Projective identification: A Kleinian perspective: DE

The term 'projective identification' was introduced into the psychoanalytic literature by Melanie Klein to describe the psychological defence mechanism revealed in phantasy, 'in which the subject inserts himself – in whole or in part – into the object in order to harm, possess or control it' (Laplanche and Pontalis, 1973: 356). In effect, projective identification involves evoking in someone else aspects of the self that are felt to be unbearable. It can be a very powerful means of communicating feelings when, for example, used by babies or infants before they are able to talk.

In therapy, projective identification can be used to attack the therapist when 'nasty' or 'mad' parts of the self are 'evoked in other people in order to destroy their comfort, their peace of mind or their happiness' (Segal, 1992: 36). During a session with a client the art therapist might, for example, feel invaded, or suddenly and dramatically filled with anger, helplessness, emptiness, or despair. The phantasies and feelings evoked within the therapist when the client is employing projective identification as a mode of communication may be very powerful. For the art therapist, the ability to help a very regressed or disturbed client who is employing projective identification as a defence may crucially depend upon their capacity to tolerate these feelings, and bring them into conscious awareness in the form of images or words. That projective identification appears to draw its communicative power through activating the inner experience (the internal objects and object relations) of the therapist has implications regarding the positive or negative use of the counter-transference.

Counter-transference; Counter-transference captivity; Negative
transference; Projective identification; Projective identification and
empathy; Scapegoat transference and projective identification

Projective identification and empathy: DE

It is important to note that projective identification involves more than
getting rid of bad feelings or hated parts of the self:

> To begin with, it is the earliest form of empathy and it is on projective
> as well as introjective identification that is based the capacity to 'put
> oneself into another person's' shoes . . . Projective identification also
> provides the basis of the earliest form of symbol-formation. By pro-
> jecting parts of the self into the object and identifying parts of the
> object with parts of the self, the ego forms its first most primitive
> symbols.
>
> (Segal, 1978b: 36)

Hannah Segal's ideas concerning the role of projective identification in
symbol formation have important implications for art therapists. Clients
may, for example, produce violent or messy images quite unconsciously in
order to provoke an emotional response such as fear or disgust in the art
therapist. Alternatively, aesthetically pleasing images may be offered as
gifts in order to seduce or captivate them. Schaverien (1987) has discussed
the issue of how images are invested with meaning or empowered, but
prefers the terms 'the scapegoat and the talisman transference' to describe
the processes involved. Mann (1989, 1990b) offers a critique of Schaverien's
ideas and suggests that projective identification provides a more useful
model for understanding.

Projective identification has, since Klein's original and far from detailed
description of it as an intrapsychic process, been extended and applied to
the understanding of interpersonal processes. Although the psychoanalytic
literature is replete with definitions of projective identification, none of
these appear entirely stable or beyond dispute (Sandler, 1993).

Empathy; Klein and creativity; Projective identification; Projective
identification: A Kleinian perspective; Reparation (two entries);
Scapegoat transference and projective identification

Psyche-social: CW

The profession has roots in social psychiatry. It developed strongly during
its second period in Britain, which was the era of social psychiatry, and
consequently it has much in common with many psychosocial interventions

in health, education, and social services. However, the approach of art therapy might be named *psyche-social*, because the profession acknowledges the role of the less conscious aspects of human experience (e.g. dreams, play, popular culture, and art). This is where the profession differs from other forms of psychosocial intervention.

Psychoanalytic accounts of the unconscious; Psychosocial approach;
Social inclusion; Social psychiatry; Unconscious

Psychiatric diagnosis as labelling: JD

Dudley (2004b) discusses the possibilities for creating more open therapeutic interactions by avoiding psychiatric labelling. The paper supports the view of Professor Mary Boyle that therapists should avoid using the shorthand of diagnosis and continually remind themselves that the person is a subject not an object. 'Non-diagnostic approaches demand a very different set of assumptions which in turn demand a different set of social and therapeutic responses' (Boyle, 1999: 88). Dudley's paper strongly suggests that this position is a good starting place for thinking about someone who is referred for art psychotherapy.

Anti-psychiatry; Diagnostic systems in psychiatry; Ideology and
psychiatric diagnosis; Social inclusion

Psychiatry: CW

The province of psychiatry is unusually broad for a medical speciality. Mental disorders may affect most aspects of a patient's life, including physical functioning, behaviour, emotions, thought, perception, interpersonal relationships, sexuality, work, and play. The disorders are caused by a poorly understood combination of biological, psychological, and social determinants. Psychiatrists are often at pains to point to the sheer range of human complexity, yet psychiatry's task is to account for the diverse sources and manifestations of mental illness. Many psychiatrists working in the public sector tend to take a liberal pragmatic approach towards the clients in a range of services. Of course there are some psychiatrists, just as there are some art therapists, who do not.

The majority of art therapists work in public services and consequently their sphere of practice and the ways in which they think about the problems of mental health are taken from an overlapping area in-between the conceptual frameworks of psychiatry (including its social work aspects) and those of psychotherapy. Art therapists need to have a broad understanding of systems of classification and diagnosis used in the public sector, and of the shortcomings of diagnostic systems. They also need to make use of cultural references as ways of understanding human distress.

Anti-psychiatry; Diagnostic systems in psychiatry; DSM systems of diagnosis; ICD systems of psychiatric diagnosis; Ideology and psychiatric diagnosis; Psychiatric diagnosis as labelling

Psychiatry, psychoanalysis, poverty, and class: CW

Doerner sees the history of medicine as tied to social and political issues. He suggests that the bourgeois classes established psychiatry specifically for the poor insane. He thinks that many themes related to the development of psychiatry 'were one aspect of the class struggle, as well as an early solution to the incipient *social question*' (Doerner, 1981: 1).

He points to the failure of sociological accounts to distinguish sufficiently between psychiatric history and that of psychoanalysis. He suggests that the failure to produce theoretical accounts of the development of psychiatry (compared with the sociological enthusiasm for theorising about psycho-analysis) is because of the harsh and complex political realities that face psychiatry. Certainly some of the client issues that face people working in psychiatry are painful to witness and hard to resolve within a purely psychological framework.

Consequently it is understandable that throughout the history of psy-chiatry it seems that: 'Praxis is limited to hard-to-verify success in indi-vidual cases, or becomes purely administrative' (Doerner, 1981: 4). This impression is relevant to contemporary debates about evidence-based prac-tice in psychiatry, and more modestly in art therapy. It also indicates the extent to which the poverty and the sheer number of clients can pervade the development of a discipline.

'Before the nineteenth century the treatment of the mad hardly consti-tuted a specialised branch of medicine' (Porter, 1997: 493). However, the French Revolution and later the development of Industrial Capitalism at the end of the eighteenth and beginning of the nineteenth century, respec-tively, see the birth of psychiatry. The many overlapping developments that accompanied industrialisation destroyed the subsistence base of small workshop workers, creating poverty and insecurity for many. Large sec-tions of the population moved to the towns and the factories and became the first members of the urban working classes; members of their ranks made up the majority of those admitted to the newly institutionalised asylums.

Evidence-based practice; Future cities; Poverty; Power; Professionalisation; Psychiatry

Psychoanalytic accounts of the unconscious: CW

Freud's method in relation to dreams has often been described with his own phrase as 'the royal road to the unconscious'. Possibly Freud's most important psychoanalytic text for art therapists is the *Interpreting Dreams* (1900). Bettleheim (1982: 65) suggests that the title is poorly translated into English and that Freud's original German indicated an attempt to grasp the deeper significance of dreams – an attempt to show the many layers of meaning and not a claim to make their meanings accessible to a simple interpretative cipher. This has resonance with regard to the ways in which images and art objects made by art therapy clients might be considered:

> The purpose of Freud's lifelong struggle was to help us understand ourselves, so that we would no longer be propelled, by forces unknown to us, to live lives of discontent, or perhaps outright misery, and to make others miserable, very much to our own detriment. In examining the content of the unconscious, Freud called into question some deeply cherished beliefs, such as the unlimited perfectibility of man and his inherent goodness; he made us aware of our ambivalences and of our ingrained narcissism, with its origins in infantile self-centeredness, and he showed us its destructive nature.
>
> (Bettleheim, 1982: 15)

Freud maintained that there are two major types of mental functioning: the primary processes characterised by the mental qualities of dreaming, and secondary processes more in keeping with rational thinking, logic, and a verifiable sense of time and place. Psychoanalytic work is often aimed at the struggle that ensues between these processes. Freud's work to uncover the unconscious was aimed at giving us a greater sense that we could choose how we respond to powerful internal impulses. His thinking developed in his later writings into a description of mental phenomena as opposed to a topological region of the mind. Nevertheless Bettelheim's (1982) inspired account of Id, Ego, and Super-ego shows how the concept can be understood within Freud's topology.

Certainly 'the notion of the unconscious is one of the few concepts that have remained relatively unchanged in the course of the development of all schools of psychoanalysis' (Hinshelwood, 1989: 467). Jung, Klein, and many later psychoanalytic theoreticians confirm that it is fundamental to psychoanalysis. Jung added the notion of a Collective Unconscious to what he saw as Freud's account of a personal unconscious.

Dreams; Ego and id; Sublimation theories in art therapy; Sublimation theories in psychoanalysis; Super-ego; Unconscious

Psycho-neuro-immunology: JHar

Psycho-neuro-immunology is an area of study combining and examining the intimate relationship between mind and body, or psyche-soma, in the fields of psychology, neurology, and immunology. 'The recent scientific research from the new field of psycho-neuro-immunology shows the deep and far reaching connection between body and mind. The image is re-emerging to take its central place again in the healing process' (Baron, 1989: 167).

Adolescence and neurological research; Brain injury; Damage to mental health; Neurological art therapy; Stroke and trauma

Psychosis and art therapy: CW

Both Killick (1991) and Greenwood (1994) consider that in the early stages of work with people who are in the midst of psychosis there is a need to suspend questions about the content of artwork made by clients. Killick argues that 'images produced by psychotic patients do not serve a symbolic purpose until a containing relationship is formed' (Killick, 1991: 6).

Killick, Greenwood, and Anna Goldsmith refer in detail to the nature of the rooms in which they meet with clients who either are in the midst of or have a history of psychosis (Killick, 1991; Goldsmith, 1986; Greenwood and Layton, 1987). The details of the rooms and the manner in which they are used all contribute to the work of containment.

Many people working for health and social care services necessarily have long relationships with clients who have a history of psychosis. Psycho-social intervention methods (which include some behavioural aspects) are to be applauded for upholding the idea of there being a need for longer case work and for the impetus for the development of assertive outreach teams, which sometimes espouse the idea of a 'caseload for life'. However, many clients remain isolated and consequently it seems wise for art therapists to adopt a supportive psychotherapeutic approach (Greenwood, 1997; Wood, 1997, 2001a). It is not feasible for art therapists single-handedly to provide an adequate container for people who have serious disorders; their work is done in conjunction with a team.

In the public sector, poverty and class influence the course of this parti-cular work (Warner, 1985), but there has still been development. Recently, evidence-based clinical guidelines (Brooker et al., 2007) for work with this client group have been produced and significant systematic research has been undertaken (e.g. the RCT by Richardson et al., 2007; and the ongoing MATISSE HTA Project, 2007).

The National Institute for Health and Clinical Excellence guidelines (NICE, 2009) recommend art therapy for this client group on the basis of a small amount of RCT research, indicating that:

Despite this small but emerging evidence base, the Guideline Development Group recognise that at present, arts therapies are the only interventions, both psychological and pharmacological, to demonstrate consistent efficacy in the reduction of negative symptoms.

(NICE, 2009: 205)

Adaptations of practice; Champernowne; Cracked pots; Diagnostic systems in psychiatry; Distributive transference and the importance of teamwork; Kusama; Psychotic processes; Rehabilitation; Social inclusion; Social psychiatry; Studios; Supportive psychotherapy; Symbolic equation and symbolic representation; Therapeutic care; Transactional object in psychosis

Psychosocial approach: DK and BL

In the contexts of political conflict, chronic poverty, HIV/AIDS, natural disaster, and social upheaval, two significant approaches have emerged that guide the interventions that offer psychological, emotional, and social support to individuals who have lived through a range of experiences:

- *a trauma approach* (also referred to as a curative/pathology model), which focuses attention on risk factors and the treatment of individual trauma;
- *a psychosocial approach* (also known as a developmental/preventative/ normalising model), which addresses individual's psychological needs through supporting groups of children, parents, family, and the wider community.

The 'psychosocial' approach is usually understood to be the most appropriate as it focuses on the resilience and resourcefulness of individuals, families, and communities, sheltering them from the effects of the above volatile environments by strengthening protective factors and coping mechanisms. Fundamental to it is a valuing of local culture and traditions. It does not deny the fact that some individuals are unable to cope and may need a particular type of specialist support, which can be offered in parallel where resources exist (Kalksma-Van-Lyth, 2007).

Adaptations of practice; Context and practice; Resilience and the psychosocial model; Social inclusion

Psychotic processes: CW

These are psychological processes in everyone that make it hard to think and they can take a number of different forms. They might involve dream-like thought processes occurring whilst awake. To experience such thinking whilst awake can be frightening or even terrifying. It might include a sense of persecution, a difficulty in thinking logically, a tendency to make strange connections, a conviction in the truth of phantasy and/or a use of symbolic equation. When someone is in the midst of a psychotic episode these kinds of mental processes can become prevalent. A number of art therapists have written about trying to help people in the midst of psychosis (e.g. collection by Killick and Schaverien, 1997). Art therapists have used both psychiatric and psychoanalytic literature in understanding such processes (Ellwood, 1995, is a helpful text that combines both).

Champernowne; Clinical guidelines in art therapy; Confusional or entangled children; Containment and counter-transference; Groups and organisations; Imagery and clay work of confusional or entangled children; Kusama; Psychosis and art therapy; Symbolic equation and symbolic representation; Thinking; Third period of British art therapy history; Transactional object in psychosis; Unconscious

Push-and-pull effect of imagery: KM

Making artwork can create the sense of a wrestling bout in which the person engaged in making artwork is fighting to get somewhere but is at the same time involved in pushing useful processes away that need longer attention. An image can ask for things, a certain push for a particular colour or a pull towards or away from a feeling or thought. This 'push-and-pull' effect is something the therapist needs be aware of and work with during the client's creation of imagery.

Art-making as a defence; Art-making leftovers; Defend; Inner art; Inner autonomy; Life of the picture; Masks; Vitality

Qualitative research: AJG

Qualitative research investigates the nature of things and uses many methods to explore research questions that are, generally speaking, oriented towards discovery. Thus, qualitative research is inductive rather than, as is usual in quantitative research, hypothetico-deductive for testing a hypothesis. Qualitative researchers enquire in depth about social and cultural issues, about real-world issues and experiences, analysing words, images, and situations and considering the researcher him/herself as a tool in the research. Thus, in qualitative research, the researcher's reflexive responses are incorporated into the project. The inclusion of the researcher's critical subjectivity can lead to qualitative research being described as 'soft', personal, and subject to all kinds of influences within the research environment. McLeod (1999) says that qualitative research gains validity through the researcher being explicit about the personal and organisational context of their research, good descriptive detail that enables replication, and the rigorous, critical subjectivity of the researcher.

A variety of views and voices are included in the process and results of qualitative research, not only that of the researcher but also those of the researched upon – the respondents, who can become co-researchers. Thus qualitative research designs can evolve and research outcomes can be negotiated.

Qualitative research does not have any underlying doctrine or preferred methodology. Instead there are many 'isms' – feminism, interactionism, social constructionism, postmodernism – and many methods of data collection and analysis: from narrative case studies to open-ended interviews and questionnaires; from heuristic to hermeneutic research; from phenomenological and historical archival research to visual and art-based methods; and from participant observation and action research to content and discourse analysis.

Case studies; Mythologies and the participant observer; Quantitative research; Seeing and looking; Sense of self; Transferable skills; Visual heuristic research; Visual research methods

Quantitative research: AJG

Quantitative research is based in the positivist tradition of the natural sciences (e.g. physics, chemistry, and biology), which assumes that there are patterns and regularities of cause and effect that will, given the same circumstances, always occur. Quantitative methods use standardised approaches in an experimental approach that considers the amount of things and collects precise measurements in order to test whether a hypothesis is true or false, the underlying assumption being that research, and the researcher, can investigate a research question or test a hypothesis in fixed, usually pre-determined ways that are objective. This leads quantitative researchers to seek validity in their research designs and reliability in their research tools and techniques.

Quantitative research can be conducted on a small or large scale. Large surveys and randomised controlled trials are used to collect exact measurements from representative samples of specific populations; smaller studies investigate cohorts of matched subjects, and single-case experimental designs and structured observation decrease the scale still further.

Audit; Clinical guidelines; Collaborative research teams; Evidence-based practice; Outcome measures; Patient choice and influence in research;

*Qualitative research; Randomised controlled trials; Research critical
appraisal; Single-case experimental designs; Systematic review; What
works for whom?*

Race and culture: MLieb

Questions that have relevance to this area of race and culture include:

- How does the race and culture of both therapist and client affect the
  process, product, and relationships in art therapy?
- How can we harness the therapeutic possibilities generated by images,
  colour, and language that reflect people's racial and cultural histories?
- What are the content and meanings of the dynamics that arise in
  intercultural art therapy?

> One of the strong themes emerging from this area of enquiry is the need
> to make connections with our respective cultures and our practice. It
> is about putting ourselves in the therapeutic frame, a position we
> have always been in, even though we have found it uncomfortable
> or hard to admit to. Our individual and cultural experiences cannot
> and should not be detached from, nor imposed on, the work we do with
> others. They should, as much as possible, be owned and acknowledged,
> so that they can creatively inform our professional (and other)
> relationships.
>
> (Campbell et al., 1999: 15–18)

*Class; Coping strategies that use dreams and art-making; Cross-cultural
influences; Power; Psychiatry, psychoanalysis, poverty, and class*

Randomised Controlled Trials (RCTs): KJ

The following explanation is taken from a review of Roth and Fonagy's
(1996) book *What Works for Whom?*:

> Randomized Controlled Trials (RCTs) are one means by which objec-
> tive links can be made between therapy and outcome. Roth and Fonagy
> (1996) make the case that by asking questions about the comparative
> benefits of two or more treatments RCTs provide the best evidence of
> these links. Users are randomly allocated to different treatment condi-
> tions and an attempt is made to control or examine for variables such
> as demographic factors, symptom severity, and level of functioning.
> Attempts are made to implement therapies under conditions, which
> reduce the number of therapist variables that can influence outcome . . .

The authors describe the limitations of the RCT . . . The demands of the research design can alter the therapy so that it no longer resembles therapy as it is normally delivered and outcome measures may not be sensitive to the particular therapy process.

RCTs are felt to answer some of the shortcomings of the single case study approach. The single case study has been an important tool in the development of art therapy. The authors acknowledge the importance of rigorous case studies in the formation of evidence for the effectiveness of a treatment . . . Results are difficult to generalize across other individuals and other therapists . . .

They stress that lack of evidence for the efficacy of a treatment in an RCT does not mean that a treatment is ineffective and recognize that improvement of clinical care will not automatically result from using empirically based treatments. However, they conclude that despite their limitations, RCTs provide the only valid, albeit limited source of evidence for the efficacy of various forms of psychological treatment.

(Jones, 1998: 75–76)

Art therapy RCTs; Case studies; Evidence-based practice; Quantitative Research; What works for whom?

Reason: PB

Reason – rhyme's twin – denotes a different approach to articulating and communicating in cognitive rather than poetic terms. It denotes our approach to the understanding of ideas, arguments, and observations encountered in the study and practice of art therapy. It is an approach to grasping the nature of 'the intelligence of feeling' conveyed to us phenomenologically through our bodies and their senses, psychologically through our relationships, surprisingly perhaps through our pathologies, and semiotically through language. It alludes to combinations of rational and empirical approaches to understanding, thus explaining relationships between psychopathology, therapy, and art. In the case of the rationales proposed for art therapy, it alludes to relationships between aesthetic theories and differing theories of psychopathology, each with its attendant account of psychotherapy.

Whereas rhyme is pertinent to the world of art, reason operates most significantly in the sciences. Importantly, reason in the context of the human sciences has to be distinguished from 'cause' because that concept is used within the physical sciences framework of causality. In their work, trainee art therapists, whose concerns continually oscillate between art and science, between rhyme and reason, need to become familiar with such distinctions, to learn to think of works of art, even the modest ones made by their clients, as 'theoretical objects' imbued with both rhyme and reason (as opposed to cultural artefacts easily relegated by colleagues to the domain of mere rhyme).

This entry was adapted from Byrne (2002).

Rhyme; Sense of self; Transferable skills

Red for Goldsworthy: CW

The following quotations were included with exhibits in the Bothy Gallery by *Andy Goldsworthy at Yorkshire Sculpture Park*:

> Colour for me is not pretty or decorative – it is raw with energy. Nor does it rest on the surface. I explore the colour within and around a rock – colour is form and space. It does not lie passively or flat. At best it reaches deep into nature – drawing on the unseen – touching the living rock – revealing the energy inside.
>
> I found and worked with red in many countries and talked of it as the earth's vein . . . The beauty of the red is its connection to life – underwritten by fragility, pain and violence – words that I would have to use in describing beauty itself.
>
> In Japan the red of the maple is one of the strongest I have found – not just for its colour but in its context. I have worked with the red leaves in the American fall, but there the colour is part of a wide variety of colours, including many different reds. The isolated Japanese maple set amongst green trees on a mountain side is so violent that it appears as an open wound.
>
> (Goldsworthy, 2007)

Colouring; Colours and active imagination; Journeying

Reductive interpretation: SH

Art therapy trainees are asked to hold on to their interpretations and to remain as open as possible to other possible ways of understanding the therapeutic encounter in order to avoid premature foreclosure of meanings. On the simplest level, art therapists practise asking open rather than closed questions: 'That letter box is in the street' says the inexperienced trainee, to which the disgruntled client responds 'It's a double-decker bus, not a letter box!'

Of course every act of understanding and every formulated question has an interpretive element. Why do I ask my client about the red mark rather than the black streak? Perhaps one feels more insistent to me, and I have indulged in an act of interpretation in getting to that point of formulating the question.

On a more profound level, psychoanalysis and object relations theory are seductive explanatory fictions. When trainees complete 'baby observations', they imagine a 'paranoid orientation' or distinguish other developmental phenomena in the baby. Someone with a different explanatory schema would *see* the baby's behaviour differently and interpret it differently. There is no such thing as theory-free observation. These explanatory schemas have important implications for the conduct of therapy. Whilst it may be quite harmless to project material onto a baby who is too young to notice, it is potentially psychologically damaging to tell a 7-year-old that she thinks her mother is a witch or that she wishes to eat her father's genitals. I have called dogmatic reductive interpretations of clients' artwork 'psychic abuse' (Hogan, 1997: 39). As Dorothy Rowe has pointed out, psychotherapists, by virtue of their training, knowledge, and special insights, sometimes feel that 'they have access to truths above and beyond the capacity of the patients . . . the psychotherapist interprets the patient's truths and tells them what they *really* mean' (Rowe, 1993: 94). Unfortunately, this [also] takes place in art therapy.

In earlier work, I questioned this phenomenon as well as giving several examples of reductive interpretation of a sort that I regard as constituting dangerous practice (Hogan, 1997: 37–42). Recently, I have produced a detailed critique of the reductive application of object relations theory (Hogan, 2010).

Interpretation as a participant in the process; Interpretation perspectives; Interpretations, Jung's approach; Metaphor (three entries); *Premature interpretation*

Reflection: MAm

We have three ways to understand reflection: reflection as faithful imitation; reflection outwards as expression or communication; and reflection meaning to turn back and look again. All three definitions have important connotations for the ways in which we perceive ourselves and our experiences, present ourselves to the world, and use our understanding of past or present experience. We can look directly at others, but to see ourselves, to know ourselves, we need the help of a reflector: 'The mind of the painter should be like a mirror which always takes the colour of the thing that it reflects and which is filled by as many images as there are things placed before it' (Leonardo da Vinci, cited by Blunt, 1940: 37).

Nor Hall (1980) suggests that the Psyche's search for meaning and completion is generally undertaken by individuals in the private space of the therapeutic encounter (Hall, 1980). To be without the means of seeing oneself can lead to a loss of self-knowledge. 'They had shut her up here in the cell without a looking glass so that she should not know how old she had grown' (White, 1979). Fonagy et al (1994) link a high reflective self-function to resilience because it facilitates stepping back and reviewing what is happening in complex interactions. In therapy this function is often seen in visual and/or verbal images (Ambridge, 2001b).

Art made by art therapists; Case Studies; Journals/sketchbooks; Looking and visual research; Reflective counter-transference; Review with images; Supervision; What works for whom?

Reflective counter-transference: CC

There are many different ways of recovering from, processing, reflecting upon and coming to an understanding of different material presented by children in therapy. I was struck by how the more primitive and non-verbal the material tended to be, how physical my means of reflecting on it were, e.g., bathing, swimming, dancing, dreaming, painting and writing. The first three, bathing, swimming, dancing come when there are few words available either to client or myself to name early pre-verbal experience, and writing normally comes as a kind of looking back after work has been completed. Supervision, verbal, is ongoing, but dreaming and painting have much more to do with 'on seeing oneself in each patient'. There are particular times in therapy where projective processes are very powerful and projective identification is being used massively by the client where client's and therapist's psyches intermingle and both have to grow to accommodate each other. The client learns the language of the therapist and the therapist learns to recognise herself in the client and has work to do to accept, often unwillingly, and own those aspects if they are going to be able to help the client understand them too.

(Case, 1994: 5–8)

Art made by art therapists; Reflection; Reflective counter-transference; Supervision; Working through

Refractive transference: CC

The term 'refractive transference' has been suggested as one way to conceptualise work with children in a 'paranoid/schizoid' position, who will be employing defences characterised by idealisation, splitting, omnipotent thinking, denial and manic activity. A 'refractive transference' would be the experience of being in a situation in the therapy room where the child has split transference to therapist, objects in the room and images made, and is also projecting parts of the self in order to manage psychic pain. The pain would be characterised by an underlying sense of depression and worthless-ness and the great difficulty of managing loving and hating feelings towards the same person hidden and disguised by an omnipotent state of mind. The term 'refractive transference' has been used to reflect thinking in progress about the room as a container for the liquid psychic state of very disturbed children. It is an umbrella term to cover the oblique projections and transference that may be split to different aspects of the setting, including the therapist.

(Case, 2000: 51)

Distributive transference and the importance of teamwork; Mise-en-scene in the therapy room; Object relations: Schizoid anxieties and claustrophobic symptoms; Studios

Rehabilitation: CW

Terry Molloy's (1997) paper about the role of art therapy in psychiatric rehabilitation continues to be pertinent. He discusses work with clients who have complex and often long-term psychiatric histories. His account is impressive because he demonstrates the range of psychotherapeutic work that is possible with clients who are rarely offered therapy of any kind. He carefully explores the ways in which art therapists might respond to, work with services, and try to provide a balance to other rehabilitative work. He sees this being achieved most effectively through close teamwork. He writes:

. . . inner emptiness . . . a psychic paralysis resulting from the terrifying confrontation of two worlds, inner and outer. In such cases no amount of practical training in coping with work and the realities of life is likely to be of much use. Art therapy can help break through the emptiness and as rehabilitation progresses, can support a patient's return to reality.

(Molloy, 1997: 242)

The establishment of psychiatric outreach teams shows that Molloy's writing in this area was prophetic.

Kraepelin; Psychiatry; Psychosis and art therapy; Social inclusion; Social psychiatry

Remembering and forgetting: DK and BL

The Russian poet Yevgeny Yevtushenko (1978) has written that things which are not expressed will be forgotten *and* will happen again. His words resonate with the sentiment we often hear in working in the context of political violence. Over time however, we have become aware of the importance of not only remembering but also forgetting in the context of trauma and resilience.

In our experience of working in countries of conflict we have found that when individuals are faced with the opportunity or the framework in which to make art and given a free choice to paint whatever they chose, some will draw or paint their horrific experiences, while most will not.

Alvarez (1992), Auerhahn and Laub (1984) all point to the importance of remembering and forgetting. Their thoughts seem to concur in relation to the individual needing to actively move between past and present so as to slowly build up a collection of memories which enable the individual to see herself as a whole person and not only defined by her trauma experience. In art therapy, the art work and the relationships that emerge can serve as intermediaries and stand between the past and the present. Art therapy can also allow the individual to work at his/her own pace. In our experience, these have served both in remembering and forgetting.

(adapted from Kalmanowitz and Lloyd, 2005: 20–22)

Complexity and pain contained in an artwork; Coping strategies that use dreams and art-making; Making meaning; Reparation (two entries)

Reparation: A Kleinian perspective: DE

Melanie Klein first introduced the term reparation into the psychoanalytic literature in her 1929 paper 'Infantile Anxiety Situations Reflected in a Work of Art and in the Creative Impulse' (Klein, 1986). In this paper, in which she discusses an opera – *L'Enfants et les sortilèges* – and the work of the Swedish painter Ruth Kjar, Klein uses the term reparation to describe the psychological process whereby feelings of guilt are alleviated through acts intended to repair, restore, or re-create internal objects that, in phantasy, have been damaged or destroyed. Reparation gained considerably in its significance when Klein later introduced the idea of the depressive position. In the depressive position the infant experiences total desolation, believing its hateful feelings have destroyed the good breast, and as a consequence feels a sense of loss and guilt. These feelings may give rise to a desire to restore and re-create the lost loved object. This promotes growth through contributing to good internal and external object relations and is believed to be the fundamental drive in creative activity. As Hanna Segal states:

> The artist's need is to create what he feels in the depth of his internal world. It is his inner perception of the deepest feeling of the depressive position that his internal world is shattered which leads to the necessity to create something that is felt to be a whole new world. This is what every major artist does – creates a world.
>
> (1991: 86)

From a clinical perspective it might be argued that an inability to acknowledge and overcome depressive anxiety may lead to inhibitions in the capacity to give expression to feelings through art, or may result in work that is lifeless or reassuringly 'pretty'.

Cosmologies; Klein and creativity; Projective identification: A Kleinian perspective; Remembering and forgetting; Reparation using ideas from Judith Herman

Reparation using ideas from Judith Herman: MAm

It is often not possible for individuals who have suffered abuse to achieve adequate reparation from the perpetrator of that abuse. Judith Lewis Herman (1994) makes a very apt comparison with war damage in her book, *Trauma and Recovery*, in which she looks at both the trauma of war and that of domestic and sexual abuse.

Herman suggests that:

> Genuine contrition in a perpetrator is a rare miracle. Fortunately, the survivor does not need to wait for it. Her healing depends on the discovery of restorative love in her own life; it does not require that this love be extended to the perpetrator.
>
> (1994: 190)

She also writes about 'the fantasy of compensation from the perpetrator' in the form of an acknowledgement, apology, or public humiliation, any of which can, paradoxically, tie the person to the perpetrator rather than free them.

During my own experience of work over many years with children and young people who have suffered physical, sexual, or emotional abuse, it has appeared that the process of reparation most often occurs between the child and her/his attachment figure (most usually mother). The journey frequently involves anger towards the mother figure at some stage; then she may need help to hold on to these feelings for her child in order to maintain their bond.

Among the aspects of harm that most often need to be addressed are:

- disruption of attachments;
- distorted family relationships;
- sexualisation of the child;
- overwhelming emotions;
- confusion in the child's inner world.

'Symbolic rescue' is particularly difficult in circumstances in which the perpetrator remains on the scene but may be achieved eventually, sometimes through a parallel process involving memories and images. Having a believing and subsequently protective parent is probably the most significant element in order that children and young people can move on from the experience of victimisation, enabling both child and carer to reach a place of reparation.

Abuse; Boundaries; Remembering and forgetting; Reparation: A Kleinian perspective; Therapeutic frame; Violation of body boundaries

Research critical appraisal: AJG

Critical appraisal is one of the key tools in the development of clinical guidelines. It is therefore a significant part of the construction of an evidence base to clinical practice.

Critical appraisal is an explicit and systematic method of reviewing a literature. As one of the first steps in the development of a clinical guideline it usually involves a group of people working together in an organised way to evaluate a literature in terms of each text's structure, rigour, and relevance to a particular topic (see Gilroy, 2006, for examples).

Texts that are not research based can be appraised. This includes the text's academic rigour, the contextualisation of the topic within an existing literature, the adequacy of description (e.g. of casework), consideration of theoretical and ethical issues, and, for art therapy, the quality of illustrations and the adequacy of their discussion. Key issues or findings from each text are identified and their application and relevance to the topic are considered. Individuals' appraisals of a text are then discussed in a reading group so that a collective critical appraisal of each text may be formed, the critical appraisal giving the basis for a text's assignment to a 'level of evidence' in the next stage of the process, that of systematic review and the positioning of the text within a hierarchy of evidence.

Clinical guidelines; Collaborative research teams; Systematic review

Resilience and the psychosocial model: DK and BL

The psychosocial model as used in contexts of political conflict, chronic poverty, HIV/AIDS, natural disaster, and social upheaval has shifted the focus of programmes away from risk factors towards a model based on coping and resilience. The psychosocial model focuses on 'protective factors' and the resourcefulness of individuals, families, and communities, and often works on a collectivist level. For an individual, it builds upon strengths, uses normalising structures to provide stability and routine, and recognises the importance of supportive factors in the environment (parental, familial, spiritual, cultural, and social). In this approach the *relationship* between the individual, his/her peers, the family, the community, the infrastructure, the culture, and setting is important. This model takes into account the constant interplay and exchange between the individual's internal world and his/her external environment.

Within the psychosocial model, access to art-making and other forms of creativity encourages the development of an individual's imagination, spontaneity, and a sense of identity; it also activates protective factors and the ability to cope, enabling individuals, families, and communities to build on resilience.

Agency; Coping strategies that use dreams and art-making; Psychosocial approach; Social action art therapy; Social inclusion; Training module in the sensitive use of art for non-art therapists; Trauma

Resonance: LR

This word has roots in the Old French *résoner*, meaning to resound or to ring again. In art psychotherapy groups, members often unknowingly influence one another and synchronously produce images with similarities. Having been intent on their own making and not consciously aware of others' work, recognition of this relationship may come as a surprise (or a shock). The phenomenon is discussed in 'Resonance in Art Groups' by Roberts (1983).

Resonance, a term used in group analytic psychotherapy as well as in arts therapies, describes relational experiences arising from unconscious interpersonal communication. This can be linked with Jung's notion of the 'collective unconscious' (Jung, 1961: 160) and Bion's concept of 'valency, an instantaneous, involuntary combination' (Bion, 1961: 153) inspired by innate human sociability. Writing about music therapy, Bunt unpacks the origins of group participation in the arts in tribal ritual, describing the combination of rhythm, harmony, physical movement, 'inner state of flow and resonance' (Bunt, 1994: 70), which, together with emotional and spiritual communion, make up a whole collective experience. Art-making shares this history as an element of the complex social matrix, where gods are appealed to and mutual support engendered.

It may also be seen as a manifestation of the transference between group members that is mediated by the images. Drawing on Foulkes and Anthony (1965), McNeilly (2006: 38) calls resonance 'the cardiovascular and nervous system of the group body or matrix'. The effect is that resonance makes the group more than the sum of its parts, rather like the moment when the individual voices in a choir blend to a spine-tingling and complex chord.

Group matrix in visual form; Group (six entries)*; Symbols and collective imagery in group analytic art therapy*

Retention of artwork by client: MEd

There are occasions when it is advisable for the client to retain their artwork, because it will keep on working for them.

Art as a discourse

Reverie: KJ

A quiet state of being in which images, bodily sensations, thoughts, words, sounds, or ideas wander in and out of awareness without any particular aim or intention.

The capacity for reverie is an important aspect of subjective development, creativity, and the therapeutic process. Bion elaborated the importance of maternal reverie in child development (Bion, 1967b). When mother developed a calm, open receptiveness to the infant's projections she was experienced as a containing object. This reverie provided a limit, which allowed the development of reflective capacities and meaning in the infant. Where anxiety or depression caused a failure of reverie, the child imagined the maternal container 'stripping' meaning from their experience, resulting in a breakdown of development (Bion, 1967a; Case, 2005a; Winnicott, 1986).

Identifying reverie with the mother perpetuates a stereotypical division of qualities between male and female and privilege a heterosexual norm. Reverie in the therapeutic space requires the therapist to move fluidly across identifications in the transference between adult and infantile sexualities (bisexual, homoerotic, and male/female cross-identifications and cross-dressings), as suggested by Dudley (2001), O'Conner and Ryan (1993), and Hogan (2003). We still do not understand how the maternal dyad and the oedipal triangle (located in family patterns lived in particular class, national, ethnic, racial, or sexual identities and structures) affect the capacity for reverie. Art therapists need to develop their capacity for social reveries or they may become a container stripping the client of meaningful reverie.

The invitation to make art in the art therapy studio provides a tranquil, protected environment in which reverie might begin. Case and Dalley (2006) describe the art therapist's reverie about group members. Sibbett links reverie to Winnicott's state of relaxed creative play and reports comments from clients about how important reverie had been in their art therapy in cancer care (Sibbett, 2005a).

Absorption in art-making; Bachelard; Containment and counter-transference; Person-centred approach to art therapy; Pleasure; Studios; Supervision; Time disappears; Unconscious and art-making in brief work

Review with images: CH

Periodically the art therapist suggests to the patient that a session be dedicated to reviewing the therapy, and because the image plays such a central role in the therapeutic relationship it makes sense to address the review through the images made in previous sessions with the patient:

> They looked again at their pictures and talked about their experience. The images evoked memories and many feelings, and they talked often with extraordinary insight and honesty, and in great detail. Images can hold their meaning and reveal more only when the person is ready to see. Words in contrast, are easily forgotten.
>
> (Dalley et al., 1987: 157)

'. . . when an image is newly exposed it needs space. The artist needs to get to know it before she can talk about it. She needs to find the words that fit' (Schaverien, 1987: 85). Matisse told Apollinaire in 1907: 'I found myself or my artistic personality by looking over my earliest works. They rarely deceive' (Matisse, 1907, in Flann, 1978: 31). A young man in a therapeutic community returned some months later for a session of reviewing all his images. He selected one image from the many. It was a large messy explosive painting: 'This is when I *sicked* it all out on the paper and I didn't feel so bad after that.'

The process of review can promote healing, integration, and therapeutic change.

Case studies; Looking and visual research; Mutative metaphor; Reflection; Time-related processing

Rhyme: PB

Rhyme is to do with a certain type of artistic understanding – of image, pattern, form, composition; of the articulations of space, mass, colour, line, tone; of facture; of rhyme-making, as in 'image-making'. Rhyme pertains to elements of time – pace, poise, holding, and releasing. It encompasses the attitudes of both maker and viewer: suspended judgement; tolerance of unlikely juxtapositions; reaching for far-fetched allusions; savouring chaotic ensembles. Also, rhyme pertains to media. Mere materials are transformed, rhymed into potent carriers of meanings – as denotations, representations, expressions, and communications. Ordinary stuff, common substances such as paints, papers, clays, are coaxed into outperforming themselves. Unlikely materials are recruited into service as art media because of their image-making potential. Scouring-pads, string, grass, chewing gum, sweet papers, any old items of garbage have served as vehicles able to effect transformation in the lives of those who have used them. Since in Britain the majority of art therapists are graduates in the visual arts, they will be instilled with knowledge and experience of such features of artistic rhyme. These will have been recognised as potent, possibly from childhood on, fashioned and refined through study and practice, now to be re-shaped into instruments to be placed at the disposal of clients and patients. This is so even when we are not aware of the extent of tacit knowledge of rhyme, built-in as part of the visual culture we often import as transferable skills from our art-making into therapeutic practice.

This entry was adapted from Byrne (2002).

Art and materials; Facture; Knowledge of materials; Reason; Reverie;
Sculptural materials; Spatial awareness and empathy; Transferable skills

Rites of Passage: TD

An exhibition at the Tate in 1996, called 'Rites of Passage', consisted of images, objects and installations which marked passages of time and made statements about the future. 'Rites of passage', an anthropological term, describes the ceremonies which mark significant changes in life in a ritualised way. This exhibition proposed that contemporary art, by responding to key experiences of life, can be analogous to such ceremonies. The art is preoccupied with states of change and with related states of identity, much of it absorbed with the greatest change of all – death. There is the use of the art objects as containers to express these ideas. I was struck by how much these images were expressive of the essence of our work as therapists, in the sense that the feelings/anxieties/preoccupations were so clearly given meaning in these pieces.

(Dalley, 2000: 96)

Complexity and pain contained in an artwork; Living and dying;
Remembering and forgetting; Rhyme; Ritual

Ritual: DW

... The roots of art therapy might also be seen as lying in the traditional rituals and practices of rural communities that have largely died out during the twentieth century in Europe. That is to say, involvement in making art objects for a specific communal purpose may have served a useful function in integrating an individual with the group . . .

Therapeutic activity has its roots in mythical, ritual, religious and sacred spheres, as well as in social practices that integrate the person into a coherent cultural milieu, which through linking every individual to the group gives meaning to each life. Our museums are full of prehistoric and Neolithic objects which have served these integrative aims. They are imbued with a powerful aesthetic.

(Waller, 1998: 93–94)

European art therapy; Evolutionary psychology and art-making;
Evolutionary psychology and cave art; Rhyme; Rites of Passage

Rodin and drawing: SAVL

The French sculptor Rodin depicted the human form mostly in the fluidity of cast bronze, to express the emotional power, predicaments, and pain of human experience. He also made dynamic, figurative drawings *for their own sake*, as well as to work out his sculptural ideas.

Drawing has sometimes been demoted to a lesser visual art form – a 'sketch' or preparatory art medium – yet for a sculptor, too, drawing is *the* most fundamental visual art form. Therefore it is perhaps unsurprising that the *tools* offered in art therapy are often, initially, drawing materials. Drawing for its own sake is a means for exploring and expressing perceptions, looking and learning spatially.

Drawing; Drawing a line

Romanticism: CW

Michael Edwards (1989) in his chapter 'Art Therapy and Romanticism' discusses the historical antecedents of ideas about healing through artistic imagery. He points to the Romantic Movement, which for a time during the late eighteenth and early nineteenth centuries touched the arts, philosophy, and even medicine (Ellenberger, 1970). 'The Movement embraced a positive conception of the imagination, gave to dreaming and fantasies the status of creative source-material, and to artistic representation of inner experience a new validity' (Edwards, 1989: 81). Although the ideas of art used in art therapy are no longer exclusively from within a romantic tradition, many aspects of the tradition resonate with its practice. Romanticism in art was characterised by a belief in the primacy of artistic freedom, originality, and self-expression. It upheld the power of imagination, subjectivity, and an affinity with nature, in opposition to the principles of Classical Art. Often the materials used reflected nature: oil, pigment, clay, earth, and stone. Many artists are associated in the popular imagination with Romanticism, including Blake, Byron, Constable, Freidrich and Delacroix, Fuseli, Goya, Shelley, and Turner.

Aesthetic philosophy in art therapy; Art and materials in contemporary aesthetic philosophy; Blake; Géricault and physiognomy; Mind-forged manacles; Muse and duende

Sanctuary: EW

Dictionary definitions include: holy place; consecrated building; place of safety and protection; place where birds or animals are left undisturbed; place of peaceful privacy; asylum; haven; protection; retreat; shelter.

This sanctuary might simply be experienced in terms of the therapy room being a safe space. This might be the first real experience of a safe space in which one can choose, or not, to begin to engage with issues and their process. One may, in consequence, begin the cautious process of re-connecting or connecting more strongly with the wounded self and soul.

Portable Studio; Process; Studios; Temenos

Sand: CC

What of sand, water, and ready-made objects as a medium of artistic expression? Sand and water can be formed into objects and can be used for play materials like clay. They cannot be transformed by fire, but they can return to their original state, which can be punched, cut, sifted, wetted sculpted, hollowed, and shaped. It can be thrown and reconstituted in the sand-tray ready for use. It can be swamped under water and return over night, dry ready to be used. It survives attack, which is a useful quality for a medium to have in therapy. It can also have a silky, delicate, sensuous feel, running smooth, moveable. It can encourage and give room for a state of reflection or waking dream, of for the business of building and construction. Like any other art medium, sand and water and objects can be non-verbal way of thinking.

(Case, 1987: 61–62)

Art and materials in contemporary aesthetic philosophy; Clay; Peat; Simplicity of materials; Terracotta

Scapegoat transference: JS

This is a form of transference specific to forms of art psychotherapy or psychotherapy where art plays a role with the therapeutic relationship. The scapegoat transference is a consequence of the embodiment of a feeling state in the artwork (see diagrammatic and embodied images) and is a form of unconscious transference of attributes and states through which a picture, or three-dimensional art object, may come to embody otherwise intolerable affects. Fragmented and split-off elements in the psyche may be unconsciously externalised and embodied in a picture. Then, as a form of scapegoat, there may follow an attempt to dispose of these by disposing of the picture. This is initially an unconscious act, lacking a symbolic dimension. With the passage of time and therapeutic interventions, including the safekeeping of the picture, the 'disposed of' affect is re-integrated. This may then be understood as a symbolic enactment and so the art object serves a positive function as a scapegoat. As a concrete object that embodies the transference, it may be understood to be a transactional object. This term was originally developed as a way of understanding the transference in art psychotherapy by Schaverien (1987, 1991) and derived from Cassirer (1955) and Frazer (1922).

Diagrammatic image; Embodied image; Scapegoat transference and projective identification; Transference

Scapegoat transference and projective identification: JS

When practising psychotherapists engage with the idea of the scapegoat transference the suggestion is, understandably, often made that what I am describing is merely a form of projective identification. The scapegoat transference, as I have discussed it, involves processes which include splitting and disposal, both fundamental aspects of projective identification. However, despite its similarity, this idea is based on a different type of understanding, drawn from anthropological researches on the one hand, and aesthetic theory on the other.

. . . Samuels (1993: 276–7) has pointed out that far from being a culturally neutral technical concept, projective identification is itself an image and, moreover, a highly culturally contingent one. The concept of projective identification rests on a whole set of given, cultural and political assumptions that propose a fundamental separateness as the basic state of affairs between people as far as communication is concerned. In projective identification something is thrown or hurled across an empty space, penetrating the other. Such an image or trend of imagery is inadequate when we come to consider the complicated psychological processes that affect the therapist and client as viewers of pictures. In circumstances where art exists, we need to recognise that there is a cultural realm to be considered.

(Schaverien, 1995a: 125–126)

Continuous projection and difficulties in symbolising; Empathy; Groups and organisations; Projective identification; Projective identification and empathy; Scapegoat transference

Schizophrenia

See *Psychosis*

Schools establishing art therapy: TBo

My own journey into the profession came as a consequence of working in schools as an environmental teacher–artist in inner-city London in the early 1980s. Children who were having difficulties in school found the art room a refuge and I witnessed the role of art in bringing a sense of well-being to an otherwise fraught school existence.

On completing the Art Therapy Diploma training in 1989 I began work in a Special School for children and adolescents with behavioural and emotional difficulties. I wrote my first paper in *Inscape: The Journal of the British Association of Art Therapists* in 1995 on an adolescent boy who had self-referred, wanting help in defending against being bullied. Through his artwork and use of metaphor his sense of self grew to the point at which he was able to find a means of self-protection.

It was here that I cut my teeth not only from a clinical perspective, but also in establishing an art therapy post with a clear pay structure; this took up time and energy. I was aware that there were many other lone art therapists out there in a similar predicament. With this in mind I set up the Art Therapy in Education (ATE) sub-group in 1992, together with Frances Prokofiev. Our aim was to introduce a benchmark that could replicate a step-by-step approach in 'setting up' in schools. Most jobs were not advertised and unless you had a teaching certificate art therapists found that they were embarking on an ongoing struggle for fair pay and working conditions that in some cases took years to establish or never materialised. Through the pooling of experience, the sub-group has become a network that contributes to and benefits those working in schools through the efforts of people like Hazel Redsull, an art therapist who gave a lot of time to establishing the work in many schools.

Adaptations of practice; Art therapy approaches for particular clients;
British Association of Art Therapists; Schools using art therapy; Third
period of British art therapy

Schools using art therapy: CW

Increasingly, art therapists are working in schools. The links between
education and art therapy are a part of the profession's origins (Waller,
1991) and a number of therapists have described their work in schools,
notably Prokofiev (1998) and Bobby Lloyd in lectures about work in
schools. A BAAT *Art Therapy in Education* leaflet (www.baat.org, 2007)
indicates that:

> Art therapy can help improve behaviour, raise achievement, encourage
> attendance, and help pupils take part more fully in school life.
>   The pupils who may benefit are those:
>
> - In danger of exclusion
> - Experiencing emotional and behavioural difficulties
> - With social and communication difficulties
> - Struggling with particular life events such as bereavement, changes
>   in family structure, and illness
> - Who are refugees or are seeking asylum
> - Who have suffered abuse, bullying or trauma
> - With learning difficulties or physical disabilities
> - With Autistic Spectrum Disorders
>
> These pupils may present as withdrawn or anxious, angry, depressed,
> moody, violent or disaffected (BAAT, 2007).
>
> Having an acknowledged therapeutic approach within a school raises
> staff awareness as to the importance of mental health in relation
> to learning. Such an approach can contribute towards a wider
> understanding of students' needs, helping to inform discussion and
> influence policy making.
>
> (Wellesby, 1998: 40)

Adaptations of practice; Adaptations of practice with adolescents;
Schools establishing art therapy

Scissors: CC

Children's struggles with aggressive impulses can be very evident when
using scissors. There are occasions when children who have been neglected

and abused by both parents cut up all their work. I have come to think of the blades as the sadistic linking of mother and father blades with the child's struggle with their own aggressive impulses. Internalisation of a good parental couple might lead to care for one's objects when cutting out. Klein (1932) has written about the sublimation of destructive feelings in fringing, where an aggressive impulse can be given expression in an acceptable way. Cutting up one's things in therapy can also enact 'feeling in pieces'. Cutting up a picture or aspects of a picture can also be isolating and separating into parts so that connections cannot be made (Case, 2002, 2005a).

Acting out; Cutting up and cutting out; Images used to convey the 'action' of violence; Sublimation theories in psychoanalysis

Sculptural materials: JM

The qualities of, say, stone, wood, metal, and clay determine how a form evolves. With stone there is a sense of resistance, a slow paring down to form; wood also involves taking down to something, or in construction a sense of building and connecting. Metal suggests the transforming fires; casting, welding, etc., a sense of taking shape and giving structure. Clay, perhaps the most versatile, can range from a sticky paint density, through vessels and modelled forms, to more complex mould-making. These materials and methods can have a powerful resonance with the evolution of the unconscious image.

Bourgeois; Clay; Peat; Rhyme; Sand; Sculpture; Size of materials; Terracotta; Three-dimensional form

Sculpture: SAVL

Sculpture's most important quality is its three-dimensional physicality and ability to relate immediately, in the round, to its surroundings and to whoever encounters it. Assembled sculptures are a 'putting together' and a 'making fit'; the process sometimes involving a 'pulling apart'. Constructing something is both an external making and an internal mending.

In the same way as the spaces in-between (the voids) are defined by the material and the physical form, the 'shape' of the space between people may define and speak of the 'form' of their relationship.

Bourgeois; Negative space; Sculptural materials; Three-dimensional form

Sculpture citing Moore: CW

'Sculpture is an art of the open air. Daylight, sunlight is necessary to it. I would rather have a piece of my sculpture put in a landscape, almost any landscape, than in or on the most beautiful building I know' (Henry Moore, on an open-air plaque: Yorkshire Sculpture Park).

Sculptural materials; Sculpture; Size of materials; Three-dimensional form; Vantage points

Second period of British art therapy history: CW

The first period had been characterised by a 'wholesome' approach to the plight of the mentally ill; with the second period in the 1960s came challenges to accepted ideas about what constituted madness. A characteristic of this period was a powerful sense of the need for change: '. . . 1968 was a year in which revolt shook at least three major governments and produced a wave of hope among young people living under many others' (Harman, 1988: vii).

The emerging humanistic schools of therapy were prevalent, as were existential ideas and social psychiatry, which seemed to foster the anti-psychiatry movement. The influence of psychoanalysis became more popularly acknowledged (in part because of its adoption by the advertising departments of large American companies).

All of these developments informed the ways in which art therapists felt able to work. The enthusiasm of the second period seemed to confirm and deepen what art therapists had been proposing during the first period. In this second period art therapists may not have understood all that was brought to them, but they respected the people who shared their art work and really paid attention to it and to them.

However, there are few descriptions of what art therapists actually did from that time. Some art therapy literature referred to the idea of a creative illness: 'There were some uncomfortable paradoxes – one person's work was drawn with extraordinary refinement and conviction at times when he was most ill, turning to pleasant but very ordinary little flower paintings in recovery' (Edwards, 1978: 12).

Art made in psychiatric hospitals was exhibited at the Oxford Museum of Modern Art in 1978. In the catalogue *The Inner Eye*, art therapists Peter Byrne, Michael Edwards, John Henzell, and Diana Halliday wrote about art therapy, posing the question whether or not the work made by clients is art or not.

From the same catalogue: 'The art therapy department in a psychiatric hospital is often an asylum within an asylum' (Holtom, 1978: 40). This was an anti-psychiatry position that often included a posturing approach to fellow psychiatric workers, one not demonstrating much understanding for them. During this period the families of psychiatric patients often felt blamed.

The ideas of Laing and Goffman were influential in art therapy training. However, although many people working in psychiatry at the time were 'anti-psychiatry', the period was one in which social psychiatry precepts were developed, much respected, and used. The mix of influences acting upon psychiatry meant that art therapists working with psychiatric teams were supported and their work flourished. In the third period, they found themselves on picket lines, cooperating with other psychiatric workers protesting about service cuts.

Advertising; First and Third periods of British art therapy history (two entries)*; Inner art; Laing and Goffman; MacGregor; Psyche-social; Seeing and looking; Simon, Rita; Social psychiatry; Withymead*

Secondary handicap: BD and RT

Sinason (1992) contributed an important re-working of Winnicott's proposition regarding the mirroring interaction between mother and infant (Winnicott, 1971b). Sinason extends the concept whereby the infant gets to know herself through the dynamic reflection of the mother's gaze and ponders the impact upon the infant where a disability co-exists. She proposes that the infant may internalise the shameful, rejecting, disappointed gaze of the traumatised parent. This conflict is resolved, as Winnicott suggests, by the infant shifting the perceptual position from being before mother's eyes to behind, in the search for what might be required to elicit the approving gaze (see Damarell, 1999). Sinason (1992) proposes that this leads to the phenomenon of the 'handicapped smile' that avoids the psychic pain first encountered during the mirror phase. It is in this area of 'secondary handicap' (Sinason, 1992) that many art therapists practise.

Emotional life for men and women with learning disabilities; Female gaze; In the box; Stupidity; Winnicott

Seeing and looking: Phenomenological perspectives: CW

The experience of *seeing* is of vital importance, and perhaps this is one of art therapy's most important contributions to general therapy even to phenomenology itself, because art therapy pays attention to the authentic experience in a twofold way. First, clients in art therapy produce an art expression that is direct experience; then they experience its appearance in their eyes and in their immediate consciousness, and this a second direct experience. In the second experience, however, they need some help, for they must learn how to look in order to see all that can be seen in their art expression . . . Slowly I began to understand the truth in Merleau Ponty's statement that '. . . to look at an object is to inhabit it and from this inhabitation to grasp all things' (Ponty, 1962: 68). This is a phenomenologist's way of looking in order to see, seeing with intentionality.

(Betensky, 1995: 5–6)

Most references cited in Betensky's book are from the second period of British art therapy history, although British art therapists refer to phenomenology in the third period and the contemporary period (e.g. Byrne, 2002; Henzell, 1994; Hills, 2007, McClelland, 1993).

Contemporary period of art therapy; Second period of British art therapy history; Sense of self

Self-harm: DN

Concepts about aggression as a component of depression are useful when trying to make sense of acts of deliberate self-harm and self-destructive, addictive, and para-suicidal behaviour. When working with people who may also have a depressive illness it can be difficult to get hold of aggressive feelings, which may be enacted, deeply buried, or masked. According to Freud (1917), in depression it is the aggressive feelings towards the lost 'object' that are turned towards the self.

However, if these 'self-reproaches' can be sought and relocated in the image, the therapeutic work of bringing what was hidden to the surface can continue. Difficult feelings can then be more easily accessed, contained, and 'worked through' (Freud, 1915) within the therapeutic relationship. Often the artwork does not express obvious feelings of aggression but those of depression. Vigorous defences against the aggression might be made.

One woman who was hospitalised for many years with an entrenched depression was under close observation due to her obsession with killing herself. In a ward group, she was gradually able to recognise and acknowledge, through her imagery, her extreme anger towards both her husband and her deceased mother. It was eventually possible to discharge her safely to her marital home and regular attendance of a long-term community-based art psychotherapy group. In the group, the anger was expressed in less destructive ways.

Aggression; Anger and art therapy; Cutting out and cutting up; Shame; Working through

Sense of self: Phenomenological, psychological, and social (nested) selves: PB

It might be useful to conceive of the artist (and the art therapist and client) as operating with three nested 'selves' – the phenomenological self nesting inside the psychological self, and both nesting inside the social self. The first of these receives and operates with sensations – colour, shape, form; the second with feeling – pleasure, repulsion, anger; and the third with thinking – attributing, sorting, appraising. The type of process varies too; the first is heuristic, the second is hermeneutic, and the third semiotic.

To explain, first there is the artist's (client's) 'existential' heuristic engagement in image-making, where W. B. Yates' question: '. . . how can we know the dancer from the dance?' applies as they immerse themselves in experiential creation. In terms of their nested selves, here the phenomenological self is trusting in the creative process itself.

In cultural terms the viewer and artist are co-creating meaning. Fruitful efforts have also been made to place such hermeneutically derived material/ processes within scientific frameworks of reliability and validity, for example, Ricoeur's (1979, cited in Byrne, 2002) clarification of relationships between *Verstehen* (understanding) and *Erklaren* (explanation) – in everyday terms, 'guessing' and 'validation'.

It is worth noting that Rose points to research strategies that encompass the audience and the social (Rose, 2001).

Aesthetic philosophy in art therapy; Heuristic research; Postmodernist art therapy; Reason; Rhyme; Seeing and looking; Transcendent function; Transferable skills

Shame: MAm

Dictionary definitions of shame include feelings of humiliation or distress and/or a sense of loss of respect or esteem. On shame experienced by the victim or survivor in relation to sexual abuse or targeting and victimisation, Joyce Carol Oates describes 'the female terror of becoming an object of male sexual desire. Shame is the emotion that most effectively blocks the memory. Amnesia is the great solace, the most available form of self-protection' (Oates, 1998: 199).

'. . . shame can be directly transmitted to a victim by a look, a posture, or any act of abusive contempt and thereby prevent disclosure as effectively as any verbal threat' (Ambridge, 2001a: 83).

On shame in the counter-transference:

> Shame is inherent in sexual abuse. Indeed, sexual abuse is the ultimate shame, and probably that is its purpose – to transfer projectively

shame from the abuser to the victim . . . The affect of shame tends to block empathy. Therapists do not want to feel this most toxic of emotions. If we empathise with the abused patient we experience shame vicariously . . .

(Mollon, 1996: 54)

Abuse; Gaze and glance; Male gaze

Sharing paper: MLieb

The shared piece of paper is a metaphor for many different kinds of sharing: territory, projects, offices, resources, and so on. Pairs are asked to share a piece of paper in silence, in any way they choose (Liebmann, 2000).

Group work models; Squiggle game

Sickness/health: MW

To embrace the insights born of experiences of illness and sickness can result in a new vision. Suddenly the healthy and the sick are no longer two completely separate categories of people, staring at one another over an unbridgeable chasm. Rather, experiences of illness and wellness turn out to be interdependent.

(Webster, 2002: 69)

Metaphors and images of illness vary with socio-cultural grouping and the body part affected, powerfully influencing interactions between family members and health-care providers.

(Altschuler, 1997: 19)

Illness can be viewed as a series of disruptive events, during which the structures and forms of knowledge that underpin daily life are changed.

(Altschuler, 1997: 132)

Cradle to grave; Health; Liminality; Living and dying; Mental health

Simon, Paul-Max: CW

MacGregor points to the work of the little known French psychiatrist Paul-Max Simon as one of the first to make a study of the art of the mental patients in his care. He is concerned to correct the erroneous impression that Lombroso's investigations preceded those of Simon (MacGregor, 1989: 103–115). Simon was writing at the end of the nineteenth century and his contribution to the study of the art made by mental patients is found in two papers: 'L'imagination dans la folie [The imagination during madness]' (1876) and 'Les écrits et les dessins des aliénés [The writings and drawings of mental patients]' (1888). MacGregor applauds Simon's work because of the quality of descriptions that pay close attention to detail. Also, as an 'artist himself, Dr Simon was less inclined to associate creativity with pathology' (MacGregor, 1989: 106). He tended rather to see everything patients did, their choice of dress, their imaginative descriptions, and their artwork, as attempts to communicate. He felt that it is 'the imagination of the patient which forms the subject of our investigation' (cited in MacGregor, 1989: 110). He also had the humility to acknowledge that he recognised aspects of his own reality in some parts of his patients' artwork. This was highly unusual for the period during the second half of the nineteenth century; it was more usual to make clear distinction between sanity and insanity.

Simon also published a study of dreams a long time before Freud: *Le Monde du Rêves [The World of Dreams]* (1882).

History of psychiatry's use of art; MacGregor

Simon, Rita: DW

> Apparently the climate of opinion towards art in hospitals was very favourable after the war. Rita Simon felt that Adrian Hill's work had been significant in producing such a climate, together with the approach to group psychotherapy for traumatised service men and the search within the health service for improved rehabilitation schemes for psychiatric patients following the war. As a member of staff at the Social Psychiatry Centre, she had continued to work with groups in an informal setting, entering into her own analysis as a way of better understanding her own and the patients' psychology. In this way she was different from both Adrian Hill and Edward Adamson, who expressed themselves not interested in this aspect of art therapy.
>
> . . . She continued to work and to write on art therapy while in Ireland, especially in the field of art therapy with children and the elderly, and on changes of style during art therapy.
>
> (Waller, 1991: 58–59)

Rita Simon (1921–2008) published two books: *The Symbolism of Style: Art as Therapy* (1992) and *Symbolic Images in Art as Therapy* (1997). These publications have been influential in Northern Ireland and they speak to an aspect of the contemporary period of art therapy that is concerned with the materiality of the art made. She was, however, mainly practising during the first and second periods of art therapy in Britain.

Contemporary period of art therapy; First and second periods of British art therapy history (two entries)*; War wounds*

Simplicity of materials: CW

'Simplicity of materials may result in more inner vitality' (Lyddiatt, 1972: 15).

Single-case experimental designs: AJG

Individual experimental case studies ($N=1$) are specifically designed to measure the outcomes of a therapy. They require controlled conditions (i.e. a consistent environment and therapeutic approach) so that the treatment can be tested specifically for its effectiveness and be systematically replicated with other individual clients in the same conditions. The entire transaction is therefore, from the outset, designed as an experiment with the client undergoing various, standard tests that measure behaviour, symptoms, social functioning, and so on, before and after the treatment. This is known as an ABA design, with A being the baseline tests and B being the treatment. Tests can also be repeated at different points during a defined follow-up period. Tests can be conducted by staff other than the art therapist, or the therapist can be involved in their administration at the beginning and the end of therapy or on a week-by-week basis. Change can also be measured indirectly, for example in schools via standard evaluations of educational attainment before and after art therapy. Change is evaluated using statistical analysis of the tests and also simple graphs (e.g. of mood change throughout the therapy). Outcomes can also be accompanied by narrative description and visual material that documents the therapeutic process.

Case studies; Qualitative research; Quantitative research

Size of materials: CW

> There is a right physical size for every idea . . . a carving may be several times over life size and yet be petty and small in feeling – and a small carving only a few inches in height can be given the feeling of huge size and monumental grandeur, because the vision behind it is big.
>
> (Henry Moore, 1937, cited in Chipp, 1968: 596)

Knowledge of materials; Simplicity of materials

Social action art therapy: CW

Social action is part of the aspiration of many mental health workers from all disciplines, because they see the damaging effects of life circumstances and stigma (prejudice). Throughout its history art therapy has been practised in ways that are motivated by improving conditions for clients. Nevertheless, it is not straightforward to be clear about the differences between politics, therapy, and social work, and what they mean for practice.

Examples of art therapy as a form of social action in the contemporary period can be seen in the work of art therapists with unemployed teenagers (e.g. Pugh, Atkins, and Turner, personal communications), with refugees (Hills, 2007; Kalmanowitz and Lloyd, 2005); and in conflict-torn areas of the world (there are an increasing number); social action could even describe aspects of the work of art therapists in schools. In these examples, parts of the therapeutic work are adapted to accommodate the dramatic circumstances of clients' lives and parts of the work seem to cross into the territory of social action.

Frances Kaplan (2007) collected a range of edited chapters, largely by American art therapists (but including Marian Liebmann from Britain), with the title *Art Therapy and Social Action*:

> Some people are still waiting to be convinced that *art* and *therapy* go together . . . *social action art therapy* is something of a contradiction in terms. After all, art therapy endeavours to facilitate inner, individual change and social action art therapy strives to make outer collective change . . .
>
> a succinct yet simplistic definition . . . social action art therapy operates outside the usual box of individual illness (mental or physical) and addresses societal problems by providing services to perpetrators, victims (potential or actual), or people who work with members of these groups. However, . . . *social action art therapy is this and more*.
>
> (Kaplan, 2007: 12–13)

Poverty; Psychiatry, psychoanalysis, poverty, and class;
Professionalization; Social inclusion

Social, economic, and cultural context for adolescence: AMB

British and European social scientists have agreed (Coleman and Hendry, 1999; Coles, 1997; Macdonald, 1997) that adolescence is a transitional period between childhood and adulthood, but there is no consensus about the sub-stages and ages of the developments within this phase. Young people, from the twentieth century onwards, experience an extension of adolescence, and delays of entry into adult functioning are prevalent. Puberty may start earlier, with consequent awareness of sexuality, adolescent feelings, behaviours, and culture. Yet entry into working life takes longer, which means that many young people are staying in the parental home with continued economic dependence into their twenties. Adolescence may commence as early as 9 or 10 years and continue until after 21 years (Coleman and Hendry, 1999: 8). European studies (Coles, 1997) conclude that the transition has become pluralised and fragmented across all countries in Europe.

Disadvantages impacting upon young people might include changes in family structure, growing up in and leaving care, migration, poverty, social exclusion, employment opportunities, racism, and political change. With all the attendant societal consequences, those severely disadvantaged 'are at risk of becoming permanently marginalised and growing up without any hope' (Coleman and Hendry, 1999: 9).

Paying attention to the individual's developmental context and recognising resources and vulnerabilities is fundamental in understanding young people's needs (Coleman and Hendry, 1999). Using a 'focal model' to view normal adolescent development is suggested by Coleman and Hendry because it allows for maximum flexibility of how young people, as agents in their own development, approach developmental tasks without fixing ideas as to age or sequence, as this may vary cross-culturally.

Agency; Adaptations of practice with adolescents; Child development; Outcomes for looked-after children; Psychosocial approach; Social psychiatry

Social inclusion: CW

> A socially inclusive approach includes recovery-oriented practice, an emphasis on social outcomes and participation, and attention to the rights of people with mental ill health, as well as to citizenship, equality and justice, and stigma and discrimination . . . This can have benefits for service users, professionals and carers, in addition to wider economic and social benefits.
>
> (Royal College of Psychiatrists, 2009: 2)

Recovery is taken to mean social recovery and not necessarily complete 'clinical' recovery, and this is an area to which art therapists continue to contribute. The social inclusion agenda is one adopted by governments of most persuasions internationally across political spectrums. The first position statement in Britain was included in the 'Mental Health and Social Exclusion Report' (Social Inclusion Unit, 2004).

Social exclusion refers to the extent to which individuals are unable to participate in key areas of economic, social and cultural life. The emphasis here is on non-participation arising from constraint, rather than choice . . .

Social exclusion is an avoidable reality in the daily lives of many people with mental health problems or intellectual disabilities. These people are among the most marginalised and stigmatised groups in our society. There is clear evidence that they may be excluded both because they have inadequate material resources and because they are unable to participate in economic or socially valuable activities. They may be isolated and excluded from social relations and the wider community, and excluded from basic civil and political processes. Importantly, they may also be excluded from basic health and social services. These social disadvantages are associated with both physical and mental health inequalities. Disadvantage in early life increases the likelihood of disadvantage in later life; disadvantage may also be transmitted across generations.

(Royal College of Psychiatrists, 2009: 1)

Access to art; Contemporary period of art therapy; Family work; Loneliness; Looked-after children; Power; Psyche-social; Psychosis and art therapy; Psychosocial approach; Rehabilitation; Resilience and the psychosocial model; Social action art therapy

Social psychiatry: CW

This model considers the relationships between individuals and society and the ways in which people's attitudes, values, and behaviours are acquired, organised, and changed through social interaction, social influence, and the social construction of knowledge. The model tries, where possible, to evade explanations relying on ideas about individual pathology alone. A social psychiatry perspective developed throughout the world after the Second World War and strengthened during the social and political upheavals of the late 1960s and 1970s.

As economic conditions got harder during the OPEC crisis (1973), the World Bank told the Wilson government to cut public sector spending and as a result a social psychiatry perspective diminished in Britain, although the ethos was retained in many European and all Scandinavian countries.

Although it is often hard to ignore the social economic circumstances that shape a client's life, it is unusual now to hear these discussed routinely in psychiatric teams in Britain. There is research evidence to suggest that rehabilitative efforts during the periods of social psychiatry (the 1960s and early 1970s) were successful (e.g. Cook and Wright, 1995; Fryers et al., 2000; Rutz, 2006; Warner, 1985). Art therapy in Britain (at that time in its second historical period of development) became established during the era of social psychiatry.

In countries that spend a greater proportion of their GDP on health, social psychiatry approaches have continued. Pilgrim and Rogers (2005) suggest that we have just passed through the decade of the brain in psychiatry, but that the prospects for social psychiatry approaches in Britain remain challenging. They wryly summarise the ideological tensions at play:

> A more optimistic scenario would require concessions on both sides. Psychiatry would need to admit its lack of reflexive capacity to understand its own theory and practice, as contentious socio-political phenomena. This would mean a re-engagement with debates about the role of psychiatry in society and the profession's reified diagnostic categories. In this respect the newer 'critical psychiatrists' who have not been ready recruits to the traditional cause of social psychiatry, are likely to play a central role. Sociologists would need to rediscover epidemiology and shed the anti-realism of post-modernism. They may discover that it is possible to be empirical without necessarily being empiricist.
>
> (Pilgrim and Rogers, 2005: 319)

Contemporary period of art therapy; Moral treatment; Postmodernist art therapy; Resilience and the psychosocial model; Social, economic, and cultural context for adolescence   -

Spatial awareness and empathy: LG

Spatial awareness is 'an ability to perceive space and modify it by thinking' (Salminen, 2005: 254; see also Gardner, 1983). In my work as an art therapist I have the strong impression of this being one of the most central areas of sensibility in my understanding of patients.

The perception of space in images and artworks is not only visual, but also multi-sensory. If we can allow ourselves to be saturated by the spatial qualities of the artwork, we receive understanding that is not narrative. This seems to matter in understanding the patient's situation.

The same spatial awareness or intelligence operates in our meetings with patients; we are conscious of where they place themselves and how they move.

Bachelard; Empathy; Rhyme; Seeing and looking; Trauma and the aesthetic dimension

Spontaneous art: TD

> . . . spontaneous art is similar to the processes of free association. It requires that 'one imagine and depict what is uppermost in one's mind and this demands both the suspension of habitual defence and a high degree of moral courage and self discipline' (Kramer, 1980: 9). However, as Kramer points out, spontaneous, expressive use of art materials is not 'untrammelled scribbling and messing' and the difference is comparable to that between aimless chatter and free association in psychoanalytic treatment. Although Freud's somewhat ambivalent view of art and artists does not incorporate this idea of spontaneous expression, the processes involved in dreams are in many ways similar to those of art activity, particularly in relation to the expression of the unconscious. The activity of art uses many of the symbols and mechanisms of displacement, condensation, splitting, etc. which Freud defined in the study of the dream . . . However, there is an obvious difference which lies in the fact that art activity is a conscious process which gives concrete form to feelings, which are often unconscious . . . 'It may be that the analysis of art can continue where the analysis of the dream left off' (Ehrenzweig, 1967: 4).
>
> (Dalley, 1984: 2–3)

Art and sublimation; Dreams; Ehrenzweig; Free association; Kramer; Lyddiatt; Naumberg; Techniques of art therapy

Squiggle game: MLieb

This game was developed by D. W. Winnicott in his work with children. Working in pairs, one person does a squiggle and then swaps with a partner, who tries to make an image out of it.

Potential Space; Winnicott

Stone: MJR

Jung describes here how his relationship with stone reveals and connects him to the eternal part of himself:

> At such times (of brooding on God and more) it was strangely reassuring and calming to sit on my stone. Somehow it would free me of all my doubts. Whenever I thought that I was the stone, the conflict ceased. 'The stone has no uncertainties, no urge to communicate, and is eternally the same for thousands of years,' I would think, 'while I am only a passing phenomenon which bursts into all kinds of emotions,

like a flame that flares up quickly and then goes out.' I was but the sum of my emotions, and the 'Other' in me was the timeless imperishable stone.

(Jung, 1961: 59)

Clay; Paint; Peat; Sand; Terracotta

Stroke and trauma: DAM

To experience the trauma of acute stroke is to experience a sudden change in your physical and psychological being that you did not anticipate and over which you have no influence or control. In psychoanalytic terms this could be said to represent a traumatic impingement on our continuity of being (Bion, 1962b; Winnicott, 1965a), leaving us struggling to make sense of experience, which may be unsymbolisable or unspeakable (Bailly, 2003).

Our capacity to make sense of trauma depends in part on our pre-existing internal resources and in part on the support and receptivity of the environment around us (Erskine and Judd, 1994). With reliable support structures, the more aggressive feelings aroused will gradually give way to more depressive ones as the process of mourning begins. However, for some, the traumatic impact of stroke may also unconsciously resonate with previous traumas, making the recovery process even more problematic. The resulting difficulties might take the form of a secondary disability where the handicap is used in the service of self to protect it from unbearable memory of trauma (Sinason, 1992).

Art therapy is particularly appropriate for those with entrenched emotional and psychosocial difficulties who might struggle to use solely verbal therapies as a source of emotional and psychological help. Stroke patients are given the opportunity to explore the colours, textures, and forms of traumatic self-experience through engagement in a responsive dialogue with the art materials and the therapist (Michaels, forthcoming). This may facilitate the *formation of a narrative* and lead to greater understanding and awareness of what has and is happening (Michaels and Weston, 2007). A wide literature is relevant (Gardner, 1996; McDougall, 1989; Miller, 1993; Von Sass Hyde, 2002; Wisdom, 1997; Wolfe et al., 1996).

Adolescence and neurological research; Brain injury; Damage to mental health; Narrative; Neurological art therapy; Secondary handicap

Studios: CW

The use of the studio in contemporary settings continues to be articulated (e.g. Hyland Moon, 2002; Wood, 2001b).

The provision of a studio makes the nature of practice clearer on a number of levels. In showing a prospective client a studio we are able to give them a tangible indication of what they might be letting themselves in for . . .

It is a strange quirk of history that as community care began in the late 1980s and the early 1990s, most of the art therapy literature appeared that mentions the places used for practice (Greenwood and Layton, 1987; Schaverien, 1989; Case and Dalley, 1992; Wood, 1992; Waller, 1993). It is a rich literature, because it tries to describe how the substantial qualities of physical space and art materials can enable clients to have a place apart in which to locate their emotional distress.

There are also a number of inspiring accounts of art therapists using studios in work with children (Case, 1987, 1990; Arguile, 1990; Prokofiev, 1998). Studio rooms are often used graphically and sym-bolically by children, with them climbing and crawling all around the rooms . . .

(Wood, 2001a: 46)

This leads to a questioning of the current relevance of a studio art therapy approach. Our former ways of working as art therapists cannot simply be forced into the framework of today's reality. What is crucial, however, is that we refrain from making the assumption that since the old ways of doing studio art therapy are no longer practical, studio art therapy must be entirely obsolete. Though the literature is sparse in regard to the use of a studio approach in short-term settings, there are models that offer effective adaptations of studio concepts . . .

(Hyland Moon, 2002: 23, 29)

'Our soul is an abode. And by remembering "houses" and "rooms" we learn to abide within ourselves' (Bachelard, 1958: xxxvii).

Absorption in art-making; Access to art; Adamson; Adaptations of practice; Group process knowledge in art therapy; Mise-en-scene; *Psychosis and art therapy; Refractive transference; Reverie; Sanctuary;* Temenos

Stupidity: SSt

Valerie Sinason (1992) explores this word in relation to the stupefying impact of trauma. It has particular relevance to the experience of learning disability. In my clinical experience in this area, a blank, numb, stupid state is often expressed within the therapeutic relationship and experienced by therapists as an attack on their own capacity to think. The therapist can feel that they are in a foggy quagmire with a strong sensation of being stupid.

The image and the creative process have a profoundly important role to play in facilitating the client to contact aspects of themselves, aspects that are not frozen and numb. A process with fluidity and movement can then begin, connections can be made, and there is a possibility for thinking to become bearable.

Emotional life for men and women with learning disabilities; In the box; Secondary handicap

Styles of practice: CW

Schaverien (1994a) offers a consideration of technical factors in different forms of art therapy. The distinctions she makes between different practices named art therapy, art psychotherapy, and analytic art psychotherapy are largely concerned with the different use of transference. Distinctions such as these are useful in thinking about the appropriate forms of therapy for clients with differing needs. However, it is not so helpful to ascribe the terms to different practitioners. They provide a way of distinguishing a range of possible technical approaches. One art therapy practitioner may use several approaches.

Adaptations of practice; Art therapy approaches for particular clients; Evidence-based practice

Sublimation theories in art therapy: KJ

'The art therapist's attitude toward the concept of sublimation must fundamentally influence both practice and theoretical outlook' (Kramer, 1987: 40). Art therapists have taken up, re-worked sublimation, and emphasised the creation of the new in relation to the dynamics of the past, and in a way that is critical of reductive applications of the concept. The focus on the different qualities of the art object in art therapy in relation to sublimation emphasises sublimation as a process of transformation that links clinical practice and the social.

The American art therapist Kramer worked with a model of sublimation derived from Kris and American ego psychology, and through her concept of the 'third hand' she emphasised the relationship between the self, others, and society (Edwards, 2004; Kramer, 1987; Kramer and Alaine, 2000). Wadeson (1980) thought that the emphasis on sublimation in Kramer's work downplayed the role of relationship in the production of art in therapy. In her later work, Kramer saw Winnicott's transitional objects as precursors of sublimated art objects, providing a necessary stage before the mature defence of sublimation could become operative (Kramer, 1979). She saw art as an aspect of reparation towards the mother as a lost object and emphasised the important role of the mother in super-ego development, laying the foundations for later sublimation.

In Britain, Greenwood (1997) used the idea of sublimation as a mature defence in the context of working with psychosis. Weir (1987) and Levens (1989) took up the Kleinian notion of mourning the lost object. Levens develops the example of scribble and smearing pictures in art therapy to suggest the deterioration in the quality of the art object that can occur when sublimation breaks down. Case and Dalley (1992) outlined the development of sublimation within a critical framework that highlighted the ambivalence towards art arising from the links made by Freud between art and symptom. Hogan (2001) also criticised the relationship between art and psychopathology in psychoanalytic theory and highlighted the inferior status assigned to women in cultural production in theories of sublimation. She further criticised the limitations of an emphasis on the determinant role of internal mental states in the production of art, to the exclusion of historical and social processes (Hogan, 2001).

Kramer thought that the art therapist's role was to function as a benign super-ego, encouraging sublimation, but warned that we must beware of sublimation as salvation (Kramer, 1987).

Art and sublimation; Artists and reparation; Art-making as a defence; Ego mechanisms of defence; Feminist art therapy; Freudian symbols; Kramer; Reductive interpretation; Spontaneous art; Sublimation theories in psychoanalysis; Transitional object; Unconscious

Sublimation theories in psychoanalysis: KJ

Where Freud had emphasised the sexual drives and the decisive importance of the father in the formation of cultural ideals (Freud, 1923), Klein emphasised sublimation as a transformation of infantile anxieties relating to the mother, the death drive, and the fear of losing the good maternal object (Klein, 1986).

Segal (1991) developed sublimation as an aspect of the depressive position and reparation, which involved a giving up of phantasy and was always accompanied by the mourning of a loss. Sublimation allowed the creation of a new object, which restored the lost object in unconscious phantasy and brought something new into the world. She emphasised the importance of the reality sense for the artist in relation to their use of art materials and the ability to tolerate anxiety and conflict in successful sublimation (Segal, 1991). In her emphasis on the role of Thanatos, the death instinct in art and creativity, Segal opens a link between sublimation and aesthetic theories of the sublime (Segal, 1952). Stokes (1963) developed the link between successful sublimation and fantasies in relation to bodily processes, sibling relationships in the family, and social context.

Laplanche described sublimation as an essential element of psychoanalytic theory that nevertheless remains incoherent and undeveloped (Laplanche, 2002–2003; Laplanche and Pontalis, 1988). Examples are: the supposed weakness of the feminine super-ego, meaning that women are not as able to become involved in cultural production (Freud, 1923); essentialist theories of sexuality and the drive within the nuclear monogamous family (Freud, 1930; Klein, 1986; Winnicott, 1971b); and the political location of different cultural artistic traditions and practices (Freud 1923, 1930; Klein 1986). While French traditions in psychoanalysis share these theoretical problems, they offer a more culturally and historically located attempt to describe sublimation. Where Freud's original account emphasised the links between sublimation and the disease at the heart of cultural development, contemporary psychoanalytic accounts of sublimation suggest the role of pleasure and terror in the transformation of both the individual and the social in the service of delight.

Art and sublimation; Delight and disgust in the abject; Freudian symbols; Lacan; Psychoanalytic accounts of the unconscious; Scissors; Sublimation theories in art therapy; Super-ego

Sublime: KJ

The historical development of the concept has seen beauty (identified with bounded form, unity, and harmony) contrasted with the unlimited, indeterminate forms of the sublime. The contrast was gendered so that the feminine was beautiful, charming, and pleasing while the masculine was dark, powerful, and sublime. McEvilley (2001) criticises contemporary theorists for confusing the beautiful and the sublime, while feminists have criticised the sublime as a masculine theory and sought different forms of transcendence (Shaw, 2006).

It was not until the second edition of Case and Dalley's handbook (2006) that the sublime and the beautiful were discussed in art therapy in relation to Winnicott's object mother and environment mother, respectively. Also Maclagan (2001) discussed the sublime in the work of Barnet Newman, Mark Rothko, and in the general relationship between symbol and referent. Both psychoanalytic and art therapy theories suggest a bridge between the sublime as an aesthetic and philosophical concept and the sublime as it might erupt into clinical experience.

Aesthetic philosophy in art therapy

Super-ego: CW

Bettleheim (1982: 58) discusses the mistranslation of Freud's concept 'super-ego': 'a controlling and often over-controlling institution of the mind which is created by the person . . . out of inner needs and external pressures that have been internalized'. The literal translation of Freud's German is the 'above-I'. Bettleheim wonders if the use of the word super-ego became more commonly used than id and ego because:

> there has been no name for that which includes not just the 'conscience' – for this the old word did admirably well – but also that wider aspect of the psyche which comprises both its conscious and fairly reasonable controlling aspects and its unconscious, unreasonable, compulsive, punitive and persecutory aspects. In Freud's system, *the I*, [ego] *the it* [id] and *the above-I* [super-ego] are but different aspects of our psyche, each of them inextricably and permanently related to one another; they cannot be separated from each other except in theory.
>
> (Bettleheim, 1982: 58)

Ego and id; Sublimation theories (two entries)*; Unconscious*

Supervision: CW

Supervision of therapeutic work is sometimes described as 'clinical supervision'. This is to distinguish it from what happens in managerial supervision. Nevertheless, much art therapy practice is not in traditional 'clinical' settings. Its supervision generally involves a collaboration between supervisor and supervisee and uses a range of subjective, reality-based, and where possible evidence-based reflection.

Supervision in the profession shares many of the features of other forms of psychotherapy supervision: the differences include the attention given to artwork made by clients and the use of art-making by the art therapist as a way of reflecting on the work of therapy. The purposes of supervision are to help the therapist to sustain their capacity to think, give good attention, and not be overwhelmed by either the internal or external plight of the client. Case describes both therapy and its supervision as working with the whole image:

> . . . recalled images, present images, body changes, and feelings are all interconnected in a process of thinking . . . conscious reflection in the session; reverie and play between supervisor and supervisee . . . These all contribute and feed back into understanding the image at the centre of the relationship in art therapy and may lead to change in the therapist's conceptualisation and approach. My interest has been in the way that images encapsulate understanding that hovers on the edge of awareness and how, following the ideas of Damasio, we can uncover this 'non-verbal narrative of knowing' lying beneath the presented verbal account of a session.
>
> (Case, 2007: 113)

When supervision is working, it seems to help practitioners to sustain a sense of agency and it makes the benefits of standing back a little in order to pay attention apparent (Wood, 2007).

Agency; Art made by art therapists; Attachment framework; Balint groups and image consultation groups; Eating disorders: Themes-based art therapy groups in specialised teams; Heterosexism and the heterosexual lens; Intuition; Supervision; Therapists' engagement with their own art practice; Witness: When the client cannot 'speak'

Supportive psychotherapy: CW

Supportive psychotherapy is referred to in relation to art therapy by Greenwood.

> A definition is offered: "'supportive psychotherapy' is a long-term psychotherapy aimed at maximising the patient's strengths, restoring his psychological equilibrium and acknowledging, but attempting to minimise, his dependence on the therapist" (Hartland 1991: 214). The goal is to help patients function independently at their optimum level with minimum input from professional carers. The key feature in this is the provision of an ongoing consistent relationship, but it is a long and complex task in preserving a balance between this and encouraging the patient to move towards a position of greater independence. In supportive psychotherapy Hartland (1991) notes how the therapist needs an inexhaustible supply of patience and optimism, as rewards are not quick in contrast with patients with a stronger ego. Change, if any, will be slow.
>
> (Greenwood, 1997: 107)

Much of the work undertaken by art therapists in public sector settings is with clients who have complex needs and difficulties. Aspects of the work are grim because of the levels of poverty, deprivation, and uncertainty in the lives of their clients. Public sector clients young and old are likely to have difficult lives in difficult circumstances. As a result, they are often struggling with fraught relationships and psychological and economic pressures. In these circumstances, it is wise for a therapist to offer a 'supportive psychotherapeutic' approach, because this is what is most feasible for a client with few external life supports.

Adaptations of practice; Advice; Interpersonal learning in groups; Psychosis and art therapy; Resilience and the psychosocial model; Therapeutic care; Third period of British art therapy history

Sustaining the therapist in cancer care: CS

> A metaphor that emerged from my experience of the cumulative impact of being a companion to the dying was that of Hermes who acted as the guide of souls (psychopomp) to Charon who then ferried the dead across the river Styx to the Underworld and who is described as 'a warden of the crossing' (Virgil's Aeneid; 29–19 BC). Interestingly, Turner (1986: 35) notes that the etymology of the word 'experience' links to meanings of 'to fear' and 'to ferry'. Stein (1983) regards Hermes as the guide of souls through liminality or threshold situations. However, what is the impact on humans taking on such a role?
>
> It is important that art therapists and other healthcare staff acknowledge the impact of such repeating and cumulative experience. It is vital that self-care processes are normalized and encouraged in the realm of liminality . . .
>
> It would be important for healthcare staff dealing with liminality, and therefore susceptible to secondary liminality, to have particular training and support in managing acute, sustained and secondary liminality and its associated characteristics.
>
> (Sibbett, 2005a: 240)

Art made by art therapists; Liminality; Metaphor (three entries)*; Transference in palliative care*

Symbol: DJ

A primary definition of symbol is something 'conventionally regarded' as representing something else. The Oxford English Dictionary states that the linkage between the two is dependent on analogy or some other association and the 'thing' represented is more likely to be abstract (an idea or quality) than material. The bread and wine of the Eucharist are cited as symbolic of the body and blood of Christ. By this definition symbols are clearly both transpersonal and culturally specific, although 'symbol' should be distinguished from 'sign' because the form of the latter may be entirely arbitrary and its meaning is always fixed.

The use of symbols has a long history as a cultural product, and most especially in religion and art. This is unsurprising as the symbol is not subject to the limitations of language and can very directly convey the metaphysical or encapsulate a feeling.

It is important to recognise that the symbol does not equate to a simple or absolute meaning. Its import extends far beyond the literal or specific, will alter according to its context, and can encompass complex or contradictory ideas. This is particularly true of the most universal symbols: water, for example, can cleanse or drown.

Jung insists that the symbol is imbued with energy and an expression of something, as yet imprecisely known, that grabs our attention (Jung, 1977: 18).

Archetype; Freudian symbols; Life of a symbol; Metaphor (linguistic); Metaphor (visual); Symbolisation

Symbolic equation and symbolic representation: DN

Hanna Segal differentiated between symbolic representation and symbolic equation. '*Symbolic representation*, in which a true symbol is substituted in the place where the original had been; its special feature is that the symbol is recognised as having its own characteristics separate from that which it symbolizes' (Segal, 1950). However, 'In the symbolic equation the symbol *becomes* the original' (Segal, 1957). The symbol is fused with the original. This kind of undifferentiated thinking is found in individuals who are unable to recognise whole 'objects' and whose self is fused with the object. These ideas are cited in Hinshelwood (1989: 447–448).

It seems to me that Nicholas Sarra offers one of the best examples from art psychotherapy of thinking in which there is no 'as if' quality. He writes:

I ask him to get down and stop exposing himself. He does so but announces that he wants to urinate in the sink. Here I make the mistake of suggesting that using the paints, he might symbolically urinate on the paper. Of course he immediately *equates* [my italics] the symbolic and concrete and proceeds to urinate on his blank piece of paper. I tell him to stop. He tells me nonchalantly that he has not yet finished. The rest of the group rapidly leave the room.

(Sarra, 1991: 79)

Continuous projection and difficulties in symbolising; Metaphor (framed and unframed); Object relations theories; Psychosis and art therapy; Psychotic Processes; Symbol; Symbolisation

Symbolisation: DE

The capacity to live in a world of symbols remote from the world of physical and biological objects is the hallmark of human development. The ability to move on to new, substitute objects (symbols) is a move out of anxiety, but it is also a developmental move.

(Hinshelwood, 1989: 447)

A symbol remains a perpetual challenge to our thoughts and feelings. That probably explains why a symbolic work is so stimulating, why it grips us so intensely, but also why it seldom affords us a purely aesthetic enjoyment.

(Jung, 1950: para. 119)

Mediating function of the art object

Symbols and collective imagery in group analytic art therapy: GMc

I slowly developed a way of working with these groups whereby the group would find its own direction and ultimately treat itself. Here each group develops its own identity within a matrix, which structures and contains it. Along with this, group cohesiveness develops and cements the group, leading to greater and more meaningful resonance. Through the use of art materials the process is illuminated, leading to an understanding of collective imagery. Group members set out to portray their own individual feelings, but what tends to happen is that they produce similar shapes, colours and symbols. Quite often, for instance, numerical imagery is influenced by the numbers in the group, or may take into account absent members. This happens both consciously and unconsciously . . .

The group-analytic art group is peculiarly sensitive to manifestations of the collective unconscious. For example if the matrix in an art group is one where the group becomes the 'Great Mother', this may emerge in the collective imagery, expressed by a series of paintings, most of which are landscapes. This is why I feel there will be stronger resonance in a theme developed spontaneously, giving natural openings for the expression of collective imagery . . .

(McNeilly, 1984b: 208–209)

Archetype; Group analytic approach to art therapy; Non-directive approach; Resonance

Systematic review: AJG

Systematic reviews are a critical part of evidence-based practice. They involve the distillation and 'grading' of the research-based literature on a given topic according to its 'quality' within a hierarchy of different kinds of 'evidence'. This comprises different kinds of research, usually quantitative, but it also includes reports of expert committees and the opinions of other 'experts', experienced practitioners, and service users.

Systematic reviews aim to make sense of and to make easily accessible, disparate, often replicated but variable research findings in a way that is as transparent and free from bias as possible (Gilbody and Sowden, 2000).

Systematic review therefore infers thoroughness, completeness, and reproducibility. It requires the gathering together and collation of every available research-based text on a topic and their subsequent assignment to different levels of evidence according to specific criteria. This enables an aggregation of findings from the critical appraisal of a literature and for judgements to be made about the validity and quality of the research, or the 'evidence', so as to identify the best that is available.

Evidence-based practice; Hierarchies of evidence; Research critical appraisal

Taking the piss (TTP): HG

Experience conducting art therapy groups for psychotic patients in a community setting first brought this form of humour to light (Greenwood and Layton, 1988). Use of TTP was a powerful characteristic of the out-patient group. TTP allows a confrontation of reality in a way that is playful and entertaining so that tension is diminished and growth is promoted. The teasing and belittling are not merely a cruel attack but, like satire, there is a transmutation of difficult feelings into humour and into play. The piss is taken out of 'valued' concerns with sympathetic cruelty. An ironic combination of acceptance and criticism is woven in an almost paradoxical juxtaposition. Deflation is an important characteristic.

Ego mechanisms of defence; Group (eight entries); Play; Psychosis and art therapy

Talisman transference: JS

This is a transference particular to forms of psychotherapy where art plays a significant part in the therapeutic relationship. It is an effect of the concrete existence of the art object. It was proposed as a term by Schaverien (1987, 1991) to describe a process observed where clients relate to their own art as an empowered object. A talisman is an object thought to have magical and protective powers. It is believed to protect the bearer from evil influences, therefore it is valued as an object. A picture may be empowered unconsciously in this way and valued as a talisman holding a feeling state live between sessions. The empowering of a picture as a talisman is related to the transference to the therapist. Unlike the *fetish*, the talisman involves a form of relatedness.

Fear (of the image); Fetish; Invocations; Magical thinking; Three-dimensional form; Transference

Techniques of art-making and psychic change: CC

Trying out techniques can parallel a first suggestion of psychic change, for instance, when I think I have seen the beginning of developing a memory. I have named as 'thought-images' those images that represent a thought on the verge of being known, such as crayon and wash/crayon rubbing of a shape under paper; both of these techniques involve the shape of something being revealed either by the crayon wash or by the crayon rubbing of a shape under the paper. In trying out these techniques there may be a first playing with depth, which provides a move towards three-dimensionality. Children who are blank and traumatised may be developing a mind in which there is a sense of depth and things below the surface – memories that could be held in an image, represented, and re-evoked. There may be a struggle to represent something that might have the qualities of a memory (Case, 2005b).

Remembering and forgetting; Techniques of art therapy; Thinking

Techniques of art therapy citing Naumburg: TD

> The techniques of art therapy are based on the knowledge that every individual, whether trained or untrained in art, has a latent capacity to project his inner conflicts into visual form. As patients picture such inner experiences, it frequently happens that they become more verbally articulate.
>
> (Naumburg, 1958: 511, cited in Dalley, 1984: xiii)

Embodied image; Kramer; Naumburg; Spontaneous art; Techniques of art-making and psychic change

Television: CW

'The Television set has become a key member of the family, the one who tells most of the stories most of the time' (George Gerbner, Hungarian born US cultural critic, 1919–2005).

The television sometimes helps to soothe a sense of loneliness, yet at other times the constant bombardment and lack of much interaction with images on screens is experienced as inhuman. For people who experience psychotic episodes the unresponsive nature of the medium can sometimes be experienced as frightening.

Widespread availability of the TV in Britain did not begin until the 1960s, and in the 1991 Census the lack of a colour TV in Britain was still an indicator of relative poverty. The availability of television has influenced imaginations and the ability to articulate feelings on a worldwide scale.

Access to art; Advertising; Computers in the art room; Graffiti; Internet;
Techniques of art therapy; Typewriter and blackboard

Temenos: EW

The ancient Greek word for 'sanctuary', *Temenos*, was given a psychological application by Jung, who drew on alchemy to elaborate and clarify
his theory. 'The house shelters daydreaming, the house protects the
dreamer, the *house* allows one to dream in peace' (Bachelard, 1958: 6).

Container/contained; Containment; Crucible; Sanctuary; Studios

Terracotta: PH

Terracotta is a smooth, textured, red-brown clay body that has been used
for pottery since prehistoric times. It is familiar, occurring in our environment in the form of flower and chimney pots and simple earthenware
utensils. This may account for its warm, unpretentious, human quality.
Also noticeable is the way that, when wet, light glances off its satiny
surface, giving it a liveliness that is lacking in dead, grey-coloured, rougher
clays. In my experience, it easily lends itself to identification with mud,
chocolate, shit, dried blood, and other substances. Direct physical contact
with it may be experienced as grounding and reassuring or, as is often the
case with sticky substances that can seem to threaten alterations in body
boundaries, disgusting or fascinatingly repellent. Its earthy colour allies it
with the soil in which plants grow, and thus to the cycle of nature. It has
an uncompromising quality that rarely elicits an intellectual response, and
the profundities of its associations are a reminder of earth, to which all
matter returns.

Clay; Paint; Peat; Rhyme; Sand; Stone

Themes: MLieb

Many people have great difficulty in starting and a theme (which is a
suggestion about focus) can enable a person to begin somewhere. Useful
themes are usually flexible enough to allow for many levels of response and
there are many situations in which themes can be helpful.

Theme-based groups meet for a common purpose to look at particular
problems or aspects of human experience (e.g. bereavement, anger, life
transitions). This way of working is particularly suited to short-life groups
that come together for this specific purpose and also for single-session art
therapy groups that are part of a longer verbal programme. Theme-based
groups can also help to introduce art therapy to people who are unfamiliar

with it (i.e. for the first few sessions of a group, before members develop their own themes). There is usually a formal structure to the group, with an introduction, the choice of a theme (by the therapist or by group members), and a time for group members to draw or paint, followed by a time of sharing (Barber, 2002; Campbell, 1993; Liebmann, 2003; Ross, 1997).

Directive and non-directive styles of work; Eating disorders: Themes-based art therapy groups in specialised teams; Group interactive art therapy; Group process knowledge in art therapy; Group work models

Therapeutic abstinence: CW

The idea of abstinence is prominently cited in relation to the prohibition on sexual relations between therapist and client. A therapist who enters into a sexual relationship with their client breaks the therapeutic frame, exploits the client's sense of trust, and introduces confusion into many aspects of the relationship. It is the responsibility of the therapist to maintain therapeutic boundaries and not exploit clients. Codes of conduct for all models of therapeutic practice cite sexual transgression by a therapist as a serious form of professional misconduct.

Therapeutic abstinence might also refer to the avoidance of physical touch in a therapeutic relationship. This is thought to help focus the relationship on the work of therapy by avoiding the provision of actual solace or gratification with a touch to the arm, handshake, or even a hug, which may provide temporary relief, but not further the work of therapy. When a client initiates touch the therapist needs to think carefully about how to restore or, if appropriate, modify the therapeutic frame.

Clients are asked to refrain from smoking or eating during sessions, because these might be habitual ways in which they distract themselves from having feelings, and their feelings could as a result become less available for therapeutic work. However, in work with clients who feel vulnerable to a psychotic episode, arrangements about eating and smoking are best left to the therapist's judgement.

Therapeutic abstinence might also reasonably extend to the avoidance of inappropriate discussion of clients by therapists.

Abuse; Acting out; Power; Professional conduct and misconduct

Therapeutic alliance: CW

This is a term used to describe the working relationship between therapist and client. It is thought that work done between the therapist and client in order to overcome difficulties and resistances in the therapy and ruptures in the relationship are particularly valuable to the strengthening of the alliance. Some 50 years of psychotherapy, psychiatric, and psychology research has cited the quality of the alliance as one of the most important factors in predicting a good outcome for the therapy (Catty, 2004; Martin, et al., 2000; Safran and Muran, 2003).

On the basis of attendance records and anecdotal evidence art therapists seem to engage well with clients, but therapeutic alliance is not much commented upon in the art therapy research literature. This is a subject worthy of future research.

Evidence-based practice; Working alliance with men and women with learning disabilities

Therapeutic care: CW

It is appropriate to the work of some art therapists that they adopt the model of 'therapeutic care'. Papadopoulos (2002) suggests this model in relation to work with refugees, but the approach is applicable to many of the clients with complicated needs that art therapists work with:

> . . . traditional psychotherapy in its fuller form may not always be available to or, dare I say, appropriate for the majority of refugees who may not have either the right motivation or symptomatology for this kind of specialist work. However, I would strongly argue that therapeutic considerations can always be useful and should be included in any kind of care plan refugees are offered. This means that regardless of their suitability for or availability of psychotherapy proper, refugees will always benefit from appropriately adjusted forms of 'therapeutic care' . . . Therapeutic care refers to the wider application of psychotherapeutic principles to any form of assistance to refugees.
>
> (Papadopoulos, 2002: 4)

Adaptations of practice; Advice; Art therapy approaches for particular clients; Portable Studio; Psychosocial approach; Supportive psychotherapy

Therapeutic frame: CW

The therapeutic frame is a concept widely used in psychotherapeutic literature as a metaphor for therapeutic or *mental* space. The therapist introduces the 'boundaries' of therapy at the earliest opportunity, preferably at the outset of meetings with the client. *Time, duration of sessions, what happens if sessions are missed, place, and the limits of confidentiality* are essential elements that are important to discuss with the client. It is in the client's interests to have clear guidance about the beginning and end of therapy sessions. This clarity conveys the idea of containment. It helps to provide modelling of the ways in which feelings can be contained: that they have a beginning and an end, and they can be lived through. Gray (1994) suggests that the way in which the framework for therapy is understood has connections with how someone was cared for in the past. She points to important metaphorical connections between establishing a clear therapeutic frame and consistent parenting, but she is clear that: 'we are therapists not parents' (Gray, 1994: 9).

The concept of frame is powerful in art and consequently artists working as therapists have much to contribute, both intuitively and intellectually, to the development of this particular metaphor (see Schaverien, 1991).

Robert Langs, an American psychoanalyst, abhors all breaks in the frame (Langs and Searles, 1980). There is a wider, less strict consensus that most breaks in the frame are unhelpful but there is room for some variation of approach.

Art therapists working in a range of settings might find that they have to adapt their approach to the frame to the circumstances of their institutional practice, but it is always important to think very carefully (in symbolic and in real terms) about any breaks in the frame that occur. This is the case even when unintentional breaks in the frame lead to some helpful insight for therapist and client alike.

Adaptations of practice; Metaphor (framed and unframed); Milner on the therapeutic frame; Picture within the frame; Temenos; Thinking; Working through

Therapeutic precision: MC

This is an image or artwork produced in art therapy that has the quality of 'therapeutic precision' – the image says it all and says it precisely. These are often key images in an art therapy.

Embodied image; Vitality

Therapist and play: DE

> The general principle seems to me to be valid that *psychotherapy is done in the overlap between the two play areas, that of the patient and that of the therapist*. If the therapist cannot play, then he is not suitable for the work. If the patient cannot play, then something needs to be done to enable the patient to become able to play, after which psychotherapy may begin. The reason why playing is essential is that it is in playing that the patient is being creative.

(Winnicott, 1971b: 63)

For Winnicott, the capacity to play is essential to the therapeutic process because:

> It is in playing and only in playing that the individual child or adult is able to be creative and to use the whole personality, and it is only in being creative that the individual discovers the self.

> (Winnicott, 1971b: 63)

Play; Play technique

Therapists' engagement with their own art practice: AJG

Therapists' engagement with their art practice has been demonstrated to enable art therapists to sustain a sense of personal and professional well-being (Gilroy, 1992, 2005). Maintaining an identity as an artist also influences and is influenced not only by art therapists' art practice but also by their engagement with thinking about 'looking' within differing social and visual contexts, be this in an art therapy session or at an exhibition (Gilroy, 2005, 2008; Mahony, 2001, 2010a, 2010b; Ryde, 2003).

It is therefore important that art therapists do not neglect an ongoing engagement with their art practice. Those who maintain their commitment are able to affirm an important aspect of their personal and professional identity. Maintaining an active relationship with art, whatever form it takes, can therefore help art therapists to preserve the uniqueness of the discipline in the face of the demands and socialisation processes within the health, social, educational, and criminal justice systems.

Art made by art therapists; Looking; Professionalization; Supervision; Therapist and play

Therapy ceremony and tea ceremony (Japanese *chado*: The path of tea): LG

The ceremonial tea master has knowledge of the tradition and the skill to perform it, but also the renewing capacity to compose the chosen elements of each individual ceremony (tea objects, flower, and calligraphy) into a well-balanced entity. The tea ceremony is said to be philosophy made visible.

Ceremony is a rite for respecting something. The process of therapy can be regarded as a transition from a disturbing and anguished situation to a new, more balanced situation. It seems to have aspects of both healing and initiation rites. In the therapy ceremony the strange, the not yet known in the patient is respected.

In the article 'The Therapy Ceremony – Encountering the Strange(r) in Art Therapy' (Girard, 2008a) some ritual aspects of therapy are discussed: 'The path of therapy in art therapy combines the practice of an aesthetic ritual of making art and a more recent ritual of psychotherapeutic treatment forming an original synthesis of them' (Girard, 2008a: 10).

Cross-cultural influences; Rites of Passage

Therapy for the therapist: TD

Logical analysis and translation of pictured ideas into words can be dangerous and destructive in the hands of inexperienced therapists. This is why a good analysis for any therapist is a great advantage. [S]He should then know how not to interfere. The art form has its own validity and to translate from one language to another is bound to bring loss or error.

(Champernowne, 1971: 141)

Group conductor role; Interpretation perspectives; Interpretations, Jung's approach; Therapist and play; Therapists' engagement with their own art practice; Training approaches

Thinking: TD

'He does not mean some abstract mental process. His concern is with thinking as a human link – the endeavour to understand, comprehend the reality of, get insight into the nature of . . . oneself and another. Thinking is an emotional experience of trying to know one's self and someone else . . .'

(O'Shaughnessy 1981: 181)

Thinking involves reflection, time, space, a container for those thoughts. This is a difficult task. Thinking together and working through can be one way. With any individual or group, when faced with anxiety and conflict, early defence mechanisms come into play. Using the Kleinian model of early development, the baby moves from the paranoid-schizoid position to the depressive position by working through the split, and only then can both good and bad be tolerated. This leads to further development, weaning and independence from mother, which enables the ability to move away from the parent. The early split in art therapy between education and psychiatry, which formed the roots or 'parental figures' of our profession, became integrated and resolved only to throw up other ones around directive and non-directive ways of working. To some extent the 'art' versus 'therapy' debate continues to be alive in our minds, but we are now moving on to accommodate this split so that we can work together, respect difference and stay within the tension . . .

However, within this overall situation there has been sufficient solidity built into the profession to enable individuals to move out on their own in their thinking and initiatives . . . The theoretical debate in art therapy is open, challenged, and continues to be well documented, which keeps the questioning in mind.

(Dalley, 2000: 86)

Psychotic processes; Working through

Third period of British art therapy history: CW

The first two periods had left art therapists with a legacy of using the same careful approach to therapeutic work – an approach that does not single out any particular client group. This began to change in the third period, with particular approaches being offered to clients with particular difficulties, such as in relation to psychosis (Killick and Greenwood, 1995; Killick and Schaverien, 1997). Special interest groups developed within the profession.

Services were preoccupied with what seemed interminable change, so that it was not always easy to maintain the basic conditions needed for the frame of therapy. It is understandable therefore that some art therapists used the majority of their energies for the ongoing need to discuss and argue for basic conditions (*see* 'Schools establishing art therapy').

What characterised art therapy in the third period were: questions of theory and technique; a general quest for more clarity of practice; and a clearer framing of practice in relation to the institutional/community context in which it is situated. The experience of increasingly working away from a team setting, often with very troubled clients, created the need for such a focus.

It was not until this third period that significant numbers of art therapists wrote or edited books about the nature of art therapy practice. These include: Case and Dalley (1990, 1992); Dalley (1984); Dalley et al. (1987, 1993); Gilroy and Dalley (1989); Gilroy and Lee (1995); Killick and Schaverien (1997); Liebmann (1990, 1994); Schaverien (1991, 1995b); Simon (1992, 1997); Skaife and Huet (1998); Thomson (1989); Waller (1991, 1993); Waller and Gilroy (1992) and Wood and Pratt (1998). The subject matter of these works indicates the wide range of practice and provides evidence of art therapists using widely differing models: art as healing (Adamson, 1984; Hill, 1948; McNiff, 1992); person-centred art therapy (Silverstone, 1995); brief art therapy (McClelland 1992; Skailes, 1990); supportive art psychotherapy (this comprises a good deal of the therapy offered to people with a history of psychosis, e.g. Charlton, 1984; Greenwood, 1994, 1997; Greenwood and Layton, 1987, 1988; Lewis, 1990; Molloy, 1997; Wood, 1997). Another example is art psychotherapy (much writing during the period can be described in this way, e.g. Case, 1994; Dalley et al., 1993; Killick, 1993). Indeed, in the early part of the contemporary period, 'Art Psychotherapist' became one of the two protected titles for the profession. Schaverien and colleagues introduced the idea of analytical art psychotherapy (1991, 1994a, 1995a, 1995b).

Work was published concerning group practice: group analytic art therapy (McNeilly, 1984a); group interactive art therapy (Waller, 1993); art psychotherapy groups (Skaife and Huet, 1998).

The increasing clarity of explanation and theory in many areas contributed to the development of practice. Adequate acknowledgement of the socio-economic circumstances of client lives, the conditions in which services operate, and the push for systematic evidence seem destined to shape the concerns of the contemporary period of art therapy.

Art therapy approaches for particular clients; Contemporary period of art therapy; First and second periods of British art therapy history (two entries)

Three-dimensional form: JM

Our sense of touch and relationship with three-dimensional form develops with us from birth. Scale, space, and time open us up to a deepened experience. In therapy, making sculpture facilitates through form and material the experiencing of a powerful, physical sense of a relationship with unconscious processes. As a transitional or talismanic object, their independent existence in space and time, mediated within the therapeutic relationship, offers an added physical dimension to the work. A sculptural form embodies aspects of the image's relationship to self, not only through its shape, context, or symbolism, but in the very materials and methods themselves.

Barbara Hepworth wrote movingly about making sculpture:

> There are fundamental shapes which speak at all times and periods in the language of sculpture. It is difficult to describe in words the meaning of forms because it is precisely this emotion, which is conveyed by sculpture alone. Our sense of touch is a fundamental sensibility which comes into action at birth – our stereognostic sense – the ability to feel weight and form and assess its significance.
>
> (Hepworth, 1970: 53)

This stereognostic sense is at work when she describes piercing through and opening up her forms, as creating an inside and outside. Her legacy continues in the work of contemporary artists such as Rachael Whiteread and her haunting casts of interior/exterior spaces.

When we consider the inner forces and energy within and around a form, it is easy to connect with metaphor and psychotherapeutic process. If, as Hepworth believed, the sense of touch vividly evokes our memory of relationship to scale, space, and time from birth, the three-dimensional form deserves our special consideration.

Bourgeois; Fetish; Invocations; Metaphor (linguistic and visual);
Sculptural materials; Sculpture citing Moore; Talisman transference;
Token; Vantage points

Time disappears: DW and CS

Writing of the death of his wife Corinne Burton at the age of 42:

> She had in those last hard months, been totally focused and implacably determined not give in. Her way was not only to live her life, and particularly, her role as a mother, to the full, until the very last gasp, but also to step up the hours of calm and concentration spent on art, especially, towards the end, in the pernickety skills of china painting. Her art took not only her full attention at a time when she might otherwise have given in to depression, but also encouraged those same virtues of calm, composure and pertinacity with which she fought against her disease. She would indeed have agreed with one of Caryl Sibbett's patient's that 'during art-making time disappears'.
>
> (Burton, 2005: ix)

> All clients reported often being absorbed in art-making and losing track of time. One client reported that during art-making 'time disappears'. Another client reported: 'When I was working I was able to just move into the art. When I went home I felt really uplifted. I was able to get a really good night's sleep'. On a research questionnaire in response to the question 'How is/was the art therapy experience for you?' another client's response included: 'No perception/awareness of time while doing art'.
>
> (Sibbett, 2005b: 20)

Absorption in art-making

Time-related processing: CT

Defining art therapy as a time-related process has become increasingly important for art therapists working in public services in the United

Kingdom (but also in other countries), because we need to clarify what we offer, for how long, for whom, and what benefits the therapy confers. To aid an understanding of their work, the art therapist encourages engagement using introductions and initial assessments, ongoing work reviews, and in ideal circumstances negotiated terminations (closure). Similarly, Budman et al. (1996) recognise the importance of group psychotherapy as being a process of phases, and Welldon (1997) believed that clarifying time-relational goals and outcomes in forensic psychotherapy is essential because most offenders will have experienced few thoughtful beginnings and endings during their lives. Amongst others, David Edwards (1997) wrote about beginnings and endings in art therapy, and Teasdale (1999) discusses the importance of setting time-related goals when working as art therapists with offenders in prisons where 'doing time' is also a factor.

Brief psychotherapy (three entries)*; Evidence-based practice; Review with images; What works for whom?*

Token: JS

> The picture which is left with the therapist between sessions may, for example, be valued as a token of affection, or a reminder of what has taken place in therapy. The significance may rest there but not necessarily.
>
> (Schaverien, 1991: 144)

Trade unions: JD

The British Association of Art Therapists (BAAT) has, throughout its history, worked alongside trade unions and continues to be strengthened by its trade union orientation (Waller, 1991: 176). In joining with the National Union of Teachers (NUT) in 1967 it was making a 'clear stand as a trade union, protecting the interests of its members and trying to secure better salaries and working conditions . . .' (Waller, 1991: 128). BAAT remained with NUT until 1976. BAAT members working in the NHS proposed a preference to join the Association of Scientific, Technical and Managerial Staff (ASTMs), which later became MSF (Manufacturing, Science and Finance), was called Amicus till late 2007, and now is called Unite. Unite remains the main union for art therapists that all BAAT members are encouraged to join.

During 1976 to 1982 ASTMs paid a key role in BAAT's campaign to enable art therapists within the NHS to become an autonomous profession, and a career and salary structure under Whitley Council was achieved in 1982 (Waller, 1991).

The professional association (BAAT) and Unite continue to work along-side each other in representing the profession, informing government policy on matters that affect art therapists within the various settings in which they may work, such as the NHS, social services, the voluntary sector, school education, higher education, and the prison system. In this context BAAT also encourages links with all the other unions that art therapists may be members of, such as UCU and Unison.

[A clear part of trade union consciousness is to understand that people working together in a whole range of roles have shared interests and that for the vast majority injury to one is injury to all. This is another sense in which there is a need for multidisciplinary work.]

Health Professions Council; Organisations regulating and representing art therapists

Training approaches: CW

Although they have a range of theoretical orientations, training courses in Britain ask students to navigate backwards and forwards between the fundamental elements of art therapy practice: the art-making and the therapeutic relationship, and the way both of these are influenced by the socio-economic circumstances of the client's life and the therapeutic setting. Students have to consider issues of effectiveness in their developing practice.

All applicants are asked to bring a portfolio of their own art-making to interview. All students have clinical placements, and all have to be in personal therapy as a significant part of training during the life of their course. Students are encouraged to understand the value of multidiscip-linary work and respect for clients and colleagues alike. Qualifying courses are at Master's Degree level and involve a combination of academic and experiential work.

Training module; Training thresholds

Training module in the sensitive use of art for non-art therapists: DK and BL

The 'sensitive use of art' is a term that has become a useful one in the context *of training non-art therapists to use art in their work*. This term was initially used in the context of training carried out by Debra Kalmanowitz and Bobby Lloyd in KwaZulu-Natal, South Africa, in 1995. Many helping professionals today recognise the benefits of including art-making in their practice and may seek training in this regard. In contexts of political conflict, natural disaster, and social upheaval this is particularly pertinent. Training local professionals in the *sensitive use of art within these often volatile contexts* must invariably embrace multiple aims. The overall aim is to better enable participants to incorporate the use of art-making into their already existing or developing scope of practice and is grounded in participants' own professional disciplines, pre-existing knowledge, limits, and strengths. The secondary outcomes of the experiential training are that it includes provision of a cathartic experience for the participants, facilitation of a time and space to replenish depleted energy, and provides an understanding of the emotional impact that the use of art can have on the people with whom they work. It also helps to build on group cohesion so that, where possible, participants can support each other after completion of the training module, both in relation to the incorporation of learning and on a wider emotional level. These secondary aims are important when working in contexts of great change and often great destruction, and cannot be avoided or denied. The primary objective however remains that each participant's personal experience will provide them with ideas, insights, and skills that will resonate in their work. It is clear from the outset that the training module is not therapy (although it may be therapeutic) and does not provide a training in art therapy. These boundaries are established at the outset and maintained accordingly.

Adaptations of practice; Art therapy and art activities; Directive and non-directive styles of work; Making meaning; Portable Studio; Psychosocial approach; Remembering and forgetting; Resilience and the psychosocial model; Supervision; Themes; Training approaches

Training thresholds: DW

In Britain, as in the USA, art therapy's roots have been in art, education, art practice and developmental psychology. Entrants to training have been over 90 per cent art graduates, bringing; with them a particular set of abilities and assumptions . . . Experience of working in various European countries, and attendance at European meetings, has demonstrated clearly that there is liable to be a very big difference in practice if, as seems to be the case in most other European countries, entrants to training are primarily medically or paramedically trained (see Waller 1984; 1992a; 1992b; Waller and Gheorghieva 1990) and they acquire the art practice element of art therapy through participation in art workshops on the course, rather than through an immersion in a four-year degree in art or design.

The socialization of art students takes a very different course from that of medical or nursing students. Attitudes towards concepts such as 'mental health' or 'treatment' are liable to vary. I have already suggested that there may be a tendency for health professionals to see art therapy as a set of techniques to be added to the primary professional role whereas for art graduates, therapy is the profession in which they can maintain their identity as artists while absorbing elements of other disciplines and synthesizing these with their art base.

(Waller, 1998: 103)

Ritual; Training approaches; Transferable skills

Transactional object: JS

The transactional object is based on anthropological explorations of the use of art in different cultures throughout the world. The word transaction implies a category where the object is used in exchange for something else. It is an object through which negotiation takes place. This may be thought to imply a conscious transaction but the process is primarily unconscious and may be magically invested. The picture is sometimes unconsciously used as an object through which transactions are acted out and channelled. Initially unconscious and therefore acting out, this may lead to a conscious attitude and enactment. The transactional object is different from the *transitional object* (Winnicott, 1971b).

The term transactional object was proposed by Schaverien (1995a) to describe a process in which art plays a mediating role in the treatment of eating disorders. In the case of eating disorders the similarity between food and art materials is that both have physical existence. Like the mother offering the child food, the art psychotherapist provides art materials for the client to use. The concrete nature of this transaction, within the therapeutic boundary, sets up a resonance with the problem. This can be observed in the use made of the materials, and often they are related to in a similar way to food. The transactional object was further developed in relation to its mediating function in the treatment of psychosis in *Art, Psychotherapy and Psychosis* (Killick and Schaverien, 1997).

Adaptations of practice; Transitional object

Transactional object in eating disorders: JS

In the treatment of eating disorders the focus on food is often central. Food is a concrete substance that often becomes the focus of transactions in the family. Parents and health professionals will try to encourage the client to eat, and this perpetuates the problem. Art psychotherapy is often helpful in treatment because here, too, concrete substances mediate between the inner experience of the client and the social environment, providing the beginning of symbolisation of a previously unsymbolised state.

This idea was introduced by Schaverien in a paper, 'The Transactional Object: Art Psychotherapy in the Treatment of Anorexia' (1994b), and developed in her book, *Desire and the Female Therapist* (1995a: 121).

Art therapy approaches for particular clients; Eating disorders; Transitional object; Transactional object in psychosis

Transactional object in psychosis: JS

In psychotic illnesses the client can feel very exposed and vulnerable. To relate directly to another person can feel threatening, and thinking is often concrete (or literal). In some such cases, art psychotherapy can offer an important means of communication because it is 'out there', separate from the body of the person. Thus it creates a space between the inner image and the outer world. In this way it offers the potential for symbolisation when symbolic thought is not yet possible. The artwork mediates between the client and the environment as a transactional object.

This idea was developed by Joy Schaverien in 'Transference and Transactional Objects in the Treatment of Psychosis' (1997: 13–37).

Art therapy approaches for particular clients; Champernowne; Psychosis and art therapy; Transactional object in eating disorders; Transitional object

Transcendent function: MEd

In 1916, the year that Jung first encouraged his patients to make pictures from their dreams and fantasies, Jung (1916) set out some of his tentative ideas about giving expression to unconscious imagery and its possibilities for healing in 'The Transcendent Function', a paper that was not published until 41 years later. The paper is particularly significant for art therapists. In the paper, he discusses the relation between 'aesthetic' and 'psychological' dimensions of images, which arise spontaneously from the unconscious:

> One tendency seems to be the regulating principle of the other; both are related in a compensatory manner. Experience confirms this formula. As far as it is possible at this stage to draw general conclusions, we would say that the tendency towards aesthetic expression seems to need the tendency towards understanding, and equally the tendency towards understanding needs that of aesthetic expression.
>
> (Jung, 1916: *CW 8*)

By 'understanding' in this context Jung appears to mean psychological insight, and by 'aesthetic expression' he means a concern for the formal properties of the image. Without something of the former, he suggests that there is a risk of empty and meaningless formalism, and without aesthetic constraints of some kind the image may be raw, chaotic, and uncontrolled.

Facture; Jung's personal uses of art; Looking; Making meaning

Transferable skills and the cultural basis of art therapy knowledge: PB

The cultural basis of art therapists' knowledge includes their understanding that the arts have created vehicles for conveying both the highest of aspirations and the direst commentaries on humankind's cruelties and foolishness. The arts provide an axis around which interior feelings and external perceptions are shaped into relationships. They enable artists (and, by proxy, art therapy clients) to locate psychological as well as phenomenological events in time and space, in the fields of perception and representation – they are/become real, are realised. Through making their own images clients can create their own psychic operators: analogous to Winnicott's (1971b) transitional objects, Kohut's (1971) self-objects, Latour's (1988) *actants*, and Gell's (1998) agents. The works made can have any degree of permanence or transience. Clients are not permanently fixed in time/space by the images they make at a particular time. One image can lead to the next in a hermeneutic spiral (Byrne, 2002).

Aesthetic philosophy in art therapy; Agency; Interpretations, Jung's approach; Reason; Rhyme; Seeing and looking; Sense of self; Training thresholds; Transcendent function; Visual culture

Transference: JS

It is through the transference that affect, [emotion] initially experienced in the past, is brought 'live' into the present. The intense form of relating which often accompanies transference mobilises affect, and it is this which offers the opportunity for transformation of the patterns of the inner world.

I propose that a similar process may be understood to occur through the patient's relation to the pictures and that, at times, it is through the pictures that affect is mobilised. When this takes place the potential for transformation is mediated primarily by means of the patient's relation to the pictures. However, this takes place within the bounds of the therapeutic relationship and so it is an integrated part of the whole experience. The relationship of the patient-artist to the picture is tempered and affected by the feeling tone of the transference to the therapist as a person.

The danger in interpreting pictures in therapy is that they may be regarded as symptoms and analysed as such. This may have the effect of reducing the patient's relationship to the picture to a mere behaviour. The complexity of the imagery and the relationships within the picture may then be ignored or pass unseen; thus the artist is diminished.

The picture is no mere illustration of the transference either, although elements of the transference may be reflected in it. It is important that both the process of image-making and the completed picture are permitted space. Their meanings may not become apparent immediately. At times these are multi-faceted and may be amplified within the therapeutic context without being fixed to any single definitive interpretation.

(Schaverien, 1991: 1).

Aesthetic counter-transference; Distributive transference and the importance of teamwork; Negative transference; Scapegoat transference; Scapegoat transference and projective identification; Transference of feelings that cannot be borne

Transference and counter-transference in group analytic art therapy: GMc

. . . Winnicott (1974) places emphasis upon how the therapist, like the mother, must be seen to survive. This is the case for the group-analytic art therapist who has to work through over-idealizations, intense anger for not supplying themes while at the same time maintaining the conductor's baton in orchestrating the subtle process of theme development. In not setting a theme, transferences of a more valid nature are promoted, rather than mere positive reactions as rewards for giving the group a nice experience. In such an experience there is limited unconscious exploration. A feeling of ease is created in giving a theme, but this has a falseness based on surface needs. It is illusory. With a group-analytic approach the art therapist who nurtures spontaneous imagery becomes fully available for a range of transference reactions. This contrasts with the directive therapist who is largely concerned with the clients' image-making. Individuation will be promoted by a non-directive approach. Power can be discovered in the patient.

(McNeilly, 1984b: 207–208)

Group analytic approach to art therapy; Group matrix in visual form; Power; Resonance; Symbols and collective imagery in group analytic art therapy; Themes; Transference; Unconscious

Transference in palliative care: DH

Traditionally, in working in the area of palliative care, there has been an emphasis on the cathartic role of the picture in the session to facilitate and contain. Writers like Connell [1998] show how effective this can be in promoting more adaptive and creative responses even in clients who are very close to death. However, failure to address transference issues is an omission, since it both underestimates the resources practitioners have to draw upon in order to 'survive' and potentially deprives them of a vital part of their practice. It is left to other writers (practitioners who do not generally work in this field) to usefully remind us of the importance of transference and counter-transference in the therapy session. They show that, far from being a source for concern, such features can and should be treated as integral to the therapy interaction. Practising in the area of palliative care is potentially fraught with problems as we continually work with people who subsequently die. As therapists we must remain aware of the effect this may be having on us as individuals, both in our professional lives and also away from work, if we are to endeavour to engage and disengage with the equanimity that our clients require. Above all, we must acknowledge that this work is difficult to sustain, for only by paying attention to our own needs can we more truly listen to those of our client. In the end I think Delmonte is right to caution that it is not necessarily the needs or motivations of the therapists who work in this area that are harmful, but their avoidance or denial (Delmonte 1995).

(Hardy, 2005: 196)

Liminality; Sustaining the therapist in cancer care

Transference of feelings that cannot be borne: DE

'The transference lets us know about that part of the client that cannot be borne by himself at the time and which seeks refuge within us until it is safe to incorporate it back in a less persecutory way' (Cantle, 1983: 9).

Negative transference

Transitional object: JS

The transitional object is a term originated by D.W. Winnicott and published in *Playing and Reality* (1971b). The transitional object is the first 'not me' object to which the infant becomes attached. It mediates between the mother and the environment. The transitional object is an actual object with a physical existence (e.g. a teddy bear or a piece of blanket) to which the infant forms an early attachment. Sustained by the transitional object, the infant begins to be able to retain a sense of the continued existence of the mother in her absence. Winnicott (1971b) demonstrates how this attachment gradually disperses and becomes sustained by the whole environment. This leads eventually to cultural life and appreciation of art.

Animals; Potential space; Sublimation theories in art therapy;
Transactional object in eating disorders; Transactional object;
Transactional object in psychosis; Transferable skills; Winnicott

Trauma: DN

The word 'traumatic' is derived from the ancient Greek word *titrosko*, which means to wound and refers to the piercing of the skin, or 'a breaking of the body envelope' as Caroline Garland (1998: 9) describes it.

She also reminds us that Freud (1921) used the word 'metaphorically to emphasise how the mind can be pierced and wounded by events' (Garland, 1998: 9). In this way the mind is thought of as being 'enveloped by a kind of skin, or protective shield' (1998: 9). A trauma can be experienced as a hole in the mind's protective shield. Some traumatic events are not experienced as devastating because the mind can protect itself, for example, through denial. At times though, a traumatic event:

> . . . is one which, for a particular individual, breaks through and overrides the discriminatory, filtering process, and overrides any temporary denial or patch-up of the damage. The mind is flooded . . . something very violent feels as though it has happened internally, and this mirrors the violence that is felt to have happened or indeed has actually happened in the external world.
>
> (Garland, 1998: 10)

National Institute for Health and Clinical Excellence guidelines (NICE, 2005: 19) recommend CBT (cognitive-behavioural therapy) or EMDR (eye movement desensitisation reprocessing) treatments for PTSD (post-traumatic stress disorder). However, there is also some empirical evidence from M. J. Horowitz (1991) to support the short-term dynamic therapy of stress response syndromes, and the results from a study of 112 people suffering from PTSD conducted by Brom et al. (1989) imply the effectiveness of brief dynamic psychotherapy (and that it is worthy of further investigation).

Beuys; Borderline personality disorder; Bourgeois; Brain injury and art
therapy; Brief dynamic art psychotherapy; Complex homelessness;
Defend; Dissociation; Mentalisation; Mise-en-scene; Negative
transference; Post-traumatic stress disorder and art psychotherapy;
Stroke and trauma; Witness: When the client cannot 'speak'

Trauma and homelessness: JJ

'There are strong connections between psychological trauma and home-lessness. Trauma can [also] occur before someone becomes homeless, in the form of childhood abuse' (Collins and Phillips, 2003). This research esti-mated that between 86–100% of people accessing homelessness services in Glasgow had experienced childhood trauma 'and whilst being homeless . . . experiences of violence, exploitation, and vulnerability' (Goodman et al., 1991). It is known that where there is a lack of early childhood containment and positive attachment, there is a higher potential for childhood abuse (Finkelhor, 1986).

Complex homelessness; Post-traumatic stress disorder and art psychotherapy; Trauma and the aesthetic dimension in art therapy

Trauma and the aesthetic dimension in art therapy: LG

There is a special usefulness of aesthetic experience in art therapy when treating trauma and dissociative problems. By means of the artworks and discussion about them, a way can be found to the amodal area of the artwork and sense data. Then, from this continuum of artworks and their associations, a stockpile of good associations can be formed. Further work then becomes possible. The patient becomes less afraid of the possibility of sudden flooding by traumatic material. Naturally careful dosage is moni-tored by the therapist.

Amodality; Post-traumatic stress disorder and art psychotherapy; Supportive Psychotherapy; Therapeutic care

Triangular relationship: ML

And, as with so much that makes art therapy unique, it is the special quality of the three way conversation between maker, image and ther-apist that lends itself. In this triangle therapist and client can, if they're lucky, form some sort of joint witness to a previously inarticulate experience.

(Learmonth, 1994: 22)

Art therapy; Mediating function of the art object; Pleasure; Without recourse to words; Witness and witnessing; Witness: When the client cannot 'speak'

Typewriter and blackboard: CW

> The blackboard may be the child's universe, outer-space, a wall for
> graffiti or even a place of learning – where the child teaches me, as often
> as not. The typewriter is one of the most subtle instruments of com-
> munication (however maltreated it may be) and I equate it with art in its
> creative power; it provides a link between visual and verbal commu-
> nication between patient and therapist. As, for instance, in the case of
> Ronnie, depressed, fearful on his first visit to the therapist. He looked
> longingly at the typewriter, so I typed 'Dear Ronnie, I like you very
> much. My name is Mrs Halliday'. Quick as a flash, he typed back: 'it like
> yoy to. what can we do. Cando somewaining now I can write it'.
>
> Others typed dreams, poems, hymns of love or hate, imaginary
> letters to employers, lawyers, expressing anxiety about jobs – or about
> parents separating. Andy (aged 10) typed a libretto for the opera he
> was writing.
>
> (Halliday, 1978: 23)

The contemporary use of the computer keyboard in art studios has similar
potential.

Art and materials in contemporary aesthetic philosophy; Computers in the
art room; Knowledge of materials; Materials and image in assessment;
Milner on using art materials; Simplicity of materials

Unconscious: CW

This ancient concept has helped to shape the development of contemporary
art therapy. In many philosophies and in many forms of art the concept has
been used to provide different explanations of the place that dreams come
from. All world religions have used the capacity for dreaming, and artists
and scientists have long drawn inspiration from them.

The notion of the unconscious held by prominent art therapists during
the first period of British art therapy history (e.g. Adamson and Lyddiatt)
linked ancient ideas about the power of the arts to heal and psychoanalytic
ideas about dreams:

> To force suppressed painful episodes into premature consciousness can
> result in a severe trauma or complete withdrawal. Painting our dreams,
> however, pays respect to the natural caution of our protective mech-
> anisms, while slowly removing them when they are blocking the way to
> change.
>
> (Adamson, 1984: 37)

During the 1960s and 1970s the profession's history in Britain was influenced by social psychiatry, the ideas of R. D. Laing and Carl Rogers. Laing (1961) denied the notion of an unconscious and Rogers (1951) did not theorise a place for it in his person-centred approach, thus although the concept was still present in the profession's practice it was less explicit in its theory. During the third period the profession consolidated its knowledge of psychotherapy and notions of the unconscious became prominent once more.

The concept of the unconscious can be helpful for therapy with all client groups. For example, in work with those who have a history of psychosis, clients often need help with the fear and disruption created by the upheavals in their unconscious as a result of a psychotic breakdown (Wood, 1997). Another example is that children can be often be helped through unconscious art-making and play in the company of a safe adult. Reference to some notion of an unconscious is often what distinguishes the work of art therapists from the work of other public sector practitioners. However, acknowledgement of the less conscious aspects of life does not mean that art therapists actively seek to uncover them; often they simply aim to help clients contain what they are experiencing.

First, second and third periods of British art therapy history (three entries)*; Psyche-social; Psychoanalytic accounts of the unconscious; Sublimation theories* (two entries)*; Unconscious phantasy*

Unconscious and art-making in brief work: LR

There is a question concerning the extent to which working with the unconscious is possible in shorter art psychotherapy. Art's ability to contain and mediate ineffable feelings is widely valued, with Michele Wood (1990) suggesting that a single session can help the terminally ill embark on grieving. She argues that the lack of time for relational development highlights the intrinsic communicative value of the images. Luzzatto (1997) sees an opportunity to offer the vulnerable some gentle 'holding' as preparation for developing their reflective skills. Springham (1992) proposes images as 'containers' for strong emotion and aggressive attacks, and McClelland (1992) actively encourages using art to 'amplify' disowned feelings, relying on a close-working multidisciplinary team to assist with containment. Atlas et al. (1992) unite cognitive approaches with Kris's (1952) notion of 'regression in the service of the ego', appreciating art's potential for reverie, and opening access to the unconscious. Riley (1999) and Riley and Malchiodi (2003) describe a collaborative process of using art to integrate both the cognitive and the unconscious.

Importantly, Luzzatto (1997) warns against premature interpretation, recognising that, particularly in brief work, one person's helpful intervention might be another's intrusion. Michele Wood is also circumspect about her interventions, seeing her function as a secular 'confessor' (1990: 32), freeing her clients from any onus of an ongoing relationship. Springham (1992) and Luzzatto (1997) both advise caution about directly addressing the unconscious in brief work, to protect more vulnerable clients from being 'out of their depth'. Whilst Atlas et al. (1992) emphasise interpretation, with care to respect the defences that young people build for survival, Riley (1999) urges its avoidance so as not to pre-empt emerging insight.

Brief and short-term art psychotherapy; Brief and short-term psychotherapy; Brief dynamic art psychotherapy; Disposal and endings in brief work; Supportive psychotherapy; Themes; Therapeutic care; Time-related processing; Witness and witnessing

Unconscious phantasy: DE

Unconscious phantasies underlie every mental process and provide the raw material from which dreams and art are fashioned. In the psychoanalytic literature the word 'phantasy' is spelled with a 'ph' rather than an 'f', in order to identify it as an unconscious mental process. Unconscious phantasies are not, like daydreams, an escape from reality, but are inextricably linked to, and are constantly interacting with, real experiences. They influence, and in turn are influenced by, our perception of reality. Not only might unconscious phantasies be said to influence our everyday lives, but they also give rise to the idealised or denigrated figures who become the heroes and demons we encounter in nightmares, fairy stories, and delusions.

In art therapy, as in everyday life, our attempts to deal with fears, wishes, and experiences may be expressed, metaphorically, through the phantasy of 'chopping up something frightening and pushing it down a hole, or putting it into a can with a lid on: the repressed impulse may be then feared as "worms" waiting to jump out and wreak havoc' (Segal, 1992: 30). It is not uncommon for clients to describe their anxiety about beginning therapy in terms of 'opening up a can of worms'.

Although it has been through the work of Melanie Klein and her followers that the concept of unconscious phantasy has been most extensively elaborated, Rycroft (1979: 118) notes: 'All schools agree that unconscious mental activity is accompanied, supported, maintained, enlivened and affected by unconscious phantasy.' Also see J. Segal (1985, 2000).

Fear (of the image); Projective identification (three entries)*; Psychoanalytic accounts of the unconscious*

Unemployment: CW

Many art therapy clients are without work. There is a vast literature on psychological consequences of unemployment (e.g. Coyle, 1984; Kelvin and

Jarrett, 1985; Townsend et al., 1988; Young and Schuller, 1991) that are deeply embedded in history and culture. Foucault claimed that historically those people who occupy the mental hospitals are those who will not work, linking confinement in a mental hospital with a process of moral correction (1967: 38).

Warner asserts that: 'Many of the negative features of chronic schizophrenia are identical with the psychological sequelae of long-term unemployment' (Warner, 1985: 148). He compares psychiatric recovery rates during large parts of the twentieth century and uses international records of hospital statistics to demonstrate that recovery in schizophrenia is linked to the economy and levels of unemployment (Warner, 1985: 72).

Class; Deserving and undeserving; Diagnostic systems in psychiatry; Poverty; Psychiatry, psychoanalysis, poverty, and class; Psychosis and art therapy; Psychosocial approach; Social action art therapy

Unfolding the meaning of artwork or *entfalten*: KM

The German word *entfalten* points to the gradual way in which the meaning of artwork can be understood. It can be translated as 'to expand' or 'to develop into', but perhaps the most useful translation is 'to unfold', implying as it does the notion of 'unveiling' (i.e. uncovering 'hidden' layers). *Entfalten* refers to thoughts and feelings that need to 'unfold' at their own pace.

Process; Process model; Therapeutic care; Visual heuristic research

Unhelpful counter-transference in forensic work: CT

In relation to service users in acute states detained in forensic settings, L. Jones noted that counter-transference mechanisms that staff can unhelpfully be drawn into include:

> Fear and appeasement; helplessness and guilt; feelings of invalidity and loss of identity; denial (not noticing); special problems of the setting; aversive reactions (to dependent clingers, entitled demanders, manipulative help rejecters, self-destructive deniers); denial of the inmate's need to test out (extinguishing of behaviour); therapeutic nihilism (hostile counter-reactions); and illusory treatment alliances.
>
> (L. Jones, 1997: 147–150)

Counter-transference captivity; Distributive transference and the importance of teamwork; Negative transference

User Movements: CW

User Movements include a range of people *using* different services in campaigns against stigma, prejudice, and discrimination, and for the rights of people with mental health problems. There is often a media-led anxiety about people with serious mental disorders living in the community. User campaigns cite statistics that demonstrate the level of media overreaction. 'From 1957 to 1995, during the period of deinstitutionalisation, the proportion of homicides committed by people with a mental disorder actually fell steadily from 35% to 11.5% according to home office figures' (from MIND: Sayce, 2000: 33).

The *Voices Movement* began in the early 1990s in The Netherlands and it has been a positive force for change. It challenges explanations of the phenomenon of 'hearing voices' and it works in a number of countries to establish networks of users who can support voice-hearers through self-help groups. Its demands are clear. It is not 'anti-psychiatry', but it does ask for a more judicious prescription of medication, more psychological intervention, and professional support in establishing self-help groups.

User Movements make it difficult to dismiss the concerns of the millions throughout the world who succumb to psychosis and other forms of mental distress. Increasingly research and service representation cannot overlook the voice of the user.

Diagnostic systems in psychiatry; Ideology and psychiatric diagnosis; Patient choice and influence in research; Patient choice in treatment

Vantage points: SAVL

Art therapy offers a different way of seeing oneself, experiencing, and approaching problems. Its three-dimensional possibilities, physicality, and materiality can offer different vantage points. In three-dimensional works the question *'What if?'* can literally be seen from different angles and perspectives.

Rhyme; Sculptural materials; Three-dimensional form

Violation of body boundaries: MAm

Violation of the body's boundaries is a frequently encountered cause of trauma that is attended to in the therapeutic intervention. Aleathea Lillitos and Ann Gillespie are art therapists who have described the effects on children abused in this way:

When the child's body is used by an adult for sexual gratification, this transgression of the child's body boundaries leads to the child losing the sense of 'self', becoming 'de-personalised' and switching off all feelings.

(Lillitos, 1990: 80)

Children who have been sexually abused have suffered a physical violation of their bodies in the breaching of the boundary between their insides and outsides. Such a physical challenge to the integrity of the body threatens the child, as a living organism, with annihilation.

(Gillespie, 2000: 89)

Abuse; Boundaries; Post-traumatic stress disorder; Therapeutic frame

Visceral: PBr

The physical bodily sense garnered from a visual object.

Delight and disgust in the abject; Ehrenzweig; Embodied/embodiment; Facture; Irigaray; Peat; Sculptural materials

Visual culture: AJG

Visual culture is concerned with all visual events, visual information, and visual pleasures that are mediated by a form of visual technology, be it through road signs, television, the internet, oil painting, or photographic journalism, in what has been described as a 'proliferation of visuality' (Mirzoeff, 1999: 3). Visual culture is global, permeating every aspect of all our lives – from traditional photography to camcorders to video surveillance in shopping malls, and from soap operas to the televising of the Gulf War. It is an interdisciplinary field that includes art history, media studies, film, and sociology, explores how the dominance of the visual influences the wider culture of everyday life in which it exists, and addresses how we picture and visualise our existence and then create meaning from it. Its espousal of a pictorial view of the world, both generally within a Western culture and specifically within the culture of contemporary mental health care (i.e. within macro and micro cultures that privilege the spoken and written word), has significant implications for the practice of art therapy. For example, how do we understand the visual culture of our clients and its influence on the representation in, and the display and viewing of, artworks made in art therapy? How does the everyday experience of the visual translate into the visual narratives that are made and then seen in the clinical setting?

Advertising; Class; Film Studio; Internet; Popular culture; Rhyme; Transferable skills

Visual heuristic research: JMa

The source of inspiration for my own art-making is the passion I feel for the substance, texture, and detail of raw materials from the natural landscape. I trained as a studio potter and my art or 'materials' practice involves ceramics and textiles, an urge to make things for use, and a love of slow labour. I used my art practice as research to provide a visual heuristic methodology for examining the art-making associated with a weekly out-patient group where I was therapist. The heuristic research methodology used visual arts practices, making it appropriate for a wide and deep exploration rather than focusing on one situation (Mahony, 2010a). In heuristic research, narratives, personal documents, artwork, journals, and poems can be used to achieve 'layers of depth and meaning' (Moustakis, 1994: 19). Art practice as research uses visual methods that come from art itself, particularly when it is studio based (Sullivan, 2005: xvii), and is particularly appropriate for exploring how art is created and what is meant by it (Gilroy, 2006: 97; Mahony 2010a). Such methods can include exhibitions, performances, texts, objects, events, dialogues, collaborations, the viewer, the artist, and the artwork. Interpretation and analysis will be located among several sources. At the heart of this art-based research model is phenomenological immersion, emphasising critical subjectivity. There is widening acceptance of art as a form of knowledge production (Morgan, 2001). Art-based research has a richness and congruence for investigating art psychotherapy (Gilroy, 2006; Mahony, 2001; McNiff, 1998).

Heuristic research; Seeing and looking; Visual research methods

Visual research methods: AJG

Visual or art-based research methods comprise a range of approaches to generating, collecting, and analysing data, and to disseminating research findings. Visual and art-based methods are commonly used in different kinds of social research, including ethnographic and anthropological research. This can involve researchers in different kinds of activities: making art-works about societies and cultures and studying them; examining existing artefacts from a society's visual and material culture for data about the society and its culture; and collaborating with others, sometimes known as 'actors', in a society to produce visual representations about their culture and society (Banks, 2001). Visual and art-based approaches are also used in art history research, and art practice per se is increasingly viewed as research (see Sullivan, 2005). Collectively these methods have much to offer art therapy research. Generally speaking they can be clustered under four main headings: looking, writing, curating, and making.

Cosmologies; Curating and visual research; Looking and visual research; Visual heuristic research

Vitality or *lebendigkeit*: KM

The German word *lebendigkeit* is normally translated as 'vitality'. Unpacked *lebendigkeit* means 'one is in it': in the play (fullness). It refers to active states of being 'fully alive', incorporating notions of spontaneity, vivacity, and movement and change. It implies an element of trust in one's own intuition and a full engagement in playfulness, sensual enjoyment, and spontaneity. It can be used to describe the quality of relating to artwork and art-making.

Absorption in art making; Inner autonomy; Intuition; Play; Pleasure

War wounds: CR and PB

In a research study, Macnair (2002) concluded that veterans that participated in killing developed more severe PTSD symptoms than the veterans that did not participate in killing. Grossman (1995) says that when rationalisation of the act of killing fails, we have PTSD . . .

The seriousness of the situation is underlined for example in *Community Care*, a British journal. The article titled *War Wounds* (12–18 October 2006: 36–37), reports that 80% of homeless people had been in the armed forces. In the Gulf War 24 men died, however after the war 107 men committed suicide. As they are discharged from the army such men face adjustment disorder. These ex-service men often suffer from isolation, alcoholism, self-harm and unemployment . . . The army creates a sense of belonging to a group, a soldier feels more responsible for the life of his fellow colleague than for his own; soldiers equate this bonding to the love that one has for a son/daughter (Grossman 1995). As these soldiers are discharged they lose this sense of belonging . . .

This is not a new situation, and here we begin to enter the world of the arts. Papadopoulos (2002) discusses Homer's *Odyssey*. Odysseus/Ulysses when returning to his homeland in Ithaca cannot recognise it, and no one can recognise him either. Even though he is in his homeland he has not yet 'arrived' there: 'Homecoming is also about the re-establishment of all meaningful connections within one's own family and own self' (Papadopoulos,

2002: 14). A further Odyssey is necessary to really get back home, and this experience can be the most difficult one: but it is one in which our work may help.

Complex homelessness; Post-traumatic stress disorder and art psychotherapy; Power of myth-making, Beuys, and the Tartars; Trauma; Trauma and homelessness; Trauma and the aesthetic dimension in art therapy

What works for whom?: KJ

The book by Anthony Roth and Peter Fonagy, *What Works for Whom? A Critical Review of Psychotherapy Research* (1996), was commissioned by the NHS executive and continues to provide a baseline of the evidence for psychotherapy with all client groups:

> . . . The authors are aware of the need to manage the tension between clinical creativity and the need for demonstrable outcomes . . . They describe an ideal EBP model for the integration of research and service delivery. Barkham (1997) suggests that Roth and Fonagy might have found space to identify the most rigorous examples of clinical effectiveness as a model of service delivery and research and thereby helped redefine the current agenda set by funders, which places almost sole reliance for evidence on RCTs.
>
> The review concludes with a list of which therapies have demonstrated clear effectiveness or have promising or limited support for their efficacy. Art therapy is not on this list and is not included or referred to in the book.
>
> . . . Although art therapy does not appear in the book it would clearly have a place under the general heading of psychodynamic psychotherapies. Here it would appear that longer term psychodynamic therapies, including child psychotherapies, have the least evidence for effectiveness in EBP terms. The outlook is better for short-term psychodynamic treatments or those that use an interpersonal psychotherapy approach.
>
> . . . EBP demands a response from our profession that can encompass the benefits of the empirical method for clinical development and service user care. It requires a political response to protect the profession from the potential abuse of EBP and to argue the case for the values which we believe have a place within the NHS.
>
> . . . Written in an accessible and thoughtful style, it allows the art therapy student or clinician approaching the question of outcome research for the first time to become a more critical judge of the literature.
>
> (Jones, 1998: 75–77)

A second fully revised edition of *What Works for Whom?* (Roth and Fonagy) was published in 2007.

Evidence-based practice; Quantitative research; Research critical appraisal; Systematic review; Randomised Controlled Trials

Wilde's *Dorian Gray*: LR

In Oscar Wilde's gothic novel *The Picture of Dorian Gray* (1891), Dorian, a young, beautiful aristocrat, sits for his portrait. Captivated, he offers his soul to change places with the portrait, to remain young whilst the portrait bears the scars of age and experience.

Dorian treats his friends and lovers cruelly; he becomes a byword for rakish morals. 'Eternal youth . . . wild joys and wilder sins – he was to have all these things. The portrait was to bear the burden of his shame: that was all' (Wilde, 1891: 102).

As the painting becomes ever more hideous, he banishes it to the attic. His friend Basil Hallward attempts to warn that he has lost his good name, and lonely with his secret Dorian shows him the gnarled portrait. Basil encourages him to pray for redemption; however, overcome by sudden fierce hatred Dorian stabs him to death.

Initially remorseless, he eventually feels sorry, but when he finds the painting has not improved he stabs it: 'it had been like conscience to him' (Wilde, 1891: 212). As he does this, he dies and his hideous corpse is found next to the now pristine portrait.

The power of painting, the pain of narcissism, and 'projective identification' are all here:

> . . . the patient splits off parts of himself in addition to impulses and anxieties and projects them into the analyst for the purpose of evacuating and emptying out the disturbing mental content, which leads to the denial of psychic reality.
>
> (Rosenfeld, 1987: 164)

Projective identification; Projective identification: A Kleinian perspective; Projective identification and empathy; Scapegoat (two entries)

Winnicott, D. W (1896–1971): TD

> Winnicott's contribution to our thinking cannot be overestimated. . . . the importance of creativity, the transitional space and the location of cultural experience for the development of the capacity to play and his clarification of early relationships between mother and child have been used extensively . . . His description of an intermediate area of

'experiencing' between inner and outer realities seems central to our understanding . . . The 'potential space' becomes the designated safe play area between mother and child which becomes in turn the 'location of cultural experience' . . .

'This gives us our indication for therapeutic procedure – to afford opportunity for formless experience, and for creative impulses, motor and sensory, which are the stuff of playing. And on the basis of playing is built the whole of man's experiential existence. No longer are we either introvert or extrovert. We experience life in the area of transitional phenomena, in the exciting interweave of subjectivity and objective observation, and in an area that is intermediate between the inner reality of the individual and the shared reality of the world that is external to individuals (Winnicott, 1971: 75)'.

(Dalley et al., 1993: 12–13)

Interpretation perspectives; Kindness; Life of the picture; Maturation in adolescence and the uses of art therapy; Object relations theories; Play; Potential space; Reverie; Secondary handicap; Squiggle game; Sublimation theories in art therapy; Therapist and play; Transitional object

Without recourse to words: JS

There are cases where the healing effect of making and viewing pictures within the bounds of a therapeutic relationship effects a change in state without recourse to words. Then the artist/patient may come to own and reintegrate the affect which was embodied in the picture without directly discussing its meaning.

(Schaverien, 1995a: 125)

Baring the phenomenon; Embodied/embodiment; Triangular relationship

Withymead centre: MEd

Withymead was a Jungian-based therapeutic community promoting psychological healing through the arts and psychotherapy founded by Irene and Gilbert Champernowne in 1942. Its importance is both historical, in that it was one of the first therapeutic communities in the Western world, and perhaps uniquely innovatory as a substantial formative influence upon the development of the art therapies in Britain. Those who worked there, as well as the diverse clients who received help over the years, gained in personal and theoretical understanding.

For 20 years, Withymead successfully pioneered a client treatment model that synthesised a flexible ongoing programme of art, music, and dance-

movement therapy with clinical support, including individual psychotherapy sessions in a community environment that sought to engender lasting
rehabilitation. The work was loosely rather than dogmatically founded in
Jung's conception of the unconscious, in that treatment models, interpretation of workshop material and dreams, and indeed the guidelines for
day-to-day living all assumed a creative and prospective role for the unconscious that included but went beyond the narrower focus of psychoanalysis.

The undoubted success of Withymead depended upon sensitive cooperation and mutual respect between clinical and arts staff, and a strong community ethos promoted by the Champernownes that was warmly and
unconditionally supportive, yet highly professional. All worked very closely
together, with frequent, long, and regular staff meetings. Many aspects of
current art therapy practices in Britain are traceable to guidelines established at Withymead. Both Waller (1991) and Hogan (2001) have discussed
the impact of the community upon art therapy.

Champernowne; First and second periods of British art therapy history
(two entries)

Witness and witnessing in art therapy: ML

The original sense of the word was 'knowledge' or 'wisdom'. A
'witness' in the religious sense represents to the world, in a deeper
sense, their truth . . . I think that one of our primary services to our
clients is as their witness, not in the sense of any absolute knowledge of
'the truth', but as the people who have received the testimony of their
experience. In this sense, all our evidence is 'hearsay'. Images are not
equivalent to Police photographs of the scene of the crime. The truth
that we are listening and looking for is the authentic experience rather
than the facts . . .

As well as this function of 'witnessing' in therapy happening in the
relationship I believe that 'bearing witness' to our own experience is a
step towards experiencing it as meaningful. As Jung pointed out, great
suffering can be borne if it is experienced as meaningful, but much less
can be experienced as intolerable if it seems meaningless. Unless people
are in possession of their stories, the lack can drive them mad. Without
some sort of inner witness, life has no shape . . .

What does this mean to our art therapy practice? I have said that a
pre-condition of witness is presence. Another may be suspending
judgement . . .

This is of course by no means the only role or tool of the therapist
(or we would risk becoming confessors without powers of absolution!).
Despite its apparent passivity however, I believe it to be a central one.
When a witness is really present, it seems that the unconscious of the

other person is somehow invited to begin to offer different tellings of old stories.

To maintain presence is an exercise in alertness . . . Fortunately art therapy has its great alliance with the image to help.

(Learmonth, 1994: 19–22)

Concentration; Image in law; Making meaning; Triangular relationship

Witness: When the client cannot 'speak': SaW

Art therapists often work with clients for whom an event or a long period of life becomes unspeakable. These might be people who have suffered abuse or trauma in childhood, or increasingly they might be refugees and asylum seekers. They may be able to use art-making at their own pace within the frame of therapy to show something of what has happened. These art objects can provide one way of facilitating psychological witness, even though it may not be possible for the client to speak.

The task of the witness is not an easy one. The 'truth' may be impossible to see. In cases of cruelty, abuse, and torture where the perpetrator relies on secrecy and a process of silencing, outsiders do not know what went on.

When working as a therapist, I have at times felt silenced. It was as if I had lost the power of speech; although my mind is active and full of thoughts and images, my therapy role seems to have been enthralled and temporarily placed under a spell. At these times I have used as many resources as I could, including painting, supervision, and poetry, to try to understand the significance of the powerful feelings I was experiencing.

Abuse; Art made by art therapists; Balint groups and image consultation groups; Heterosexism and the heterosexual lens; Intuition; Supervision; Therapists' engagement with their own art practice; Witness and witnessing in art therapy

Words written on a picture: JS

The words written on pictures also reflect the transference. They could be understood as controlling the irrational expressive function. Words written on pictures may be employed as a decoy; they may mystify, mislead or confuse or set a false trail in order to preserve the self. The picture offers the advantage that, whatever the feelings or thoughts attributed to it, they may be safely contained 'out there', separate from the artist. The words and images exist in space and time and remain within the picture until the artist is ready to own the rejected element. Pictures which contain words in addition to images might be understood to exhibit the perpetual interplay between the need to change and the need to remain the same.

(Schaverien, 1997: 35)

Art-making as a defence; Collage; Transactional object; Transactional object in psychosis; Transference

Working alliance with men and women with learning disabilities: BD and RT

The ability (verbal and non-verbal) and the motivation to communicate affects the therapy in obvious ways, but the work is also influenced by the capacity for explorative, functional, and symbolic play (the ability to generate and use representations and signs). A lack of engagement or inhibition in the use of art materials is sometimes present, as is a repetitiveness and a defensive use of materials.

Despite the difficulties, the tangible concrete nature of the materials, the processes, and the products opens the possibility of transcending memory losses, cognitive deficiencies, and verbal understandings. The object (the lump of clay, paint on paper) is not lost and can be re-examined and revisited in each encounter. Exchanges centred around objects and materials can lead to shared reflections and a shift in gaze, allowing individuals to maintain autonomy and regulate interactions, developing relationships at a comfortable pace.

Establishing a working alliance where severe challenging behaviours are present can be hazardous, and safety can be threatened. The art therapist has to think very carefully about her own communications, and may need to consider how the limits of their current theoretical understandings represent a barrier to understanding. It is vital to recognise that this work is difficult and complex. Particular counter-transference experiences of struggling to think are often reported in the literature, and art therapists working with this client group often feel devalued and unsupported. Learning disabled people deserve no less than well-trained and properly supported therapists.

Communication with men and women with learning disabilities; Counter-transference; Counter-transference captivity; Gaze; Gaze and glance; Power; Review with images; Secondary handicap; Stupidity; Therapeutic alliance

Working through: CW

 . . . there may be an increase in the level of distress and pain as previously hidden feelings and buried aspects of self become uncovered.

One of the tasks of being in therapy is to be able to withstand this and work it through.

Working through is an important process that is central to our practice and involves attending therapy even when it is difficult. It means enabling the client to experience his feelings, anxieties and past situations over and over again in relation both to the therapist and to different people and situations in his past and present life. However painful, uncomfortable or confusing an experience, if the client can stay with these difficult feelings, some understanding will take place and a more resolved position will be reached. Normal patterns of behaviour, such as running away and avoiding conflict, may be used in an attempt to block out the emotional pain, but this merely compounds the problems with the repetition of previous patterns of relating. As Sandler *et al.* (1973) point out, working through is additional to uncovering conflicts and resistances. Intellectual insight without working through is not regarded as sufficient, as the tendency to repeat previous ways of functioning would remain.

(Dalley et al., 1993: 11)

... The image absorbs, contains and also communicates and symbolises the intense experience ... it can be seen how images can hold on to feelings in a different way which can facilitate the process of working through.

(Dalley et al., 1993: 83)

Anticipatory guidance in art therapy; Anticipatory guidance, worse/better paradigm; Reflective counter-transference; Self-harm; Thinking

Works of art: MEd

A work of art is abundant, spills out, gets drunk, sits up with you all night and forgets to close the curtains, dries your tears, is your friend, offers you a disguise, a difference, a pose. Cut it through and through and there is a still a diamond at the core. Skim the top and it is rich. The inexhaustible energy of art is a transformation for a worn-out world.

(Winterson, 1996: 65)

Non-art

References

Abram, J. (1996) *The Language of Winnicott*. London: Karnac.

Ackroyd, P. (1995) *Blake*. St Ives: Quality Paperback Direct.

Adams, J. (1979) *Conceptual Blockbusting*. New York: Norton.

Adams, P. (2003) *Art: Sublimation and Symptom*. London: Karnac.

Adamson, E. (1984) *Art as Healing*. London: Coventure.

Aldridge, F. (1998) 'Chocolate or Shit: Aesthetics and Cultural Poverty in Art Therapy with Children', *Inscape: The Journal of the British Association of Art Therapists*, 3: 2–9.

Allen, P. B. (1992) 'Artist-in Residence: An Alternative to "Clinification" for Art Therapists', *Art Therapy: Journal of the American Art Therapy Association*, 9: 22–29.

Allen, P. B. (1995) *Art is a Way of Knowing: A Guide to Self-Knowledge and Spiritual Fulfilment through Creativity*. Boston, MA: Shambala Books.

Altschuler, J. (1997) *Working with Chronic Illness*. London: Macmillan.

Alvarez, A. (1992) *Live Company: Psychoanalytic Psychotherapy with Autistic Borderline, Deprived and Abused Children*. London: Routledge.

Alvesson, M. and Skoldberg, K. (2000) *Reflective Methodology: New Vistas for Qualitative Research*. London: Sage.

Ambridge, M. (2001a) 'The Reflective Image', in J. Murphy and D. Waller (eds.) *Art Therapy with Young Survivors of Sexual Abuse*. London: Brunner-Routledge: 69–85.

Ambridge, M. (2001b) 'Monsters and Angels', in S. Richardson and H. Bacon (eds.) *Creative Responses to Child Sexual Abuse: Challenges and Dilemmas*. London: Jessica Kingsley: 167–182.

American Psychiatric Association (1994) *Diagnostic and Statistical Manual of Mental Disorders* (DSM-IV-TR). Washington, DC: APA.

Ansdell, G. and Pavlicevic, M. (2001) *Beginning Research in the Arts Therapies: A Practical Guide*. London: Jessica Kingsley.

Arlow, J. A. (1979) 'Metaphor and the Psychoanalytic Situation', *Psychoanalytic Quarterly*, 48: 363–385.

Arnheim, R. (1954) *Art and Visual Perception: A Psychology of the Creative Eye*. Berkeley, CA: University of California Press.

Arnheim, R. (1969) *Visual Thinking*. Berkely, CA: University of California Press.

Atkins, M. (2007) 'Using Digital Photography to Record Clients' Art Work', *International Journal of Art Therapy: Inscape*, 12: 79–87.

Atlas, J. A., Smith, P. and Sessoms, L. (1992) 'Art and Poetry in Brief Therapy of Hospitalized Adolescents', *The Arts in Psychotherapy*, 19: 279–283.

Auerhahn, N. and Laub, D. (1984) 'Annihilation and Restoration: Post-Traumatic Memory as Pathway and Obstacle to Recovery', *International Review of Psychoanalysis*, 11: 327–344.

Aveline, M. (2001) 'Very Brief Dynamic Psychotherapy', *Advances in Psychiatric Treatment: Journal of Continuing Professional Development Royal College of Psychiatrists*, 7: 373–380.

Bachelard, G. (1958) *The Poetics of Space*. New York: Orion Press [reprinted and translated from French in 1964 and reprinted in 1969 and 1994 by Beacon Press, Boston].

Bachelard, G. (1967) *La Poetique de la Rêverie*. Boston: Beacon Press [translated in 1988 as *On Poetic Imagination and Reverie* and reprinted in 1961 and 1971].

Bailly, L. (2003) 'A Psychodynamically Orientated Intervention Strategy for Early Reactions to Trauma', in R. Orner and U. Schnyder (eds.) *Reconstructing Early Intervention after Trauma: Innovations in the Care of Survivors*. Oxford: Oxford University Press: 95–105.

Balbernie, R. (2001) 'Circuits and Circumstances: The Neurobiological Consequences of Early Relationships and How they Shape Later Behaviour', *Journal of Child Psychotherapy*, 27: 237–255.

Balint, M. and Balint, E. (1961) *Psychotherapeutic Techniques in Medicine*. London: Tavistock.

Banks, M. (2001) *Visual Methods in Social Research*. London: Sage.

Banon, E., Evan-Grenier, M. and Bond, M. (2001) 'Early Transference Interventions with Male Patients in Psychotherapy', *Journal of Psychotherapy Practice and Research*, 10: 79–92.

Barber, V. (2002) *Explore Yourself through Art: Creative Projects to Promote Personal Insight, Growth and Problem-solving*, London: Carroll & Brown.

Barham, P. (1995) 'Manfred Bleuler and the Understanding of Psychosis', in J. Ellwood (ed.) *Psychosis: Understanding and Treatment*. London: Jessica Kingsley: 23–33.

Barkham, M. (1997) 'NHS. Modern, Dependable', *British Journal of Clinical Psychology*, 36: 462.

Barkham, M. (2007, March) *Written Evidence for Parliamentary Committee on Health*, submitted by Professor Michael Barkham and others (NICE 83). London: NICE.

Barnes, M. and Berke, J. (1973) *Mary Barnes: Two Accounts of a Journey through Madness*. Harmondsworth: Penguin.

Baron, P. H. (1989) 'Fighting Cancer with Images', in H. Waddison, J. Durkin and D. Perach (eds.) *Advances in Art Therapy*. New York: Wiley: 148–168.

Bateman, A. and Fonagy, P. (2002) *Psychotherapy for Borderline Personality Disorder*. Oxford: Oxford University Press.

Bateman, A. and Fonagy, P. (2006) *Mentalization-Based Treatment for Borderline Personality Disorder: A Practical Guide*. Oxford: Oxford University Press.

Bateman, A. and Holmes, J. (2002) *Introduction to Psychoanalysis: Contemporary Theory and Practice*. London: Brunner-Routledge.

Beck, A. T. (1976) *Cognitive Therapy and Emotional Disorders*. New York: International Universities Press.

Bell, C. E. and Robbins, S. J. (2007) 'Effect of Art Production on Negative Mood: A Randomized, Control Trial', *Art Therapy: Journal of the American Art Therapy Association*, 24: 71–75.

Berger, J. (1972) *Ways of Seeing BBC*. London: Penguin.

Bergin, A. E. and Garfield, S. L. (1994) *Handbook of Psychotherapy and Behaviour Change*. New York: Wiley.

Betensky, M. G. (1995) *What Do You See? Phenomenology of Therapeutic Art Expression*. London: Jessica Kingsley.

Bettleheim, B. (1982) *Freud and Man's Soul*. London: Pelican/Penguin.

Beveridge, W. (1942) *Social Insurance and Allied Services*. London: HMSO.

Bick, E. (1968) 'The Experience of Skin in Early Object Relations', *International Journal of Psychoanalysis*, 49: 484–486.

Biddulph, S. (1994) *Manhood: An Action Plan for Changing Men's Lives*. Stroud: Hawthorn Press.

Bindman, D. (2007) *Mind-Forged Manacles; William Blake and Slavery*. Hayward Gallery Touring Exhibition Catalogue, British Museum Partnership.

Bion, W. R. (1959) 'Attacks on Linking', *International Journal of Psycho-Analysis*, 40: 93–101.

Bion, W. R. (1961) *Experiences in Groups and Other Papers*. London: Tavistock [reprinted in 1996 by Routledge].

Bion, W. (1962a) 'A Theory of Thinking', *International Journal of Psycho-Analysis*, 43: 306–310.

Bion, W. R. (1962b) *Learning from Experience*. London: Heinemann.

Bion, W. R. (1963) 'Container and Contained', in *Elements of Psychoanalysis*. London: Heinemann [reprinted in 1984 by Karnac: 1–4].

Bion, W. (1967a) *Second Thoughts*. London: Heinemann [reprinted in 1990 by Maresfield].

Bion, W. (1967b) 'Notes on Memory and Desire', in E. B. Spillius (ed.) (1998) *Melanie Klein Today. Vol. 2 Mainly Practice*. London: Routledge: 17–21.

Bion, W. R. (1973–1974) *Brazilian Lectures, Numbers 1 and 2*. Rio de Janeiro: Imago Editora [reprinted in 1990 by Karnac].

Bion, W. R. (1984a) *Attention and Interpretation*. London: Karnac.

Bion, W. R. (1984b) *Transformations*. London: Karnac.

Blackwell, D. (1994a) 'The Psyche and the System', in D. Brown and L. Zinkin (eds.) *The Psyche and the Social World: Developments in Group Analytic Therapy*. London: Routledge: 232–252.

Blackwell, D. (1994b) 'Group Analysis and Sport', *Group Analysis*, 27: 227–229.

Bleuler, M. (1972) *The Schizophrenic Disorder: Long-Term Patient and Family Studies*. New Haven, CT: Yale University Press [reprinted and translated from German in 1978].

Bloch, S. and Crouch, E. (1985) *Therapeutic Factors in Group Psychotherapy*. Oxford: Oxford University Press.

Blos, P. (1962) *On Adolescence*. New York: Free Press.

Blunt, A. (1940) *Artistic Theory in Italy 1450–1600*. Oxford: Oxford University Press.

Bollas, C. (1987) *The Shadow of the Object: Psychoanalysis of the Unknown Thought*. London: Free Association Books.

Bollas, C. (1999) *The Mystery of Things*. London: Routledge.

Bolton K. G. (2005) *The Urban Canvas: Art and Identity in the Urban Landscape and Beyond. Investigating Graffiti in Relation to Art Psychotherapy Practice*, MA Dissertation, Northern Programme.

Borer, A. (1996) *The Essential Joseph Beuys*. London: Thames & Hudson.

Boronska, T. (2000) 'Art Therapy with Two Sibling Groups Using an Attachment Framework', *Inscape: The Journal of the British Association of Art Therapists*, 5: 2–10.

Boronska, T. (2008) 'I'm the King of the Castle: The Sibling Bond: Art Therapy with Sibling Groups with Children in Care', in C. Case and T. Dalley (eds.) *Art Therapy with Children: From Infancy to Adolescence*. London: Routledge: 54–68.

Bourgeois, L. (1998) *Louise Bourgeois: Destruction of the Father/Reconstruction of the Father: Writings and Interviews 1923–1997*. Cambridge, MA: MIT Press.

Boyd, W. (2007, 31 December) 'Start the Week', *BBC Radio Four*.

Boyle, M. (1999) 'Diagnosis', in C. Newnes, G. Holmes and C. Dunn (eds.) *This is Madness: A Critical Look at Psychiatry and the Future of the Mental Health Service*. Ross on Wye: PCCS Books: 75–90.

Bragg, M. (2004, 10th July) 'Britain in a Box', *BBC Radio 4*.

British Museum Exhibition Catalogue (2003) *Living and Dying*. London: Wellcome Trust and British Museum.

Britton, R. (1998) *Belief and Imagination – Explorations in Psychoanalysis*. London: Routledge.

Brom, D., Kleber, R. J. and Defares, P. B. (1989) 'Brief psychotherapy for posttraumatic stress disorders', *Journal of Consulting and Clinical Psychology*, 57: 607–612.

Brooker, J., Cullum, M., Gilroy, A., McCombe, B., Mahony, J., Ringrose, K., et al. (2007) *The Use of Artwork in Art Psychotherapy with People Prone to Psychotic States: A Clinical Practice Guideline*. London: Goldsmiths College, University of London.

Brown, A. (2005) 'Survey of Art Therapists Working with Adolescents in the NHS in Great Britain', *British Association of Art Therapy ATPRN Symposium*, London.

Brown, C., Meyerowtiz-Katz, J. and Ryde, J. (2003) 'Thinking with Image-Making in Supervision', *Inscape: The Journal of the British Association of Art Therapists*, 8: 71–78.

Brown, C., Meyerowtiz-Katz, J. and Ryde, J. (2007) 'Thinking with Image-Making: Supervising Art Therapy Students', in J. Schaverien and C. Case (eds.) *Supervision of Art Psychotherapy*. Hove: Routledge: 167–181.

Bryson N. (1983) *Vision and Painting: The Logic of the Gaze*. London: Macmillan.

Budman, S. H., Cooley, S., Demby, A., Koppenaal, G., Koslof, J. and Powers, T. (1996) 'A Model of Time-Effective Group Psychotherapy for Patients with Personality Disorders', *International Journal of Group Psychotherapy*, 26: 329–355.

Bunt, L. (1994) *Music Therapy: An Art Beyond Words*. London: Routledge.

Burton, M. (2005) 'Foreword', in *Facing Death: Art Therapy and Cancer Care*. Maidenhead: Open University Press.

Butler, R. and Parr, H. (1999) *Mind and Body Spaces: Geographies of Illness*. London: Routledge.

Butler, R. W. and Satz, P. (1999) 'Depression and its Diagnosis and Treatment', in K. Langer, L. Laatsch and L. Lewis (eds.) *Psychotherapeutic Interventions for Adults with Brain Injury or Stroke: A Clinician's Treatment Resource*. Madison, CT: Psychosocial Press: 97–112.

Byrne, P. (2002) *Art Therapy: A Developmental Narrative, from Symptoms and Theory to Cultural Paradigms*, PhD Thesis, University of Edinburgh Library.

Calvino, I. (1998) *Six Memos for the Next Millennium*. Cambridge, MA: Harvard University Press.

Campbell, J. (1993) *Creative Art in Group Work*, Bicester: Speechmark Publishing (formerly Winslow Press).

Campbell, J., Liebmann, M., Brooks, F., Jones, J. and Ward, C. (1999) *Art Therapy, Race and Culture*. London: Jessica Kingsley.

Cantle, T. (1983) 'Hate in the Helping Relationship: The Therapeutic Use of an Occupational Hazard', *Inscape: The Journal of the British Association of Art Therapists*, October: 2–10.

Cape, J. and Parry, G. (2000) 'Clinical Practice Guidelines Development in Evidence-Based Psychotherapy', in N. Rowland and S. Goss (eds.) *Evidence-Based Counselling and Psychological Therapies*. London: Routledge: 171–190.

Cardinal, R. (1972) *Outsider Art*. London: Studio Vista.

Carrel, C. and Laing, J. (1982) *The Special Unit: Barlinnie Prison*. Glasgow: Third Eye Centre.

Case, C. (1987) 'A Search for Meaning: Loss and Transition in Art Therapy with Children', in T. Dalley et al. (eds.) *Images of Art Therapy: New Developments in Theory and Practice*. London: Tavistock: 36–73.

Case, C. (1994) 'Art Therapy in Analysis: Advance/Retreat in the Belly of a Spider', *Inscape: The Journal of the British Association of Art Therapists*, 1: 3–10.

Case, C. (2000) '"Our Lady of the Queen": Journeys Around the Maternal Object', in A. Gilroy and G. McNeilly (eds.) *The Changing Shape of Art Therapy: New Developments in Theory and Practice*. London: Jessica Kingsley: 15–54.

Case, C. (2002) 'Animation and the Location of Beauty', *Journal of Child Psychotherapy*, 28: 327–343.

Case, C. (2003) 'Authenticity and Survival: Working with Children in Chaos', *Inscape: The Journal of the British Association of Art Therapists*, 8: 17–28.

Case, C. (2005a) 'Observations of Children Cutting Up, Cutting Out and Sticking Down', *International Journal of Art Therapy: Inscape*, 10: 53–62.

Case, C. (2005b) 'The Mermaid: Moving Towards Reality after Trauma', *Journal of Child Psychotherapy*, 31: 335–351.

Case, C. (2005c) *Imagining Animals: Art, Psychotherapy and Primitive States of Mind*. London: Routledge.

Case, C. (2007) 'Imagery in Supervision: The Non-Verbal Narrative of Knowing', in J. Schaverien and C. Case (eds.) *Supervision of Art Psychotherapy: A Theoretical and Practical Handbook*. London: Routledge: 95–115.

Case, C. (2008) 'Playing Ball: Oscillations within the Potential Space', in C. Case and D. Dalley (eds.) *Art Therapy with Children: From Infancy to Adolescence*. London: Routledge: 103–122.

Case, C. and Dalley, T. (1990) *Working with Children in Art Therapy*. London: Routledge.

Case, C. and Dalley, T. (1992) *The Handbook of Art Therapy*. London: Routledge.

Case, C. and Dalley, T. (2006) *The Handbook of Art Therapy: Second Edition*. London: Tavistock/Routledge.

Case, C. and Dalley, T. (2008) *Art Therapy with Children: From Infancy to Adolescence*. London: Routledge.

Cassirer, E. (1955) *Mythical Thought: Vol. 11. The Philosophy of Symbolic Forms*. New Haven, CT: Yale University Press.

Cassirer, E. (1957) *The Phenomenology of Knowledge: Vol. III. The Philosophy of Symbolic Forms*. New Haven, CT: Yale University Press.

Catty, J. (2004) 'The Vehicle of Success: Theoretical and Empirical Perspectives on the Therapeutic Alliance in Psychotherapy and Psychiatry', *Psychology and Psychotherapy: Theory Research and Practice*, 77: 255–272.

Chalfant, H. and Prigoff, J. (1987) *Spraycan Art*. London: Thames & Hudson.

Champernowne, I. (1971) 'Art and Therapy: An Uneasy Partnership', *American Journal of Art Therapy*, 10: 131–143; also published in *Inscape: Journal of the British Association of Art Therapists*, 1: 2–14.

Charlton, S. (1984) 'Art Therapy with Long Stay Residents of Psychiatric Hospitals', in T. Dalley (ed.) *Art as Therapy*. London: Tavistock: 173–190.

Chipp, H. B. (1968) *Theories of Modern Art: A Source Book by Artists and Critics*. Berkeley, CA: University of California Press.

Clarkson, P. (1999) *Gestalt Counselling in Action*. London: Sage.

Cohen, G. D. (2006) 'The Impact of Professionally Conducted Cultural Programs on the Physical Health, Mental Health, and Social Functioning of Older Adults', *The Gerontologist*, 46: 726–734.

Cole, P. (1984) 'Psychopathology Illustrated through Art Therapy', in *Art Therapy as Psychotherapy in Relation to the Mentally Handicapped?*, Conference Proceedings. St Albans: Hertfordshire College of Art: 161–178.

Coleman, J. C. and Hendry, L. B. (1999) 'The Nature of Adolescence', *Adolescence and Society Series*. London: Routledge.

Coles, B. (1997) 'Vulnerable Youth and Processes of Social Exclusion', in J. Bynner, L. Chisholm and A. Furlong (eds.) *Youth, Citizenship and Social Change in a European Context*. Aldershot: Ashgate Publishing: 69–88.

Collins, M. and Phillips, J. (2003) 'Disempowerment and Disconnection: Trauma and Homelessness', Glasgow Homelessness Network.

Coltart, N. (1987) 'Diagnosis and Assessment for Suitability for Psychoanalytic Psychotherapy', *British Journal of Psychotherapy*, 14: 127–134.

Coltart, N. (1988) 'The Assessment of Psychological-Mindedness in the Diagnostic Interview', *British Journal of Psychiatry*, 153: 819–820.

Coltart, N. (1993) *How to Survive as a Psychotherapist*. London: Sheldon Press.

Connell, C. (1998) *Something Understood: Art Therapy in Cancer Care*. Wrexham: Wrexham Publications.

Cook, J. A. and Wright, E. R. (1995) 'Medical Sociology and the Study of Severe Mental Illness: Reflections on Past Accomplishments and Directions for Future Research', *Journal of Health and Social Behaviour*, 35: 95–114.

Copley, B. (1993) *The World of Adolescence*. London: Free Association Books.

Cordess, C. (1996) 'Introduction: The Multidisciplinary Team in Forensic Psychotherapy', in C. Cordess and M. Cox (eds.) *Forensic Psychotherapy: Crime, Psychodynamics and the Offender Patient*, Vol. 2. London: Jessica Kingsley: 97–99.

Cortazzie, D. and Gunsburg, H. C. (1969) 'The Bottom of the Barrel', *Journal of Mental Subnormality*, XV: 3–10.

Cox, J. (1996) *Julia Margaret Cameron*. London: Christopher Hudson.

Cox, M. (1996) 'Supportive and Interpretive Psychotherapy in Diverse Contexts', in C. Cordess and M. Cox (eds.) *Forensic Psychotherapy: Crime, Psychodynamics and the Offender Patient*, Vol. 2. London: Jessica Kingsley 83–93.

Coyle, A. (1984) *Redundant Women*. London: The Women's Press.

Creed, B. (1993) *The Monstrous Feminine: Film, Feminism and Psychoanalysis*. London: Routledge.

Critchley, S. (2007) *Outsider Art and Graffiti*, MA Dissertation, Northern Programme.

CSIP (2006) *Our Choices in Mental Health: A Framework for Improving Choice for People who Use Mental Health Services and their Carers; a Set of Good Practice Guidelines*. London: Sainsbury Centre for Mental Health.

Cupples, M., Bradley, T., Sibbett, C. and Thompson, W. (2002) 'The Sick General Practitioner's Dilemma – to Work or Not to Work?', *British Medical Journal*, 324: 139s.

Dalley, T. (1984) *Art as Therapy*. London: Tavistock.

Dalley, T. (2000) 'Back to the Future: Thinking about Theoretical Developments in Art Therapy', in A. Gilroy and G. McNeilly (eds.) *The Changing Shape of Art Therapy: New Developments in Theory and Practice*. London: Jessica Kingsley: 84–98.

Dalley, T. and Gilroy, A. (1989) *Pictures at an Exhibition*. London: Tavistock/ Routledge.

Dalley, T., Case, C., Schaverien, J., Weir, F., Halliday, D., Nowell Hall P., et al. (eds.) (1987) *Images of Art Therapy: New Developments in Theory and Practice*. London: Tavistock.

Dalley, T., Rifkind, G. and Terry, K. (1993) *Three Voices of Art Therapy: Image, Client, Therapist*. London and New York: Routledge.

Damarell, B. (1999) 'Just Forging or Seeking Love and Approval?', *Inscape: The Journal of the British Association of Art Therapists*, 4: 44–50.

Damasio, A. (1994) *Descartes' Error: Emotion, Reason and the Human Brain*. New York: Putman.

Deco, S. (1998) 'Return to the Open Studio Group: Art Therapy Groups in Acute Psychiatry', in S. Skaife and V. Huet (eds.) *Art Psychotherapy Groups*, London: Routledge: 88–108.

Delmonte, H. (1995) 'Why Work with the Dying?', in C. Lee (ed.) *Lonely Waters*. Oxford: Sobell: 10–24.

Denscombe, M. (1998) *The Good Research Guide for Small-scale Research Projects*. Buckingham: Open University Press.

Derrida, J. (1976) *Of Grammatology*. London: John Hopkins University Press [republished 1997].

Descartes, R. and Maclean, I. (2006) *Discourse on Method*. Oxford: Oxford University Press.

Dexter, E. and Bush, K. (1994) *Mise en Scène*. London: ICA.

Dickinson, C. (2004) *Disguise*. Manchester: City Galleries.

Dickman, S., Dunn, J. and Wolf, A. (1996) 'The Use of Art Therapy as a Predictor of Relapse in Chemical Dependency Treatment', *Art Therapy: Journal of the American Association of Art Therapists*, 13: 232–237.

Dickson, C. (2007) 'An Evaluation Study of Art Therapy Provision in a Residential Addiction Treatment Programme (ATP)', in *International Journal of Art Therapy: Inscape*, 12: 17–27.

Digby, J. and Digby, J. (1985) *The Collage Handbook*. London: Thames & Hudson.

Dissanayake, E. (1985) *What is Art For?* Seattle: University of Washington.

Dissanayake, E. (1995) *Homo Aestheticus*. Seattle: University of Washington.

Doerner, K. (1981) *Madmen and the Bourgeoisie: A Social History of Insanity and Psychiatry*. Blackwell: Oxford.

DOH (1999) *NHS Framework for Mental Health*. London: HMSO.

DOH (2000) *The NHS Plan: A Plan for Investment, A Plan for Reform* London: HMSO.

DOH (2001a) *Treatment Choice in Psychological Therapies*. London: HMSO.

DOH (2001b) *Valuing People*. London: HMSO.

DOH (2004) *Organising and Delivering Psychological Therapies*. London: HMSO.

DOH (2007) *Improving Access to Psychological Therapies: Specifications for the Commissioner-Led Pathfinder Programme*. London: HMSO.

DOH (2009, March) *New Horizons: Mental Health Strategy*. London: HMSO.

Dokter, D. (1994) *Arts Therapies and Clients with Eating Disorders: Fragile Board*. London: Jessica Kingsley.

Donati, F (1989) 'A Psychodynamic Observer in a Chronic Psychiatric Ward', *British Journal of Psychotherapy*, 5: 317–329; also in R. D. Hinshelwood and W. Skogstad (eds.) *Observing Organisations – Anxiety, Defence and Culture in Healthcare*. London: Routledge: 29–43.

Dow, J. (1986) 'Universal Aspects of Symbolic Healing: A Theoretical Synthesis', *American Anthropologist* 88: 56–69.

Dower, N. and Williams, E. (2000) *Cynthia Pell: The Bexley Hospital Drawings*. London: The Cynthia Pell Account.

Dubowski J. (1985) *An Investigation of the Pre-representational Drawing Activity of Certain Severely Retarded Subjects Within an Institution Using Ethological Techniques*, PhD Thesis, University of Hertfordshire School of Art and Design.

Dubuffet, J. (1995) *Art Brut*. Switzerland: Booking International.

Dudley J. (2001) 'The Co Therapist Relationship – A Married Couple?', *Inscape: The Journal of the British Association of Art Therapists*, 6: 12–22.

Dudley, J (2004a) 'Politics and Pragmatism Proposing the Use of the Title Arts Psychotherapies for All', *BAAT Newsbriefing*. London: BAAT.

Dudley, J. (2004b). 'Art Psychotherapy and the Use of Psychiatric Diagnosis: Assessment for Art Psychotherapy', *Inscape: The Journal of the British Association of Art Therapists*, 9: 14–25.

Duncan, C. (1995) *Civilizing Rituals Inside Public Art Museums*. London: Routledge.

Eagleton, T. (1990) *The Ideology of the Aesthetic*. Oxford: Blackwell.

Edwards, B. (2001) *Drawing on the Right Side of the Brain*. New York: Harper Collins.

Edwards, D. (1997) 'Endings', *Inscape: The Journal of the British Association of Art Therapy*, 2: 49–56.

Edwards, D. (2004) *Art Therapy*. London: Sage.

Edwards, M. (1978) 'Art Therapy in Great Britain', in D. Elliot (ed.) *The Inner Eye*. Oxford: Museum of Modern Art Catalogue: 12–20.

Edwards, M. (1989) 'Art Therapy and Romanticism', in A. Gilroy and T. Dalley (eds.) *Pictures at an Exhibition: Selected Essays on Art and Art Therapy*. London: Routledge: 74–83.

Edwards, M. (1998) 'Ways In and Ways Out', *Harmony and Discord, Champernowne Trust Conference*, Cumberland Lodge, Windsor.

Edwards, M. (1999) *Without Virtue or Virtuosity*, Champernowne Trust Summer School, Windsor.

Edwards, M. (2001) *Drawing the Line*, Champernowne Trust Summer School, Windsor.

Edwards, M. (2005) Lecture with the title 'Withymead' given to the Art Therapy Northern Programme in Sheffield.

Ehrenzweig, A. (1967) *The Hidden Order of Art*. London: Paladin.

Elkins, J. (2000) *What Painting Is*. London: Routledge.

Ellenberger, H. F. (1970) *The Discovery of the Unconscious*. New York: Basic Books.

Elliot, D. (1978) *The Inner Eye*. Oxford: Catalogue Museum of Modern Art.

Ellis, A. (1993) *Better, Deeper and More Enduring Brief Therapy: The REBT Behavioural Therapy Approach*. New York: Brunner/Mazel.

Ellwood, J. (1995) *Psychosis: Understanding and Treatment*. London: Jessica Kingsley.

Elo, I. (2009) 'Class Differentials in Mortality and Morbidity' [electronic version], *Annual Review of Sociology*, 35.

Erskine, A. and Judd, D. (1994) *The Imaginative Body: Psychodynamic Therapy in Health Care*. London: Whurr.

Etherington, K. (1995) *Adult Male Survivors of Childhood Sexual Abuse*. London: Pitman.

Euroqol Group (2008) *EQ-5D Clinical Outcome Measure* (http://www.euroqol.org/).

Evans, K. and Dubowski, J. (2001) *Art Therapy with Children on the Autistic Spectrum: Beyond Words*. London: Jessica Kingsley.

Fairbairn, W. R. D. (1952) *Psycho-Analytic Studies of the Personality*. London: Routledge.

Faulkner, A. and Layzell, S. (2000) *Strategies for Living: A Report of User-Led Research into People's Strategies for Living with Mental Distress*. London: Mental Health Foundation.

Feltham, C. and Dryden, W. (2006) *Brief Counselling: A Practical Integrative Approach*. Maidenhead: Open University Press.

Finkelhor, D. (1986) *Sourcebook on Child Sexual Abuse*. Los Angeles, CA: Sage.

Flann, J. D. (1978) *Matisse on Art*. London: Phaidon Press.

Fonagy, P. (1991) 'Thinking about Thinking: Some Clinical and Theoretical Considerations in the Treatment of a Borderline Patient', *International Journal of Psycho-Analysis*, 72: 639–656.

Fonagy, P., Steele, M., Steele, H., Higgit, A. and Target, M. (1994) 'The Theory and Practice of Resilience', *Journal of Child Psychology and Psychiatry*, 35: 231–257.

Fonagy, P., Gergely, G., Jurist, E. and Target, M. (2002) *Affect Regulation, Mentalization, and the Development of the Self*. New York: Other Press.

Foucault, M. (1967) *Madness and Civilization: A History of Insanity in the Age of Reason*. London: Tavistock [reprinted by Routledge in 1989].

Foulkes, S. H. (1964) *Therapeutic Group Analysis*. London: George Allen & Unwin.

Foulkes, S. H. (1975) *Group Analytic Psychotherapy: Method and Principles*. London: Gordon & Breach [reprinted in 1991 by Karnac].

Foulkes, S. H. and Anthony, E. J. (1965) *Group Psychotherapy, the Psychoanalytic Approach*. Harmondsworth: Penguin.

Fox, L. (1998) 'Lost in Space', in M. Rees (ed.) *Drawing on Difference*. London: Routledge: 73–90.

Francis, D., Kaiser, D. and Deaver, S. (2003) 'Representations of Attachment Security in the Bird's Nest Drawings of Clients with Substance Abuse Disorders', *Art Therapy: Journal of the American Association of Art Therapists*, 20: 125–137.

Frankl, V. (1984) *Man's Search for Meaning*. New York: Washington Square Press.

Franks, M. and Whitaker, R. (2007) 'The Image, Mentalization and Group Art Psychotherapy', *'International Journal of Art Therapy: Inscape*, 12: 3–16.

Frazer, J. G. (1922) *The Golden Bough*. London: Macmillan [abridged in 1933].

Freud, A. (1966) *The Ego and Mechanisms of Defence*. New York: International Universities Press.

Freud, S. (1900) *Interpreting Dreams*. London: Penguin [translation by J. A. Underwood published in 2006].

Freud, S. (1907) 'Creative Writers and Day Dreaming', *Art and Literature: Penguin Freud Library*, Vol. 14. Harmondsworth: Penguin: 129–143.

Freud, S. (1915) 'Remembering, Repeating and Working Through', *Standard Edition*, Vol. 12. London: Hogarth Press: 97–108.

Freud, S. (1915–1917) *Introductory Lectures on Psychoanalysis*. London: Hogarth Press [republished in 1979 as *The Pelican Freud Library*, Vol. 1. Harmondsworth: Penguin].

Freud, S. (1917) 'Mourning and Melancholia', in A. Philips (ed.) *Sigmund Freud, On Murder, Mourning and Melancholia*. London: Penguin: 201–218 [new translation by Shaun Whiteside].

Freud, S. (1921) 'Group Psychology and the Analysis of the Ego', in *Civilisation, Society and Religion: Penguin Freud Library*, Vol. 12. Harmondsworth: Penguin.

Freud, S. (1923) 'The Ego and the Id', *On Metapsychology: Penguin Freud Library*, Vol. 11. Harmondsworth: Penguin.

Freud, S. (1928) 'Fetishism', *Standard Edition*, Vol. 21. London: Hogarth Press.

Freud, S. (1930) 'Civilisation and its Discontents', *Civilization, Society and Religion: Penguin Freud Library*, Vol. 12. Harmondsworth: Penguin.

Freud, S. (1940a[1938]) *An Outline of Psychoanalysis, Standard Edition*, Vol. 23. London: Hogarth Press.

Fryers, D., Meltzer, D. and Jenkins, R. (2000) *Mental Health Inequalities Report 1: A Systematic Literature Review*. London: DOH.

Gardner, H. (1983) *Frames of Mind – The Theory of Multiple Intelligences*. London: Heinemann.

Garland, C. (1998) 'Thinking about Trauma', in *Understanding Trauma: A Psychoanalytical Approach*. London: Tavistock: 9–31.

Garner, R. L. (1966) 'Factors in Neuropsychological Rehabilitation', *American Journal of Art Therapy*, 34: 107–111.

Gedo, J. (1989) *Portraits of the Artist*. Hillsdale, NJ: Lawrence Erlbaum Associates.

Gell, A. (1998) *Art and Agency: An Anthropological Theory*. Oxford: Clarendon Press.

Gilbody, S. and Sowden, A. (2000) 'Systematic Reviews in Mental Health', in N. Rowland and S. Goss (eds.) *Evidence-Based Counselling and Psychological Therapies*. London: Routledge: 241–249.

Gillespie, A. (2000) 'Into the Body', in J. Murphy and D. Waller (eds.) *Art Therapy with Young Survivors of Childhood Sexual Abuse: Lost for Words*. London: Brunner-Routledge: 86–100.

Gilroy, A. (1992) *Art Therapists and their Art. From the Origins of an Interest in Art to Occasionally Being Able to Paint*, DPhil Thesis, University of Sussex.

Gilroy, A. (1996) 'Our Own Kind of Evidence', *Inscape: The Journal of the British Association of Art Therapists*, 1: 52–60.

Gilroy, A. (2005) 'On Occasionally Being Able to Paint', *Inscape: The Journal of the British Association of Art Therapists*, 9: 72–78.

Gilroy, A. (2006) *Art Therapy, Research and Evidence-Based Practice*. London: Sage.

Gilroy, A. (2008) 'Taking a Long Look at Art. Reflections on the Production and Consumption of Art in Art Therapy and Allied Organisational Settings', *International Review of Art and Design Education*, 27 [also available at http://eprints.goldsmiths.ac.uk/224].

Gilroy, A. and Dalley, T. (1989) *Pictures at an Exhibition: Selected Essays on Art and Art Therapy*. London: Routledge.

Gilroy, A. and Lee, C. (1995) *Art and Music: Therapy and Research*. London: Routledge.

Gilroy, A. and McNeilly, G. (2000) *The Changing Shape of Art Therapy: New Developments in Theory and Practice*. London: Jessica Kingsley.

Girard, L. (2008a) 'The Therapy Ceremony – Encountering the Strange(r) in Art Therapy', unpublished Finnish paper.

Girard, L. (2008b) 'The Aesthetic Dimension in Art Therapy', unpublished Finnish Paper.

Glossop, M., Marsden, J. and Stewart, D. (2001) *After Five Years: Changes in Substance Use, Health and Criminal Behaviour*. London: National Addiction Centre.

Glover, N. (2000) *Psychoanalytic Aesthetics: The British School* (http://human-nature.com/free-associations/glover/index.html).

Godfrey, H. (2008) 'Androcles and the Lion: Prolific Offenders on Probation', in M. Liebmann (ed.) *Art Therapy and Anger*. London: Jessica Kingsley: 102–116.

Goffman, I. (1961) *Asylums*. Harmondsworth: Penguin.

Golberg, D. and Thornicroft, G. (1998) *Mental Health in Our Future Cities*. Hove: Psychology Press.

Goldsmith, Anna. (1986) 'Substance and Structure in the Art Therapeutic Process – Working with Mental Handicap', *Inscape: The Journal of the British Association of Art Therapists*, Summer: 18–22.

Goldsworthy, A. (2007) 'Bothy Gallery', *Andy Goldsworthy at Yorkshire Sculpture Park*.

Gomez, L. (1997) *An Introduction to Object Relations*. London: Free Association Books.

Goodman, L., Saxe, L. and Harvey, M. (1991). 'Homelessness as Psychological Trauma', *American Psychologist*, 46: 1219–1225.

Gray, A. (1994) *An Introduction to the Therapeutic Frame*. London: Routledge.

Gray, J. (1985) 'The Conscious and Unconscious Process – Parallel Aspects of Art Therapy in Mental Handicap', *Inscape: The Journal of the British Association of Art Therapists*, Winter: 3–7.

Greenberg, J. R. and Mitchell, S. A. (1983) *Object Relations in Psychoanalytic Theory*. Cambridge, MA: Harvard University Press.

Greenwood, H. (1994) 'Cracked Pots', *Inscape: The Journal of the British Association of Art Therapists*, 1: 11–14.

Greenwood, H. (1997) 'Psychosis and the Maturing Ego', in K. Killick and J. Schaverien (eds.) *Art, Psychotherapy and Psychosis*. London: Routledge: 106–127.

Greenwood, H. (2000) 'Captivity and Terror in the Therapeutic Relationship', *Inscape: The Journal of the British Association of Art Therapists*, 5: 53–61.

Greenwood, H. and Layton, G. (1987) 'An Out-Patient Art Therapy Group', *Inscape: The Journal of the British Association of Art Therapist*, Summer: 12–19.

Greenwood, H. and Layton, G. (1988) 'Taking the Piss', *British Journal of Clinical and Social Psychiatry*, 6: 74–84.

Greenwood, H., Leach, C., Lucock, M. and Noble, R. (2007) 'The Process of Long-Term Art Therapy: A Case Study Combining Artwork and Clinical Outcome', *Psychotherapy Research*, 17: 588–599.

Grosskurth, P. (1987) *Melanie Klein: Her World and Her Work*. London: Hodder & Staughton.

Grossman, D. (1995) *On Killing: The Psychological Cost of Learning to Kill in War and Society*. New York: Back Bay Books.

Gunderson, J. and Sabo, A. (1993) 'The Phenomenal and Conceptual Interface between Borderline Personality Disorder and PTSD', *American Journal of Psychiatry*, 150: 19–27.

Guntrip, H. (1986) *Schizoid Phenomena Object Relations and the Self*. London: Hogarth Press.

Haesler, M. P. (1989) 'Should Art Therapists Create Artwork Alongside Their Clients?', *American Journal of Art Therapy*, 27: 70–79.

Hagood, M. (1992) 'Group Art Therapy with Adolescent Sex Offenders', in M. Liebmann (ed.) *Art Therapy with Offenders*. London: Jessica Kingsley: 197–219.

Hall, N. (1980) *The Moon and the Virgin*. London: The Women's Press.

Hallam, J. (1983) 'Complicity and Dissent within a Mental Handicap Hospital', *Inscape: The British Journal of the Association of Art Therapists*, October: 13–15.

Hallam, J. (1984) 'Regression and Ego Integration in Art Therapy with Mentally Handicapped People', *Art Therapy as Psychotherapy? In Relation to the Mentally Handicapped*, Conference at Hertfordshire College of Art and Design.

Halliday, D. (1978) 'The Use of Therapeutic Art in Child Guidance', in D. Elliot (ed.) *The Inner Eye*. Oxford: Catalogue Museum of Modern Art: 21–26.

Halliday, D. (1988) 'My Art Healed Me', *Inscape: The Journal of the British Association of Art Therapists*, Spring: 18–22.

Hardy, D. (2005) 'Creating Through Loss: How Art Therapists Sustain their

Practice', in D. Waller and C. Sibbett (eds.) *Facing Death: Art Therapy and Cancer Care*. Maidenhead: Open University Press: 185–198.

Harlan, V. (2004) *What is Art*. Forest Row: Fairview Books.

Harman, C. (1988) *The Fire Last Time: 1968 and After*. London: Bookmarks.

Hartland, S. (1991) 'Supportive Psychotherapy', in J. Holmes (ed.) *Textbook of Psychotherapy in Psychiatric Practice*. Edinburgh: Churchill Livingstone: 213–235.

Haslam, J. (1810) *Illustrations of Madness: Exhibiting a Singular Case of Insanity and a No Less Remarkable Difference in Medical Opinion*. London: Hayden Press.

Hass-Cohen, N. and Carr, R. (2008) *Art Therapy and Clinical Neuroscience*. London: Jessica Kingsley.

Hawkes, T. (1972) *Metaphor: The Critical Idiom*. London: Methuen.

Heidegger, M. (1962) *Being and Time*. Oxford: Blackwell [1st English edition translated from 7th edition by J. Macquarrie and E. Robinson].

Henzell, J. (1978) 'Art and Psychopathology', in D. Elliot (ed.) *The Inner Eye*. Oxford: Catalogue Museum of Modern Art: 27–34.

Henzell, J. (1984) 'Art, Psychotherapy, and Symbol Systems', in T. Dalley (ed.) *Art as Therapy*. London: Tavistock.

Henzell, J. (1994) 'Art as an Ally in Therapy', in J. Laing and P. Byrne (eds.) *Starting from Scratch. Proceedings of the First Scottish International Art Therapy Conference*. Edinburgh: University Settlement.

Henzell, J. (1997) 'Art, Madness and Anti-Psychiatry: A Memoir', in K. Killick and J. Schaverien (eds.) *Art, Psychotherapy and Psychosis*. London: Routledge.

Hepworth, B. (1970) *Pictorial Biography*. London: Tate/Bowness Hepworth Estate.

Herman, J. L. (1994) *Trauma and Recovery*. London: Pandora.

Herman, J. L. (2001) *Trauma and Recovery: From Domestic Abuse to Political Terror*. London: Rivers Oram Press/Pandora List.

Higgins, R. (1996) *Approaches to Research*. London: Jessica Kingsley.

Hill, A. (1948) *Art versus Illness: A Story of Art Therapy*. London: George Allen & Unwin.

Hill, A. (1951) *Painting Out Illness*. London: Williams & Norgate.

Hillman, J. (1998) *The Myth of Analysis: Three Essays in Archetypal Psychology*. Evanston, IL: Northwest University.

Hills, M. (2006) *An inquiry into the relationship between the visual arts and psychotherapy in post-revolutionary Cuba*, PhD Thesis, Queen Margaret University College Library.

Hindele, D. and Vaciago Smith, M. (1999) *Personality Development: A Psychoanalytic Perspective*. London: Routledge.

Hinshelwood, R. D. (1987) *What Happens in Groups?* London: Free Association Books.

Hinshelwood, R. D. (1989) *A Dictionary of Kleinian Thought*. London: Free Association Books.

Hinshelwood, R. D. and Skogstad, W. (2000) *Observing Organisations – Anxiety, Defence and Culture in Healthcare*. London: Routledge.

HMSO (2006) *Care Matters: Transforming the Lives of Children and Young People in Care*. London: HMSO.

Hobson, R. F. (1985) *Forms of Feeling: The Heart of Psychotherapy*. London: Tavistock.

Hodson, P. (1984) *Men: An Investigation into the Emotional Male*. London: British Broadcasting Corporation (BBC).

Hogan, S. (1997) *Feminist Approaches to Art Therapy*. London: Routledge.

Hogan, S. (2001) *Healing Arts: The History of Art Therapy*. London: Jessica Kingsley.

Hogan, S. (2003) *Gender Issues in Art Therapy*. London: Jessica Kingsley.

Hogan, S. (2010) 'Postmodernist but Not Post-Feminist! A Feminist Postmodernist Approach to Working with New Mothers', in H. Burt (ed.) *Current Trends and New Research in Art Therapy: A Postmodernist Perspective*. Canada: Wilfred Laurier.

Hollins, S. and Esterhuyzen, A. (1997) 'Bereavement and Grief in Adults with Learning Disabilities', *British Journal of Psychiatry*, 17: 497–501.

Holmes, J. (1999) *John Bowlby & Attachment Theory*. London: Brunner-Routledge.

Holtom, R. (1978) 'Springfield Hospital, London, Art therapist Robin Holtom', in D. Elliot (ed.) *The Inner Eye*. Oxford: Museum of Modern Art Catalogue: 40.

Hoptman, L. (2000) *Yayoi Kusama: Exhibition Catalogue*. London: Serpentine Gallery.

Horowitz, M. J. (1991) *Person Schemas and Maladaptive Interpersonal Patterns*. Chicago: University of Chicago Press.

Houghton-Broderick, A. (1948) 'Introduction', in R.-J. Moulin (ed.) *Prehistoric Painting*, English Edition. Geneva: Edito-Services.

Houzel, D. (1995) 'Precipitation Anxiety', *Journal of Child Psychotherapy*, 21: 65–78.

Hughes, R. (1980) *The Shock of the New*. London: Thames & Hudson.

Hughes, R. (1988) 'Transitional Phenomena and the Potential Space in Art Therapy with Mentally Handicapped People', *Inscape: The Journal of the British Association of Art Therapists*, Summer: 4–8.

Hyland Moon, C. (2007) *Studio Art Therapy*. London: Jessica Kingsley.

Irigaray, L. (2004) *Key Writings*. London: Continuum.

Isaak, J. A. (1996) *Feminism and Contemporary Art. The Revolutionary Power of Women's Laughter*. London: Routledge.

Jackson, J. (2007) *Can Art Therapy provide a sense of 'home' for people with complex homelessness issues?*, MA Dissertation, Northern Programme.

Jackson, M. and Williams, P. (1994) *Unimaginable Storms: A Search for Meaning in Psychosis*. London: Karnac.

Jacobi, J. (1942) *The Psychology of C. G. Jung*. London: Routledge.

Jaques, E. (1955) 'Social Systems as a Defence against Persecutory and Depressive Anxiety', in M. Klein, P. Heimann and R. Money-Kryle (eds.) *New Directions in Psychoanalysis*. London: Tavistock: 478–498.

Jones, K. (1972) *A History of Mental Health Services*. London: Routledge & Kegan Paul.

Jones, Kevin. (1998) 'Review of "*What works for Whom*"', *Inscape: The Journal of the British Association of Art Therapists*, 3: 75–77.

Jones, L. (1997) 'Developing Models for Managing Treatment Integrity and Efficacy in a Prison Based Therapeutic Community', in E. Jones, L. Cullen and R. Woodward (eds.) *Therapeutic Communities for Offenders*. Chichester: Wiley: 121–160.

Juilliard, K. (1995) 'Increasing Chemically Dependent Patients' Beliefs in Step One Through Expressive Therapy', *American Journal of Art Therapy*, 33: 110–119.

Jung, C. G. (1916) 'The Transcendent Function', in *The Structure and Dynamics of the Psyche: CW 8*, Bollingen Series XX. Princeton: Princeton University Press [published in 1957].

Jung, C. G. (1918) *The Role of the Unconscious: CW 10*. Princeton: Princeton University Press.

Jung, C. G. (1921) *Psychological Types: CW 6*, Bollingen Series XX. Princeton: Princeton University Press.

Jung, C. G. (1933) *Modern Man in Search of a Soul*. Oxford: Trowbridge & Esher [reprinted as a Routledge paperback in 1961].

Jung, C. G. (1946) *Psychology of the Transference: CW 16*, Bollingen Series XX. Princeton: Princeton University Press.

Jung, C. G. (1950) 'Psychology and Literature', in *The Spirit in Man, Art and Literature: CW 15*, Bollingen Series XX. Princeton: Princeton University Press.

Jung, C. G. (1953–1966) *The Collected Works of C. G. Jung* (20 Volumes). London: Routledge & Kegan Paul [reprinted in 1969].

Jung, C. G. (1955–1956) *Mysterium Coniunctionis: CW 14*, Bollingen Series XX. Princeton: Princeton University Press.

Jung, C. G. (1958) *Flying Saucers a Modern Myth: CW 10*, Bollingen Series XX. Princeton: Princeton University Press.

Jung, C. G. (1961) *Memories, Dreams and Reflections*. London: Random House/Routledge [reprinted by Fontana paperback in 1967].

Jung, C.G. (1977) *Miscellany: Posthumous and Other Miscellaneous Works: CW 18*. Princeton: Princeton University Press.

Kahlo, F. (2006) *The Diary of Frieda Kahlo: An Intimate Self-Portrait*. New York: H. N. Abrams.

Kalksma-Van-Lyth, B. (2007) 'Psychosocial Interventions for Children in War Affected Areas: The State of the Art', *Intervention*, 5: 3–17.

Kalmanowitz, D. and Lloyd, B. (1997) *The Portable Studio: Art Therapy and Political Conflict: Initiatives in former Yugoslavia and South Africa*. London: Health Education Authority.

Kalmanowitz, D. and Lloyd, B. (1999) 'Fragments of Art at Work: Art Therapy in the Former Yugoslavia', *The Arts in Psychotherapy*, 26: 15–25.

Kalmanowitz, D. and Lloyd, B. (2005) *Art Therapy and Political Violence: With Art, Without Illusion*. London: Routledge.

Kalmanowitz, D., Lloyd, B., Beagley, S., Miller, F., Kälin, A. and Murphy, J. (2002) 'Inhabiting the Uninhabitable: The use of Art Making with Teachers in South West Kosovo', *The Arts in Psychotherapy*, 29: 41–52.

Kaplan, F. (2007) *Art Therapy and Social Action*. London: Jessica Kingsley.

Karkou, V. and Sanderson, P. (1997) 'An Exploratory Study of the Utilisation of Creative Arts Therapies in Treating Substance Dependence', *Journal of Contemporary Health*, 5: 56–60.

Karkou, V. and Sanderson, P. (2006) *Arts Therapies: A Research-Based Map of the Field*. New York: Elsevier.

Kelly, G. A. (1955) *Theory of Personality: The Psychology of Personal Constructs*. New York: Norton [reprinted in 1963 by Norton and in 1991–2000 by Routledge].

Kelly, O. (1984) *Community, Art and the State: Storming the Citadels*. London: Comedia Publishing.

Kelvin, P. and Jarrett, J. E. (1985) *Unemployment: Its Social Psychological Effects*. Cambridge: Cambridge University Press.

Kernberg, O. (1984) *Severe Personality Disorders: Psychotherapeutic Strategies*. New Haven, CT: Yale University Press.

Killick, K. (1991) 'The Practice of Art Therapy with Patients in Acute Psychotic States', *Inscape: The Journal of the British Association of Art Therapists*, Winter: 2–6.

Killick, K. (1993) 'Working with Psychotic Processes in Art Therapy', *Psychoanalytic Psychotherapy*, 7: 25–36.

Killick, K. and Greenwood, H. (1995) 'Research into Art Therapy with People who have Psychotic Illnesses', in A. Gilroy and C. Lee (eds.) *Art and Music: Therapy and Research*. London: Routledge: 101–116.

Killick, K. and Schaverien, J. (1997) *Art, Psychotherapy and Psychosis*. London: Routledge.

King, E. and Bradley, F. (2001) *Paula Rego: Celestina's House*. Kendal: Abbott Hall Art Gallery.

Klein, M. (1932) 'Early Stages of the Oedipus Conflict and Super-Ego Formation', in M. Klein (ed.) *The Psychoanalysis of Children*. London: Hogarth Press: 123–148 [reprinted in 1975].

Klein, M. (1940) 'Mourning and its Relation to Manic-Depressive States', in *The Writings of Melanie Klein: Volume 1, Love, Guilt and Reparation*. London: Hogarth Press: 344–369.

Klein, M. (1946) 'Notes on Some Schizoid Mechanisms', *International Journal of Psycho-Analysis*, 27: 99–110.

Klein, M. (1955) 'The Psycho-Analytic Play Technique: Its History and Significance', in M. Klein, P. Heinmann and R. E. Money-Kryle (eds.) *New Directions in Psycho-Analysis: The Significance of Infant Conflict in the Pattern of Adult Behaviour*. London: Tavistock: 3–22.

Klein, M. (1975) *The Writings of Melanie Klein* (4 Volumes). London: Hogarth Press.

Klein, M. (1986) 'Infantile Anxiety Situations Reflected in a Work of Art and in the Creative Impulse', in J. Mitchell (ed.) *The Selected Melanie Klein*. London: Penguin: 84–94.

Klingman, A., Shalev, R. and Pearlman, A. (2000) 'Graffiti: A Creative Means of Youth Coping with Collective Trauma', *The Arts in Psychotherapy*, 27: 209–307.

Knights, B. (1995) *The Listening Reader: Fiction and Poetry for Counsellors and Psychotherapists*. London: Jessica Kingsley.

Kohon, G. (1988) *The British School of Psychoanalysis: The Independent Tradition*. London: Free Association Books.

Kohut, H. (1971) *The Analysis of the Self: A Systematic Analysis of the Treatment of the Narcissistic Personality Disorders*: New York: International Universities Press.

Kramer, E. (1979) *Art as Therapy with Children*. New York: Schocken.

Kramer, E. (1980) 'Symposium: Integration of Divergent Points of View in Art Therapy', in E. Ulman and C. Levy (eds.) *Art Therapy Viewpoints*. New York: Schocken Books.

Kramer, E. (1987) 'Sublimation and Art Therapy', in J. A. Rubin (ed.) *Approaches to Art Therapy*. New York: Brunner/Mazel.

Kramer, E. and Alaine, G. L. (2000) *Art as Therapy: Collected Papers Edith Kramer*. London: Jessica Kingsley.

Kris, E. (1952) *Psychoanalytic Explorations in Art*. New York: International Universities Press.

Kristeva, J. (1982) *Powers of Horror*. New York: Columbia University Press.

Kristeva, J. (1989) *Black Sun*. New York: Columbia University Press.

Lacan, J. (1949) 'The Mirror Stage as Formative of the Function of the I as Revealed in Psychoanalytic Experience', in J. Lacan (ed.) *Ecrits: A Selection*. London: Tavistock: 1–7.

Lacan, J. (1977) *Ecrits: A Selection*. London: Tavistock.

Lachman-Chapin, M. (1979) 'Kohut's Theories on Narcissism: Implications for Art Therapy', *American Journal of Art Therapy*, 19: 3–9.

Laine, R. (2007) 'Image Consultation', in J. Schaverien and C. Case (eds.) *Supervision of Art Psychotherapy: A Theoretical and Practical Handbook*. London: Routledge: 119–137.

Laing, R. D. (1959) *The Divided Self*. London: Tavistock [reprinted in 1965 by Penguin].

Laing, R. D. (1961) *The Self and Others*. London: Tavistock [reprinted in 1965 by Penguin].

Lakoff, G. and Johnson, M. (1980) *Metaphors We Live By*. Chicago, IL: University of Chicago Press.

Langer, K. G., Laatsch, L. and Lewis, L. (1999) *Psychotherapeutic Interventions for Adults with Brain Injury or Stroke: A Clinician's Treatment Resource*. Madison, CT: Psychosocial Press.

Langer, S. (1957) *The Problems of Art*. London: Routledge & Kegan Paul.

Langs, R. and Searles, H. F. (1980) *Intrapsychic and Interpersonal Dimensions of Treatment: A Clinical Dialogue*. London: Aronson.

Lanham, R. (1998) 'The Life and Soul of the Image', *Inscape: The Journal of the British Association of Art Therapists*, 3: 48–54.

Laplanche, J. (2002–2003) 'Sublimation and/or Inspiration', *New Formations: A Journal of Culture/Theory/Politics*, 48: 30–50.

Laplanche, J. and Pontalis, J. B. (1973) *The Language of Psychoanalysis*. London: Hogarth Press.

Laplanche, J. and Pontalis, J. B. (1988) *The Language of Psychoanalysis*. London: Karnac.

Latner, J. (1992) 'The Theory of Gestalt', in E. Nevis (ed.) *Gestalt Therapy: Perspectives and Applications*. New York: Garden Press [republished by Routledge in 1996: 13–56].

Latour, B. (1988) 'Mixing Humans and Non-Humans Together: The Sociology of a Door Closer', *Social Problems*, 35: 3.

Lawrence, M. (1984) *The Anorexic Experience*. London: The Women's Press.

Leach, B. (1978) *Beyond East and West*. London: Faber & Faber.

Learmonth, M. (1994) 'Witness and Witnessing in Art Therapy', *Inscape: The Journal of the British Association of Art Therapists*, 1: 19–22.

Learmonth, M. (1999) 'Taoism and Art Therapy: Flowing and Stuckness', in J.

Campbell, M. Liebmann, F. Brooks, J. Jones and C. Ward (eds.) *Art Therapy, Race and Culture*. London: Jessica Kingsley: 192–206.

Leary, D. E. (1992) *Metaphors in the History of Psychology*. Cambridge: Cambridge University Press.

Lee, J. (1991) *At My Father's Wedding*. New York: Bantam.

Lertzman, D. A. (2002) 'Rediscovering Rites of Passage: Education, Transformation, and the Transition to Sustainability', *Conservation Ecology*, 5: 30.

Levens, M. (1989) 'Working with Defence Mechanisms in Art Therapy', in A. Gilroy and T. Dalley (eds.) *Pictures at an Exhibition*. London: Tavistock/Routledge: 143–146.

Levens, M. (1995) *Eating Disorders and Magical Control of the Body: Treatment Through Art Therapy*. London: Routledge.

Lewis, S. (1990) 'A Place to Be: Art Therapy and Community-Based Rehabilitation', in M. Liebmann (ed.) *Art Therapy in Practice*. London: Jessica Kingsley: 72–89.

Liebmann, M. (1990) *Art Therapy in Practice*. London: Jessica Kingsley

Liebmann, M. (1994) *Art Therapy with Offenders*. London: Jessica Kingsley.

Liebmann, M. (1996) *Arts Approaches to Conflict*. London: Jessica Kingsley.

Liebmann, M. (2000) *Mediation in Context*. London: Jessica Kingsley.

Liebmann, M. (2003) 'Working with Men', in S. Hogan (ed.) *Gender Issues in Art Therapy*. London: Jessica Kingsley: 108–125.

Liebmann, M. (2007) 'Anger Management Group Art Therapy for Clients in the Mental Health System', in F. Kaplan (ed.) *Art Therapy and Social Action: Treating the World's Wounds*. London: Jessica Kingsley: 125–141.

Liebmann, M. (2008) *Art Therapy and Anger*. London: Jessica Kingsley.

Liebmann, M., Buddery, H., Curtis, P., Drucker, P., Ford, J., Holst, K., et al. (1985) 'A Review of Gerry McNeilly's Article "Directive and Non-Directive Approaches in Art Therapy", in *Inscape* 1984', *Inscape: The Journal of the British Association of Art Therapists*, 1: 23–25.

Lillitos, A. (1990) 'Control, Uncontrol, Order, and Chaos', in C. Case and T. Dalley (eds.) *Working with Children in Art Therapy*. London: Routledge: 72–88.

Little, M., Jordens, C. F., Paul, K., Montgomery, K. and Philipson, B. (1998) 'Liminality: A Major Category of the Experience of Cancer Illness', *Social Science and Medicine*, 47: 1485–1494.

Loake, J. (1984) 'A Non-Directive Approach to Art Therapy with Mentally Handicapped People', in *Art Therapy as Psychotherapy in Relation to the Mentally Handicapped?*, Conference Proceedings. St Albans: Hertfordshire College of Art: 60–70.

London, P. (1989) *No More Second Hand Art – Awakening the Artist Within*. London: Shambala Books.

Long, J. (1996) 'Working with Lesbians, Gays and Bisexuals: Addressing Heterosexism in Supervision', *Family Process*, 35: 377–388.

Loth-Rozum, A. and Malchiodi, C. (2003) 'Cognitive Behavioural Approaches', in C. Malchiodi (ed.) *Handbook of Art Therapy*. New York: Guilford Press: 72–81.

Luzzatto, P. (1994) 'Art Therapy and Anorexia – The Mental Double Trap of the Anorexic Patient. The Use of Art Therapy to Facilitate Psychic Change', in D. Dokter (ed.) *Arts Therapies and Clients with Eating Disorders Fragile Board*. London: Jessica Kingsley: 60–75.

Luzzatto, P. (1997) 'Short-Term Art Therapy on the Acute Psychiatric Ward: The Open Session as a Psychodynamic Development of the Studio-Based Approach', in *Inscape: The Journal of the British Association of Art Therapists*, 2: 2–10.

Lyddiatt, E.M. (1972) *Spontaneous Painting and Modelling – A Practical Approach in Therapy*. New York: St Martin's Press.

MacDonald, N. (2001) *The Graffiti Subculture: Youth, Masculinity and Identity in London and New York*. Basingstoke: Palgrave.

Macdonald, R. (1997) *Youth, the Underclass and Social Exclusion*. London: Routledge.

Mace, C. (1995) *The Art and Science of Assessment in Psychotherapy*. London: Routledge.

MacGregor, J. (1989) *The Discovery of the Art of the Insane*. Princeton, NJ: Princeton University Press.

Mackie, B. (1992) 'Art Therapy – An Alternative to Prison', in M. Liebmann (ed.) *Art Therapy with Offenders*. Jessica Kingsley: 220–223.

Maclagan, D. (2001) *Psychological Aesthetics*. London: Jessica Kingsley.

Maclagan, D. (2005) 'Re-Imagining Art Therapy', *Inscape: The Journal of the British Association of Art Therapists*, 10: 23–30.

Macnair, R. (2002) *Perpetration-Induced Traumatic Stress: The Psychological Consequences of Killing*. Lincoln: iUniverse.

Mahdi, L. C., Christopher, N. G. and Meade, M. (1996) *Crossroads: The Quest for Contemporary Rites of Passage*. La Salla, IL: Open Court Publishing.

Mahony, J. (1992) 'The Organizational Context of Art Therapy', in D. Waller and A. Gilroy (eds.) *Art Therapy: A Handbook*. Buckingham: Open University Press: 49–70.

Mahony, J. (1999) 'Art Therapy and Art Activities in Alcohol Services', in D. Waller and J. Mahony (eds.) *Treatment of Addiction – Current Issues for Arts Therapies*. London: Routledge: 117–140.

Mahony, J. (2001) 'Three Commentaries: Experiences at Three Exhibitions', *Inscape: The Journal of the British Association of Art Therapists*, 6: 51–62.

Mahony, J. (2010a) 'Artefacts Related to an Art Psychotherapy Group: The Therapist's Art Practice as Research', in A. Gilroy (ed.) *Evidence in Art Therapy*. London: Langer.

Mahony, J. (2010b) *'Reunion of Broken Parts' (Arabic al-jabr) – A Therapist's Personal Art Practice and its Relationship to an NHS Outpatient Art Psychotherapy Group: An Exploration Through Visual Arts Practice*, PhD Thesis, Goldsmiths College, London University.

Mahony, J. and Waller, D. (1992) 'Art Therapy in the Treatment of Alcohol and Drug Abuse', in D. E. Waller and A. Gilroy (eds.) *Art Therapy: A Handbook*. Buckingham: Open University Press: 173–188 [reprinted in 1994].

Malan, D. H. (1976) *The Frontier of Brief Psychotherapy*. New York: Plenum Press.

Malchiodi, C. A. (1997) 'Invasive Art. Art as Empowerment for Women with Breast Cancer', in S. Hogan (ed.) *Feminist Approaches to Art Therapy*. London: Routledge: 49–64.

Mann, D. (1989) 'The Talisman or Projective Identification in Art Therapy', *Inscape: The Journal of the British Association of Art Therapists*, Winter: 33–35.

Mann, D. (1990a) 'Art as a Defence Mechanism Against Creativity', *British Journal of Psychotherapy*, 7: 5–14.

Mann, D. (1990b) 'Some Further Thoughts on Projective Identification? A Critique', *Inscape: The Journal of the British Association of Art Therapists*, Autumn: 11–15.

Mann, D. (1997) *Psychotherapy an Erotic Relationship: Transference and Counter-Transference Patterns*. London: Routledge.

Mann, J. (1973) *Time-Limited Psychotherapy*. Cambridge, MA: Harvard University Press.

Mann, T. (1996a) *Clinical Audit in the NHS. Using Clinical Audit in the NHS: A Position Statement*. Wetherby: NHS Executive.

Mann, T. (1996b) *Clinical Guidelines. Using Clinical Guidelines to Improve Patient Care Within the NHS*. Wetherby: NHS Executive.

Manners, R. (1989) 'Art and Art Therapy for People who have Learning Difficulties', in *Art Therapy for People with Severe to Marginal Learning Difficulties*, Conference Proceedings, Leicester.

Marien, M. W. (2002) *Photography: A Cultural History*. London: Laurence King.

Marrone, M. (1998) *Attachment and Interaction*. London: Jessica Kingsley.

Martin D. J., Garske J. P. and Davis M. K. (2000) 'Relation of the Therapeutic Alliance with Outcome and Other Variables: A Meta-Analytic Review', *Journal of Consulting and Clinical Psychology*, 68: 438–450.

Marx, K. (1844) 'Economic and Philosophic Manuscripts of 1844', *Classics in Politics: Marx and Engels ElecBook*. London: The Electric Book Company.

MATISSE HTA Project (2007) *A Multi Site Randomized Control Study Evaluating the Use of Art Therapy for People with a Diagnosis of Schizophrenia*. London: Imperial College London.

May, R. (1953) *Man's Search for Himself*. New York: Norton.

McClelland, S. (1992) 'Brief Art Therapy in Acute States: A Process Orientated Approach', in D. Waller and A. Gilroy (eds.) *Art Therapy: A Handbook*. Buckingham: Open University Press: 189–208.

McClelland, S. (1993) 'The Art of Science with Clients', in H. Payne (ed.) *Handbook of Inquiry in the Arts Therapies*. London: Jessica Kingsley: 104–129.

McDougall, J. (1989) *Theatres of the Body: A Psychoanalytic Approach to Psychosomatic Illness*. London: Norton.

McEvilley, T. (2001) 'Turned Upside Down and Torn Apart', in B. Beckley (ed.) *Sticky Sublime*. New York: Allworth Press: 52–83.

McEwan, J. (1992) *Paula Rego*. London: Phaidon Press.

McGraw, M. (1989) 'Art Therapy with Brain-Injured Patients', *American Journal of Art Therapy*, 28: 37–44.

McIntosh, P. (1987) *Sport in Society*. London: West London Press.

Mclay, J. (2008) *Love, Desire and Teen Spirit: Reflections on the Dynamic Force of Adolescent Eros*. Exeter: Insider Art.

McLeod, J. (1999) *Practitioner Research in Counselling*. London: Sage.

McNeilly, G. (1984a) 'Directive and Non-Directive Approaches in Art Therapy', *Inscape: The Journal of the British Association of Art Therapists*, December: 7–12.

McNeilly, G. (1984b) 'Group-Analytic Art therapy', *Group Analysis*, 17: 204–210.

McNeilly, G. (1987) 'Further Contributions to Group Analytic Art Therapy', *Inscape: The Journal of the British Association of Art Therapists*, Summer: 8–11.

McNeilly, G. (1989) 'Group Analytic Art Groups', in A. Gilroy and T. Dalley (eds.) *Pictures at an Exhibition*. London: Tavistock/Routledge: 156–166.

McNeilly, G. (2000) 'Failure in Group Analytic Art Therapy', in A. Gilroy and G. McNeilly (eds.) *The Changing Shape of Art Therapy*. London: Jessica Kingsley: 143–171.

McNeilly, G. (2006) *Group Analytic Art Therapy*. London: Jessica Kingsley.

McNiff, S. (1992) *Art as Medicine: Creating a Therapy of the Imagination*. Boston: Shambala Books.

McNiff, S. (1998) *Art-Based Research*. London: Jessica Kingsley.

Menzies-Lyth, I. (1959) 'The Functioning of Social Systems as a Defence Against Anxiety: A Report on a Study of the Nursing Services of a General Hospital', *Human Relations*, 13: 95–112.

Menzies-Lyth, I. (1988) *Containing Anxiety in Institutions*. London: Free Association Books.

Merleau-Ponty, M. (1962) *Phenomenology of Perception*. Routledge & Kegan Paul.

Mészáros, I. (1970) *Marx's Theory of Alienation*. London: Merlin Press.

Michaels, D. A. (forthcoming) 'A Space for Linking: Art Therapy and Stroke Rehabilitation', *International Journal of Art Psychotherapy*, in press.

Michaels, D. A. and Weston, S. (2007) *Case Study: The Role of Art Therapy as a Potential Space for the Processing of Psychological and Physical Experience Following Stroke*. London: BAAT (www.baat.org/CaseStudyStroke.pdf).

Miedzian, M. (1992) *Boys Will Be Boys: Breaking the Link Between Masculinity and Violence*. London: Virago Press.

Miller, L. (1993) *Psychotherapy of the Brain-Injured Patient: Reclaiming the Shattered Self*. New York: Norton.

Miller, L. (1998) *Shocks to the System: Psychotherapy of Traumatic Disability Syndromes*. New York: Norton.

Milner, M. (1950) *On Not Being Able to Paint*. London: Heinemann [reprinted by Routledge in 2010].

Milner, M. (1952) 'Aspects of Symbolism and Comprehension of the Not-Self', *International Journal of Psychoanalysis*, 33: 181–195.

Milner, M. (1955) 'The Role of Illusion in Symbol Formation', in M. Klein, P. Heinmann and R. E. Money-Kryle (eds.) *New Directions in Psycho-Analysis*. London: Tavistock: 82–108.

Milner, M. (1969) *The Hands of the Living God*. London: Virago [reprinted by Routledge in 2010].

Milner, M. (1978) 'D. W. Winnicott and the Two-Way Journey', in S. A. Grolnick and L. Barkin (eds.) *Transitional Objects and Phenomena Between Reality and Fantasy*. Lanham: Aronson: 37–42.

Milner, M. (1996) *The Suppressed Madness of Sane Men*. London: Routledge.

Mind (2002) *My Choice Campaign*. London: Mind.

Mirzoeff, N. (1999) *An Introduction to Visual Culture*. London: Routledge.

Mitchell, J. (1975) *Psychoanalysis and Feminism*. Harmondsworth: Pelican.

Mitchell, J. (1986) *The Selected Melanie Klein*. Harmondsworth: Peregrine/Penguin.

Mithen, S. (1996) *The Prehistory of the Mind: A Search for the Origins of Art, Religion and Science*. Phoenix: University of Washington Press.

Mollon, P. (1996) *Multiple Selves, Multiple Voices: Working with Trauma, Violation and Dissociation*. Chichester: Wiley.

Molloy, T. (1997) 'Art Therapy and Psychiatric Rehabilitation, Harmonious

Partnership or Philosophical Collision', in K. Killick and J. Schaverien (eds.) *Art Psychotherapy and Psychosis*. London: Routledge: 237–259.

Monti, D. A. (2006) 'A Randomized Controlled Trail of Mindfulness-Based Art Therapy (MBAT) for Women with Cancer', *Psycho-Oncology*, 15: 363–373.

Morgan, S. (2001) 'A Terminal Degree: Fine Art and the PhD', *Journal of Visual Art Practice*, 1: 6–15.

Morin, S. F. (1977) 'Heterosexual Bias in Psychological Research on Lesbianism and Male Homosexuality', *American Psychologist*, 10: 629–637.

Morter, S. (1997) 'Where Words Fail: A Meeting Place', in K. Killick and J. Schaverien (eds.) *Art Psychotherapy and Psychosis*. London: Routledge: 219–236.

Moustakas, C. (1990) *Heuristic Research: Design, Methodology and Applications*. Los Angeles, CA: Sage.

Moustakis, C. (1994) *Phenomenological Research Methods*. London: Sage.

Muller-White, L. (2002) *Printmaking as Therapy: Frameworks for Freedom*. London: Jessica Kingsley.

Murphy, J. (1984) 'The Use of Art Therapy in the Treatment of Anorexia Nervosa', in T. Dalley (ed.) *Art as Therapy*. London: Routledge: 96–110.

Naumburg, M. (1958) 'Art Therapy: Its Scope and Function', in E. F. Hammer (ed.) *Clinical Application of Projective Drawing*. Springfield, IL: Thomas: 511–517.

Nhat Hanh, T. (2008) *The Miracle of Mindfulness: The Classic Guide to Meditation*. London: Rider.

NICE (National Institute for Health and Clinical Excellence) (2009) *Schizophrenia Update* (http://www.nice.org.uk/Guidance/CG82/).

Nightingale, A. (2006) 'Mimesis: Ancient Greek Literary Theory', in P. Waugh (ed.) *An Oxford Guide: Literary Theory and Criticism*. Oxford: Oxford University Press: 37–47.

Nitsun, M. (1996) *The Anti-Group*. London: Routledge.

O'Conner, N. and Ryan, J. (1993) *Wild Desires and Mistaken Identities*. London: Virago Press.

O'Hara, N. (1995) *Find a Quiet Corner*. New York: Warner Brothers.

O'Shaughnessy, E. (1981) 'A Comprehensive Essay on W. R. Bion's Theory of Thinking', *Journal of Child Psychotherapy*, 7: 181–186.

Oakley, C. (2007) *Football Delirium*, London: Karnac.

Oates, J. C. (1998) 'After Amnesia', *Granta*, 63: 188–200.

Obholzer, A. and Roberts, V. Z. (1994) *The Unconscious at Work*. London: Routledge.

Ogden, T. H. (1982) *Projective Identification and Psychotherapeutic Technique*. London: Karnac.

Ogden, T. H. (1988) 'On the Dialectical Structure of Experience: Some Clinical and Theoretical Implications', *Contemporary Psychoanalysis*, 24: 17–45.

Ogden, T. H. (1992a) 'The Dialectically Constituted/Decentred Subject of Psychoanalysis. 1. The Freudian Subject', *International Journal of Psychoanalysis*, 73: 517–526.

Ogden, T. H. (1992b) 'The Dialectically Constituted/Decentred Subject of Psycho-analysis. 2. The Contributions of Klein and Winnicott', *International Journal of Psychoanalysis*, 73: 613–626.

Orbach, S. (1986) *Hunger Strike*. London: Faber.

Oster, I. (2006) 'Art Therapy Improves Coping Resources: A Randomized, Control Study among Women with Breast Cancer', *Palliative Support Care*, 4: 57–64.

Othen-Price, L. (2006) 'Making their Mark: A Psychodynamic View of Adolescent Graffiti Writing', *Psychodynamic Practice*, 12: 5–17.

Packard, V. (1957) *The Hidden Persuaders*. Harmondsworth: Pelican.

Palmer, F. (1975) *Monoprint Techniques*. London: Batsford.

Panofsky, E. (1972) *Studies in Iconology: Humanistic Themes in the Art of the Renaissance*. New York: Harper & Row.

Papadopoulos, R. (2002) *Therapeutic Care for Refugees and Asylum Seekers: No Place Like Home*. London: Karnac.

Parry, G. (1998) 'Psychotherapy Services, Health Care Policy and Clinical Audit', in R. Davenhill and M. Patrick (eds.) *Re-Thinking Clinical Audit. The Case of Psychotherapy Services in the NHS*. London: Routledge: 7–23.

Parry, G. (2001) *Treatment Choice in Psychological Therapies and Counselling*. Wetherby: NHS Executive.

Pell, C. (2008) Unpublished MA Dissertation, Goldsmiths College, London University.

Perls, F., Hefferline, R. and Goodman, P. (1951) *Gestalt Therapy: Excitement and Growth in the Human Personality*. New York: Julian Press.

Perring, C. (2003) *Review of Advancing DSM: Dilemmas in Psychiatric Diagnosis*. (http://human-nature.com/nibbs/03/dsm.html).

Phillips, A. (1988) *Winnicott*. London: Fontana Press.

Phillips, A. and Taylor, B. (2009) *On Kindness*. London: Penguin.

Pickford, R. W. (1940) 'The Psychology of the History and Organization of Association Football – Part II', *British Journal of Psychology*, 31: 129–143.

Pilgrim, D. and Rogers, A. (1996) *Mental Health Policy in Britain: A Critical Introduction*. London: Macmillan.

Pilgrim, D. and Rogers, A. (2005) 'Social Psychiatry and Sociology', *Journal of Mental Health*, 14: 317–320.

Pinel, P. (1801) *Traité Medico-philosophique Sur l'Aliénation Mentale Ou La Manie* [translated by D. D. Davis as *A Treatise on Insanity* and reprinted in 1806]. London: Cadell & Davis.

Piper, W. E., Azim, F. A., Joyce, S. A., Mccallum, M., Nixon, G. and Segal, P. S. (1991) 'Quality of Object Relations versus Interpersonal Functioning as Predictions of Alliance and Outcome', *Journal of Nervous and Mental Disease*, 179: 432–438.

Pollock, G. (1995) 'The View from Elsewhere', in P. Florence and D. Reynolds (eds.) *Feminist Studies and Multi-Media*. Manchester: Manchester University: 3–38.

Pollock, G. (1999) *Differencing the Canon – Feminist Desire and the Writing of Art's Histories*. London: Routledge.

Ponty, M. (1962) *Phenomenology of Perception*. London: Routledge.

Porter, R. (1997) *The Greatest Benefit to Mankind: A Medical History of Humanity from Antiquity to the Present*. London: Harper Collins.

Powell, T. (2001) *Head Injury: A Practical Guide*. Milton Keynes: Speechmark.

Power, M. (1998) 'The Audit Fixation: Some Issues for Psychotherapy', in R. Davenhill, R. and M. Patrick (eds.) *Re-Thinking Clinical Audit: The Case of Psychotherapy Services in the NHS*. London: Routledge.

Preble, D. and Preble, P. (1994) *Art Forms*. New York: Harper Collins.

Prigatano, G. P. (1991) 'Disordered Mind, Wounded Soul: The Emerging Role of Psychotherapy in Rehabilitation after Head Trauma', in *Journal of Head Trauma Rehabilitation*, 6: 1–10.

Prigatano, G. P. (1999) *Principles of Neuropsychological Rehabilitation*. New York: Open University Press.

Proctor, G. (2002) *The Dynamics of Power in Counselling and Psychotherapy*. Ross on Wye: PCCS Books.

Prokofiev, F. (1998) 'Adapting the Art Therapy Group For Children', in V. Huet and S. Skaife (eds.) *Art Psychotherapy Groups: Between Pictures and Words*. London: Routledge: 44–68.

Punamaki, R. (2000) 'Personal and Family Resources Promoting Resiliency among Children Suffering from Military Violence', in L. van Willigen (ed.) *Health Hazards of Organized Violence in Children, Volume 2: Coping and Protective Factors*. Utrecht: Pharos: 29–41.

Rafael, C. and Byrne, P. (forthcoming) 'Post-Traumatic-Stress-Disorder and Modes of Reparation: Reintegrating the Sense of Meaning in Ex-Soldiers through Myth Making in Art Therapy', *ATOL: Art Therapy Online*.

Ramm, A. (2005) 'What is Drawing? Bringing the Art into Art Therapy', *Inscape: The Journal of the British Association of Art Therapists*, 10: 63–77.

Rank, O. (1932) *Art and Artists: Creative Urge and Personality Development*. New York: Knopf.

Reed, H. (1937) *Art and Society*. London: Faber & Faber.

Rees, M. (1995) 'Making Sense of Marking Space – Researching Art Therapy with People who have Severe Learning Difficulties', in G. Gilroy and C. Lee (eds.) *Art and Music Therapy Research*. London: Routledge: 117–137.

Rees, M. (1998) *Drawing on Difference – Art Therapy with People who have Learning Difficulties*. London: Routledge.

Rhodes, C. (2000) *Outsider Art: Spontaneous Alternatives*. London: Thames & Hudson.

Richards, B. (1992) *Disciplines of Delight: The Psychoanalysis of Popular Culture*. London: Free Association Books.

Richardson, P., Jones, K., Evans, C., Stevens, P. and Rowe, A. (2007) 'Exploratory RCT of Art Therapy as an Adjunctive Treatment in Schizophrenia', *Journal of Mental Health*, 16: 483–491.

Richardson, S. (1997) *Colourful Language: Examining the Role of Participant Observer in Art Therapy*, MA Dissertation, University of Hertfordshire.

Riley, S. (1999) 'Brief Therapy: An Adolescent Intervention', in *Art Therapy: Journal of the American Art Therapy Association*, 16: 112–120.

Riley, S. and Malchiodi, C. (2003) 'Solution-Focused and Narrative Approaches', in C. Malchiodi (ed.) *Handbook of Art Therapy*. New York: Guilford Press: 82–92.

Robbins, A. (2001) 'Object Relations and Art Therapy', in J. A. Rubin (ed.) *Approaches to Art Therapy: Theory and Technique*. London: Brunner-Routledge: 54–65.

Roberts, J. P. (1983) 'Resonance in Art Groups', *Group Analysis*, 17: 211–220.

Rogers, C. R. (1951) *Client-Centred Therapy*. London: Constable.

Rogers, C. R. (1959) 'A Theory of Therapy, Personality and Interpersonal Relationships, as Developed in the Client-Centred Framework', in S. Koch (ed.)

Psychology: A study of science. Vol. 3. Formulation of the Person and the Social Context. New York: McGraw-Hill: 184–256.

Rogers, C. (1966) 'Client-Centred Therapy', in S. Arieti (ed.) *American Handbook of Psychiatry*, Vol. 3. New York: Basic Books: 183–200.

Rogers, M. (2002) 'Absent Figures: A Personal Reflection on the Value of Art Therapists' Own Image-Making', *Inscape: The Journal of the British Association of Art Therapists*, 7: 59–71.

Rosal, M. L. (1993) 'Comparative Group Art Therapy Research to Evaluate Changes in Locus of Control in Behaviour Disordered Children', *The Arts in Psychotherapy*, 20: 231–241.

Rose, G. (2001) *Visual Methodologies: An Introduction to the Interpretation of Visual Materials*. London: Sage.

Rosenberg, H. (1952) 'The American Action Painters', reprinted in 1962 in *The London Magazine*, I(4).

Rosenfeld, H. (1971) 'A Clinical Approach to the Psychoanalytical Theory of the Life and Death Instincts: An Investigation into the Aggressive Aspects of Narcissism', *International Journal of Psycho-Analysis*, 52: 169–178.

Rosenfeld, H. (1987) *Impasse and Interpretation – Therapeutic and Anti-Therapeutic Factors in the Psychoanalytic Treatment of Psychotic, Borderline and Neurotic Patients*. London: Tavistock.

Rosenthal, M. (1984) *Joseph Beuys Actions, Vitrines, Environments*. London: Tate Publishing.

Rosenthal, N., Saatchi, C. and Franquelli, S. (1998) *Sensation*. London: Royal Academy of Arts.

Ross, C. (1997) *Something to Draw On: Activities and Interventions using an Art Therapy Approach*. London: Jessica Kingsley.

Roth, A. and Fonagy, P. (1996) *What Works for Whom?: A Critical Review of Psychotherapy Research*. New York: Guilford Press [reprinted in 2007].

Rothwell, K. (2009) 'Lost in Translation: Art Psychotherapy with Patients Presenting Suicidal States', *International Journal Art Therapy: Inscape*, 13: 2–12.

Rowe, D. (1993) 'Foreword', in J. Masson (ed.) *Against Therapy*. London: Harper Collins.

Royal College of Psychiatrists (2009) *Mental Health and Social Inclusion: Making Psychiatry and Mental Health Services Fit for the 21st Century*. London: Royal College of Psychiatrists.

Ruddy, R. and Milnes D. (2003) 'Art Therapy for Schizophrenia or Schizophrenia-Like Illnesses', *Cochrane Database of Systematic Reviews*, Issue 3.

Rust, M. (1992) 'Art Therapy in the Treatment of Women with Eating Disorders', in D. Waller and A. Gilroy (eds.) *Art Therapy: A Handbook*. Oxford: Oxford University Press: 155–172.

Rutz, W. (2006) 'Social Psychiatry and Public Mental Health: Present Situation and Future Objectives – Time for Rethinking and Renaissance?', *Acta Psychiatrica Scandinavica*, 113: 95–100.

Ryan, R. E. (2002) *Shamanism and the Psychology of C. G. Jung: The Great Circle*. New York: Vega.

Rycroft, C. (1979) *A Critical Dictionary of Psychoanalysis*. Harmondsworth: Penguin.

Rycroft, C. (1981) *The Innocence of Dreams*. London: Hogarth [reprinted in 1981 by Oxford University Press].

Ryde, J. (2003) 'Rothko – Reflections on an Aesthetic Moment', *Journal of the British Association of Psychotherapists*, 41: 56–61.

Safran J. D. and Muran, J. C. (2003) *Negotiating the Therapeutic Alliance: A Relational Treatment Guide*. London: Guilford Press.

Salminen, A. (2005) *Pääjalkainen – Kuva ja havainto [Picture and Perception]*. Finland.

Samuels, A. (1993) *The Politics of the Psyche*. London: Routledge.

Samuels, A., Shorter, B. and Plaut, F. (1986) *A Critical Dictionary of Jungian Analysis*. London: Routledge & Kegan Paul.

Sanders, M. R., Gooley, S. and Nicholson, J. (2000) *Early Interventions in Conduct Problems in Children*. The Australian Early Intervention Network for Mental Health in Young People.

Sandler, J. (1993) 'On Communication from Patient to Analyst: Not Everything is Projective Identification', *International Journal of Psycho-Analysis*, 74: 1097–1107.

Sarra, N. (1991) 'Connection and Disconnection in the Art Therapy Group: Working with Forensic Patients in Acute States on a Locked Ward', in V. Huet and S. Skaife (eds.) *Art Psychotherapy Groups: Between Pictures and Words*. London: Routledge: 79.

Sartorius, N. (1998) 'Nearly Forgotten: The Mental Health Needs of an Urbanised Planet', in D. Goldberg and G. Thornicroft (eds.) *Mental Health in our Future Cities*. London: Psychology Press: 3–12.

Sarup, M. (1993) *An Introductory Guide to Post-Structuralism and Postmodernism*, 2nd Edn. London: Harvester Wheatsheaf Pearson Education.

Sayce, L. (2000) *From Psychiatric Patient to Citizen: Overcoming Discrimination and Social Exclusion*. London: Macmillan Press.

Schaverien, J. (1987) 'The Scapegoat and the Talisman: Transference in Art Therapy', in T. Dalley et al. (eds.) *Images of Art Therapy: New Developments in Theory and Practice*. London: Tavistock: 74–108.

Schaverien, J. (1989a) 'The Picture Within the Frame', in A. Gilroy and T. Dalley (eds.) *Pictures at an Exhibition*. London: Tavistock/Routledge: 147–155.

Schaverien, J. (1989b) 'Transference and the Picture: Art Therapy in the Treatment of Anorexia Nervosa', *Inscape: The Journal of The British Association of Art Therapists*, Spring: 14–18.

Schaverien, J. (1990) *Transference and Counter-Transference in Art Therapy: Mediation, Interpretation and the Aesthetic Object*, PhD Thesis. Birmingham University Library.

Schaverien, J. (1991) *The Revealing Image: Analytical Art Psychotherapy in Theory and Practice*. London: Routledge.

Schaverien, J. (1993) 'The Retrospective Review of Pictures: Data for Research in Art Therapy', in H. Payne (ed.) *Handbook of Inquiry in the Arts Therapies. One River, Many Currents*. London: Jessica Kingsley: 91–103.

Schaverien, J. (1994a) 'Analytical Art Psychotherapy: Further Reflections on Theory and Practice', *Inscape: The Journal of The British Association of Art Therapists*, 2: 41–49.

Schaverien, J. (1994b) 'The Transactional Object: Art Psychotherapy in the Treatment of Anorexia', *British Journal of Psychotherapy*, 11: 46–60.

Schaverien, J. (1995a) *Desire and the Female Therapist: Engendered Gazes in Psychotherapy and Art Therapy*. London: Routledge.

Schaverien, J. (1995b) 'Analytical Art Psychotherapy and the Dialectics of Art Therapy', *Inscape: The Journal of The British Association of Art Therapists*, 2: 28.

Schaverien, J. (1997) 'Transference and Transactional Objects in the Treatment of Psychosis', in K. Killick and J. Schaverien (eds.) *Art, Psychotherapy and Psychosis*. London: Routledge: 13–37.

Schaverien, J. (1999) *The Revealing Image: Analytical Art Psychotherapy in Theory and Practice*. London: Jessica Kingsley.

Schaverien, J. (2000) 'The Triangular Relationship and the Aesthetic Counter transference in Analytical Art Psychotherapy', in A. Gilroy and G. McNeilly (eds.) *The Changing Face of Art Therapy*. London: Jessica Kingsley: 55–83.

Schaverien, J. (2002) *The Dying Patient in Psychotherapy: Desire, Dreams and Individuation*. Basingstoke: Palgrave.

Scottish Executive (2000) *The Same as You? A Review of Services for People with Learning Disabilities*. Edinburgh: Scottish Government: document modified in 2006.

Sedgwick, P. (1982) *Psycho-Politics*. London: Pluto Press.

Segal, H. (1950) 'Some Aspects of the Analysis of a Schizophrenic', *International Journal of Psycho-Analysis*, 31: 268–278.

Segal, H. (1952) 'A Psychoanalytical Approach to Aesthetics', *International Journal of Psycho-Analysis*, 33: 196–207.

Segal, H. (1957) 'Notes on Symbol-Formation', *International Journal of Psycho-Analysis*, 38: 391–397.

Segal, H. (1975) 'A Psycho-Analytic Approach to the Treatment of Schizophrenia', in M. Lader (ed.) *Studies of Schizophrenia*. Ashford: Headley Bros.: 94–97.

Segal, H. (1978a) 'On Symbolism', *International Journal of Psycho-Analysis*, 55: 315–319.

Segal, H. (1978b) *Introduction to the Work of Melanie Klein*, 2nd Edn. London: Hogarth Press/Institute of Psycho-Analysis.

Segal, H. (1991) *Dream, Phantasy, Art*. London: Tavistock/Routledge.

Segal, J. (1985) *Phantasy in Everyday Life*. Harmondsworth: Penguin.

Segal, J. (1992) *Melanie Klein*. London: Sage.

Segal, J. (2000) *Phantasy*. Cambridge: Icon Books.

Segal, Z. V., Williams, J. M. G. and Teasdale J. D. (2002) *Mindfulness-Based Cognitive Therapy for Depression. A New Approach to Preventing Relapse*. New York: Guilford Press.

Seligman, M. E. P. (1995) 'The Effectiveness of Psychotherapy: The Consumer Reports Study', *American Psychologist*, 50: 965–974.

Shaw, P. (2006) *The Sublime*. London: Routledge.

Shazer, S. de (1988) *Clues: Investigating Solutions in Brief Therapy*. New York: Norton.

Shelton, J. L. and Ackermann, J. M. (1974) *Homework in Counselling and Psychotherapy*. Springfield, IL: Thomas.

Shore, C. and Wright, S. (2000) 'Coercive Accountability: The Rise of Audit Culture in Higher Education', in M. Strathern (ed). *Audit Cultures*. London: Routledge: 57–90.

Sibbett, C. (2005a) 'An Art Therapist's Experience of Having Cancer: Living and Dying with the Tiger', in D. Waller and C. Sibbett (eds.) *Facing Death: Art Therapy and Cancer Care*. Maidenhead: Open University Press: 223–247.

Sibbett, C. (2005b) 'Betwixt and Between: Crossing Thresholds', in D. Waller and C. Sibbett (eds.) *Facing Death: Art Therapy and Cancer Care*. Maidenhead: Open University Press: 12–37.

Sibbett, C. H. (2006) 'Art Therapy in Cancer Care: Revelatory Expression and Inclusion of Liminal and Taboo Issues', in D. Spring (ed.) *Art in Treatment: Transatlantic Dialogue*, Vol. 7. Springfield, IL: Thomas: 124–142.

Silverstone, L. (1995) *Art Therapy – The Person Centred Way: Art and the Development of the Person*. London: Autonomy Books [reprinted in 1993 and 1997 by Jessica Kingsley].

Simon, P. (1876) 'L'imagination dans la folie: Etude sur les dessins, plans, descriptions, et costumes des aliénés', *Annales médico psychologiques*, 16: 358–390.

Simon, P. (1882) *Le Monde du Rêves*. Paris: Bibliotheque Scientifique Contemporaine.

Simon, P. (1888) 'Les écrits et les dessins des aliénés', *Archivio di antropologia criminelle psichiatria et medicina legale*, 3: 318–355.

Simon, R. (1992) *The Symbolism of Style: Art as Therapy*. London: Routledge.

Simon, R. (1997) *Symbolic Images in Art as Therapy*. London: Routledge.

Sinason, V. (1992) *Mental Handicap and the Human Condition – New Approaches from the Tavistock*. London: Free Association Books.

Skaife, S. (1995) 'The Dialectics of Art Therapy', *Inscape: The Journal of the British Association of Art Therapists*, 1: 2–7.

Skaife, S. (2000) 'Keeping the Balance: Further thoughts on the Dialectics of Art Therapy', in A. Gilroy and G. McNeilly (eds.) *The Changing Shape of Art Therapy*. London: Jessica Kingsley: 115–142.

Skaife, S. (2008) 'Off Shore: A Deconstruction of David Maclagan's and David Mann's "Inscape" papers', *International Journal of Art Therapy: Inscape*, 13: 44–52.

Skaife, S. and Huet, V. (1998) *Art Psychotherapy Groups: Between Pictures and Word*. London: Routledge.

Skailes, C. (1990) 'The Revolving Door: The Day Hospital and Beyond', in M. Liebmann (ed.) *Art Therapy in Practice*. London: Jessica Kingsley: 58–71.

Skogstad, W. (1997) 'Working in a World of Bodies', *Psychoanalytic Psychotherapy*, 11: 221–240.

Smail, D. (1987) *Taking Care*. London: Dent.

Smail, D. (1995) 'Power and the Origins of Unhappiness: Working with Individuals', *Journal of Community and Applied Social Psychology*, 5: 347–356.

Social Inclusion Unit (2004) *Mental Health and Social Exclusion*. London: Crown Publications.

Springham, N. (1992) 'Short-Term Group Processes in Art Therapy for People with Substance Misuse Problems', *Inscape: The Journal of the British Association of Art Therapists*, Spring: 8–16.

Springham, N. (1994) 'Research into Patients' Reactions to Art Therapy on a Drug and Alcohol Programme', *Inscape: The Journal of the British Association of Art Therapists*, 2: 36–40.

Springham, N. and Huet, V. (2004) *Off the Peg Audit Pack*. London: BAAT/Art Therapy Practice Research Network.

Stack, M. (1996) 'Humpty Dumpty had a Great Fall', *Inscape: The Journal of the British Association of Art Therapists*, 1: 1–13.

Stack Sullivan, H. (1953) *The Interpersonal Theory of Psychiatry*. New York: Norton.

Steiner, G. (2003) *Lessons of the Masters*. Cambridge, MA: Harvard University Press.

Steiner, J. (1993) *Psychic Retreats: Pathological Organisations in Psychotic, Neurotic and Borderline Patients*. London: Routledge.

Stern, D. (1985) *The Interpersonal World of the Infant*. New York: Basic Books [reprinted by Karnac in 1998].

Stevens, A. (1986) *Withymead: A Jungian Community for the Healing Arts*. London: Coventure.

Stokes, A. (1963) *Painting and the Inner World*. London: Tavistock.

Stokes, A. (1965) *The Invitation in Art*. London: Tavistock.

Stokes, A. (1972) *The Image in Form*. Harmondsworth: Penguin.

Stoller, R. J. (1975) *Sex and Gender*. London: Hogarth Press.

Stott, J. and Males, B. (1984) 'Art Therapy for People who are Mentally Handicapped', in T. Dalley (ed.) *Art as Therapy – An Introduction to the Use of Art as a Therapeutic Technique*. London: Tavistock: 111–126.

Strand, S. (1990) 'Counteracting Isolation: Group Art Therapy for People with Learning Difficulties', *Group Analysis*, 23: 255–263.

Sturdee, P. (2001) 'Evidence, Influence or Evaluation? Fact and Value in Clinical Science', in M. Mace, S. Moorey and B. Roberts (eds.) *Evidence in the Psychological Therapies. A Practical Guide for Practitioners*. London: Brunner-Routledge: 60–77.

Sullivan, G. (2005) *Art Practice as Research: Inquiry in the Visual Arts*. London: Sage.

Tantam, D. (1995) 'Why Assess?', in C. Mace (ed.) *The Art and Science of Assessment in Psychotherapy*. London: Routledge: 9–26.

Teasdale, C. (1995a) 'Creating Change: Art Therapy as Part of a Treatment Service to Counter Criminality', *Prison Service Journal*, 99: 6–12.

Teasdale, C. (1995b) 'Reforming Zeal or Fatal Attraction: Why should Art Therapists work with Violent Offenders', *Inscape: The Journal of the British Association of Art Therapists*, 2: 2–9.

Teasdale, C. (1997) 'Art Therapy as a Shared Forensic Investigation', in *Inscape: The Journal of the British Association of Art Therapists*, 2: 32–40.

Teasdale, C. (1999) 'Developing Principles and Policies for Arts Therapists Working in United Kingdom Prisons', *Arts in Psychotherapy*, 26: 265–270.

Teasdale, C. (2002) 'Guidelines for Arts Therapists Working in Prisons', *Home Office: HM Prison Service for England & Wales*, (revised edition). London: Crown Publications.

Thatcher, M. (1987) Interview for *Woman's Own*, 23 September 1987, as reproduced on the Margaret Thatcher Foundation website (http://www.margaretthatcher.org/).

Thévoz, M. (1995) 'Forward', in J. Dubuffet (ed.) *Art Brut*. Switzerland: Booking International.

Thomas, N. (1998) 'Foreword', in A. Gell (ed.) *Art and Agency: An Anthropological Theory*. Oxford: Clarendon Press: vii–xiii.

Thomashoff, H.-O. (2004) 'A Work of Art is a Work of Art Whoever Created It', in H.-O. Thomashoff and N. Sartorius (eds.) *Art Against Stigma: A Historical Perspective*. New York: Schattauer: 73–74.

Thomson, M. (1989) *On Art and Therapy*. London: Virago Press [reprinted by Free Association Books in 1998].

Thornicroft, G., Rose, D., Huxley, P., Dale, G. and Wykes, T. (2002) 'What are the Research Priorities of Mental Health Service Users?', *Journal of Mental Health*, 11: 1–5.

Thyme, K. E. (2007) 'The Outcome of Short-term Psychodynamic Art Therapy Compared to Short-Term Psychodynamic Verbal Therapy for Depressed Women', *Psychoanalytic Psychotherapy*, 21: 250–264.

Tipple, R. (1992) 'Art Therapy with People who have Severe Learning Difficulties', in A. Gilroy and D. Waller (eds.) *Art Therapy A Handbook – Psychotherapy Handbooks*. Buckingham: Open University Press: 105–124.

Tipple, R. (1993) 'Challenging Assumptions: The Importance of Transference Processes in Work with People with Learning Difficulties', *Inscape: The Journal of the British Association of Art Therapists*, Summer: 2–9.

Townsend, C. (1998) *Vile Bodies*. Channel 4 Video.

Townsend, P., Davidson, N. and Whitehead, M. (1988) *Inequalities in Health: The Black Report and The Health Divide*. London: Penguin.

Tuke, S. (1813) *Description of the Retreat, An Institution Near York for Insane Persons*. London: Process Press [reprinted in 1996].

Turkle, S. (1992) *Psychoanalytic Politics: Jaques Lacan and Freud's French Revolution*. London: Free Association Books.

Turner, V. W. (1967) *The Forest of Symbols: Aspects of Ndembu Ritual*. Ithaca, NY: Cornell University Press.

Turner, V. W. (1975) *Dramas, Fields, and Metaphors: Symbolic Action in Human Society*. Ithaca, NY: Cornell University Press

Turner, V. W. (1982) *From Ritual to Theatre: The Human Seriousness of Play*. New York: Performing Arts Journal Publications.

Turner, V. W. (1988) *The Anthropology of Performance*. New York: Performing Arts Journal Publications.

Turner, V. W. (1995) *The Ritual Process: Structure and Anti-Structure*. New York: Aldine de Gruyter.

Tustin, F. (1992) *Autistic States in Children* (revised edition). London: Tavistock/Routledge.

Ulman, E. (1983) 'Obituary of Margaret Naumburg', *American Journal of Art Therapy*, (22)4.

Vance, C. (1991) *Pleasure and Danger: Exploring Female Sexuality*. London: Pandora Press.

Vintage, P. (1983) *Penguin Medical Encyclopaedia*. Harmondsworth: Penguin.

Von Sass Hyde, I. (2002) *The Janus Response: Art Therapy within a Neuro-Rehabilitation Setting*, MA Dissertation, University of Sheffield.

Wadeson, H. (1980) *Art Psychotherapy*. New York: Wiley.

Waddell, M. (1998) *Inside Life: Psychoanalysis and the Growth of the Personality*. London: Tavistock.

Waller, D. (1974) 'Naïve Artists or Naïve Critics?', *Inscape: The Journal of the British Association of Art Therapists*, 14.

Waller, D. (1990) 'Special Section: Group Analysis and the Arts Therapies 1', *Group Analysis*, 23: 211–214.

Waller, D. (1991) *Becoming a Profession: The History of Art Therapy in Britain 1940–82*. London: Routledge.

Waller, D. (1993) *Group Interactive Art Therapy: Its Use in Training and Treatment*. London: Routledge.

Waller, D. (1998) *Towards a European Art Therapy*. Buckingham: Open University Press.

Waller, D. (1999) 'Executive Summary of Research into Art Therapy with People with Dementia', *BAAT Newsletter*. London: BAAT.

Waller, D. (2002) *Arts Therapies and Progressive Illness: Nameless Dread*. London: Brunner-Routledge.

Waller, D. (2004) 'Problems of Looking: An Exploration of the Art of the Other', in H. O. Thomashoff (ed.) *Human Art Project*. Stuttgart: Schattauer: 43–46.

Waller, D. (2009a) *Art Therapy and the Psychopathology of Expression: An Uneasy Alliance?*, Jubilee publication to celebrate the 50th anniversary of the International Society for Psychopathology of Expression. Paris: La Société Française de Psychopathologie de l'Expression et d'Art-Thérapie.

Waller, D. (2009b) 'The Influence of Culture on Aesthetic Preferences: An Art Therapist's Perspective', in H. O. Thomashoff and E. Sukhanova (eds.) *The Person in Art: Conceptual and Pictorial Frames on Art and Mental Health*. New York: Nova Science Publications: 57–69.

Waller, D. (2010) *Textiles from the Balkans (Fabric Folios)*. London: British Museum Press.

Waller, D. and Gilroy A. (1992) *Art Therapy: A Handbook*. Buckingham: Open University Press.

Waller, D. and Mahony, J. (1999) *Treatment of Addiction: Current Issues for Art Therapies*. London: Routledge.

Waller, D. and Sheppard, L. (2006) *Guidelines for Art Therapists Working with Older People with Dementia*. London: Goldsmiths College.

Waller, D. and Sibbett, C. (2005) *Facing Death: Art Therapy and Cancer Care*. Maidenhead: Open University Press.

Waller, D., Rusted, J. and Sheppard, L. (2006) 'A Multi-Centre Randomized Control Trial on the Use of Art Therapy for people with Dementia', *Group Analysis*, 39: 517–536.

Warner, R. (1985) *Recovery from Schizophrenia: Psychiatry and Political Economy*. London: Routledge & Kegan Paul.

Waterfield, J. and Brown, A. (1996) 'Every Picture Tells a Story: A Joint Approach Using Art and Educational Therapy', in M. Barrett and U. Varma (eds.) *Educational Therapy in the Clinic and the Classroom*. London: Whurr.

Webster, A. R. (2002) *Wellbeing: Church and Society*. Canterbury: SCM Books.

Webster University (2004) 'Margaret Naumberg and Florence Cane', in *Women's*

Contributions to the Mind and Society (www.webster.edu/~woolflm/naumburgcane. html).

Weich, S. and Lewis, G. (1998) 'Poverty, Unemployment and Common Mental Disorders', *British Medical Journal*, 317: 115–119.

Weir, F. (1987) 'The Role of Symbolic Expression in its Relation to Art Therapy: A Kleinian Approach', in T. Dalley et al. (eds.) *Images of Art Therapy*. London: Tavistock: 109–127.

Welldon, E. V. (1997) 'Let the Treatment Fit the Crime: Twentieth Century Annual Foulkes Lecture', *Group Analysis*, 30: 9–26.

Wellesby, C. (1998) 'A Part of the Whole: Art Therapy in a Girl's Comprehensive School', *Inscape: The Journal of the British Association of Art Therapists*, 3: 33–40.

Weston, S. (1999) 'Issues of Empowerment in a Multi-Cultural Art Therapy Group', in J. Campbell, M. Liebmann, F. Brooks, J. Jones and C. Ward (eds.) *Art Therapy, Race and Culture*. London: Jessica Kingsley: 177–191.

Whitehurst, T. (1984) 'The Involvement of Mentally Handicapped People in Art Psychotherapy', *Art Therapy as Psychotherapy in Relation to the Mentally Handicapped*, Conference Proceedings. St Albans: Hertfordshire College of Art: 8–15.

Wilde, O. (1891) *The Picture of Dorian Gray*. London: Penguin.

Wilkinson, M. (2006) *Coming into Mind: The Mind Brain Relationship – a Jungian Perspective*. London: Routledge.

Willner, A. (2002) 'Imperviousness in Anorexia – The No-Entry Defence', *Psychoanalytic Psychotherapy*, 16: 125–141.

Winnicott, D. W. (1965a) *The Maturational Processes and the Facilitating Environment*. London: Hogarth Press.

Winnicott, D.W. (1965b) *The Family and Individual Development*. London: Tavistock.

Winnicott, D. W. (1971a) 'Playing: A Theoretical Statement', in D. W. Winnicott (ed.) *Playing and Reality*. London: Tavistock: 44–61.

Winnicott, D. W. (1971b) *Playing and Reality*. London: Tavistock [reprinted by Penguin in 1974, 1980, 1982, 1993].

Winnicott, D. W. (1986) *Home is Where We Start From* (compiled and edited by Clare Winnicott). London: Penguin [published posthumously].

Winslade, J. (1996, March) *Stories That Bind*. Paper presented at the Counselling and Passion Conference, University of Durham.

Winterson, J. (1996) *Art Objects*. London: Vintage.

Wisdom, C. (1997) 'Art Therapy', in J. Goodwill, M. A. Chamberlain and C. Evans (eds.) *Rehabilitation of the Physically Disabled Adult*. Cheltenham: Stanley Thornes.

Wittgenstein, L. (1978) *Philosophical Investigations*, 3rd Edn. Oxford: Blackwell.

Wolfe, C., Rudd, T. and Beech, R. (1996) *Stroke Services and Research: An Overview with Recommendations for Future Research*. London: The Stroke Association.

Wood, C. (1985) 'Psychiatrica Democratica and the Problems of Translation', *Inscape: The Journal of the British Association of Art Therapists*, 1: 9–16.

Wood, C. (1986) 'Milk White Panic: What Do we Do to People When we Ask Them to Draw and Paint?', *Inscape: The Journal of the British Association of Art Therapists*, Winter: 2–7.

Wood, C. (1990) 'The Triangular Relationship (1): The Beginnings and Endings of Art Therapy Relationships', *Inscape: The Journal of the British Association of Art Therapists*, Winter: 7–13.

Wood, C. (1991) 'A Personal View of Laing and His Influence on Art Therapy', *Inscape: The Journal of the British Association of Art Therapist*, Winter: 15–19.

Wood, C. (1997) 'A History of Art Therapy and Psychosis, 1938–1995', in K. Killick and J. Schaverien (eds.) *Art Psychotherapy and Psychosis*. London: Routledge: 144–175.

Wood, C. (1999a) 'Class Issues in Therapy', in M. Liebmann et al. (eds.) *Art Therapy, Race and Culture*. London: Jessica Kingsley: 135–156.

Wood, C. (1999b) 'Gathering Evidence: Expansion of Art Therapy Research Strategy', *Inscape: The Journal of the British Association of Art Therapists*, 4: 51–61.

Wood, C. (2001a) *Art, Psychotherapy and Psychosis: The Nature and the Politics of Art Therapy*, PhD Thesis, University of Sheffield Library.

Wood, C. (2001b) 'The Significance of Studios', *Inscape: The Journal of the British Association of Art Therapists*, 5: 41–53.

Wood, C. (2005) *Convivencia: A Medieval Idea with Contemporary Relevance*. Buckland Hall, Brecon Beacons: Champernowne Trust Conference Publications.

Wood, C. (2007) 'Agency and Attention: Purposes of Supervision', in J. Schaverien and C. Case (eds.) *Supervision of Art Psychotherapy: A Theoretical and Practical Handbook*. London: Routledge: 185–199.

Wood, C. (2010a) 'Convivencia: A Medieval Idea with Contemporary Relevance', *ATOL: Art Therapy Online*, 1: 1–33 (http://eprints-gojo.gold.ac.uk/atol.html).

Wood, C. (2010b) 'The Evolution of Art Psychotherapy in Relation to Psychosis and Poverty', in A. Gilroy (ed.) *Evidence in Art Therapy*. London: Langer.

Wood, M. (1990) 'Art Therapy in One Session – Working with People with AIDS', in *Inscape: The Journal of the British Association of Art Therapists*, Winter: 31–35.

Wood, M. (1996) 'Art Therapy and Eating Disorders: Theory and Practice in Britain', *Inscape: The Journal of the British Association of Art Therapists*, 1: 13–19.

Wood, M. (2005) 'Shoreline: The Realities of Working in Cancer and Palliative Care', in D. Waller and C. Sibbett (eds.) *Facing Death: Art Therapy and Cancer Care*. Maidenhead: Open University Press: 82–102.

Wood, M. and Pratt, M. (1998) *Art Therapy in Palliative Care: The Creative Response*. London: Routledge.

Wright, E. (1998) *Psychoanalytic Criticism: A Reappraisal*. Oxford: Blackwell.

Yalom, I. (1983) *In-Patient Group Psychotherapy*. New York: Basic Books.

Yalom, I. (1985) *The Theory and Practice of Group Psychotherapy*. New York: Basic Books.

Yevtushenko, Y. (1978) *Early Poems*. London: Marion Boyars.

Young, M. and Schuller, T. (1991) *Life After Work: The Arrival of the Ageless Society*. London: Harper Collins.

Young, R. M. (1994) *Mental Space*. London: Process Press.

Young, R. M. (1999) 'Between Nosology and Narrative: Where should we be?'. Paper given to the Toronto Psychoanalytic Society. (http://human-nature.com/rmyoung/).

Zulueta, F. (1998) *The Traumatic Roots of Destructiveness from Pain to Violence.* London: Whurr.